GERMANY,
AUSTRIA & SWITZERLAND'S

BEST TRIPS
----
33 AMAZING
ROAD TRIPS

Marc Di Duca, Anthony Ham, Anthony Haywood,
Catherine Le Nevez, Ali Lemer, Craig McLachlan, Hugh
McNaughtan, Leonid Ragozin, Andrea Schulte-Peevers,
Benedict Walker, Kerry Walker

SYMBOLS IN THIS BOOK

✓	Top Tips	📖	History & Culture	📷	Essential Photo
§	Link Your Trips	👫	Family	🏃	Walking Tour
◯	Tips from Locals	🍷	Food & Drink	🍴	Eating
↱	Trip Detour	🌳	Outdoors	🛏	Sleeping

📞 Telephone Number	@ Internet Access	📖 English-Language Menu
🕓 Opening Hours	📶 Wi-Fi Access	👪 Family-Friendly
P Parking	🥕 Vegetarian Selection	🐾 Pet-Friendly
⊖ Nonsmoking	🏊 Swimming Pool	
❄ Air-Conditioning		

MAP LEGEND

Routes
- ▬▬ Trip Route
- ▬ ▬ Trip Detour
- ░░░ Linked Trip
- ► Walk Route
- Tollway
- Freeway
- Primary
- Secondary
- Tertiary
- Lane
- Unsealed Road
- ✕ Plaza/Mall
- ⁞⁞⁞ Steps
-)⸗ ⸗ Tunnel
- Pedestrian Overpass
- ─ ─ Walk Track/Path

Boundaries
- ─ ─ International
- ─ ─ State/Province
- ⌐⌐ Cliff

Hydrography
- River/Creek
- Intermittent River
- Swamp/Mangrove
- Canal
- Water
- Dry/Salt/ Intermittent Lake
- Glacier

Highway Markers
- (A20) Highway marker

Trips
- 1️⃣ Trip Numbers
- 9️⃣ Trip Stop
- 🔄 Walking tour
- ↱ Trip Detour

Population
- ✪ Capital (National)
- ◉ Capital (State/Province)
- ● City/Large Town
- ◯ Town/Village

Areas
- Beach
- Cemetery (Christian)
- Cemetery (Other)
- Park
- Forest
- Reservation
- Urban Area
- Sportsground

Transport
- ✈ Airport
- Cable Car/ Funicular
- Ⓜ Metro station
- Ⓟ Parking
- Ⓢ S-bahn station
- Train/Railway
- Tram
- Ⓤ U-bahn station

Note: Not all symbols displayed above appear on the maps in this book

---

PLAN YOUR TRIP

ON THE ROAD

NORTHEASTERN GERMANY 33

CONTENTS

Northeastern Germany p33

Northwestern Germany p121

Southern Germany p189

Austria p273

Switzerland p335

Contents cont.

ROAD TRIP ESSENTIALS

Classic Trips

Look out for the Classic Trips stamp on our favourite routes in this book.

WELCOME TO

GERMANY, AUSTRIA & SWITZERLAND

Grandiose cities, storybook villages, vine-stitched valleys and dreamy Alpine landscapes that beg you to toot your horn, leap out of the car and jump for joy – road-tripping in this Germanic part of Western Europe is a mesmerising kaleidoscope of brilliant landscapes and experiences.

The 33 trips in this book take you for a spin from Germany's edgy capital to its bracing northern coast and fabled Rhine and Moselle Valley vineyards, from Bavaria to the Black Forest, and beyond to the sparkling shores of Lake Constance and into Austria and Switzerland. Motor the castle-strewn banks of Europe's greatest rivers and within a whisker of its mightiest glacial peaks.

Whether you want to navigate hairpins with attitude on high-altitude mountain passes, taste wine, or cool off in romantic cobalt-blue lakes, we have something for you. And if you only have time for one trip, make it one of our eight Classic Trips, which take you to the very best of Germany, Austria and Switzerland. Turn the page for more.

Hallstatt (p320), Austria
SORINCOLAC / GETTY IMAGES ©

GERMANY, AUSTRIA & SWITZERLAND

Classic Trips

IAN TROWER / AWL-IMAGES.COM © SCULPTOR: RUI CHAFES

16

What is a Classic Trip?

All of our trips show you the best of the region, but we've chosen some as our all-time favourites. These are our Classic Trips – the ones that lead you to the most iconic sights, the top activities and the uniquely German, Austrian and Swiss experiences. Turn the page to see the map, and look out for the Classic Trips stamp throughout the book.

Above: Town hall in the Altstadt (old town; p208), Bamberg
Left: Arosa (p367), Switzerland

GERMANY, AUSTRIA & SWITZERLAND HIGHLIGHTS

Classic Trip 8
German Avenues Route
Follow one of Germany's most picturesque, tree-lined driving routes. **5–7 DAYS**

Classic Trip 16
German Castle Road
Castles, palaces and fortresses galore along this route from Mannheim to Bayreuth. **7 DAYS**

Classic Trip 10
German Fairy-Tale Road
Learn the fantasies and the horrors in the stories of the Brothers Grimm. **5 DAYS**

Classic Trip 12
Romantic Rhine Fall under the spell of the castle-lined riverscape along the world-famous Rhine. **5–7 DAYS**

POLAND

Szczecin

Binz
Stralsund

Rostock

BERLIN ★
Potsdam

Cottbus
Hoyerswerda

Dresden
Chemnitz
Zwickau

Lutherstadt Wittenberg
Magdeburg
Dessau-Rosslau
Halle
Leipzig
Freyburg
Gera
Jena
Erfurt
Gotha
Suhl

Wismar
Schwerin

Elbe

Wolfsburg
Braunschweig
Hildesheim

Broken (1141m)

Göttingen

Lübeck
Hamburg
Lüneburg

Kiel

DENMARK
Flensburg

Bremerhaven
Bremen

Werra

Hanover

Kellerwald-Edersee National Park
Kassel
Kellerwald National Park

GERMANY

200 km
100 miles

Norddeich
Jever
Wilhelmshaven
Oldenburg

Groningen

Leeuwarden

NETHERLANDS

Enschede

Osnabrück
Bielefeld
Münster

Dortmund
Gelsenkirchen
Duisburg
Krefeld
Düsseldorf
Wuppertal
Solingen
Bergisch Gladbach
Cologne
Aachen

Ems

Siegen
Giessen

Bonn

Hohe Acht (747m)

Nijmegen
Rhine (Rhein)

BELGIUM

Wasserberg (501m)
Signal de Botrange (694m)

10

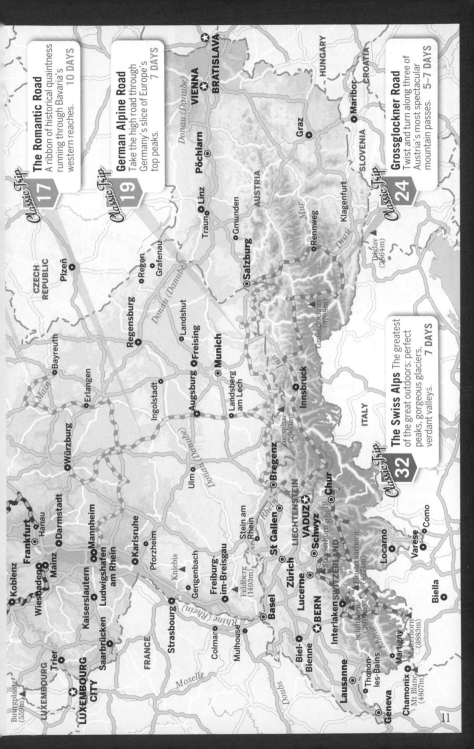

Classic Trip
17 The Romantic Road
A ribbon of historical quaintness running through Bavaria's western reaches. **10 DAYS**

Classic Trip
19 German Alpine Road
Take the high road through Germany's slice of Europe's top peaks. **7 DAYS**

Classic Trip
24 Grossglockner Road
Twist and turn along three of Austria's most spectacular mountain passes. **5–7 DAYS**

Classic Trip
32 The Swiss Alps The greatest of the great outdoors: perfect peaks, gorgeous glaciers, verdant valleys. **7 DAYS**

11

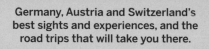

Germany, Austria and Switzerland's best sights and experiences, and the road trips that will take you there.

GERMANY, AUSTRIA & SWITZERLAND HIGHLIGHTS

Berlin

It can bookend either end of **Trip 6: Berlin & the Jewels of Eastern Brandenburg** – and what a bookend it is! Berlin is a bon vivant feasting on the smorgasbord of urban life. It oozes glamour and grit, and teems with top museums and world-famous landmarks (such as the Berlin Wall and Brandenburg Gate) that have to be seen. If you love great nightlife, you might ditch the car and never leave.

Trip 6

Berlin Brandenburg Gate (p116)

Vienna Schloss Schönbrunn (p306)

The Black Forest

Few spots soul-soothe like Germany's Black Forest. Each bend in the road on **Trip 22: Schwarzwaldhoch-strasse** unveils a surprise: half-timbered fairy-tale-like villages, thunderous waterfalls and cuckoo clocks the size of houses. Inhale pine-scented air, navigate roller-coaster roads to middle-of-nowhere lakes, frolic in waterfalls and dine in fine restaurants.

Trips 21 22

Romantic Rhine

The Rhine has long mesmerised artists, illustrated by the 19th-century paintings in Koblenz on **Trip 12: Romantic Rhine**. From Düsseldorf and Cologne, the majestic river snakes through churning whirlpools, castle-capped cliffs, medieval villages and vineyards. Trails lead to forests and fortresses, or to evenings sipping Rieslings under chestnut trees.

Trips 11 12

Vienna

There is no finer approach to Austria's elegant capital than through farmland, forest and vineyard-streaked hills on **Trip 23: Along the Danube**. In Vienna, park up and indulge in pedestrian meanderings around imperial Habsburg palaces and castles of unimaginable grandeur. Track down Mozart, and talk, read, dream and indulge, as Trotsky and Freud did, in a Viennese coffee house.

Trips 23 26

Northwestern Germany Bacharach (p165) on the Rhine

BEST ROADS FOR DRIVING

Schwarzwaldhochstrasse Altitude trip from Baden-Baden to Freudenstadt past forested peaks and glacial lakes. **Trip** 22

St Gotthard Pass Spectacular drive, partly on cobblestones, over Switzerland's famous mountain pass (2108m). **Trip** 33

Route 28 Wild Alpine scenery in the Swiss National Park. **Trip** 33

Grossglockner Road Heart-in-your-mouth Alpine adventure on a legendary Austrian road. **Trip** 24

Lake Geneva

Europe's largest lake is rarely out of sight on **Trip 30: Lake Geneva & Western Switzerland**. The urban viewpoint is cosmopolitan, French-speaking Geneva, where yellow 'seagulls' ferry locals across the water, overlooked by the icy peak of Mont Blanc. East along the shore, nothing prepares for the dazzling spectacle of emerald vines marching uphill from the water in the Lavaux wine region.

Trips

15

HIGHLIGHTS ★

Switzerland Matterhorn (p374)

The Swiss Alps

You'd think after motoring through 537km of mind-blowing Alpine scenery with **Trip 32: The Swiss Alps** that you'd seen it all. Wrong. After a relentless succession of dramatic green peaks, Alpine lakes, glacial ravines and other amazing natural landscapes, you finally pull into your final destination: Zermatt, a highly desirable Alpine resort built around the iconic, one-of-a-kind Matterhorn. *Nothing* prepares you for that first unforgettable glance.

Trips `30` `31` `32`

BEST PICTURESQUE VILLAGES

Soest Medieval village in luminous green stone. **Trip** `11`

Annweiler A German mountain gem with waterways and wooden wheels. **Trip** `14`

Rothenburg ob der Tauber Bavarian beauty from the Middle Ages. **Trips** `16` `17`

Ottenhöfen Black Forest storybook village amid hills and watermills. **Trip** `22`

Gruyères Swiss hilltop village with châteaux, dairies and meringues. **Trip** `30`

HIGHLIGHTS ★

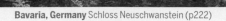

Bavaria, Germany Schloss Neuschwanstein (p222)

Switzerland Zürich (p362)

Schloss Neuschwanstein

King Ludwig II's crazy castle rises from the forest like a storybook illustration. Inside, confection outdoes even the flashiest oligarch's palazzo. Said to have inspired Walt's castle at Disney World, it now inspires tourist masses to make the pilgrimage along **Trip 17: The Romantic Road**, which culminates at its gates.

Trip 17

Zürich

Ending **Trip 31: Geneva to Zürich** here is the perfect antidote to wild motoring through dairy pasture, lake and mountain. Zürich is one of Europe's most liveable cities, and this German-speaking Swiss city is a hipster delight with a quaint old town, great art and shopping, waterfront bars and dancing till dawn in Züri-West.

Trip 31

Salzburg

Mozart's birthplace is a fitting finale to **Trip 25: Tyrol & Vorarlberg**, a drive with a 'Wow!' at every turn. Salzburg – baroque masterpiece, classical music legend, Austria's spiritual heartland – is just as grand. The city stands proud on the banks of the Salzach River, above which rise the Altstadt (old town) and clifftop-fortress Festung Hohensalzburg in their architectural glory.

Trips 24 25

Dresden

This Saxon city is dubbed 'Florence on the Elbe' for good reason. Reconstructed architectural jewels pair with stunning art collections to justify Dresden's place in the pantheon of European cultural capitals. Packaged with superb museums, baroque architectual gems and a tiara of villas and palaces lined up along the river, **Trip 4: Highlights of Saxony** is one handsome road trip.

Trip 4

Moselle Valley

With its Roman ruins and Unesco World Heritage status, Germany's oldest city Trier opens **Trip 13: Moselle Valley**. The downstream drive along the serpentine Moselle River is a go-slow, curvaceous affair with drop-dead-gorgeous castles and storybook half-timbered villages. It's topped by exhilarating walks through some of the world's steepest vineyards and tasting the valley's famed white wine.

Trip 13

(left) **Northwestern Germany** Calmont, Europe's steepest vineyard (p172)

(below) **Dresden, Northeastern Germany** Frauenkirche (p69, p119)

Frankfurt

After the natural splendour of **Trip 7: Via Regia**, urbanites need a dose of city life. Frankfurt, Germany's financial capital, brims with cultural, culinary and shopping excitement beneath a corporate demeanour. Discover its soul with an espresso in an old-time cafe, museum-hop along the riverbank, or wash down hearty local fare with tart *Ebbelwei* (apple wine) in an old-world wood-panelled tavern.

Trip 7

BEST FOR WINE LOVERS

Traben-Trarbach Moselle wine town with *Jugendstil* (Art Nouveau) architecture and wisteria. **Trip** 13

Bad Dürkheim German spa town with perfumed parks, vineyard trails and wine fest. **Trip** 14

St-Saphorin Bewitching village with a tasting cellar among vineyards. **Trip** 30

Rust Nesting storks, reed-filled lake and renowned Austrian wines. **Trip** 26

21

IF YOU LIKE

Black Forest gateau

History

With a history harking back several millennia, the region is littered with reminders of its turbulent past – ancient and uncannily recent.

6 Berlin & the Jewels of Eastern Brandenburg
Explore history's dark side in a concentration camp and on the largest WWII battlefield on German soil.

11 Cologne & the Ruhr Valley Romans to 20th-century postindustrialisation in northwest Germany.

13 Moselle Valley
Germany's finest ensemble of Roman remains.

17 The Romantic Road
Ancient walled towns, medieval castles and historic churches bejewel Bavaria's romantic east.

Food & Drink

Pepper road trips with sausages and dumplings, Black Forest gateau, Swiss chocolate and creamy Alpine cheeses. The 'homegrown and seasonal' mantra is picnic-perfect.

14 German Wine Route
Eat and drink your way through vine-planted hills in Germany's Palatinate region.

22 Schwarzwaldhoch-strasse Menus sing with earthy, seasonal flavours – from wild game to mushrooms – in this southern Germany foodie region.

25 Tyrol & Vorarlberg
Visit cheesemakers along Austria's Bregenz Forest Cheese Road.

33 Graubünden & Ticino
Distinct local flavours and rare Swiss wines create a notable culinary experience.

Mountains

Buckle up for Europe's greatest Alpine drives. On sunny days, icy mountain peaks and shimmering white glaciers are spellbinding. Keep your eyes firmly on the hairpin-laced road and go slow.

15 Bergstrasse
Germany's historic 'mountain road', a Roman trade route, shadows the forested Odenwald mountain range.

19 German Alpine Road
This dramatic road trip through the Bavarian Alps showcases Germany's mightiest peaks.

24 Grossglockner Road
A feat of 1930s engineering, this road swings giddily around 36 switchbacks in the Austrian Alps.

32 The Swiss Alps All the big names are here: Matterhorn, Eiger, Mönch, Jungfrau, Schilthorn and Titlis.

Swiss Alps (p365) Off-piste skiing

Castles

Romantic castles and feudal fortresses enhance the region's natural good looks. Teetering on rocky crags, clifftops or lacing a lake shore, their settings are picture-perfect.

5 Central Germany's Castles & Palaces Motor between mystical ruins, robust fortresses and exquisite palaces on this scenic trip.

10 German Fairy-Tale Road Yes, this trip is straight out of a Brothers Grimm fairy tale: aspiring princesses, let your hair down!

16 German Castle Road Castle-hop in southern Germany along 600km of scenic road and a thousand years of history.

26 Castles of Burgenland Castles abound on this drive through eastern Austria's wine country.

Lakes & Rivers

Stock up on superlatives and ensure camera batteries are charged. Few parts of Europe have so many of the longest, biggest, deepest...

3 Lakes & Treasures of Mecklenburg–Western Pomerania Take your foot off the pedal along a string of beautiful lakes.

12 Romantic Rhine Powerhouse riverside cities and castle-capped cliffs; this German journey along Europe's longest river is epic.

23 Along the Danube Abbeys, castles and Austria's resplendent capital unfurl riverside.

30 Lake Geneva & Western Switzerland Vineyards, villages, beaches and castles embellish Europe's largest Alpine lake.

Art & Architecture

Romanesque cathedrals, baroque palaces, timber granaries on stilts and chalet farmsteads in the Alps: the region's artistic and architectural legacy will be a memorable part of your trip.

2 Design for Life: Bauhaus to VW Unique Bauhaus and other design-related sights in central Germany.

8 German Avenues Route Renaissance palaces, baroque cathedrals and art-rich 'Florence on the Elbe'.

25 Tyrol & Vorarlberg Ecofriendly contemporary design contrasts with traditional chocolate-box chalets in Austria.

29 Northern Switzerland Human-made wonders are showcased in this art trip, with museum-rich Basel at its helm.

NEED TO KNOW

CURRENCY
Germany & Austria: euro (€)
Switzerland: Swiss franc
(CHF, also Sfr)

LANGUAGE
German region-wide, plus
French, Italian, Romansch in
Switzerland

VISAS
Generally not required for
stays of up to 90 days;
some nationalities require a
Schengen visa.

FUEL
Petrol stations are common
on major roads and in
larger towns. Unleaded
in Germany/Austria
costs around €1.50/1.25
per litre, diesel around
€1.30/1.20. Expect to pay
around Sfr1.42 and Sfr1.65
respectively in Switzerland.

RENTAL CARS
Auto Europe (www.
autoeurope.com)

Avis (www.avis.com)

Europcar (www.europcar.com)

Hertz (www.hertz.com)

IMPORTANT NUMBERS
Europe-wide emergency,
covering police, fire and
ambulance (📞112)

Climate

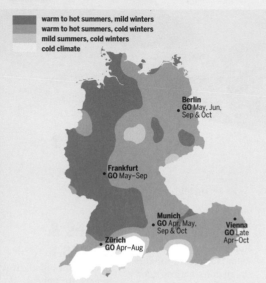

warm to hot summers, mild winters
warm to hot summers, cold winters
mild summers, cold winters
cold climate

Berlin
GO May, Jun,
Sep & Oct

Frankfurt
GO May–Sep

Munich
GO Apr, May,
Sep & Oct

Vienna
GO Late
Apr–Oct

Zürich
GO Apr–Aug

When to Go

High Season (Jul & Aug)
» Main holiday season – expect increased traffic on roads and
Alpine walking trails.

» Late December to early April is high season in Swiss and
Austrian ski resorts.

» Christmas and New Year are busy – warm cockles with
Glühwein (hot mulled wine) at alfresco Christmas markets.

Shoulder Season (May, Jun & Sep)
» Accommodation rates drop by at least 30% in popular
tourist areas.

» September's grape harvest ushers in the year's new wine in
vineyards region-wide – it's also the month of Munich's famous
'Oktober' fest.

Low Season (Oct–Mar)
» Expect heavy discounts on accommodation.

» Snow covers the Alps – Alpine-ski-resort hotels sometimes
close October to early December, depending on snow
conditions.

Your Daily Budget

Budget: Less than €100/Sfr200

» Double room in a budget hotel: €50–80/Sfr80–170

» Picnic, dinner out: €15/Sfr25

» Free entry to some museums first Saturday or Sunday of month

Midrange: €100–200/ Sfr200–300

» Double room in a midrange hotel: €80–160/Sfr170–350

» Dish of day or two-course menu: €15–30/Sfr25–50

» Museum entry: €5–15/ Sfr5–10

Top End: More than €200/Sfr300

» Luxury double room: more than €200/Sfr350

» Three-course dinner in top restaurant: €50/Sfr100

Eating

Cafes Coffee, drinks, snacks.

Bistros Light meals to full-blown dinners.

Restaurants Simple eateries to Michelin-starred temples.

Vegetarian Few wholly vegetarian places; limited choices on most menus.

The following prices indicate the cost of a two-course set menu:

€	less than €15/Sfr25
€€	€15-30/ Sfr25–50
€€€	more than €30/Sfr50

Sleeping

Hotels From budget to luxury; breakfast included unless indicated.

B&Bs *Chambres d'hôte* in French-speaking Switzerland, *Pensionen* elsewhere; rates include breakfast.

Hostels In cities and large towns; private or HI-affiliated.

Price symbols indicate the cost of a double room with private bathroom in high season:

€	less than €80/ Sfr170
€€	€80–160 (Germany), €80–200 (Austria), Sfr170–350
€€€	more than €160/200 (Germany/Austria), more than Sfr350

Arriving in the Region

Major car-rental agencies offer competitive rates at the airports.

Frankfurt Airport

S-Bahn Commuter rail lines S8 and S9 from Flughafen Regionalbahnhof to Frankfurt centre, 4.30am to 12.30am (€4.95, 10 minutes).

Taxis €25 to €35; 20 minutes to centre.

Vienna Airport

Trains & S-Bahn To city centre every 30 minutes, 6am to 11.30pm (€4.20 to €11, 15 to 30 minutes).

Taxis €25 to €50; 30 minutes to centre.

Zürich Airport

Trains To Zürich centre, 6am to midnight (Sfr7, 12 minutes).

Taxis Sfr50 to Sfr70; 20 minutes to centre.

Mobile Phones

All European and some Australian phones function; those from outside Europe should turn off roaming to avoid data charges and buy a local SIM.

Internet Access

Wi-fi (usually free) is available to guests in most hotels, B&Bs and hostels. Also offered at many cafes, bars, train stations and other public spaces.

Money

ATMs are widespread. Most major credit cards are accepted. Larger cities have money-exchange bureaus.

Tipping

Restaurant and bar prices include a service charge but locals still tip. Taxis expect 10%.

Useful Websites

Lonely Planet (lonelyplanet.com) Travel tips, accommodation, travellers' forum and more.

Germany (www.germany.travel) German tourist board.

Austria (www.austria.info) Austrian tourist board.

My Switzerland (www.myswitzerland.com) Swiss tourist board.

ADAC (www.adac.de) Driving info for Germany and neighbouring countries.

For more, see Road Trip Essentials (p390).

CITY GUIDE

BERLIN

Berlin's glamour-grit combo mesmerises. Allow a couple of days to get your teeth into its vibrant culture, cutting-edge architecture, fabulous food, legendary party scene and tangible history. After all, this city staged a revolution, was headquartered by Nazis, bombed, divided by a wall and finally reunited – all in the 20th century.

Berlin *Worlds People* by Schamil Gimajew, East Side Gallery (p83)

Getting Around

Driving in Berlin is a hassle. The key areas are compact and easily navigated on foot, bike or public transport. Jump on the U-Bahn or, for longer distances, the S-Bahn. A single/day ticket starts at €2.80/7.

Parking

Parking is expensive and scarce. Hotel parking (€25 per day) is rare; on the street is limited to three hours (€2 to €3 per hour); garage parking in commercial areas costs €3 per hour. Central Berlin is a low-emission zone – vehicles must display an Umweltplakette.

Where to Eat

Enjoy *Currywurst* (sausage in tomato ketchup sprinkled with curry powder), *Eisbein* (pork hock with sauerkraut and boiled potatoes) and other classics in historic Mitte. Prenzlauer Berg has a lively cafe scene or enjoy the street-food craze at a weekly market: Markthalle 9 (Thursday), Bite Club (Friday) or Neue Heimat (Sunday).

Where to Stay

Base yourself in Scheunenviertel's web of narrow lanes in Mitte, packed with trendy boutiques, restaurants and bars, and in walking distance of the sights. Cool Kreuzberg is for party animals and those on a budget.

Useful Websites

Visit Berlin (www.visitberlin.de)

Lonely Planet (www.lonelyplanet.com/berlin)

Trips Through Berlin: 6

For more, check out our city and country guides. www.lonelyplanet.com

TOP EXPERIENCES

➡ **Reichstag Panorama**
Ride the free lift up the Reichstag, home to Germany's parliament, for close-ups of the landmark's famous glass dome and dazzling city panorama.

➡ **Berlin Wall**
Trail the legacy of the world's most infamous wall, torn down in 1989, at Checkpoint Charlie, the Gedenkstätte Berliner Mauer, and East Side Gallery with its colourful murals.

➡ **The Holocaust Relived**
Stand in the very room where the Holocaust was planned and feel the presence of uncounted souls at the heart-wrenching Holocaust Memorial and its subterranean exhibit.

➡ **Museum Island**
Explore 6000 years of art and cultural history, from the Stone Age to the 19th century, in the five museums on the Unesco World Heritage site Museumsinsel.

➡ **Schloss Charlottenburg**
Fall in love with Berlin's largest and loveliest royal palace, a baroque beauty in a romantic park with carp pond, rhododendron-lined paths, a mausoleum and two smaller palaces.

➡ **Berlin Afloat**
Explore the city with a laid-back boat cruise through its historic core or further afield to the lakes.

➡ **High-Octane Nightlife**
Party until sunrise or beyond in one of Berlin's legendary electro-music clubs, some housed in old bits of the city's infrastructure and factories.

Stephansdom (p333) Tiled roof

VIENNA

Austria's capital city is a timeless, oh-so-elegant cocktail of imperial history, exciting contemporary museums, lively eating and infectious nightlife. Be it clip-clopping in a horse-drawn carriage past majestic monuments, waltzing through the Habsburgs' summer palace or spinning on the iconic Ferris wheel, Viennese life is uncannily cinematic. Play the part!

Getting Around

Stick with the excellent public transport system, one of Europe's most efficient. Tickets that are good for trams, buses, the underground (U-Bahn) and regional trains (S-Bahn) cost €2.40/8 for a single/day validate on board.

Parking

Pay for street parking with prepaid parking tickets (first 15 minutes free, then €2.10 per hour) sold at tobacconists, petrol stations and U-Bahn stations; street parking is free from 10pm to 9am. Well-signposted car parks cost around €4 per hour. Few city hotels offer parking.

Where to Eat

Kaffeehäuser (coffee houses) abound in the historic Innere Stadt. They're as good for a fine meal as they are for a traditional coffee and cake – don't skip the slice of *Sacher Torte* (rich chocolate cake with apricot jam). For goulash and other traditional Austrian dishes hit a *Beisl* (bistro pub). Vienna's historic Naschmarkt, with its food stalls, is a foodie heaven.

Where to Stay

The Innere Stadt is ideal for getting around the main sights, eateries and bar-spiked MuseumsQuartier on foot. Money-conscious road-trippers will appreciate the good value offered by accommodation around the Ringstrasse (ring road), and its excellent public transport.

Useful Websites

Vienna Tourism (www.vienna.info)

Falter (www.falter.at)

Trips Through Vienna:

Zürich (p362) Walking through the old town

ZÜRICH

Switzerland's largest metropolis is one of Central Europe's hippest destinations, with a postindustrial edge. World-class art in the Kunsthaus and Marc Chagall's stained-glass cathedral windows suit culture vultures, while Zürich's Bahnhofstrasse is shopping paradise. Few urban experiences climax like Zürich: with a swim 'n' tipple at a lake or river bath cum bar.

Getting Around

Dump the car at the hotel or in a car park and navigate one of the world's most liveable cities on foot or public transport – Zürich's public transport system works like a dream. Pay Sfr2.70/8.80 for a single/day ticket.

Parking

Street parking (Sfr1.50 per 30 minutes, free 9pm to 8am) is limited to between 30 minutes and four hours. For all-day parking try a car park run by **Parking Zürich AG** (www. parkingzuerichag.ch); pay around Sfr4 per hour or Sfr45 per day.

Where to Eat

The narrow streets of Niederdorf on the Limmat River's east bank are crammed with restaurants cooking up the rich local cuisine, epitomised by Zürich's signature dish, *Zürcher Geschnetzeltes* (sliced veal in a creamy mushroom and white-wine sauce). Swiss chocolate, coffee and cakes at **Café Sprüngli** (www.spruengli. ch), dating to 1836, are obligatory.

Where to Stay

Accommodation in reborn hip hood Züri-West – epicentre of nightlife, with bags of late-night eateries, bars and dance venues – is as good value as it gets in this expensive city.

Useful Websites

Zürich Tourism (www. zuerich.com)
New in Zürich (www. newinzurich.com)

Trips Through Zürich:

GERMANY, AUSTRIA & SWITZERLAND
BY REGION

From zigzagging snail-pace up spectacular Alpine mountain passes to speeding – foot down – along German autobahn, this is a driver's dream. Here's your guide to what each country has to offer, along with suggestions for our top road trips.

Northwestern Germany (p121)

A place for outdoor lovers and wine aficionados: the Rhine and Moselle rivers carve past castles, villages and vineyards. Park and hike, cycle, or hit North Sea beaches for alfresco beauty. Culture vultures find industrial history in the Ruhr Valley and the Grimm stuff (fairy tales) in Lower Saxony.

Taste star Rieslings on Trips 12 and 13

Switzerland (p335)

The epic beauty of this tiny country, with four languages and cosmopolitan cities, is completely disproportionate. Toss your walking boots in the car and rev up for spine-tingling motoring across Alpine passes, around cobalt-blue lakes, and through lush meadows strewn with chalets and wildflowers.

Ogle at the iconic Matterhorn on Trip 32

Northeastern Germany (p33)

Surf's up on the bracing Baltic Sea. Sand beaches and dunes lace the coastline of red-brick Hanseatic jewels Lübeck and Wismar. Motoring south, lakes and forests jockey with world-class architectural treasures in Bauhaus meccas Weimar and Dessau, comeback city Dresden and capital Berlin.

Feast on seafood on Trip 1

Admire architecture on Trip 2

Southern Germany (p189)

Southern Germany keeps its promise with lofty castles, mountains and forests fit for witches. The road ribbons through Bavaria and Baden-Württemberg, from romantic palace to medieval town, glass art to glacial peak, railway to waterway. Every journey ends in a tree-shaded beer garden.

Drink water from Germany's highest lake on Trip 19

Austria (p273)

Austria meanders the banks of Strauss' beautiful 'blue' Danube. It plays off spectacular natural landscapes against elegant urban vignettes like coffee in a Viennese *Kaffeehaus* or imperial-palace strolls. The cultural might of the Habsburgs is felt everywhere, while rural landscapes are rugged, exhilarating and charged with outdoor adventure.

Explore ice caves on Trip 24

Ice-dive on Trip 28

Northeastern Germany

DRIVE INTO THE SPIRITUAL HEART OF GERMANY on these trips, which are found in the regions in and around the compelling capital of Berlin. There's natural beauty galore: Baltic shores feature endless beaches and beautiful surf; inland, pristine lakes abound amid ancient beech forests.

But it's the proud and ancient cities that really stand out. Dresden is a baroque wonderland of buildings and churches. Beguiling, strollable Lübeck was the Hanseatic League capital, which once made this region one of the world's richest and most civilised. And the riches weren't limited to the coasts – wealthy potentates built lavishly from the Harz Mountains to the sea.

On these drives, you'll discover hulking castles, opulent palaces and magnificent gardens, along with excellent German food and drink.

Ariel view of Lübeck (p38)

1 **Along the Baltic Coast 5 Days**
From Lübeck to Rügen Island, celebrate the bracing, beautiful Baltic.

2 **Design for Life:**
Bauhaus to VW 2–4 Days
Drive through the evocative industrial heart of the old East Germany (GDR).

3 **Lakes & Treasures of**
Mecklenburg–Western Pomerania 2–3 Days
Palaces and jewel-box towns spread across land dotted with lakes.

4 **Highlights of Saxony 5–7 Days**
Follow one of Germany's great rivers, past palaces and fortresses, to Dresden.

5 **Central Germany's Castles & Palaces 3–5 Days**
Through Germany's heartland from Leipzig to Kassel, with castles and lavish palaces.

6 **Berlin & the Jewels of**
Eastern Brandenburg 4 Days
A tantalising tour to a watery forest, WWII sites and medieval marvels.

7 **Via Regia 5–7 Days**
The German portion of the longest historic road link across Europe.

Classic Trip
8 **German Avenues Route 5–7 Days**
Follow one of Germany's most picturesque, tree-lined driving routes, including Dresden and Leipzig.

 DON'T MISS

Dresden
Saxony's capital has superb museums, baroque architectural gems and a dynamic alternative scene in its funky Neustadt.
Trips **4** **7** **8**

Lübbenau & the Spreewald
Take a punt in the slow lane in this rivulet-laced forest, inhabited by exotic locals with a passion for pickles.
Trip **6**

Berlin
Germany's thriving capital has a past that's operatic in its drama. See how the entire 20th century is writ large here.
Trip **6**

Ahrenshoop
Feel the Baltic Sea's surging surf pound the shore, as little beach towns like Ahrenshoop shelter behind the dunes. Trip **1**

Schwerin
Like a box of chocolates, regal Schwerin is studded with surprises and delights. Walk the gardens, tour the lakes and make discoveries.
Trip **3**

Along the Baltic Coast

Head to Germany's north because you love the water. The fabled, historic Baltic towns – like Lübeck, Wismar and Stralsund – mix with long stretches of wave-tossed sand.

TRIP HIGHLIGHTS

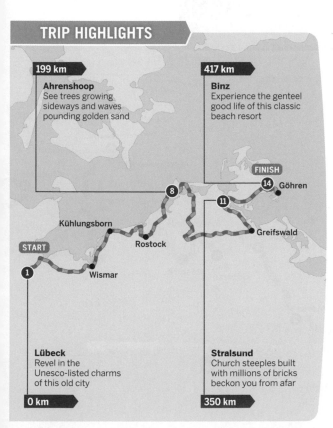

199 km

Ahrenshoop
See trees growing sideways and waves pounding golden sand

417 km

Binz
Experience the genteel good life of this classic beach resort

FINISH
14 Göhren

8
11

Kühlungsborn
Rostock
Greifswald

START
1

Wismar

Lübeck
Revel in the Unesco-listed charms of this old city

0 km

Stralsund
Church steeples built with millions of bricks beckon you from afar

350 km

---

5 DAYS
417KM / 259 MILES

GREAT FOR...

BEST TIME TO GO
April to October for the best weather.

ESSENTIAL PHOTO
Lübeck's Holstentor, with the city's iconic church steeples rising up behind.

BEST FOR FAMILIES
Riding the Molli steam train along the Baltic coast.

Along the Baltic Coast

The Hanseatic cities along the Baltic coast are some of the most beautiful in Germany, perfect for evocative strolling amid huge architectural treasures made from untold millions of bricks. In between, this drive takes you along the wave-tossed coast with its rugged beaches and long sandy vistas. But there are also great places to take a dip, like the fabled promenade at Binz.

TRIP HIGHLIGHT

1 Lübeck

A 12th-century gem boasting more than 1000 historical buildings, Lübeck's picture-book appearance is an enduring reminder of its role as one of the founding cities of the mighty Hanseatic League and its moniker as the 'Queen of the Hanse'. Behind its landmark 1464 **Holstentor** (Holsten Gate), you'll find streets lined with medieval merchants' homes

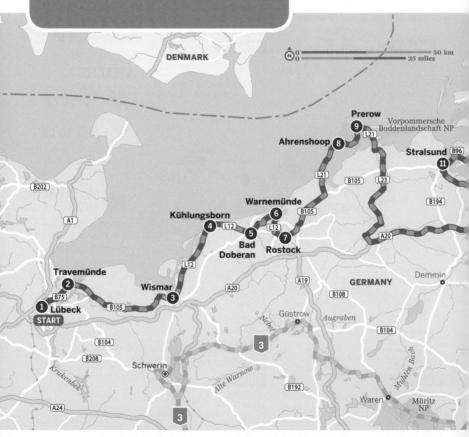

and spired churches forming Lübeck's 'crown'.

The fine Gothic **Marienkirche** (St Mary's Church; 📞0451-397 700; www.st-marien-luebeck.com; Marienkirchhof 1; adult/child €2/free; 🕐10am-6pm Apr-Sep, to 5pm Oct, to 4pm Nov-Mar) boasts the world's highest brick-vaulted roof and was the model for dozens of churches in northern Germany. A WWII bombing raid brought down the church's bells, which have been left where they fell in 1942 and have become a famous symbol of the city.

Thanks to a lift, even the fitness-phobic get to enjoy panoramic views from the 50m-high platform in the tower of the 13th-century **Petrikirche** (Church of St Peter; 📞0451-397 730; www.st-petri-luebeck.de; Petrikirchhof 1; tower adult/child €4/2.50; 🕐church 10am-4pm, tower 9am-8pm Mar-Sep, 10am-7pm Oct-Dec, 10am-6pm Jan & Feb).

In the north of the old town the brilliant **Europäisches Hansemuseum** (European Hanseatic Museum; 📞0451-809 0990; www.hansemuseum.eu; An der Untertrave 1; adult/child €13/7.50; 🕐10am-6pm) tells the remarkable story of the Hanseatic League, Lübeck and the region. Transfixing exhibits use every modern technology to tell a story as dramatic as anything in *Game of Thrones*.

 p45

The Drive >> Take the B75 northeast for 19km to Travemünde.

----

② Travemünde

Writer Thomas Mann declared that he spent his happiest days in Travemünde, just outside Lübeck (which bought it in 1329 to control the shipping coming into its harbour). Its 4.5km of sandy beaches at the point where the Trave River flows into the Baltic Sea make it easy to see why. Water sports are the main draw, along with a colourful **sailing regatta** (www.travemuender-woche.com) in mid-July.

The town is all wide streets and has a certain 1960s feel. Vorderreihe on the waterfront is lined with upscale shops and cafes.

The town takes great pride in its historic four-masted sailing ship turned museum, **Passat** (📞04502-122 5202; www.rettetdiepassat.de; Am Priwallhafen 16a; adult/child €5/2.50; 🕐10am-5pm Apr-Oct), which used to do the run around South America's

🔗 LINK YOUR TRIP

3 **Lakes & Treasures of Mecklenburg–Western Pomerania**

From Greifswald, found on both routes, discover the inland charms and surprises of the region.

6 **Berlin & the Jewels of Eastern Brandenburg**

It's only 180km south (under two hours on A20) from Greifswald to hit this route's Kloster Chorin, a 13th-century abbey.

Cape Horn from the early to mid-20th century.

The Drive » Take the very short but fun car-ferry ride across the Trave River, then take the Siedlung road southeast for 10km to the junction with the B105, which you follow for 39km east to Wismar.

- - - - - - - - - - - - - - -

❸ Wismar

With its gabled facades and cobbled streets, this small, photogenic city looks essentially Hanseatic. But although it joined the Hanseatic trading league in the 13th century, it spent most of the 16th and 17th centuries as part of Sweden. There are numerous reminders of this era all over town. The entire **Altstadt** (old town) was Unesco-listed in 2002.

The sober red-brick **St-Nikolai-Kirche** (St-Nikolai-Kirchhof; www.kirchen-in-wismar.de; St-Nikolai-Kirchhof; €2; ☺8am-8pm Mon-Sat, from 11.30am Sun May-Sep, 10am-6pm Mon-Sat, from 11.30am Sun Apr & Oct, 11am-4pm Mon-Sat, from 11.30am Sun Nov-Mar) is the largest of its kind in Europe. Its linden-tree-shaded churchyard is next to a small canal and is Wismar's loveliest spot.

Dominating the middle of the **Markt** is the 1602-built Wasserkunst (waterworks), an ornate, 12-sided well that supplied Wismar's drinking water until 1897. Today it remains the town's landmark. The large **Rathaus**

(Town Hall; exhibition adult/child €4/2.50; ☺exhibition 9am-5pm Apr-Sep, 10am-4pm Oct-Mar) at the Markt's northern end was built between 1817 and 1819.

🛏 p45

The Drive » Sand dunes and forests add accents to placidly flat expanses as you head to the coast. Head north for 42km on the L12 via Neubukow to Kühlungsborn.

- - - - - - - - - - - - - - -

❹ Kühlungsborn

Get some beach time in Kühlungsborn, one of the most atmospheric beach resorts along this starkly beautiful coast.

Molli (Mecklenburger Bäderbahn Molli; ☎038293-431 331; www.molli-bahn.de; Bad Doberan Bahnhof; return adult/child €15.50/11.50; 🚃) is a popular tourist train that travels along the coast from Kühlungsborn and Bad Doberan. Alternate taking the train and walking between stops for a gorgeous day out along the often-wild Baltic shore before you set out driving again.

The Drive » Enjoy the coastal plains and glimpses of the Baltic as you take the Pfarrweg and L12 16km east to Bad Doberan.

- - - - - - - - - - - - - - -

❺ Bad Doberan

The former summer ducal residence of Bad Doberan was once the site of a powerful Cistercian monastery and is now home to a fantasy in brick. Construction

of the magnificent Gothic **Münster Bad Doberan** (☎038203-627 16; www.muenster-doberan.de; Klosterstrasse 2; adult/child €3/free; ☺9am-6pm Mon-Sat, from 11am Sun May-Sep, 10am-5pm Mon-Sat, 11am-5pm Sun Mar, Apr & Oct, 10am-4pm Mon-Sat, from 11am Sun Nov-Feb) started in 1280 but the scale of the building meant it wasn't consecrated until 1368. Its treasures include an intricate **high altar** and an **ornate pulpit**.

The Drive » Leave town driving north on the L12, which curves around to the east for 16km until it meets the B103. Turn north for 3km to Warnemünde.

- - - - - - - - - - - - - - -

❻ Warnemünde

Genteel Warnemünde is all about promenading, eating fish, sipping cocktails and lazing on its long, wide and startlingly white **beach**. Perfect for the last of these activities is the *Strandkorb,* the iconic German wicker beach chair, complete with its own roof and awning to deflect seaside breezes. Rent one and get cosy on most public beaches.

Walking along **Alter Strom**, the boat-lined main canal, you'll pass a row of quaint cottages housing restaurants.

The Drive » Drive south on the Werftallee for 10km through Rostock's interesting industrial docklands to the centre.

THE HANSEATIC LEAGUE

The legacy of the Hanseatic League lives on in many of the towns and cities on this route, including Lübeck, Wismar, Stralsund, Greifswald and more. Its origins go back to various guilds and associations established from about the mid-12th century by out-of-town merchants to protect their interests. After Hamburg and Lübeck signed an agreement in 1241 to protect their ships and trading routes, they were joined in their league by Lüneburg, Kiel and a string of Baltic Sea cities east to Greifswald. By 1356 this had grown into the Hanseatic League, encompassing half a dozen other large alliances of cities, with Lübeck playing the lead role.

At its zenith, the league had about 200 member cities. It earned a say in the choice of Danish kings after fighting two wars against the Danes between 1361 and 1369. The resulting Treaty of Stralsund in 1370 turned it into northern Europe's most powerful economic and political entity. Some 70 inland and coastal cities – mostly German – formed the core of the Hanseatic League, but another 130 beyond the Reich maintained a loose association, making it truly international. During a period of endless feudal squabbles in Germany, it was a bastion of political and social stability.

By the 15th century, however, competition from Dutch and English shipping companies, internal disputes and a shift in the centre of world trade from the North and Baltic Seas to the Atlantic had caused decline. The ruin and chaos of the Thirty Years' War in the 17th century delivered the final blow, although Hamburg, Bremen and Lübeck retained the 'Hanse City' title. Since reunification, however, well over a dozen cities have decided to adopt the title once again.

7 Rostock

Rostock was devastated in WWII and later pummelled by socialist architectural 'ideals'. But this large port city still has small but attractive historic enclaves. Perhaps the best feature is the vibrant energy provided by the 11,000 university students.

Central Rostock's pride and joy is the 13th-century **Marienkirche** (☏0381-453 325; www.marienkirche-rostock.de; Am Ziegenmarkt; requested donation €2; ⊙10am-6pm Mon-Sat, 11.15am-5pm Sun May-Sep, 10am-4pm Mon-Sat, 11.15am-12.15pm Sun Oct-Apr), the only main Rostock church to have survived WWII unscathed (although restorations are ongoing). Behind the main altar, the church's 12m-high astrological clock was built in 1472 by Hans Düringer.

Red-brick and pastel-coloured buildings on the large **Alter Markt** hark back to the 14th- and 15th-century Hanseatic era.

✖ 🛏 p45

The Drive ›› Drive 22km on the B105. Just before the village of Borg, look for the turn north on the L21 and follow this beautiful coastal road 22km north to Ahrenshoop.

8 Ahrenshoop

Nature lovers and artists will be captivated by the Darss-Zingst Peninsula. This far-flung splinter of land has a seaside that is raw and bracing, with trees growing sideways away from the constant winds. The artists' village of Ahrenshoop is a great place to wander. It has some of the region's most strikingly painted reed-thatched houses.

The Drive ›› Drive 8km northeast on the L21, then turn due north for 7km to Prerow, right on the coast.

⑨ Prerow

The tiny town of Prerow is renowned for its model-ship-filled seafarers' church and lighthouse. Look for charming 'captains' houses' – reed-thatched dwellings with colourfully painted doors depicting sunflowers, fish and other regional motifs. Also common are *Zeesenboote* (drag-net fishing boats) with striking brown sails.

The Drive ›› Take the L21 and L23 44km south via Löbnitz to the A20. Now you get to open up the car while heading east for 31km to exit 25, where you'll take the B109 25km east to Greifswald.

⑩ Greifswald

The skyline of this compact former Hanseatic city is defined by three churches: the 'Langer Nikolas' (Long Nicholas), 'Dicke Marie' (Fat Mary) and 'Kleine Jakob' (Small Jacob). Don't miss climbing the tower of the first, 14th-century **Dom St Nikolai** (☎03834-2627; www.dom-greifswald.de; Domstrasse 54; tower adult/child €3/1.50; ⏱10am-4pm Mon-Sat, 11.30am-3pm Sun), for sweeping views.

The richly ornamented buildings ringing the **Markt** hint at Greifswald's stature in the Middle Ages. The **Rathaus**, at the western end, started life as 14th-century shops. Among the red-brick gabled houses on the eastern side, the **Coffee House** (No 11) is gorgeous and a good example of a combined living-and-storage house owned by Hanseatic merchants.

✕ ⌕ p61

The Drive ›› It's an easy 36km northwest on the B105 to Stralsund. Watch for the huge church spires as they appear on the horizon.

TRIP HIGHLIGHT

⑪ Stralsund

Stralsund was once the second-most-important member of the Hanseatic League, after Lübeck, and its square gables interspersed with Gothic turrets, ornate portals and vaulted arches make it one of the leading examples of *Backsteingotik* (classic red-brick Gothic gabled architecture) in northern Germany.

This vibrant city's historic cobbled streets and many attractions make it an unmissable stop. The main square, **Alter Markt**, is a hub of its architectural treasures. The soaring 1270 **Nikolai-kirche** (Church of St Nicholas; ☎03831-299 799; www.hst-nikolai.de; adult/child €3/free; ⏱10am-7pm Mon-Sat, noon-4pm Sun Jun-Aug, 10am-6pm Mon-Sat, noon-4pm Sun Apr, May, Sep & Oct, 10am-4pm Mon-Sat, noon-3pm Sun Nov-Mar) is a masterpiece of medieval architecture. Its interior is colourful and filled with art treasures.

Seven copper turrets and six triangular gables grace the red-brick Gothic facade of the splendid 1370 **Rathaus**.

DETOUR: PEENEMÜNDE

Start: ⑩ Greifswald

Amid the sandy dunes and bleak expanses of Usedom Island, the notorious village of Peenemünde is at the end of a scenic 52km drive via the B109 and B111.

It was here, on the island's western tip, that Wernher von Braun developed the V2 rocket, first launched in October 1942. It flew 90km high and a distance of 200km before plunging into the Baltic – the first time in history that a flying object exited the earth's atmosphere. Displays at the **Historisch-Technisches Museum** (Historical & Technological Museum; ☎038371-5050; www.peenemuende. de; Im Kraftwerk; adult/concession €9/6; ⏱10am-6pm Apr-Sep, 10am-4pm Tue-Sun Oct-Mar) – some in surviving buildings – do a good job of showing how the rockets were developed and the destruction they caused.

Wismar Buildings in the Markt (p40)

In an arctic-white wavelike building that leaps out from the surrounding red-brick warehouses, the state-of-the-art **Ozeaneum** (☑03831-265 0610; www.ozeaneum.de; Hafenstrasse 11; adult/child €17/8, combined ticket incl Meeresmuseum €23/12; ⊗9.30am-8pm Jun-Sep, to 6pm Oct-May) takes you into an underwater world of creatures from the Baltic and North Seas and the Atlantic Ocean.

Stroll the nearby harbour area for lots of stands selling smoked fish.

✕ 🛏 p45

The Drive » Soar over the water on the bridge to Rügen Island on the B96. Once on the island (7km from Stralsund) turn southeast on the L29 and drive through a canopy of trees. Pass through villages for 36km to the B196, where another 10km southeast brings you to Göhren.

⑫ Göhren

Göhren's stunning 7km-long **beach** – divided into the sleepier Südstrand and the more developed Nordstrand – lives up to its hype as Rügen's best resort beach.

Göhren is the eastern terminus of the **Rügensche Bäderbahn** (RBB; www.ruegensche-baederbahn.de) steam train that chuffs between Putbus and Göhren. En route, it stops in Binz, Jagdschloss Granitz, Sellin and Baabe. Much of the narrow track passes through sun-dappled forest. Its nickname is the ironic 'Rasender Roland' (Rushing Roland).

The Drive » Take the B196 northwest for a mere 12km to the L29, then turn east for the final 3km to the Jagdschloss Granitz car park.

⑬ Jagdschloss Granitz

A grandiose hunting palace built in 1723 on top of the 107m-high Tempelberg, **Jagdschloss Granitz** (☑038393-667 10; www.jagdschloss-granitz.de; adult/child €6/free; ⊗10am-6pm May-Sep, to 5pm Apr & Oct, to 4pm Tue-Sun Nov-Mar) was significantly enlarged and altered by Wilhelm Malte I in 1837. The results will remind you of salt and pepper shakers or a phallic fantasy, depending on your outlook. Malte's flights of fancy also gave Rügen the grandiose **Putbus**.

The RBB steam train stops at Jagdschloss and Garftitz, which serve the palace. Get off at one, enjoy some lovely hiking and reboard at the other for a trip to either Göhren or Binz (where you might have left your

LOCAL KNOWLEDGE: CLASSIC ROADSIDE ATTRACTION: KARLS

Gloriously hokey, **Karls** (☎0382-024 050; www.karls.de; Purkshof 2, off B105; ⊗8am-8pm May-Sep, to 7pm Oct-Apr; 🚻) is a roadside attraction in the cheesiest tradition. The schtick here is fruit – strawberries to be exact. In this sprawling hodgepodge of petting zoo, shops, playgrounds, cafes and, yes, strawberry fields, you will find something for anyone in the family. The fresh-strawberry ice cream is really good. Watch them make preserves, then listen to the mechanical bears sing Elvis. Karls is about 12km northeast of Rostock.

car). The palace parking itself is 2km from the complex.

The Drive » It's only 2km northwest on the L29 to the beachy pleasures of Binz.

TRIP HIGHLIGHT

⑭ Binz

Rügen's largest and most-celebrated seaside resort, 'Ostseebad' (Baltic Sea spa) Binz is an alluring confection of ornate, white Victorian-era villas, white sand and blue water. Its roads are signed in Gothic script and lined with coastal pines and chestnut trees. Even if all signs of 21st-century capitalism abound, espe-

cially along jam-packed Hauptstrasse, you can still feel the pull of history amid the modern-day crowds.

A highlight of Binz is simply strolling its 4km-long north–south **Strandpromenade** lined with elegant villas. At the southern end of the built-up area, you'll find the palatial **Kurhaus**, a lovely-looking 1908 building containing a luxury hotel. In front of it is the long pier. Strandpromenade continues further south from here, and becomes markedly less busy. Join the mobs and stop frequently for ice creams.

✕ 🛏 p45

Eating & Sleeping

Lübeck ❶

✖ Schiffergesellschaft   German €€€

(☎0451-767 76; www.schiffergesellschaft.
de; Breite Strasse 2; mains €15-31; ☺10am-
midnight) In the historic seafarers' guild hall
(1535), Lübeck's most atmospheric restaurant
is a veritable museum. Ships' lanterns, old
model ships and revolving Chinese-style
silhouette lamps dangle from the dining room
ceiling. White-aproned waitstaff deliver regional
specialities to tables here or in the hidden
garden out back. Book ahead for dinner.

⛏ Hotel Haase   Boutique Hotel €€

(☎0451-7074 90 1; www.hotel-haase-luebeck.de;
Glockengiesserstrasse 24; s/d from €90/106; 🛜)
Gorgeous rooms with exposed brick walls and
polished hardwood floors inhabit this beautifully
restored 14th-century home in the heart of
town. The public areas in particular sparkle with
character, and service never misses a beat.

Wismar ❸

⛏ Hotel Reingard   Hotel €€

(☎03841-284 972; www.hotel-reingard.de;
Weberstrasse 18; s/d from €72/87; P🛜)
Wismar's most-charming hotel has a dozen
artistic rooms, a little garden and wonderfully
idiosyncratic touches – such as a light show to
classical music that plays across the facade
daily at 8.30pm. The breakfast includes apples
from the orchard and eggs from the chickens.

Rostock ❼

✖ Zur Kogge   German €€

(☎0381-493 4493; www.zur-kogge.de;
Wokrenterstrasse 27; mains €9-23; ☺ noon-
11pm Mon-Sat, to 9pm Sun; 👶) At this Rostock
institution, cosy wooden booths are lined with
stained-glass Hanseatic coats of armour and
monster fish threatening sailing ships, and
ships' lanterns are suspended from the ceiling.

⛏ Hotel Verdi   Hotel €€

(☎0381-252 240; www.hotel-verdi.de;
Wollenweberstrasse 28; s/d/apt €69/89/99; 🛜)

Opening to an umbrella-shaded, timber-decked
terrace is this sparkling little hotel near the
Petrikirche and Alter Markt, with a handful
of attractively decorated rooms (some with
kitchenettes), and two apartments with views.

Stralsund ⓫

✖ Speicher 8   German €€

(☎03831-288 2898; www.speicher8.de;
Hafenstrasse 8; mains €17-26; ☺10am-10pm)
Simply roasted fish is one of the stars of this
excellent casual restaurant in an old turreted
building on the waterfront. There are great
tables out front; inside it's all glass and exposed
wood. Celebrate your love by ordering a
beautifully presented meat or fish platter for
two. Sushi and veggie fare are also on offer.

⛏ Hotel Scheelehof   Boutique Hotel €€

(☎03831-283 300; www.scheelehof.com;
Fährstrasse 23-25; d €95-170; 🛜) The
Scheelehof's 94 rooms are all individually
decorated and scattered about several
adjoining historic buildings. Furnishings have
a luxurious period feel (although we also like
those with a more contemporary feel and
exposed brick walls) and there is a small spa.
The hotel is noted for its bars and restaurants.

Binz ⓮

✖ Fischräucherei Kuse   Seafood €€

(☎038393-2970; www.fischraeucherei-kruse.
de; Strandpromenade 3; mains from €10; ☺3-
7pm Mar-Dec) For some of the most delicious
and certainly the cheapest fish on Rügen, follow
your nose – literally – to the southeast end of
the Strandpromenade, where fish has been
freshly smoked since 1900. Choose from fish
sandwiches and meals; dine at indoor tables,
or out on the terrace.

⛏ Pension Haus Colmsee   Pension €€

(☎038393-214 25; www.hauscolmsee.de;
Strandpromenade 8; r €75-110; P😊🛜) Relax
in the leafy, quieter and more pleasant eastern
edge of town at this family-run historic 1902
villa. Some of the comfy but unadorned rooms
have sea views.

Design for Life: Bauhaus to VW

2

This pilgrimage for lovers of modern architecture and design goes from the birthplace of Bauhaus to Volkswagen's global HQ, visiting game-changing sites that shaped today's world.

TRIP HIGHLIGHTS

320 km

Wolfsburg
Global HQ of Volkswagen and home to superb museums

158 km

Dessau-Rosslau
Birthplace of Bauhaus and paradise found for lovers of design

FINISH
6

4

Magdeburg

2

Hanover
A green city of music, arts and culture

487 km

START
Weimar

2–4 DAYS
487KM /304 MILES

GREAT FOR...

BEST TIME TO GO
Long days and clear skies from May to September mean bonus hours.

ESSENTIAL PHOTO
Design-heads' Holy Grail: Bauhausgebäude signage.

BEST FOR FAMILIES
Wolfsburg's fun museums delight young and old.

Magdeburg Grüne Zitadelle facade (p50)

2

Design for Life: Bauhaus to VW

Fans of modern architecture, design and technology will find this easy, engaging trip hard to resist. You'll take in the history of the Bauhaus movement in Dessau-Rosslau, where it all took off, get a taste of German Art Deco and quirky Austrian architect Hundertwasser's off-the-wall ideas in Magdeburg, explore the world's first modern factory in Alfeld, and delve into German automotive genius, firsthand, in Wolfsburg.

---

❶ Weimar

Weimar is best known as the stomping ground for cultural heavyweights Goethe and Schiller, and its post-WWI dalliance with international fame as the place where the constitution of the German Reich (the Weimar Republic) was drafted. Weimar is teeming with historical sights and museums, and is home to the **Bauhaus Museum** (☏03643-545 400; www. klassik-stiftung.de; Stéphane-Hessel-Platz 1; adult/child €11/7; ☺9am-2.30pm Mon, to 6pm Tue-Sun), **which is why you're here**. Although the movement did most of its work from Dessau-Rosslau, it was founded

here by Walter Gropius in 1919. The tiny **Haus am Horn** (☏03643-582 019; www.hausamhorn.de; Am Horn 61; ☺10am-6pm Wed-Mon Apr-Oct, to 4pm Nov-Mar) is the only remaining Bauhaus structure in Weimar, but the fascinating Art Nouveau **Haus Hohe Pappeln** (☏03643-545 400; www.klassik-stiftung. de; Belvederer Allee 58; adult/ concession €3.50/2.50; ☺11am-5pm Tue-Sun Apr-Oct) predates the movement and is considered a pioneer of modernity.

 p53, 79

The Drive » Take the B7 for 7.5km east to the village of Umpferstedt, where you'll pick up the B87, heading north. Follow the B87 for 50km as it winds through fields and

forests to the pretty Saale River township of Naumburg: a nice place to stop. Take the B180 east for 14km to the A9 autobahn for the remaining 90km north into Dessau-Rosslau.

TRIP HIGHLIGHT

❷ Dessau-Rosslau

Welcome to the birthplace of Bauhaus, the most influential design

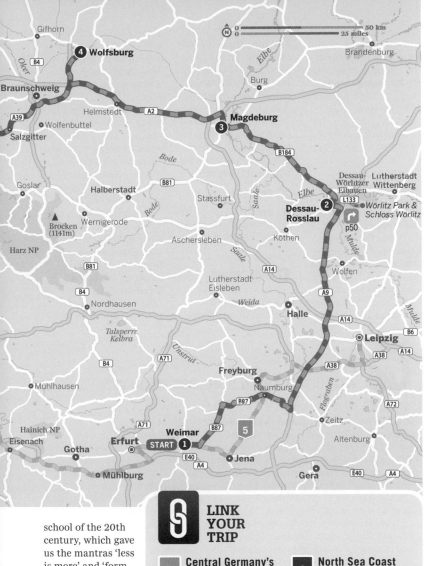

school of the 20th century, which gave us the mantras 'less is more' and 'form follows function'. Nowhere else will you find a greater concentration of structures from Bauhaus' most creative period, 1925 to 1932. If you're a student of

LINK YOUR TRIP

5 **Central Germany's Castles & Palaces**

Fancy some medieval with your modern? From Weimar, take our castles and palaces trip, too.

9 **North Sea Coast**

If you do like to be beside the seaside, follow the autobahn for 130km northwest from Hanover to Bremen for this nautical jaunt.

architecture or design, you might not want to leave. Pick up a tour at the epicentre of activity, the **Bauhausgebäude** (Bauhaus Building; ☎0340-650 8250; www.bauhaus-dessau.de; Gropiusallee 38; exhibition adult/concession €8.50/5.50, tour €7; ☺9am-6pm, tours 11am & 2pm daily, plus noon & 4pm Sat & Sun, in English noon Fri), erected in 1925–26 as the school of Bauhaus art, design and architecture. Next, check out the **Meister-häuser** (Masters' Houses; www.bauhaus-dessau.de; Ebertallee; combined ticket adult/concession €8.50/5.50, tour €7; ☺10am-5pm daily, tours 12.30pm & 3.30pm daily, plus

1.30pm Sat & Sun, in English 1.30pm Fri) where the likes of Kandinsky and Gropius once lived. Proceed to the 300-plus homes of the **Törten Estate** (Am Dreieck 1; tour €4; ☺ tours 3.30pm daily, in English Fri), prototype of the first-ever housing estate. To complete the experience, why not spend the night?

🍴 🛏 p53

The Drive » Follow the B184 through farms and canola fields for 63km, into Magdeburg.

----

❸ Magdeburg

Few people could deny that Magdeburg is aesthetically challenged, thanks to WWII bombs and socialist city planners in love with sparse boulevards and prefab concrete apartment blocks (the so-called Plattenbauten). Yet this is one of the country's oldest cities, founded some 1200 years ago, and its imposing **Dom** (www.magdeburgerdom.de; Am Dom 1; tour adult/concession €6/4; ☺10am-6pm May-Sep, shorter hours Oct-Apr) is the first Gothic cathedral on German soil. The reason you're here, however, is the love-it-or-hate-it, whimsical **Grüne Zitadelle** (Green Citadel; ☎0391-5975 5941; www.gruene-zitadelle.de; Breiter

DETOUR: WÖRLITZ PARK & SCHLOSS WÖRLITZ

Start: ❷ **Dessau-Rosslau**

The 112-hectare **Wörlitz Park & Schloss Wörlitz** (☎039404-310 09; www.woerlitz-information.de; Förstergasse 26, Wörlitz; tour €8; ☺10am-6pm Tue-Sun May-Sep, 11am-5pm Oct-Apr) is the pinnacle of Prince Leopold III's so-named Gartenreich Dessau-Wörlitz (Garden Realm), one of the finest garden ensembles in Germany. A visit, to contemplate Bauhaus in contrast to the culture from which it emerged, is highly recommended. Allow at least a half-day including travel time to appreciate the beauty on display. To get here from Dessau-Rosslau, take the B185 east until the junction with the L133. Follow the L133 for 14.5km until you reach the park.

There are five other parks belonging to the Gartenreich Dessau-Wörlitz: Oranienbaum, Luisium, Georgium, Mosigkau and Grosskühnau. Scattered over 142 sq km, each comes with its own palace and other buildings, in styles ranging from neoclassical to neo-Gothic, and reflects the vision of Prince Leopold III Friedrich Franz von Anhalt-Dessau (1740–1817). A highly educated man, he travelled to the Netherlands, Italy, France and Switzerland, gaining inspiration to apply the philosophy of the Enlightenment to the design of a landscape that would create a harmony of nature, architecture and art.

The gardens were added to Unesco's World Heritage list in 2000 and are protected under the Biosphärenreservat Mittelelbe (www.mittelelbe.com). All parks are free and can be roamed during daylight hours, but the palaces charge admission and have their own opening hours.

Dessau Bauhausgebäude (p50)

Weg 9; tour adult/concession €8//; ☺tours 11am, 3pm & 5pm Mon-Fri, hourly 11am-5pm Sat & Sun Apr-Oct, 11am & 3pm daily plus 1pm Sat & Sun Nov-Mar), the last building of eccentric artist-architect Friedensreich Hundertwasser. For a little more architectural contrast, stop to admire the ornately detailed dark-green walls of **Die Saison** (☏0391-850 80; www.herrenkrug.de; Herrenkrug Parkhotel an der Elbe, Herrenkrug 3; mains €12.50-30; ☺noon-2pm & 6-10pm), or dine alfresco and admire the hotel's handsome Art Deco facade and immaculate gardens.

🛏 p53

The Drive » Follow the B71 north for 10km, then pick up the A2 autobahn at exit 69 Magdeburg-Kannenstieg. It's 69km of autobahn action until exit 58 Kreuz Wolfsburg/Königslutter, before heading north for 15km on the A39 into Wolfsburg.

- - - - - - - - - - - - - -

TRIP HIGHLIGHT

❹ Wolfsburg

Volkswagen is the world's second-largest vehicle manufacturer, and its global headquarters employ about 40% of Wolfsburg's residents: you can't miss the massive VW emblem on the side of the textbook post-war factory building. Designed by Ferdinand Porsche under Hitler's orders, the Volkswagen Beetle (or 'People's Car') influenced the automobile industry in much the same way as the Bauhaus movement influenced architecture. Of Wolfsburg's numerous shiny state-of-the-art museums, loved by adults and kids alike, you'll want to check out Volkswagen's own **AutoMuseum** (☏05361-520 71; www.automuseum-volkswagen.de; Dieselstrasse 35; adult/concession/family €8/4/20; ☺10am-5pm Tue-Sun; 🚌212 to Automuseum), or the big draw for rev-heads, **Autostadt** (Car City; 📞05361-400; www.autostadt. de; Stadtbrücke; adult/child €15/6; ☺9am-6pm; 🚌201, 202, 213 to Autostadt), a celebration of all things automobile spread across 25 hectares. To see where design and science meet, head straight to the informative and engaging **Phaeno** (📞05361-890 100; www.phaeno.de; Willy-Brandt-Platz 1; adult/child €14/9; ☺9am-5pm Tue & Wed, 10am-6pm Thu-Sun), or swap your smarts for the arty side of modern design at the **Kunstmuseum** (Art Museum; 📞05361-266 90; www.kunstmuseum-wolfsburg. de; Hollerplatz 1; adult/concession €10/8; ☺11am-6pm Tue-Sun; 🚌201, 202, 213 to Kunstmuseum).

📖 p53

The Drive » Follow the A39 south for 76km to exit 65 Bockenem. Take the B243 north to the tiny village of Nette, then scoot west on the L493 for 6km to another tiny village, Bodenburg. Drive the less than 1km across town to pick up the L490, which winds through picturesque hills and fields for 17km to the township of Alfeld. Your next stop, Fagus Werk, is clearly signposted.

- - - - - - - - - - - - - - - -

⑤ Fagus Werk, Alfeld

Designed and built by Bauhaus founder

Walter Gropius in 1911, the **Fagus Werk** (Fagus Factory; 📞05181-7914; www. fagus-werk.com; Hannoversche Strasse 58; adult/child €7/5; ☺10am-5pm Apr-Oct, to 4pm Nov-Mar) has been producing shoe lasts – the basic moulds around which shoes are made – for over a century. It's regarded as the first building in the world to conform to the modern architectural style and is the last Bauhaus stop on your pilgrimage. Given Unesco World Heritage status in 2011, sections of the building have been turned into a gallery which focuses on Gropius' life, the Bauhaus movement, the history of the Fagus company and footwear in general. Guided factory tours are recommended.

The Drive » The B3 runs north for 45km where it merges with the B6 and proceeds for 5km into the heart of Hanover.

- - - - - - - - - - - - - - - -

TRIP HIGHLIGHT

⑥ Hanover

Capital of the state of Lower Saxony, Hanover boasts a wealth of cultural attractions, pretty parks and plenty of top-notch nosh. Few realise that from 1714, monarchs from the house of Hanover also ruled the entire British Empire, for over a century. In a cruel irony,

extensive Allied bombing in 1943 wiped out much of Hanover's rich architectural and cultural heritage. But there are a few highlights to round out your trip. The **Neues Rathaus** (Trammplatz 2; lift adult/child €3.50/2; ☺9am-6pm Mon-Fri, from 10am Sat & Sun, lift closed mid-Nov–Mar; Ⓤaegidientorplatz), completed in 1913, features a curved lift – the only one of its kind in the world – that travels 98m to four observation platforms offering panoramic views. For something completely different architecturally, the 1979 **Sprengel Museum** (📞0511-438 75; www.sprengel-museum. com; Kurt-Schwitters-Platz; adult/child €7/free, Fri free; ☺10am-6pm Wed-Sun, to 8pm Tue; 🚌100 to Maschsee/ Sprengel Museum) houses one of Germany's finest art collections. Complete your visit with a stroll through the grandiose, baroque **Herrenhäuser Gärten** (📞0511-1683 4000; www.herrenhaeuser-gaerten. de; Herrenhäuser Strasse 4; ☺9am-6pm Apr-Oct, to 4.30pm Nov-Mar, grotto to 5.30pm Apr-Oct, to 4pm Nov-Mar; Ⓤ4, 5 to Herrenhäuser Gärten), the city's pride and joy.

Eating & Sleeping

Weimar ❶

✗ Gretchen's Cafe
& Restaurant   Cafe €€

(📞03643-457 9877; www.gretchens-weimar.de;
Seifengasse 8; mains around €20; ⊙8am-11pm
Tue-Sat, to 6pm Sun & Mon; 👪) Located on the
ground floor of the Familienhotel (p79), and
thus family-friendly, this passionately locavore
cafe offers great alternatives to the Thuringian
standards available across Weimar. For those
intent only on snacking and chatting, it serves
great cakes, tea and coffee, but the meals
(including great-value €7.50 midday specials
such as salmon en papillote, with abundant
salad) are wholesome and delightful.

🛏 Casa dei Colori   Pension €€

(📞03643-489 640; www.casa-colori.de; Eisfeld
1a; d from €120; 🅿 🛜) Possibly Weimar's most
charming boutique *Pension,* the 'House of
Colours' convincingly imports Mediterranean
style to Central Europe. Run by an Italophile
and decorated with framed testaments from
delighted guests, it offers 10 good-sized rooms
dressed in bold colours and kitted out with small
desks, comfy armchairs and stylish bathrooms.

Dessau-Rosslau ❷

✗ Kornhaus   Cafe €€

(📞0340-6501 9963; www.kornhaus-dessau.de;
Kornhausstrasse 146; mains €14-25; ⊙noon-
10pm) This striking Bauhaus riverside beer-
and-dance hall was designed by Carl Flieger,
an assistant to the school's founder, Walter
Gropius. Apart from being a piece of modern
architectural history, it offers the perfect spot to
sit and enjoy a beer and some refreshingly light,
modern German fare in the sun.

🛏 Bauhaus 'Prellerhaus'   Hostel €€

(📞0340-650 8318; www.bauhaus-dessau.de;
Gropiusallee 38; s/d from €40/60; 🅿) One
for the architecture and design purists, who'll
first need to come to terms with the fact that
all rooms share showers and toilets. If you
can swallow that, you'll be able to channel
your modernist dream into something highly
functional by staying in these minimally
supercool former students' quarters.

Magdeburg ❸

🛏 Grüne Zitadelle   Boutique Hotel €€

(📞0391-620 780; www.arthotel-magdeburg.
de; Breiter Weg 9; s/d from €100/105; 🅿 ❄ 🛜)
Housed inside the Green Citadel (p50), a
design by Austrian architect Friedensreich
Hundertwasser, this hotel has bold colours,
organic shapes and all-natural materials. The
nicest rooms face the inner courtyard and
access a grassy terrace. Those facing the street
are air-conditioned.

Wolfsburg ❹

🛏 Innside by Melia   Hotel €€

(📞05361-609 00; www.melia.com; Heinrich-
Nordhoff-Strasse 2; s/d from €135/150) This
spotless, stylish property is a hop, skip and
a jump from the train station. Its slick, sleek
black-and-steel guest rooms afford every
comfort and convenience, including ports in
all the right places, wi-fi and a killer LED smart
TV. There's also a fitness room and sauna. Find
discounts by booking online through the hotel
website.

🛏 Ritz-Carlton Wolfsburg   Hotel €€€

(📞05361-607 000; www.ritzcarlton.
com; Parkstrasse 1; r/ste from €230/350;
🅿 ❄ 🛜 🏊) A hard act to beat, this hotel forms
a stunning arc on one side of Autostadt, while
its swimming pool is integrated into the canal's
harbour basin, giving it a lakeside feel. The
decor is elegant and breathes natural tones.
Expect full five-star facilities, complemented
by a Michelin-starred restaurant and numerous
bars. You can take high tea overlooking the
harbour.

Lakes & Treasures of Mecklenburg–Western Pomerania

3

Beautiful old towns mix with pastoral landscapes on this drive through the heart of one of Germany's oldest provinces. You can almost see the knights riding in the mists.

TRIP HIGHLIGHTS

127 km

Schwerin
The local dukes left a grand palace for this beautiful town

190 km

Güstrow
A tiny town that's big on art and architecture

FINISH Greifswald

4

3

Neubrandenburg

5

Neustrelitz

1 **START** Ludwigslust

Lüneburg
Enjoy wandering an old town where the buildings look drunk

0 km

Waren
Get back to nature in the heart of the lakes district

249 km

2–3 DAYS
387KM / 240 MILES

GREAT FOR...

BEST TIME TO GO

May to October, the beautiful forests and lakes are at their best.

📷 ESSENTIAL PHOTO

Schwerin's Schloss at dawn, with the stones glowing rose.

☑ BEST FOR FAMILIES

Exploring Schwerin's lakes and gardens on a family bike ride.

Lakes & Treasures of Mecklenburg–Western Pomerania

3

During the 15th century, the dukes of Mecklenburg–Western Pomerania built palaces across the lake-strewn plains of Germany's north so they could luxuriate in their wealth. Get a taste of their coddled lives, while you also taste the hearty fare of the north at the many excellent restaurants and cafes. Walk it off in the ancient and fabled beech forests of Müritz National Park.

TRIP HIGHLIGHT

❶ Lüneburg

An off-kilter church steeple, buildings leaning on each other and houses with swollen 'beer-belly' facades: in parts it looks like the charming town of Lüneburg has drunk too much of the pilsner lager it used to brew. Of course, the city's wobbly angles and uneven pavements have a more prosaic cause: shifting ground and subsidence due to salt mining has

caused many buildings to tilt sideways.

The medieval **Rathaus** (Town Hall; ☎04131-207 6620; tours adult/child €5/4; ⊘ tours 11am & 2pm Tue-Sun Jan-Mar, noon & 3pm Tue-Sat, 11am & 2pm Sun Apr-Dec) on the **Markt** has a spectacular baroque facade, added in 1720 and decorated with coats of arms and three tiers of statues. The top row represents (from left to right) Strength, Trade, Peace (the one with the staff), Justice and Moderation.

The cobbled, slightly wobbly street and square

Am Sande is full of red-brick buildings with typically Hanseatic stepped gables.

✕ p61

The Drive » Take the B5 north and east 89km to Ludwigslust. At 20km watch for the crossing of the historic Elbe River, which flows towards Hamburg.

- - - - - - - - - - - - - - - -

❷ Ludwigslust

Such was the allure of the grand palace, **Schloss Ludwigslust** (☎03874-571 90; www.schloss-ludwigslust. de; Schloss Strasse; adult/child €6.50/free; ⊘10am-6pm Tue-

Sun mid-Apr–mid-Oct, to 5pm mid-Oct–mid-Apr), that when the ducal seat moved 36km north to Schwerin in 1837, some family members continued living here until 1945. Now part of the Schwerin State Museum, its high point is the stately, gilt-columned, high-ceilinged Golden Hall.

A planned baroque town, Ludwigslust showcases a neat, orderly layout that is an attraction in itself.

The Drive » Go straight north for 38km on the B106. As you near Schwerin, you'll start to see some of the lakes that make the district famous, like the Ostorfer See, Fauler See and Schweriner See.

- - - - - - - - - - - - - - - -

TRIP HIGHLIGHT

❸ Schwerin

Picturesquely sited around seven lakes

LINK YOUR TRIP

1 Along the Baltic Coast

This trip ends in Greifswald where you can join the coastal trip.

10 German Fairy-Tale Road

From Lüneburg it's only 141km on the A39 and A1 to Bremen in the west, where you can plunge into the world of the Brothers Grimm.

(possibly more, depending how you tally them), Schwerin is the unofficial capital of the lakes district. The centrepiece of this engaging city is its **Schloss** (☏0385-525 2920; www.schloss-schwerin. de; Burg Island; adult/child €8.50/free; ☉10am-6pm Tue-Sun mid-Apr–mid-Oct, to 5pm mid-Oct–mid-Apr), a castle built in the 14th century during the city's six centuries as the former seat of the Grand Duchy of Mecklenburg. It's an appealing mishmash of architectural styles and is crowned by a gleaming golden dome. Nowadays the Schloss earns its keep as the state's parliament building. Crossing the causeway south from the palace-surrounding **Burggarten** brings you to the baroque **Schlossgarten** (Palace Garden), intersected by several canals.

Schwerin has an upbeat, vibrant energy on its restored streets that befits its role as the capital of Mecklenburg–Western Pomerania. Cafes, interesting shops and flashes of its regal past make wandering the **Altstadt** (old town) a delight. The bustling **Markt** is home to the Rathaus and the colonnaded neoclassical Neues Gebäude (1780–83).

Schwerin's central lake, the **Pfaffentiech**, was created by a dam in the 12th century. Through the centuries it was surrounded by some of the city's most elegant buildings. At the southwest corner, the vividly orange **Arsenal** dates from 1840. You can cross the waters on a small **ferry** (adult/child €2/1; ☉10am-6pm Tue-Sun May-Sep).

✗ 🛏 p61

The Drive » Drive directly east for 63km on the B104. As you go, the land becomes increasingly moist, with rivers and tiny lakes appearing in profusion.

TRIP HIGHLIGHT

❹ Güstrow

This charming town is over 775 years old and is a great place to explore on foot. The fabulous Renaissance 16th-century **Schloss Güstrow** (☏03843-7520; www. schloss-guestrow.de; Franz-Parr-Platz 1; adult/child €6.50/free; ☉11am-5pm Tue-Sun) is home to a historical museum, luxe rooms and formal **gardens**.

Built between 1226 and 1335, the richly ornamented Gothic **Güstrow Dom** (☏03843-682 433; www.dom-guestrow. de; Philipp-Brandin-Strasse 5; ☉10am-5pm mid-May–mid-Oct, shorter hours rest of year) is an old-town highlight.

Famed 20th-century sculptor Ernst Barlach spent most of his working life in Güstrow. You can view his deeply felt, humanist works in the **Gertrudenkapelle**

(☏03843-844 000; Gertrudenplatz 1; adult/child €6/4; ☉10am-5pm Tue-Sun Apr-Oct, 11am-4pm Tue-Sun Nov-Mar) and at the **Atelierhaus** (☏03843-822 99; www.ernst-barlach-stiftung.de; Heidberg 15; adult/child/family €6/4/15; ☉10am-5pm Tue-Sun Apr-Oct, 11am-4pm Tue-Sun Nov-Mar).

✗ p61

The Drive » Drive due south for 20km on the B103. At Krakow-am-See (and its large lake) turn southeast for 14km on the L204, then continue east for another 14km on the Kastanienallee to the B108, which you take southeast to Waren.

Schwerin Castle statue detail

TRIP HIGHLIGHT

❺ Waren

Right on the sparkling blue waters of **Lake Müritz**, Waren is a lovely village and one of the more popular in the lakes region. You can stroll streets lined with half-timbered buildings, poke in and out of churches and best of all, relax at a waterfront cafe while you watch small sailboats darting past.

Large-scale renovation schemes have restored much of the 16th-century feel to the town. Should the waters beckon, there are several places where you can rent a kayak or small boat to explore the chain of lakes that includes the **Tiefwarensee** and the **Kölpinsee**.

The Drive ❱❱ Leave Waren on Kargower Weg and plunge right into the heart of the Müritz National Park. Drive for 32km following the signs for Neustrelitz via Kratzeburg, then turn south for 10km on the B193.

❻ Neustrelitz

Situated on the Zierker See within the national park, the pretty, planned baroque town of Neustrelitz centres on its circular **Markt**, from which streets radiate like the spokes of a wheel.

The town's Schloss fell victim to WWII damage, but its beautiful **Schlossgarten** retains its 18th-century orangery (with a restaurant open Tuesday to Sunday May to September), and hosts the **Schlossgartenfestspiele**, a series of classical music and other concerts in summer.

The **national park office** (☎03981-253 106; www.mueritz-nationalpark.de; Strelitzerstrasse 1; ⊙9am-6pm Mon-Fri, 9.30am-1pm Sat & Sun May-Sep, 9am-noon & 1-4pm Mon-Thu, 9am-noon Fri Oct) is a good stop as it has a

MÜRITZ NATIONAL PARK

Müritz is commonly known as the land of a thousand lakes. While that's an exaggeration, there are well over 100 lakes here, as well as countless ponds, streams and rivers in this beautiful area midway between Berlin and Rostock.

The serene **Müritz National Park** (www.mueritz -nationalpark.de) consists of bog and wetlands, and is home to a wide range of waterfowl, including ospreys, white-tailed eagles and cranes. Its two main sections sprawl over 300 sq km to the east and (mainly) west of Neustrelitz, where the park's waterway begins on the Zierker See. Boardwalks and other features let you get close to nature.

The country roads between Waren and Neustrelitz cut through the heart of the park and offer plenty of places to stop and admire the Unesco-recognised **beech forests**.

lot of information on the lakes, forests and park in English. Fish plucked fresh from the lake is the highlight at simple restaurants along the shore, near the centre.

The Drive ⟩⟩ For more than half your 31km drive on the B96 to Neubrandenburg, you'll be passing by a beautiful lake, the Tollensesee.

- - - - - - - - - - - - - - - - -

❼ Neubrandenburg

Neubrandenburg bills itself as 'the city of four gates on the Tollensee Lake', and you'll see why during this enjoyable stop. A largely intact medieval **wall**, with those gates, encircles the city, which was founded in 1248. Made of stone, the wall is 2.3km in circumference and averages 7.5m in height. To navi-

gate it, consider the wall as the rim of a clock face, with the train station at 12 o'clock.

The **Friedländer Tor** (2 o'clock), begun in 1300 and completed in 1450, was the first gate. **Treptower Tor** (9 o'clock) is the largest and contains an archaeological collection. At the southern end of the city is the gaudy **Stargarder Tor** (6 o'clock). The simple brick **Neues Tor** (3 o'clock) fronts the east side of the Altstadt. Southwest of the train station is the city's former dungeon, the **Fangelturm** (11 o'clock). You'll recognise it by its pointy tower.

Wedged into the stone circumference are the 27 sweet half-timbered houses, the remains of the original sentry posts.

Most of the surviving homes are now craft shops, galleries and cafes.

✖ p61

The Drive ⟩⟩ Fertile fields keep the view from your car green as you go 65km straight north on the L35 to Greifswald.

- - - - - - - - - - - - - - - - -

❽ Greifswald

The old university town of Greifswald, south of Stralsund, was largely unscathed by WWII thanks to a courageous German colonel who surrendered to Soviet troops (a move usually punishable by execution).

This former Hanseatic city is small and easy to explore on foot. Start at the **Markt** and be sure to see its three famous churches: the 'Langer Nikolas' (Long Nicholas), 'Dicke Marie' (Fat Mary) and the 'Kleine Jakob' (Small Jacob).

Trade the fresh water encountered on this drive for the salt variety with a visit to Greifswald's pretty harbour in the charming district of **Wieck**, reached by a Dutch-style wooden drawbridge; its medieval city walls have been turned into a wide, tree-shaded promenade. If forsaking the car, it's easily reached via a 5km foot/bike path. More paths follow the pretty and sinuous waterfront.

✖ ⊨ p61

Eating & Sleeping

Lüneburg ❶

✖ Zum Alten Brauhaus   German €€€

(☎04131-721 277; www.brauhaus-lueneburg.
de; Grapengiesserstrasse 11; mains €11-29;
🕑noon-11pm Tue-Sat) This old-style *Brauhaus*
(brewery) has been around in some form since
the 16th century. Dishes flit effortlessly between
tradition and outside influences. It's right in the
centre, just off the western end of Am Sande.

Schwerin ❸

✖ Buschérie   European €€

(☎0385-3945 6092; www.buscherie.de;
Buschstrasse 9; mains €12-24; 🕑11.30am-11pm)
Although historic and half-timbered, Buschérie
is very much the modern bistro. Enjoy seasonal,
regional foods at an outdoor table with the Dom
seeming to loom overhead. From mains to small
plates, everything is well priced. Come for a
glass of wine and listen to live jazz some nights.

✖ Rösterei Fuchs   Cafe €

(www.roesterei-fuchs.de; Am Markt 4; mains €7-
12; 🕑9am-8pm Mon-Fri, to 6pm Sat & Sun) The
aroma of fresh coffee fills this chic cafe, which
roasts its own coffee in-house and sells beans
as well as gourmet chocolates. Drop by for an
espresso or other hot drink. Breakfasts are
fresh and healthy, while sandwiches, quiches
and beautiful baked goods fill out the day.

🛏 Hotel Niederländischer Hof   Hotel €€

(☎0385-591 100; www.niederlaendischer-hof.
de; Karl-Marx-Strasse 12-13; s €95-155, d
€150-230; P 🛜) Overlooking the Pfaffenteich,
this regal 1901-established hotel has 33
elegant rooms with black marble bathrooms,
a library warmed by an open fire, and a lauded
restaurant. The decor is plushly period with
whimsical touches.

🛏 Zur guten Quelle   Hotel €€

(☎0385-565 985; www.gasthof-schwerin.de;
Schusterstrasse 12; s/d from €60/85; P 🛜) One
of Schwerin's prettiest half-timbered houses,
bang in the heart of the Altstadt, Zur guten
Quelle is known for its cosy traditional restaurant

and beer garden. It also has six simple but
comfortable rooms, many with ancient timbers
running right through the rooms.

Güstrow ❹

✖ WunderBar   Cafe €€

(☎0384-776 927; www.wunderbar-guestrow.de;
Krönchenhagen 10; mains from €8; 🕑11am-late)
Much loved by locals for its rare combination
of cool, classy and warmth, WunderBar is part
cafe, part bar (great cocktails!) and very much
a hub of local life. The menu consists of light
meals (usually with a veg or vegan option) and
the cooking is assured.

Neubrandenburg ❼

✖ Wiekhaus 45   German €€

(☎0395-566 7762; www.wiekhaus45.de;
4th Ringstrasse 44; mains €14-20; 🕑11am-
11.30pm) The most appealing place to eat in
Neubrandenburg is this renovated guardhouse
set into the wall. Waiters zip up and down the
narrow stairwell carrying huge portions of
Mecklenburg specialities (start with the tasty
onion soup served with fresh bread; look for fresh
herring in season). Outside tables in summer.

Greifswald ❽

✖ Fischer-Hütte   Seafood €€

(☎03834-839 654; www.fischer-huette.de; An
der Mühle 12, Wieck; mains €8-22; 🕑11.30am-
11pm; 🚗) An exquisitely presented meal at the
'fisher's house' might start with Wieck-style
fish soup and move onto the house speciality –
smoked herring. You know everything is fresh
as you can see the boats pulling up to the dock
right outside.

🛏 Hotel Galerie   Hotel €€

(☎03834-773 7830; www.hotelgalerie.de;
Mühlenstrasse 10; s/d €80/110; P 🛜) The
13 rooms in this sparkling modern property
are filled with a changing collection of works
by contemporary artists. Room design is a cut
above the usual hotel standard.

Highlights of Saxony

4

Saxony's romantic mountains and castles compete for your attention on this wonderful and varied drive, from the perfectly preserved city of Görlitz to the cultural giant that is Leipzig.

TRIP HIGHLIGHTS

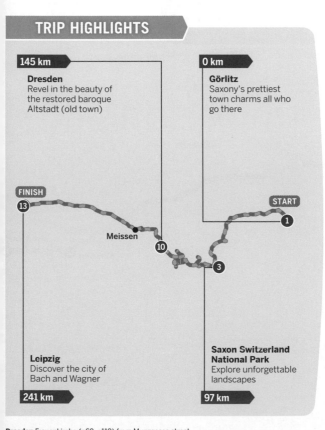

145 km

Dresden
Revel in the beauty of the restored baroque Altstadt (old town)

0 km

Görlitz
Saxony's prettiest town charms all who go there

FINISH
13

START
1

Meissen
10

3

Leipzig
Discover the city of Bach and Wagner

241 km

Saxon Switzerland National Park
Explore unforgettable landscapes

97 km

5–7 DAYS
241KM / 134 MILES

GREAT FOR...

BEST TIME TO GO
April to October for warmer hiking weather.

 ESSENTIAL PHOTO
The extraordinary view over the Elbe River from the Bastei lookouts.

☑ **BEST FOR HISTORY**
The silhouette of the magnificently rebuilt Altstadt in Dresden.

Dresden Frauenkirche (p69, p119) from Munzgasse street

63

4 Highlights of Saxony

On this unforgettable journey through the state of Saxony, you'll see castles and fortresses, one of Germany's great rivers, impossibly shaped sandstone mountains, and several magical baroque cities and palaces along the way. These extraordinary landscapes then give way to magnificent Dresden, the erstwhile 'Florence of the North', then to charming cool-kid Leipzig, one-time home to Bach and Wagner but long touted as the 'New Berlin'.

TRIP HIGHLIGHT

❶ Görlitz

This border town (half of which, on the other side of the Neisse River, became Polish territory after WWII), is an utter beauty and easily one of Saxony's most charming cities. Having miraculously survived the war intact, Görlitz has been used on numerous occasions as the backdrop to several Hollywood movies, and one look at its skyline of medieval towers and baroque

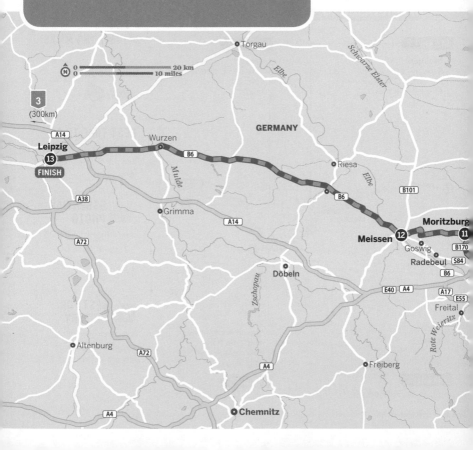

churches will tell you why. The **Reichenbacher Turm** (www.goerlitzer -sammlungen.de; Platz des 17 Juni; adult/concession €3/2; ⏰10am-5pm Tue-Thu, to 6pm Fri-Sun May-Oct) and the interesting **Barock-haus** (☎03581-671 355; www.goerlitzer-sammlungen. de; Neissstrasse 30; adult/ concession €5/3.50; ⏰10am-5pm Tue-Thu, to 6pm Fri-Sun) are the two most obvious sights, but nearly all visitors simply enjoy strolling around. In the last decade Görlitz has grown enormously as a weekend destination and consequently has some excellent restaurants and accommodation options.

✗ ⮆ p71

The Drive ⟫ It's an easy 50km drive due west out of Görlitz along the A4/E40 directly to Bautzen.

LINK YOUR TRIP

3 Lakes & Treasures of Mecklenburg– Western Pomerania

From Leipzig, take the A14 and then the B71 northwest for 300km to Lüneburg for this verdant slice of northeastern Germany.

6 Berlin & the Jewels of Eastern Brandenburg

From Dresden, take the A13 north for the 103km drive to Lübbenau to discover this fascinating and multifaceted region.

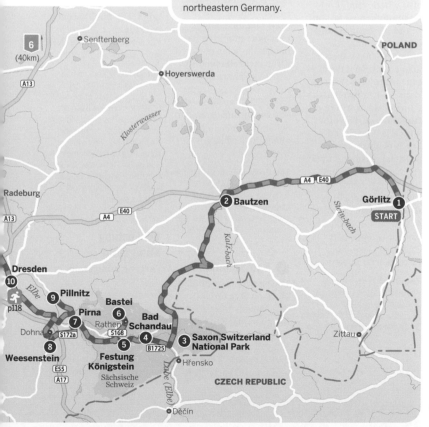

② Bautzen

Quirky Bautzen has an attractive cobblestone old town surrounding a fairy-tale castle and attracts visitors for three main, rather diverse reasons. It's home to the Sorbian people, an ethnic minority within Germany that has its own Slavic language and very distinct cultural identity – best explored at the **Sorbisches Museum** (☏03591-270 8700; www.sorbisches-museum.de; Ortenburg 3-5; adult/concession €5/2.50; ⊙10am-6pm Tue-Sun). It's also where you'll find Germany's most famous brand of mustard (and on top of numerous mustard shops, there's also an all-mustard restaurant to try!). Finally, Bautzen has two prisons – one of them still operational today. The other, which is now closed but previously hosted political prisoners under the Nazi and communist governments, is the focus of a compelling **Gedenkstätte** (☏03591-404 74; www.gedenkstaette-bautzen.de; Weigangstrasse 8a; ⊙10am-6pm, to 8pm Fri), or memorial museum.

The Drive ≫ Take the picturesque S154 through Neustadt towards the gorgeous scenery of the Saxon Switzerland National Park.

TRIP HIGHLIGHT

③ Saxon Switzerland National Park

Saxony may only have one national park, but Saxon Switzerland is a real stunner. There is an enormous number of hiking and climbing opportunities here, including some 700 peaks to climb and 400 sq km of hiking routes. The entire place is simply stunning, with ethereal sandstone formations that look quite unlike anything else in Europe. It's best to park outside the park itself then take public transport into it, in particular the solar-powered **Kirnitzschtalbahn** (www.ovps.de; Kurpark; adult/concession €5/2.50, day pass €8/4; ⊙9.30am-7.30pm Apr-Oct) which runs from Bad Schandau to Beutehnfall along the Kirnitzsch River.

The Drive ≫ From the national park, take the B172 from Schmilka to Bad Schandau, a gorgeous 8km drive that runs along the banks of the Elbe with mountains visible on both sides.

④ Bad Schandau

The charming 'capital' of Saxon Switzerland, this friendly little town is a good place to bed down for the night after a day of walking in the national park. There's a wonderful early 20th-century lift, the **Person-enaufzug** (Rudolf-Sendig Str; adult/concession return €2.80/2.20; ⊙9am-6pm Apr & Oct, to 8pm May-Sep, to 5pm Nov-Mar), which takes you to the town's highest point for some breathtaking views. Hikers should not miss the glorious trek to the **Schrammstein-aussicht**, a moderate-to-strenuous trail that leads to a fantastic viewpoint of the rocks, the Elbe Valley and national park beyond. The first 20 minutes up the steep **Obrigensteig** are tough but then the trail levels out and leads through fabulous rock formations. The final 'ascent' is straight up the rocks via a one-way network of steel stairs and ladders.

The Drive ≫ Leaving Bad Schandau, cross the Elbe at the bridge outside of town and continue along the B172 to Königstein. This charming small town is a good spot to stop for breakfast or lunch before continuing up to the famous Königstein Fortress high above the town. Park in the car park and walk five minutes to the fortress entrance.

⑤ Festung Königstein

Festung Königstein (☏035021-646 07; www.festung-koenigstein.de; adult/concession Apr-Oct €12/9, Nov-Mar €10/7, audioguide €3; ⊙9am-6pm Apr-Oct, to 5pm Nov-Mar; 🚲) is the largest intact fortress in Germany, and so imposing

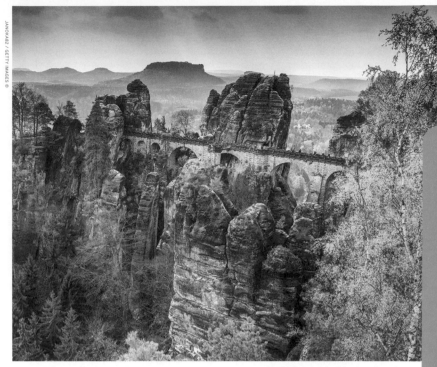

JANOKABZ / GETTY IMAGES ©

Bastei Basteibrücke, Felsenburg Neurathen

and formidable that no one in history has ever even bothered to attack it, let alone managed to conquer it. Begun in the 13th century, it was repeatedly enlarged and is now a veritable textbook in military architecture, with 30 buildings spread across 9.5 hectares. Inside, the main highlight is the **In Lapide Regis**, a superb permanent exhibition that tells the dramatic story of the fortress in an engaging and interactive way.

The Drive » Drive back down into the valley along the S168 and in a couple of kilometres you'll come to Rathen. Park in the car park here and take the ferry across the Elbe.

----

6 Bastei

The resort town of Rathen, in the northwestern corner of the national park, is the access point for the Bastei, the most famous rock formations in the Elbe Valley, and also the most popular spot in the park to visit. It's an easy and gentle hike up to the magnificent **Felsenburg Neurathen** (adult/concession €2/1; ☺9am-6pm), a partly reconstructed medieval castle in the Bastei, from which there are numerous lookouts and viewpoints, including a stunning panorama over the Elbe hundreds of metres below. The much-photographed Basteibrücke, a sandstone bridge built in 1851, leads through the rocks, though this is the busiest part of the park. Try taking the 5km loop back to Rathen to escape the crowds.

The Drive » After returning to Rathen, where there are numerous spots for a meal, cross the Elbe again to get back to your car, then take the S168 to Pirna. It's a short drive through some lovely countryside.

67

❼ Pirna

Pirna is a charming town on the Elbe, famous as Canaletto's home during his years in Saxony, and a friendly and easy-going place today. The big attraction in town is the excellent **DDR Museum** (☎03501-774 842; www.ddr-museum-pirna.de; Rottwerndorferstrasse 45; adult/child €8/6; ◷10am-4pm Tue-Fri, to 5pm Sat & Sun Apr-Oct, Sat & Sun only Nov-Mar), in a former army barracks on the outskirts of town. You can wander around a fully furnished East German apartment, sit in a classroom with GDR president Walter Ulbricht glowering at you, or find out how much a Junge Pioniere youth organisation uniform cost.

The Drive ≫ It's just 10km along the B172a to Weesenstein, and a lovely drive that wends its way between valleys along the river.

❽ Weesenstein

With its gorgeous setting towering above the valley, **Schloss Weesenstein** (☎035027-6260; www.schloss-weesenstein.de; Am Schlossberg 1, Müglitztal; adult/concession €7.50/6, audioguide €2; ◷10am-6pm) has an unforgettable setting and looks as fairy-tale perfect as can be. The castle itself is an amazing alchemy of styles, blending medieval roots with Renaissance and baroque embellishments. This resulted in an architectural curiosity where the banquet halls ended up beneath the roof, the horse stables on the 5th floor and the residential quarters in the cellar. There's lots to see inside, with an entire wing of the castle still filled with furniture and an exhibition on life here over the centuries. There's also a wonderful formal garden to explore.

The Drive ≫ Take the B172a then cross the Elbe at Pirna and follow the signs to Pillnitz. The drive should take around 15 minutes and the views while crossing the river are superb.

❾ Pillnitz

Right on the banks of the Elbe, **Schloss & Park Pillnitz** (☎0351-261 3260; www.schlosspillnitz.de; Aug-Böckstiegel-Strasse 2; park 9am-6pm adult/concession €3/2.50, park, museums & greenhouses €8/6; ◷park 6am-dusk, museums 10am-6pm Tue-Sun mid-Apr-Oct) is a delightful baroque pleasure palace festooned with fanciful Chinese flourishes. This is where the Saxon rulers once lived it up during long, hot Dresden summers. Explore the wonderful formal gardens, then learn about the history of the palace and life at court in the Schlossmuseum inside the palace itself. Two other buildings, the **Wasserpalais** and the **Bergpalais**, house the **Kunstgewerbemuseum**, which is filled with various valuables from the Saxon court, including Augustus the Strong's throne.

The Drive ≫ Take the Pillnitzer Landstrasse from the palace towards Dresden. It's a half-hour, 14km journey that in parts runs along the Elbe's edge. Cross the river at Loschwitz and follow signs for Dresden's Altstadt.

TRIP HIGHLIGHT

❿ Dresden

There are few city silhouettes more striking than Dresden's. The classic view from the Elbe's northern bank takes in spires, towers and domes belonging to palaces, churches and stately buildings, and indeed it's hard to believe that the city was all but wiped off the map by Allied air raids in 1945. There's an enormous amount to see in the relatively small area that makes up Dresden's **Altstadt** (old town). First on the list should be the **Zwinger** (☎0351-4914 2000; www.der-dresdner-zwinger.de; Theaterplatz 1; ticket for all museums adult/concession €12/9, courtyard free; ◷6am-10pm Apr-Oct, to 8pm Nov-Mar), the incredible pleasure palace of the Saxon electors, which now contains three superb museums. Next up, visit the **Residenzschloss** (☎0351-4914 2000; www.skd.museum; Schlossplatz; adult/child €12/free, incl Historisches Grünes Gewölbe €21/free;

⊙10am-6pm Wed-Mon), the seat of power of the Saxon electors and now the setting for several impressive museums, the most important of which is the **Historisches Grünes Gewölbe** (Historic Green Vault; ☑0351-4914 2000; www.skd. museum; Residenzschloss; €12; ⊙10am-6pm Wed-Mon), which displays some 3000 precious items on shelves and tables (without glass protection) in a series of increasingly lavish rooms. Finally, be sure not to miss the famous **Frauenkirche** (☑0351-6560 6100; www. frauenkirche-dresden.de; Neumarkt; audioguide €2.50, cupola adult/student €8/5; ⊙10am-noon & 1-6pm Mon-Fri, weekend hours vary), which graced the Dresden skyline for two centuries before collapsing after the February 1945 bombings. It was rebuilt from a pile of rubble between 1994 and 2005, and is now Dresden's most enduring symbol.

See p118 for a walking tour of Dresden.

✕ ⌷ p71, p99, p115

The Drive ❱❱ Take the B170 for 16km to reach Moritzburg. It's a picturesque drive through some charming countryside. Park in the car park in the centre of the village and you'll see the castle in the distance ahead of you.

- - - - - - - - - - - - - - - -

⑪ Moritzburg
Schloss Moritzburg
(☑035207-8730; www.

schloss-moritzburg.de; Schlossallee; adult/concession €8.50/6.50; ⊙10am-6pm, to 5pm Sat & Sun Mar) is the third of the famous palaces surrounding Dresden, but in many ways it's the most impressive, set in the middle of an enormous lake that doubles as a moat, and standing magnificently overlooking a huge park. It was the preferred hunting palace of the Saxon rulers, and its interiors are dominated by hundreds of framed antlers, which are quite a sight to behold in the sumptuous state rooms. Prized trophies include the antlers of an extinct giant stag and bizarrely misshapen ones in the **Hall of Monstrosities**. Considerably prettier is the legendary

Federzimmer (Feather Room) downstairs, whose centrepiece is a bed made from over a million colourful duck, pheasant and peacock feathers. A walk through the gorgeous formal gardens and then through the wilder, forested park around the ornamental lake will return you to the car park.

The Drive ❱❱ It's an easy 16km drive to Meissen along Köhlerstrasse.

- - - - - - - - - - - - - - - -

⑫ Meissen
Straddling the Elbe around 25km upstream from Dresden, Meissen is the cradle of European porcelain manufacturing and still hitches its tourism appeal to the world-famous china first

---

DRESDEN & WWII

Between 13 and 15 February 1945, British and US planes unleashed 3900 tonnes of explosives on Dresden in four huge air raids. Bombs and incendiary shells whipped up a mammoth firestorm, and ashes rained down on villages 35km away. Historians still argue over whether or not this constituted a war crime committed by the Allies on an innocent civilian population. Some claim that with the Red Army at the gates of Berlin, the war was effectively won, and the Allies gained little military advantage from the destruction of Dresden. Others have said that as the last urban centre in the east of the country left intact, Dresden could have provided shelter for German troops returning from the east and was a viable target. What's undeniable though, is that when the blazes had died down and the dust settled, tens of thousands of Dresdners had lost their lives and 20 sq km of this once-elegant baroque city lay in smouldering ruins.

cooked up in its imposing castle in 1710. But even those left unmoved by August the Strong's 'white gold' will find the impressive position of the town, dominated by its soaring Gothic cathedral, impressive fairy-tale-like castle and wonderful Elbe valley views, quite compelling. Most visitors will want to head straight up the hillside to glorious **Albrechtsburg** (☎03521-470 70; www.albrechtsburg-meissen.de; Domplatz 1; adult/concession incl audioguide €8/6.50, with Dom €11/8; ☺10am-6pm Mar-Oct, to 5pm Nov-Feb), Meissen's enormous castle, and the home of European porcelain. After a stroll through the delightful old town, end the day with a visit to the superb **Erlebniswelt Haus Meissen** (☎03521-468 208; www.erlebniswelt-meissen.com; Talstrasse 9; adult/concession €10/6; ☺9am-6pm May-Oct, to 5pm Nov-Apr), *the* place to witness the astonishing artistry that makes Meissen porcelain unique.

The Drive ⟫ Head out of Meissen and take the B6, a pleasant alternative to the motorway, directly to Leipzig.

The drive is 88km and takes 1½ hours.

TRIP HIGHLIGHT

⓭ Leipzig

The final destination on this trip is Leipzig, a fascinating combination of cultural powerhouse and contemporary creative hothouse. Head to the storied Altstadt to explore the city's dramatic past, from the choir once led by Bach, which still goes strong at the **Thomaskirche** (☎0341-222 240; www.thomaskirche.org; Thomaskirchhof 18; tower €2; ☺church 9am-6pm, tower 1pm, 2pm & 4.30pm Sat, 2pm & 3pm Sun Apr-Nov), to the chilling **Stasi Museum** (☎0341-961 2443; www.runde-ecke-leipzig.de; Dittrichring 24; ☺10am-6pm) and the first-class **Zeitgeschichtliches Forum** (Forum of Contemporary History; ☎0341-222 0400; www.hdg.de/leipzig; Grimmaische Strasse 6; ☺9am-6pm Tue-Fri, from 10am Sat & Sun), which gives a detailed account of the creation and collapse of East Germany. Another museum not to miss is the excellent **Museum der Bildenden Künste** (Museum of Fine Arts; ☎0341-216 990; www.mdbk.de; Katharinenstrasse 10; adult/concession €10/7; ☺10am-6pm Tue & Thu-Sun, noon-8pm Wed), a first-class art collection in an amazing building. Visit the famous **Oper Leipzig** (☎0341-126 1261; www.oper-leipzig.de; Augustusplatz 12) or see the **Thomanerchor** (☎0341-984 4211; www.thomaskirche.org; Thomaskirchhof 18; tickets €2) perform, before discovering Leipzig's relaxed nightlife and contemporary art and music scenes in the studenty-creative neighbourhoods of the Südvorstadt and Plagwitz. Stroll down Karli, the main street of the Südvorstadt, or Karl-Heine-Strasse, Plagwitz' main thoroughfare, both of which are packed with bars, restaurants, cafes and clubs. Finally, don't miss the amazing **Völkerschlachtdenkmal** (Monument to the Battle of the Nations; ☎0341-241 6870; www.stadtgeschichtliches-museum-leipzig.de; Strasse des 18 Oktober 100; adult/child €8/6; ☺10am-6pm Apr-Oct, to 4pm Nov-Mar; ⊞2 or 15 to Völkerschlachtdenkmal), the mother of all war monuments.

🍴 🛏 p71 , p99, p115

Eating & Sleeping

Görlitz ❶

✖ Miódmaliny — Eastern European €

(✆in Poland 0756-418 090; www.facebook.com/miodmaliny; Daszyńskiego 17, Zgorzelec; mains €6-15; ⏰11.30am-10.30pm) A short walk to the Polish side of town and you can gorge on culinary delights with a big discount. Furnished as grandma's parlour, this cosy cafe is strong on Central European classics, with a local touch. Try Polish duck with apples or beef roulette, both served with Silesian dumplings, and don't bypass *nalewki* – delightful fruity liqueurs.

⌂ Hotel Börse — Hotel €€

(✆03581-764 20; www.boerse-goerlitz.de; Untermarkt 16; s/d from €80/115; P ☎) Four-poster beds, sparkling glass chandeliers, marble bathrooms, patterned parquet floors and elegant antiques are the hallmarks of this stylish hotel in an 18th-century Palais. With its absolutely perfect location, old-world atmosphere and surprisingly affordable rates, this is our best bet for a comfortable and memorable stay in Görlitz.

Dresden ❿

✖ brennNessel — Vegetarian €€

(✆0351-494 3319; www.brennnessel-dresden.de; Schützengasse 18; mains €10-16; ⏰11am-midnight; 🖋) This popular, largely vegetarian gastropub in a miraculously surviving 350-year-old building is an oasis in the otherwise empty and anodyne streets of the Altstadt. Indeed, reserve for lunch if you'd like to eat outside in the charming, sun-dappled courtyard, as it's a favourite hang-out for off-duty Semperoper musicians and office workers.

✖ Raskolnikoff — International €€

(✆0351-804 5706; www.raskolnikoff.de; Böhmische Strasse 34; mains €10-15; ⏰11am-10.30pm) An artist squat in the 1980s, Raskolnikoff now brims with grown-up artsy-bohemian flair, especially in the sweet little

garden at the back, complete with bizarre water feature. The seasonally calibrated menu showcases the fruits of the surrounding land in globally inspired dishes, including a variety of *pelmeni* (Russian dumplings), which proudly represent the Dostoyevsky character the establishment is named after.

⌂ Gewandhaus Hotel — Boutique Hotel €€€

(✆0351-494 90; www.gewandhaus-hotel.de; Ringstrasse 1; d from €125; P ✳ @ ☎ ⛟) Revamped as a boutique hotel a few years ago, the stunning Gewandhaus, an 18th-century trading house of tailors and fabric merchants that burned down in 1945, boasts sleek public areas, beautiful and bright rooms, and a breakfast that sets a high bar for the city.

Leipzig ⓭

✖ Auerbachs Keller — German €€€

(✆0341-216 100; www.auerbachs-keller-leipzig.de; Mädlerpassage, Grimmaische Strasse 2-4; mains Keller €15-30, Weinstuben €30-40; ⏰Keller noon-11pm daily, Weinstuben 6-11pm Mon-Sat) Founded in 1525, Auerbachs Keller is one of Germany's best-known restaurants. It's cosy and touristy but the food's actually quite good and the setting memorable. There are two sections: the vaulted Grosser Keller for hearty Saxonian dishes and the four historic rooms of the Historische Weinstuben for upscale German fare. Reservations are highly advised.

⌂ Meisterzimmer — Boutique Hotel €€

(✆0341-2270 4063; www.meisterzimmer.de; Spinnereistrasse 7; s/d from €80/90) Somewhere between a hotel and a designer Airbnb loft, this selection of minimalist but style-conscious rooms is inside a massive converted factory that houses half of Leipzig's creative industries. If you don't enjoy public areas in hotels, but love a light-bathed converted factory, this is the place for you. Booking ahead is essential.

Central Germany's Castles & Palaces

From medieval to romantic, this trip twists through bucolic fields, rustic villages and alongside sparkling rivers, uncovering mystical ruins, robust fortresses and exquisite palaces.

TRIP HIGHLIGHTS

305 km

Kassel
Three palaces and the amazing Herkules fountain

0 km

Leipzig
A vibrant city rich in history and culture

8 FINISH

1 START

7

Erfurt

3

Drei Gleichen

Eisenach
Home to the Wartburg, one of Germany's best-loved castles

225 km

Dornburger Schlösser
A trio of spectacular hilltop palaces

97 km

3–5 DAYS
305KM / 224 MILES

GREAT FOR...

BEST TIME TO GO
May to September has crisp, clear skies and luminous canola fields.

ESSENTIAL PHOTO
The Saale River valley from Dornburger Schlösser's clifftop perch.

BEST FOR FOODIES
Dine in classic style at Weimar's romantic AnnA.

Central Germany's Castles & Palaces

Journey into the historical and geographical heartland of Germany, where cultural titans Goethe and Schiller once deliberated. You'll pass through ancient forests and villages, alongside sparkling rivers and working farms to visit spectacular castles and palaces in medieval, Renaissance, baroque and rococo styles. The magnificent Wartburg castle, inspiration for Ludwig II's famous Neuschwanstein, is one of Germany's finest.

TRIP HIGHLIGHT

❶ Leipzig

Leipzig could well be Germany's 'it' city, a playground for no-madic young creatives displaced by the fast-gentrifying German capital, but it's also a city of enormous history, set solidly in the sights of music lovers due to an intrinsic connection to the lives and works of Bach, Mendelssohn and Wagner. There's much to see and do here. At the very least, you'll want to

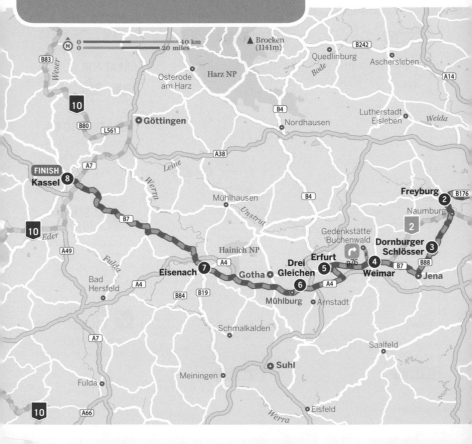

check out the enormous art collection of **Museum der Bildenden Künste** (p70) in its modernist glass cube home (for a little architectural contrast), and get an overview of this rapidly changing city in the **Stadtgeschichtliches Museum** (City History Museum; ☎0341-965 130; www. stadtgeschichtliches-museum -leipzig.de; Markt 1; adult/ concession €6/4; ◷10am-6pm Tue-Sun), housed in Leipzig's beautiful Renaissance town hall.

✕ 🏠 p71 , p99, p115

The Drive ≫ Take the B2 south out of Leipzig until you reach the A38 at exit 31, for some 33km of autobahn action west to exit 26. Head south on the B91 until the junction with the B176 outside Burgwerben. Follow the B176 west for 17km until you reach a roundabout: head straight through then turn left on Merseburger Strasse into Freyburg.

- - - - - - - - - - - - - - - - - -

 Freyburg

With its cobblestone streets and medieval castle clinging to vine-covered slopes, Freyburg puts the 'r' in rustic. Sparkling-wine production has been the town's focus since the mid-19th century. Pop into **Rotkäppchen Sektkellerei** (☎034464-340; www.rotkaeppchen.de; Sektkellereistrasse 5; 45 min tour €6; ◷tours 11am & 2pm daily, also 12.30pm & 3.30pm Sat & Sun) to toast the start of your trip with a glass of Germany's best-known homegrown bubbles, then head to

the imposing medieval **Schloss Neuenburg** (☎34464-355 30; www. schloss-neuenburg.de; Schloss 25; adult/concession €6.50/4, with tour €8.50/6, tower €2.50/1.50; ◷10am-6pm daily, tower Tue-Sun), on the hill above town. There's an excellent museum, a rare Romanesque two-storey chapel and a free-standing tower, the Dicker Wilhelm, with splendid views over the Saale River valley. It's possible to spend the night in one of two charming apartments within the castle walls: book ahead if this tickles your fancy.

The Drive ≫ Take the B180 south for 11km to the pretty town of Naumburg. Pick up the B88 for 15km until it meets the Saale River at Camburg. Cross the bridge and follow the scenic L1059 for 9km until you reach a tiny hamlet belonging to Saaleplatte village, where you'll drop south along Wilsdorfer Strasser for 5km to Dornburg.

 LINK YOUR TRIP

2 **Design for Life: Bauhaus to VW**

Have some Bauhaus with your baroque, on this exploration of modern German design and architecture that begins in Weimar.

10 **German Fairy-Tale Road**

Delve into the world of the Brothers Grimm in Kassel, heading north or south along Germany's beloved Fairy-Tale Road.

TRIP HIGHLIGHT

❸ Dornburger Schlösser

There are few places in the world where you can get a snapshot of three distinct historical periods, side by side. The **Dornburger Schlösser** (☏036427-215 130; www. dornburg-schloesser.de; Max-Krehan-Strasse 2, Dornburg; adult/concession combination ticket €6/4; ⊙10am-5pm Thu-Tue Apr-Oct) is one – a hillside trilogy of superbly restored palaces in medieval, Renaissance and rococo styles, with stunning views and immaculate gardens. The **Altes Schloss**, the oldest,

blends Romanesque, late-Gothic and baroque elements but can only be viewed from the outside. You can enter both the 1539 **Renaissance Palace** (where Goethe once stayed) and the gorgeous **Rococo Palace**. It's free to stroll around the magnificent gardens, to enjoy the wonderful views and admire the palaces from the outside.

The Drive ≫ Head south on the B88 for 12km through the picturesque Saale valley. The road hugs the river, even meeting for a brief kiss here and there, until it reaches the outskirts of Jena, where you'll pick up the B7 heading west. Follow it for 21km until you reach Weimar.

❹ Weimar

A pantheon of intellectual and creative giants lived and worked in Weimar: historical epicentre of the German Enlightenment. Goethe, Schiller, Bach, Nietzsche and Kandinsky are all memorialised throughout town. History buffs may want to linger here a few days. The **Herzogin Anna Amalia Bibliothek** (☏03643-545 400; www. klassik-stiftung.de; Platz der Demokratie 1; adult/concession €8/6.50; ⊙9.30am-2.30pm Tue-Sun) displays precious tomes in its magnificent Rokokosaal (Rococo Hall), including some once used by several of the aforementioned creators whose busts and paintings still keep watch over the collection. About 4km south of town, baroque **Schloss Belvedere** (☏03643-545 400; www. klassik-stiftung.de; Schloss und Park Weimar-Belvedere; adult/concession €6.50/5; ⊙11am-5pm Tue-Sun Apr-Oct; 🅿) is set among manicured grounds and has a museum of artefacts from the 17th and 18th centuries. Complete your visit with a comprehensive overview of Weimar's beloved genius at the **Goethe-Nationalmuseum** (☏03643-545 400; www. klassik-stiftung.de; Frauenplan 1; adult/concession €12.50/9; ⊙9.30am-6pm Tue-Sun Apr-Oct, to 4pm Nov-Mar).

🍴 🛏 p53, p79

DETOUR: GEDENKSTÄTTE BUCHENWALD

Start: ❹ **Weimar**

A visit to the sombre **Gedenkstätte Buchenwald** (☏03463-4300; www.buchenwald.de; Buchenwald; ⊙9am-6pm Apr-Oct, to 4pm Nov-Mar; 🅿) memorial, in the former concentration camp 10km northwest of Weimar, might be the most memorable of your trip. Drive north out of town along Ettersburger Strasse to Blutstrasse and head west. You'll first pass the striking memorial to your left: be sure to approach the massive hillside monument to fully appreciate it. Publications from the museum store explain the symbolic significance of its many elements. Follow the road for 1km into the camp towards the visitor centre, then wander around the numerous intact structures to deepen your understanding of the horrors that played out here. Between 1937 and 1945, hidden from Weimarers and surrounding villagers, some 56,500 of the 250,000 men, women and children who were incarcerated here lost their lives.

HANS BLOSSEY / ALAMY STOCK PHOTO ©

Kassel *Herkules* statue, Schloss Wilhelmshöhe (p78)

The Drive » Take the B7 west through fields of canola and wind turbines for 22km, directly into Erfurt.

⑤ Erfurt

Thuringia's capital is a scene-stealing mix of sweeping squares, cobblestone alleyways, perky church towers, idyllic river scenery and pan-generational architecture. It's a great place to stop for a meal or two and makes a good base if you decide to explore the area over a few days. Perched on the only hill above town, Erfurt's **Zitadelle Petersberg** (☎0361-664 00; Petersberg

3; tour adult/concession €9/6; ◷10am-6pm Tue-Sun) ranks among Europe's largest and best-preserved baroque fortresses. It sits above a honeycomb of tunnels, which can be explored on guided tours. It's free to roam the external grounds and enjoy the fabulous views.

✕ 🍴 p79, p99, p115

The Drive » Head south on the L1052 for 9km. Pick up the A4 autobahn at exit 47a Erfurt-Ost, heading west in the direction of Frankfurt. Stay on the A4 until you reach exit 43 Wandersleben, then head south into the pretty village of Mühlburg. You'll be able to see Burg Gleichen to the north.

⑥ Drei Gleichen

Allow a few hours to enjoy this fascinating medieval stop comprising three similar hilltop castles, collectively known as Drei Gleichen, each within eyesight of the other. North of the autobahn, **Burg Gleichen** (☎036202-824 40; www.drei-gleichen.de; Wandersleben; €3; ◷10am-6pm Apr-Oct) makes a rewarding visit for castle fans, but it's a 30-minute uphill climb from the car park to the ruins. Of the three castles, **Mühlburg** (☎0160-225 0918; www.drei-gleichen.de; Mühlberg; adult/concession

77

€2/1.50; ⏰10am-5pm Mon-Fri, to 6pm Sat & Sun Mar-Oct) is the oldest and closest, dating to around 704. Its moat walls, drawbridge and 22m-high castle tower are intact. **Veste Wachsenburg** (📞03628-742 40; www.wachsenburg. com; Amt Wachsenburg; ⏰restaurant 11am-8pm Tue-Sat, to 5pm Sun), **10km south** of the A4, is fully preserved, housing a hotel, restaurant and museum; it's possible to drive right up to the castle gate.

The Drive ››› Take the A4 autobahn west towards Frankfurt for 36km, to exit 40a Eisenach Ost. From here, follow the signs for Eisenach/Wartburg for another 10km.

TRIP HIGHLIGHT

7 Eisenach

Hilly Eisenach, on the edge of the Thuringian forest, is best known for its Unesco World Heritage castle **Wartburg** (📞03691-2500; www.wartburg-eisenach. de; Auf der Wartburg 1; tour adult/concession €10/7; ⏰tours 8.30am-5pm Apr-Oct, 9am-3.30pm Nov-Mar, English tour 1.30pm), **where Martin Luther hid** while his controversial theses brought about the Reformation. This huge, medieval fortress is magnificently preserved, offering much by way of its permanent and visiting exhibitions, intact structure and breathtaking views over little Eisenach, the forest and beyond. Allow at least two hours: one for the guided tour, the rest

for the museum and the views. If you love classical music, you'll also want to take a look at **Bachhaus** (📞03691-793 40; www.bachhaus.de; Frauenplan 21; adult/concession €10/6; ⏰10am-6pm) and the **Reuter-Wagner Museum** (📞03691-743 293; Reuterweg 2; adult/concession €4/2; ⏰2-5pm Wed-Sun), while rev-heads won't want to miss **Automobile Welt Eisenach** (📞03691-772 12; www.awe-stiftung.de; Friedrich-Naumann-Strasse 10; adult/concession €6/3.50; ⏰10am-6pm Apr-Oct, 11am-5pm Nov-Mar, closed Mon).

✕ 🛏 p79, p114

The Drive ››› Head north on Mühlhäuser Strasse for 2km, then pick up the B19 heading west. Follow the B19 north for 5km until the start of the B7. Follow the B7 northwest as it winds through forests, farmlands and pretty villages for 75km towards Kassel.

TRIP HIGHLIGHT

8 Kassel

Although WWII bombing and postwar reconstruction left Kassel looking undeniably utilitarian, you'd hardly know it today. This culture-rich city on the Fulda River boasts some impressive attractions. The palatial **Schloss Wilhelmshöhe** (📞0561-316 800; www. museum-kassel.de; Schlosspark 1; adult/concession €6/4, Weissenstein wing incl tour €4/3, audioguide €3; ⏰10am-5pm Tue-Sun, to 8pm Wed; 🅿) contains a premier

baroque art collection – time your visit to coincide with the Wednesday and Sunday operation of the spectacular **Herkules** (📞visitor centre 0561-3168 0781; www.museum-kassel. de; Schlosspark Wilhelmshöhe 26, Herkules-Terrassen; adult/concession €6/4; ⏰10am-5pm Tue-Sun mid-Mar–mid-Nov, daily May-Sep; 🅿 🚌) fountain. Both are within **Bergpark Wilhelmshöhe** (📞0561-3168 0751; www. museum-kassel.de; Wilhelmshöher Allee 380, visitor centre; ⏰9am-sunset, visitor centre 10am-5pm May-Sep, to 4pm Sat & Sun Oct-Apr; 🅿 🚌), as is the smaller, equally adored **Löwenburg** (Lion Castle; 📞0561-3168 0244; www.museum-kassel. de; Schlosspark 9; adult/concession €4/3; ⏰tours hourly 10am-4pm Tue-Sun Mar-mid-Nov, 10am-3pm Fri-Sun mid-Nov-Feb; 🚌) or 'Lion Castle'. Round out your visit with some fun and fantasy in Kassel's fairytale **Grimmwelt** (📞0561-598 6190; www.grimm welt.de; Weinbergstrasse 21; adult/concession €8/6; ⏰10am-6pm Tue-Sun, to 8pm Fri; 🚌), paying homage to the Brothers Grimm. Or make a 10km side trip to **Schloss Wilhelmsthal** (📞05674-6898; www. museum-kassel.de; Calden; adult/concession €4/3; ⏰hourly tours 10am-4pm Tue-Sun Mar–mid-Nov, 10am-3pm Fri-Sun mid-Nov–Feb; 🅿), in Calden; almost due north of Wilhelmshöhe, it's one of Germany's finest rococo palaces.

Eating & Sleeping

Weimar ❹

✗ Restaurant
AnnA International €€€

(📞03643-8020; https://hotelelephantweimar.
de/restaurant; Hotel Elephant, Markt 19;
mains €32-39; ⏰ noon-10pm) Inside the
Hotel Elephant Weimar, this highly acclaimed
gourmet act is one for those who appreciate a
true fine-dining experience. Dress to impress,
expect the chef to wow your palate, wait for the
staff to make you feel more important than you
know you are, and leave plenty of room on the
credit card.

🛏 Familienhotel Hotel €€

(📞03643-457 9888; www.familienhotel-weimar.
de; Seifengasse 8; apt from €100; 📶) This
timber-fronted, multistoried hotel in Weimar's
historical centre has won awards for its
ecological principles and family-friendly
attitude (kids are welcome, and given space to
play). There are 11 apartments, and the equally
agreeable Gretchen's Cafe (p53) is downstairs.
Parking nearby is €6 per night.

Erfurt ❺

✗ Zum Wenigemarkt 13 German €€

(📞0361-642 2379; www.wenigemarkt-13.de;
Wenigemarkt 13; mains €10-20; ⏰11.30am-
11pm) This upbeat restaurant in a delightful
spot serves traditional and updated takes on
Thuringian cuisine, starring regionally hunted
and gathered ingredients where possible.
Tender salt-encrusted pork roast and trout
drizzled with tangy caper-and-white-wine sauce
are both menu stars.

🛏 Hotel
Brühlerhöhe Boutique Hotel €€

(📞0361-241 4990; www.hotel-bruehlerhoehe
-erfurt.de; Rudolfstrasse 48; s/d from €90/100;
🅿📶) This Prussian officers' casino turned
chic city hotel gets high marks for its opulent
breakfast spread (€12.50) and smiling, quick-
on-their-feet staff. Rooms are cosy and modern
with chocolate-brown furniture, thick carpets
and sparkling baths. It's a short tram ride into
the town centre.

Eisenach ❼

✗ Weinrestaurant
Turmschänke German €€€

(📞03691-213 533; www.turmschaenke
-eisenach.de; Karlsplatz 28; mains €16-28,
3-/4-course menu €37/45; ⏰6-11pm Mon-Sat)
Going strong since 1910 – when the hotelier of
the Kaiserhof connected his premises to the
11th-century defensive tower next door – and
persisting through the GDR years, this hushed
hideaway scores a perfect 10 on the 'romance
metre'. Walls of polished oak, beautiful table
settings and immaculate service complement
Ulrich Rösch's flavour-packed concoctions,
which finely balance the trendy and the
traditional.

🛏 Hotel
Villa Anna Boutique Hotel €€

(📞03691-239 50; www.hotel-villa-anna.de; Fritz-
Koch-Strasse 12; s/d from €75/105; 🅿😊📶)
In a handsome three-storey townhouse built in
1907, this fantastic boutique hotel at the foot of
the Wartburg has 15 classy, spacious rooms that
design heads will love. The beds are ultracomfy,
most rooms feature a decent desk and the
breakfast buffet is more than generous.

Berlin & the Jewels of Eastern Brandenburg

6

This tour wraps a lot that's great about Germany into one neat package: vibrant metropolis, romantic forest, spirit-lifting gardens and monasteries, and awe-inspiring technology.

TRIP HIGHLIGHTS

366 km

Gedenkstätte & Museum Sachsenhausen
Sobering concentration camp

285 km

Schiffshebewerk Niederfinow
Marvel of technology

FINISH **9**

Kloster Chorin **7**

START **1**

Gedenkstätte Seelower Höhen

0 km

Berlin
Capital of culture and cool

Frankfurt (Oder)

Stift Neuzelle

89 km

Lübbenau & the Spreewald
Enchanting watery forest

2

Schloss Branitz, Cottbus

4 DAYS
366KM / 250 MILES

GREAT FOR...

BEST TIME TO GO
Any time is possible, but April to October has better weather.

📷 ESSENTIAL PHOTO
Capture a traditional Sorb village in Lehde in the Spreewald.

✔️ BEST FOR HISTORY
The heart-wrenching memorial exhibit at Sachsenhausen concentration camp.

6 Berlin & the Jewels of Eastern Brandenburg

This trip gets your head spinning in scintillating Berlin, then slows you back down on a leisurely tour around sparsely populated eastern Brandenburg. You'll meet the Sorbs, a traditional Slavic people at home in the Spreewald, a rivulet-laced fairy-tale forest. You'll visit gardens created by an eccentric prince, soul-stirring monasteries, a technological marvel and socialist model cities. WWII comes hauntingly alive in a concentration camp and on the largest battlefield on German soil.

TRIP HIGHLIGHT

❶ Berlin

Your adventure starts in the German capital, an intoxicating cocktail of culture, history, offbeat experiences and nightlife. Tick off sightseeing blockbusters as you Stretch Your Legs (p116), then devote time to exploring the city's grand museum landscape. A good bet are the five treasure chests on Museum Island that showcase 6000 years of art and cultural history,

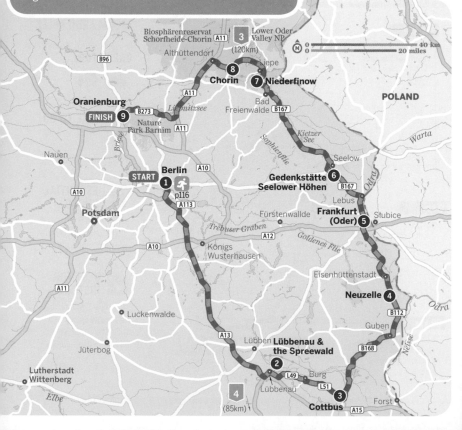

including the ethereal 3300-year-old bust of Egyptian Queen Nefertiti at the **Neues Museum** (New Museum; ☎030-266 424 242; www.smb.museum; Bodestrasse 1-3; adult/concession/under 18yr €12/6/free; ⏱10am-6pm Fri-Wed, to 8pm Thu; ☐100, 200, TXL, ⑤Hackescher Markt, Friedrichstrasse, ⓊFriedrichstrasse), and the radiantly blue Babylonian Ishtar Gate at the **Pergamonmuseum** (☎030-266 424 242; www.smb.museum; Bodestrasse 1-3; adult/concession/under 18yr €19/9.50/free; ⏱10am-6pm Fri-Wed, to 8pm Thu; ☐100, 200, TXL, ⑤Hackescher Markt, Friedrichstrasse, ⓊFriedrichstrasse). To come to grips with Berlin's division during

the Cold War, there's no better place than the **Gedenkstätte Berliner Mauer** (Berlin Wall Memorial; ☎030-467 986 666; www.berliner-mauer-gedenkstaette.de; Bernauer Strasse btwn Schwedter Strasse & Gartenstrasse; ⏱visitor & documentation centre 10am-6pm Tue-Sun, open-air exhibit 8am-10pm daily; ⑤Nordbahnhof, Bernauer Strasse, Eberswalder Strasse), an indoor-outdoor exhibit along 1.4km of the former barrier. To see the longest remaining Wall vestige, head to the mural-festooned **East Side Gallery** (www.eastsidegallery-berlin.de; Mühlenstrasse btwn Oberbaumbrücke & Ostbahnhof; ⏱24hr; ⓊWarschauer Strasse, ⑤Ostbahnhof, Warschauer Strasse).

✗ ⊨ p87

The Drive » From Berlin, it's a quick one-hour drive to Lübbenau via the A100, A113 and A13, where you leave the autobahn at exit 9.

TRIP HIGHLIGHT

❷ Lübbenau & the Spreewald

Lübbenau is the main town in the Spreewald, a unique ice-age-formed landscape of jungle-like forest and marshland crisscrossed by some 300 channels fed by the Spree River – a German Everglades, if you will, minus the alligators. About 100km southeast of Berlin, this is the traditional homeland of

the Sorbs, a Slavic tribe whose members maintain their age-old customs, costumes and language (all signs are bilingual).

Until the first road was built in 1936, Spreewald villages were accessible only by flat-bottomed punt boats. Today, exploring the Unesco biosphere reserve in a *Kahn* piloted by a ferryman in traditional garb is a Spreewald must-do. Trips last from one hour to all day and depart from various spots, including the **Grosser Hafen** (☎03542-2225; www.grosser-kahnhafen.de; Dammstrasse 77a; boat tours €12-28; ⏱8.30am-7pm Mon-Thu, 9am-5pm Fri-Sun May-Sep, shorter hours Oct-Apr). A particularly nice one goes to the Sorb village of Lehde, whose **Freilandmuseum** (Open-Air Museum Lehde; ☎Apr-Oct 03542-871 508, Nov-Mar 03542-2472; www.museum-osl.de; An der Giglitza 1a; adult/concession €5/3.50; ⏱10am-6pm Apr-Sep, to 5pm Oct) gives you a good sense of what rural life in the Spreewald was like a century ago. DIY types can also rent a canoe or kayak, including from **Bootsverleih Richter** (☎03542-3764; www.bootsverleih-richter.de; Dammstrasse 75; kayak per person 2hr €12, day €17-20; ⏱9am-6pm late-Mar–mid-Oct).

✗ ⊨ p87

The Drive » The A15 takes you from Lübbenau to Cottbus in 30 minutes. For the scenic drive through Sorb heartland,

LINK YOUR TRIP

3 Lakes & Treasures of Mecklenburg–Western Pomerania

From Berlin, head north on the B96 for 120km to pick up this route in Neustrelitz, through the heart of one of Germany's oldest provinces.

4 Highlights of Saxony

From Lübbenau, head 100km south on the A13 to jewel-like Dresden and on to whimsical sandstone formations.

head south on the L49, turn left on Radduscher Bahnhofstrasse (L51) and follow it via Burg for about 28km to Cottbus.

- - - - - - - - - - - - - - - - -

❸ Schloss Branitz, Cottbus

Cottbus has a handsomely restored historic centre but its star attraction is **Park & Schloss Branitz** (☏0355-751 50; www.pueckler-museum.de; Robinienweg 5; park free, Schloss adult/concession €6.50/4.50; ⏱10am-6pm daily Apr-Oct, 11am-4pm Tue-Sun Nov-Mar; **P**; 🚃10 to Branitz Schloss) on the southeastern edge of town. The sprawling park-and-palace ensemble was dreamed up by Prince Hermann von Pückler-Muskau, a kooky 19th-century aristocrat, writer, ladies' man and renowned garden architect. For over 20 years, he feverishly turned his ancestral family estate into an Arcadian English-style landscape park by shaping hills, digging canals and lakes, and building earthen pyramids, one of which serves as his tomb. Exhibits in the Schloss (by Gottfried Semper, of Dresden opera house fame) and outer buildings tell the story of the man and his ultimate pet project.

The Drive » The 60km-ride to Neuzelle (which has a feel-good eating option) takes you northeast on the B168 past the Peitzer Teiche, a huge network of carp-farming ponds, and through the southern reaches of the romantic Schlaube Valley Nature Park, a hikers' and cyclists' paradise. At Schenkendobern turn north onto the B112.

- - - - - - - - - - - - - - - - -

❹ Stift Neuzelle

Having hit the three-quarters-of-a-millennium mark in 2018, the Cistercian **Stift Neuzelle**

JUERGEN SACK / GETTY IMAGES ©

(Neuzelle Abbey; ☏033652-6102; www.stift-neuzelle.de; Stiftsplatz 7, Neuzelle; €7.50; ⏱10am-6pm Apr-Oct, to 4pm Nov-Mar) wears the moniker 'Brandenburg's baroque miracle' with pride. Gothic at its core, it received a baroque makeover in the 18th century that included the addition of exuberant gardens with water features, terraced hillsides and an orangery. A museum presents scenes from the **Passion of Christ** composed of 250-year-old vividly painted, life-sized cut-out figures dramatically arranged in a 'heavenly theatre'.

LOCAL KNOWLEDGE: GHERKIN COUNTRY

The Spreewald is world-renowned for its pickled cucumbers, cherished by connoisseurs for their low acidity, crunchy texture and delicate spicing. The official name 'Spreewälder Gurke' is even an EU-certified Protected Designation of Origin, just like Champagne and Cognac. Flemish clothmakers introduced the pickle seeds that thrive in the region's watery and humus-rich soil. Only about 20 companies, each using their own 'secret' family recipe, are allowed to produce the vegetable. Discover more pickle secrets on the 260km-long Gurken-Radweg (Gherkin Cycle Path) or at the Gurkenmuseum in Lehde.

Spreewald (p83) Cruise in Lehde

Make your pilgrimage to the Neuzeller Kloster **brewery** to try its *Bock*, porter, pilsner or 'anti-ageing' beer.

✗ p87

The Drive » Follow the B112 north for 36km to Frankfurt (Oder), perhaps stopping briefly in Eisenhüttenstadt, a once-thriving East German 'socialist model city'.

- - - - - - - - - - - - - - - - -

❺ Frankfurt (Oder)

Germany's 'other' Frankfurt sits on the Oder River right on the Polish border. WWII bombs and socialist reconstruction wiped out most vestiges of its one-time grandeur as a medieval trading centre

and university town. Still, the scenic river setting and unique sightseeing gems invite a quick stopover. The Gothic **Marienkirche** (Church of St Mary; ☎0335-224 42; www. st-marien-ffo.de; Oberkirchplatz; ⏰10am-6pm May-Sep, to 4pm Oct-Apr), for instance, boasts stunning medieval stained-glass windows that were squirrelled away by the Soviets as WWII booty and only returned in 2007. For the world's most comprehensive collection of East German art, drop by the **Museum Junge Kunst** (☎0335-2839 6183; www.blmk.de; Marktplatz 1; adult/concession €4/3; ⏰11am-5pm Tue-Sun). If

it's cheap(er) vodka and cigarettes you're after, walk across the Oder to Słubice, Frankfurt's Polish twin town.

✗ ⏹ p87

The Drive » Follow the B112 north for 10km to Lebus, then continue west for 18km on the B167 past hillsides and grassland carpeted in wildflowers from spring to autumn.

- - - - - - - - - - - - - - - - -

❻ Gedenkstätte Seelower Höhen

The **Seelow Heights Memorial Exhibit** (☎03346-597; www.gedenkstaette -seelower-hoehen.de; Küstriner Strasse 28a, Seelow; adult/

concession €4/3; ☺10am-5pm Tue-Sun Apr-Oct, to 4pm Nov-Mar) documents one of the last major battles of WWII, which took place on this 48m-high plateau above the Oder River valley in April 1945. Some 100,000 German troops fought tooth and nail – but in vain – to stave off a million Soviet soldiers. After three days of fighting, an estimated 50,000 on both sides had fallen. Imagine the horrors of this brutal battle as you climb to the military cemetery with its striking **memorial**, then pick your way past military vehicles and artillery pieces to the **museum** for the full low-down.

The Drive » Follow the B167 northwest for 55km via Neuhardenberg, with its palace turned hotel (p87), and past the Kietzer See birders' paradise. In Niederfinow, turn right on Hebewerkstrasse to arrive at the ship lift.

TRIP HIGHLIGHT

⑦ Schiffshebewerk Niederfinow

The tiny town of Niederfinow is famous for its spectacular ship lift, the **Schiffshebewerk Niederfinow** (☎033362-215; www.schiffshebewerk-niederfinow.info; Hebewerkstrasse 52; adult/concession €3/2; ☺9.30am-5.30pm late Mar-Oct, 10am-4pm Nov, Dec & Mar, closed Jan & Feb), which links the Oder River and the Oder-Havel Canal. This remarkable engi-

neering feat was completed in 1934 and measures 60m high, 27m wide and 94m long. Cargo barges sail into a sort of giant bathtub, which is then raised or lowered 36m, water and all. Visitors can enjoy the ride aboard tourist boats operated by **Fahrgastschifffahrt Neumann** (☎03334-244 05; www.schiffshebewerk-niederfinow.info/neumann; Hebewerkstrasse; adult/child €7/4; ☺11am, 1pm & 3pm late Mar-Oct). To accommodate larger and multiple barges, an even bigger ship lift is being built adjacent to the historic one. A boat-shaped info centre has details about this ambitious project.

The Drive » Head north on Hebewerkstrasse as far as Liepe, then turn left on Brodowiner Strasse and continue for 17km through the Schorfheide-Chorin Unesco World Biosphere Reserve (Biosphärenreservat), whose woods, ponds and swamps are a haven for storks, cranes, beavers and other critters.

⑧ Kloster Chorin

A romantically ruined abbey, **Kloster Chorin** (☎033366-703 77; www.kloster-chorin.org; Amt Chorin 11a; adult/concession €6/3.50; ☺9am-6pm Apr-Oct, 10am-4pm Nov-Mar; P) was built by Cistercian monks over six decades starting in 1273, and is widely considered one of the finest red-brick Gothic structures in northern Germany. In summer, the abbey forms

an enchanting backdrop for the classical concert series **Choriner Musiksommer** (☎03334-818 472; www.musiksommer-chorin.de; ☺Jun-Aug).

The Drive » Pick up the A11 in Althüttendorf, drive south to exit 14 and follow the B273 toward Oranienburg, which takes you through the Nature Park Barnim with its many crystal-clear swimming lakes, including the enchanting Liepnitzsee.

TRIP HIGHLIGHT

⑨ Gedenkstätte & Museum Sachsenhausen

Only 30km north of central Berlin, **Sachsenhausen** (☎03301-200 200; www.sachsenhausen-sbg.de; Strasse der Nationen 22, Oranienburg; ☺8.30am-6pm mid-Mar–mid-Oct, to 4.30pm mid-Oct–mid-Mar, museums closed Mon mid-Oct–mid-Mar; P; S Oranienburg) was built by prisoners and opened in 1936 as a prototype for other concentration camps. Some 200,000 people passed through its sinister gates, most of them political opponents, Roma, Jews and POWs. By 1945, tens of thousands had died here from hunger, exhaustion, illness, exposure, medical experiments and executions. A tour of the grounds, remaining buildings and exhibits will leave no one untouched. Key stops include the **infirmary barracks**, the **prisoners' kitchen** and the execution area called **Station Z**.

Eating & Sleeping

Berlin ❶

🛏 Michelberger Hotel — Hotel €€

(📞030-2977 8590; www.michelbergerhotel.
com; Warschauer Strasse 39; d from €105;
🅿😊📶; 🆄Warschauer Strasse, 🆂Warschauer
Strasse) Offering the ultimate in creative crash
pads, Michelberger perfectly encapsulates
Berlin's offbeat DIY spirit without being self-
consciously cool. Rooms don't hide their factory
pedigree, but are comfortable and come in
sizes suitable for lovebirds, families or rock
bands. Staff are friendly and clued-up, and the
restaurant (3-course lunch €12, dinner dishes
€8-15; 😊7-11am, noon-2.30pm & 6.30-11pm;
📶🍴) is popular with both guests and locals.

Lübbenau ❷

🍴 Schlossrestaurant
Linari — International €€€

(📞03542-8730; www.schloss-luebbenau.de;
Schlossbezirk 6; mains €18-30, 3-course menu
from €32; 😊11.30am-10.30pm) This delightful
restaurant in the **Lübbenau Palace** (d €100-
180; 🅿📶) is elegant without being stuffy, and
the chef keeps the innovative menu in flux with
seasonal and regionally hunted-and-gathered
ingredients. In summer, the terrace with a full
view of the gardens is the place to sit, while in
winter the Sunday roast and goose feasts make
reservations de rigueur.

Neuzelle ❹

🍴 Restaurant
Prinz Albrecht — German €€

(📞033652-813 22; www.hotel-prinz-albrecht.de;
Frankfurter Strasse 34; mains €11-30; 😊11am-
10pm) Attached to a hotel, this country-style
restaurant with garden terrace has a feel-good
menu that includes such local dishes as pork

marinated in *Bock* (from the abbey brewery), or
smoked trout from the nearby Schlaube Valley.
Portions are generous.

Frankfurt (Oder) ❺

🍴 Restaurant Turm 24 — German €€

(📞0335-2301 0024; http://turm24.business.
site; Logenstrasse 8; mains €5-30; 😊7am-
10pm Mon-Fri, 10am-11pm Sat & Sun) Some
locals joke that the best thing about this smart
restaurant on the 24th floor of the Oderturm
is that you can't see the Oderturm, Frankfurt's
tallest building. Perhaps. But the panoramic
views from up here are indeed fabulous and the
German-Polish food is solid. It's also a good
spot for breakfast.

🛏 Hotel zur Alten Oder — Hotel €

(📞0335-556 220; www.zuraltenoder.de;
Fischerstrasse 32; s/d from €50/60; 🅿😊📶;
🚃1 Stadion) No two rooms are exactly alike in
this little hotel in a historical building, but all
have coral-coloured carpet, tasteful art and big
windows. Breakfast costs €9.50 but is a lavish
affair that should tide you over until the early
afternoon. It's about 1.5km south of the city
centre.

Neuhardenberg

🛏 Hotel Schloss
Neuhardenberg — Hotel €€€

(📞033476-6000; www.schlossneuhardenberg.
de; Schinkelplatz; r from €80; 🅿😊📶) Spend
the night in a palace built in 1786, modified by
Prussian starchitect Karl Friedrich Schinkel a
few years later and beautified with a garden
designed by Prince Hermann von Pückler-
Muskau. Rooms exude understated elegance
and come with a gamut of creature comforts.
The two on-site restaurants, one serving hearty
regional cuisine, the other Mediterranean, are
also recommended.

Via Regia

This road trip pays homage to the German section of the Via Regia or 'Kings Road', the oldest and longest transport route between Western and Eastern Europe.

7

TRIP HIGHLIGHTS

148 km

Mainz
Mainz' elegance is a throwback to its Napoleonic occupation

358 km

Eisenach
Much loved for its medieval pile, Wartburg Castle

FINISH
Görlitz

286 km

Fulda
Get your camera ready for Fulda's beautiful baroque styling

Saarbrücken
START

193 km

Frankfurt
Wine, dine and shop till you drop in fast-paced Frankfurt

5–7 DAYS
875KM / 544 MILES

GREAT FOR...

BEST TIME TO GO
Fit more in when days are longest from May to July.

ESSENTIAL PHOTO
Fulda's baroque Dom, crowdless at twilight.

✓ **BEST FOR FAMILIES**
Frankfurt's myriad attractions entertain young and old.

Frankfurt (p92) Traditional German architecture

7 Via Regia

Beginning in Saarbrücken and ending in Görlitz, this spirited west–east romp cuts through the heart of the nation. It juxtaposes Frankfurt's big-city excitement with Fulda's tranquil lanes, gets cultured in Weimar, Dresden and Leipzig, lingers on quiet country highways and roars along autobahn, visiting the key outposts of a road no longer in existence, but once the way of kings.

❶ Saarbrücken

Vestiges of Saarbrücken's 18th-century heyday survive in the city's beautiful baroque townhouses and churches. The historic centre around **St Johanner Markt** brims with fine restaurants and cafes. Start with a visit to the **Historisches Museum Saar** (📞0681-506 4506; www.historisches-museum. org; Schlossplatz 15; adult/ child €6/free; ⏰10am-6pm Tue & Thu-Sun, to 8pm Wed), housed in the basement of the **Saarbrücker Schloss**, where you can descend

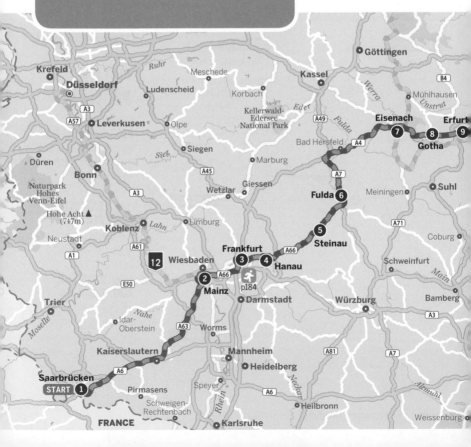

to the castle's massive bastions and casemates. Exhibits look at Saarland from the 1870s, and periods under French and Nazi rule. The Saarland Museum's **Alte Sammlung** (📞0681-954 050; www.kulturbesitz.de; Schlossplatz 16; adult/child €5/free, after 3pm Tue free; 🕙10am-6pm Tue & Thu-Sun, to 10pm Wed), or 'old collection', displays a millennium of paintings and artefacts from southwest Germany and France's Alsace-Lorraine. Before you hit the road, why not spend a few minutes' quiet contemplation in the dazzling Catholic church, **Basilika St Johann** (www.pfarrei-st-johann.de; Gerberstrasse 31; 🕙9.30am-7.15pm Mon, Fri & Sat, from 8.30am Tue, Thu & Sun, 8.30am-5pm Wed), with its gold altars, pulpit, organ case and overhead rayburst design?

The Drive ≫ Head south out of town on the A620 for 6km until it becomes the A6 autobahn. Stay on the A6 for 66km until exit 16a Dreieck Kaiserslautern, merging on to the A63 towards Frankfurt. Stay on the A63 for 70km until you reach the outskirts of Mainz, where the road becomes the B40. Keep heading straight for 4km into Mainz.

LINK YOUR TRIP

8 **German Avenues Route**

Link in with this amazing loop that intersects at Dresden and you have central Germany covered.

12 **Romantic Rhine**

Hook up with the Rhine while crossing paths in Mainz for some real river romance.

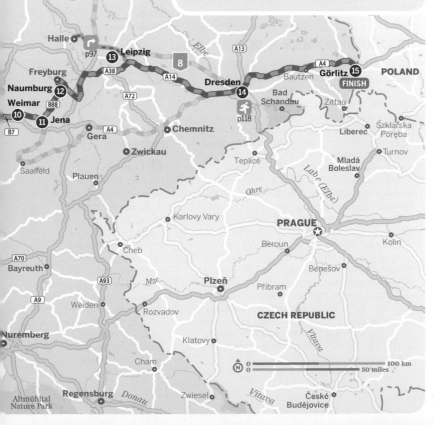

TRIP HIGHLIGHT

2 Mainz

Mainz is located at the confluence of the Rhine and Main rivers, its elegance a throwback to its Napoleonic occupation. Strolling along the Rhine and sampling local wines in an **Altstadt** (old town) tavern are as essential as viewing the fabulous Romanesque **Mainzer Dom** (☎06131-253 412; www.mainzerdom.bistummainz.de; Markt 10; ⊙9am-6.30pm Mon-Fri, to 4pm Sat, 12.45-6.30pm Sun Mar-Oct, 9am-5pm Mon-Fri, to 3pm Sat, 12.45-3pm & 4-5pm Sun Nov-Feb), with its oc-

tagonal tower; Chagall's ethereal windows in **St-Stephan-Kirche** (https://bistummainz.de/pfarrei/mainz-st-stephan/; Kleine Weissgasse 12; ⊙10am-5pm Mon-Sat, from noon Sun Mar-Oct, 10am-4.30pm Mon-Sat, from noon Sun Nov-Feb); or the first printed Bible in the **Gutenberg-Museum Mainz** (☎06131-122 503; www.gutenberg-museum.de; Liebfrauenplatz 5; adult/child €5/2, audioguide €3.50; ⊙9am-5pm Tue-Sat, from 11am Sun), commemorating the native son who perfected movable type. If you're not claustrophobic, head to the dungeon-like **Heiligtum der Isis und**

Mater Magna (☎06131-600 7493; www.roemisches-mainz.de; Römerpassage 1; ⊙10am-6pm Mon-Sat) archaeological site, with its brilliantly illuminated artefacts uncovered in 1999 during the construction of the Römer Passage mall. If you're desperate for more, head to the **Landesmuseum Mainz** (☎06131-285 70; www.landesmuseum-mainz.de; Grosse Bleiche 49-51; adult/child €6/3, audio/multimedia guide €1/2; ⊙10am-5pm Wed-Sun, to 8pm Tue) for outstanding collections of Renaissance and 20th-century German paintings, baroque porcelain and furniture.

The Drive ≫ Cross the Rhine on the Theodor Heuss Bridge then pick up the B455 at the roundabout and follow it north for 5km to the junction with the A66 autobahn at exit 6 Weisbaden-Erbenheim. Follow the A66 towards Frankfurt for 30km until exit 21 Frankfurt am Main-Miquelallee.

TRIP HIGHLIGHT

3 Frankfurt

Beneath the glinting glass, steel and concrete, you'll discover Frankfurt is an unexpectedly traditional city, with its medieval **Altstadt**, village-like neighbourhoods, attractive gardens, riverside paths and wealth of museums. The Main flows from east to west, with the city centre on its northern banks. The **Römerberg** ([U]Dom|Römer),

---

FRANKFURT: THEN & NOW

Around 2000 years ago Frankfurt was a Celtic and Germanic settlement and then a Roman garrison town. Mentioned in historical documents as far back as AD 794, Frankfurt was an important centre of power in the Holy Roman Empire. With the election of Friedrich I (Barbarossa) in 1152, the city became the customary site of the selection of German kings. In 1372 Frankfurt became a 'Free Imperial City', a status it enjoyed until the Prussian takeover of 1866.

It's hard to believe that about 80% of Frankfurt's medieval city centre was destroyed by WWII Allied bombing raids in March 1944; over 1000 people lost their lives. The area around Römerberg was reconstructed in its original style and, phoenix-like, the city returned to prominence as a thriving contemporary centre of commerce. Frankfurt's first international trade fairs began in the 12th century and continue to attract tens of thousands each year; its airport is the third-busiest in Europe. Frankfurt's first stock exchange began operating in 1585 and is now in the world's top 10. In the 1760s, the Rothschild banking family began their ascent from Frankfurt, and the city is today home to the gleaming HQ of the European Central Bank.

LOCAL KNOWLEDGE: FRANKFURT FOR KIDS

Frankfurt is a fun place to linger a little if you've got youngsters in your party: they'll jump at the chance to get out of the car. There are plenty of parks to picnic in and several museums have kid-friendly exhibits. Favourites include the following:

Senckenberg Museum (☎069-754 20; www.senckenberg.de; Senckenberganlage 25; adult/child €10/5, audioguide €3; ☺9am-5pm Mon, Tue, Thu & Fri, to 8pm Wed, to 6pm Sat & Sun; ⓤBockenheimer Warte) Fossils and dinosaurs.

Frankfurt Zoo (Zoologischer Garten; ☎069-2123 3735; www.zoo-frankfurt.de; Bernhard-Grzimek-Allee 1; adult/child €12/6; ☺9am-7pm Apr-Oct, to 5pm Nov-Mar; ♿; ⓤZoo) Animals galore.

PalmenGarten (www.palmengarten.de; Siesmayerstrasse 63; adult/child €7/2; ☺9am-6pm Feb-Oct, to 4pm Nov-Jan; ⓤPalmengartenstrasse) Parkland and fountains.

Junges Museum (Young Museum Frankfurt; ☎069-2123 5154; www.kindermuseum.frankfurt. de; Historisches Museum Frankfurt, Saalhof 1; adult/child €8/free; ☺10am-6pm Tue, Thu & Fri, to 9pm Wed, 11am-7pm Sat & Sun; ♿; ⓤRömer) Specifically designed for children...and to give wise old elders a break!

Frankfurt's ornately gabled central square, with the **Gerechtigkeitsbrunnen** (Fountain of Justice), marks the Altstadt's centre. To its north, shop till you drop along the **Zeil**, linking **An der Hauptwache** and **Konstablerwache** public squares. Must-sees include the photogenic town hall **Römer** (Römerberg; ⓤDom|Römer), comprised of three step-gabled 15th-century houses; Frankfurt's red-sandstone **Kaiserdom** (Imperial Frankfurt Cathedral; www.dom-frankfurt.de; Domplatz 1; tower adult/child €3/1.50; ☺church 9am-8pm Sun-Thu, from 1pm Fri, tower 9am-6pm Apr-Oct, 10am-5pm Nov-Apr; ⓤDom|Römer), dominated by a 95m-high Gothic tower (which you can climb, via 324 steps!); and the

world-renowned **Städel Museum** (☎069-605 098; www.staedelmuseum.de; Schaumainkai 63; adult/concession €14/12; ☺10am-7pm Tue, Wed, Sat & Sun, to 9pm Thu & Fri; 🚃15|16 Otto-Hahn-Platz), founded in 1815 and housing outstanding works by Dürer, Rembrandt, Rubens, Renoir, Picasso and Cézanne.

See p184 for a walking tour of Frankfurt.

🍴🛏 p99

The Drive » Head south on the B44 for 6.5km to the A3 autobahn at exit 51 Frankfurt Süd. Take the A3 east for 19km until exit 54 Hanau, then follow the B45 for 10km north.

❹ Hanau

There are two reasons you've stopped by Hanau: first, because brothers Jacob and Wilhelm Grimm were born here, com-

memorated by a statue located on the **Markt**; and second, for the wonderful **Historisches Museum Schloss Philippsruhe** (☎06181-295 564; www.museen-hanau.de; Philippsruher Allee 45; adult/concession €4/3; ☺11am-6pm Tue-Sun; Ⓟ), located within Philippsruhe Palace. Dating from the early 18th century, this museum has displays on town history, arts and crafts. The parks and gardens are beautiful for a stroll.

The Drive » Pick up the A66 autobahn at exit 36 Hanau Nord for 48km towards Fulda until exit 47 Steinau an der Strasse.

❺ Steinau

Steinau (an der Strasse) has been a stop on the Via Regia for centuries (*an der Strasse* means 'on the road'). At the old-town entrance, you'll see two sandstone pillars commemorating the Via Regia. While you're here, stop by the twinned museums **Brüder Grimm-Haus and Museum Steinau** (☎06663-7605; www.brueder-grimm-haus. de; Brüder Grimm-Strasse 80; adult/concession €6/3.50; ☺10am-5pm), in a house where the Grimm family lived from 1791 to 1796.

The Drive ❯❯ Return to the A66 at exit 47 Steinau an der Strasse and follow it for 21km until exit 51 Neuhof-Süd. At the roundabout, veer right onto Hanauer Strasse and follow it through the village of Neuhof for 1.6km until the road forks. Take the left fork and follow Alte Heerstrasse for 7km towards Fulda: you're now driving on an original Via Regia roadway! Turn left at the junction with the K103 then right onto the L3418 until you reach Frankfurter Strasse: follow it for 3km into Fulda.

TRIP HIGHLIGHT

❻ Fulda

Founded in 744, photogenic Fulda boasts a treasure trove of sumptuous baroque architecture and a delightfully relaxed atmosphere, with plenty of selfie ops and a handful of top spots to pause for a meal or a glass of wine. Fulda's spectacular **Stadtschloss** (☎0661-102 1814; adult/concession €3.50/2.50; ☺10am-5pm Tue-Sun) was built (1706–21) as the prince-abbots' residence. Visitors can enter ornate historic rooms and the octagonal

Schlossturm (April to October) for great views of the magnificent gardens where locals bronze themselves in summer. Inside the baroque **Dom** (☎0661-874 57; www.bistum-fulda.de; Domplatz 1; ☺10am-6pm Mon-Fri, to 3pm Sat, 1-6pm Sun Apr-Oct, to 5pm Mon-Fri Nov-Mar), a cathedral built from 1704 to 1712, you'll find gilded furnishings, statues and the tomb of St Boniface, who died a martyr in 754.

The Drive ❯❯ Take the B27 for 5km north to meet the A7 autobahn at exit 91 Fulda Nord. Follow the A7 north for 35km then merge onto the A4 towards Berlin/Dresden at interchange 86 Kirchheimer Dreieck. Follow the A4 for 60km to exit 39 Eisenach West. Take the B19 south for 6km into Eisenach.

TRIP HIGHLIGHT

❼ Eisenach

Historically, Eisenach was an important stop on the Via Regia, and its Wartburg (p78) castle is one of Germany's most significant medieval sites: it held Martin Luther while his actions brought about the Reformation and was the inspiration for better-known Neuschwanstein (p222), whose creator, Ludwig II, saw it and wanted to build a fortress even more grandiose and impenetrable. Eisenach proudly remembers the birth of Johann Sebastian Bach in the wattle-and-daub home now housing the museum **Bachhaus**

(☎03691-793 40; www.bachhaus.de; Frauenplan 21; adult/concession €10/6; ☺10am-6pm), and also celebrates its automotive history (the world's first BMW rolled off the assembly line here in 1929): check out **Automobile Welt Eisenach** (☎03691-772 12; www.awe-stiftung.de; Friedrich-Naumann-Strasse 10; adult/concession €6/3.50; ☺10am-6pm Apr-Oct, 11am-5pm Nov-Mar, closed Mon) if four wheels and six cylinders kick-start your heart.

✕ 🛏 p79, p114

The Drive ❯❯ Head north on Mühlhäuser Strasse for 2km then turn right on to the L1021 for 6km to the junction with the

Frankfurt Gerechtigkeitsbrunnen (Fountain of Justice; p93)

A4 at exit 40a Eisenach Ost. Head south on the A4 for 9.5km to exit 40b Sättelstädt. Follow the L3007 east for 15km through the small villages of Teutleben and Aspach into Gotha.

- - - - - - - - - - - - - - - - -

❽ Gotha

Gotha is no longer Thuringia's wealthiest and most beautiful city, as it was once described, but its focal point remains the enormous **Schloss Friedenstein** (☎03621-823 40; www.stiftungfriedenstein. de; adult/concession €10/4, audioguide €2.50; ⏲10am-5pm Tue-Sun Apr-Oct, to 4pm Nov-Mar; Ⓟ Ⓗ), built by Duke Ernst I of House Saxe-Coburg-Gotha (his descendants reinvented

themselves as the House of Windsor after WWI and now sit upon the British throne). Inside the palace you'll find the exuberantly stucco-ornamented Festival Hall, a neoclassical wing, a curio cabinet jammed with exotica, the Palace Church, and stunning Ekhof-Theater, one of Europe's oldest baroque theatres. Gotha's **Hauptmarkt** is dominated by the picturesque **Rathaus** (Town Hall; tower €1; ⏲11am-6pm Apr-Oct, to 4pm Nov-Mar), with its colourful Renaissance facade and 35m-tall tower.

The Drive » Follow Weimarer Strasse, which becomes

Eisenacher Strasse, for 21km east, into Erfurt.

- - - - - - - - - - - - - - - - -

❾ Erfurt

Founded as a bishopric on the little Gera River in 742, Erfurt was catapulted to prosperity in the Middle Ages when it began producing a precious blue pigment from a woad plant. In 1392 rich merchants founded Erfurt's university, whose most famous graduate was Martin Luther. There's plenty to enjoy here, with the town's history and modernity complementing each other. Head to the **Krämerbrücke** (Merchants'

Bridge), a charming 1325 stone bridge flanked by cute half-timbered houses. Erfurt's is the only one of its kind north of the Alps that's still inhabited. Linger a while in the delightful eateries of nearby **Wenigemarkt**, and consider a visit to the **Augustinerkloster** (☏0361-576 600; www. augustinerkloster.de; Auginerstrasse 10; public German-language tour €7.50; ⊘tours 9.30am-5pm Mon-Sat & 11am Sun Apr-Oct, 9.30am-3.30pm Mon-Sat & 11am Sun Nov-Mar); this is where Luther lived from 1505 to 1511, was ordained as a monk and read his first Mass. Be sure to stroll about the gorgeous houses on **Fischmarkt** and onwards to the spectacular **Domplatz** and Erfurt's famous **Dom** (Mariendom; ☏0361-646 1265; www.dom-erfurt.de; ⊙9.30am-6pm Mon-Sat, 1-6pm Sun May-Oct, to 5pm Nov-Apr).

✕ ⮐ p79, p99, p114

The Drive ⟫ Take the B7 22km east, through fields of canola and wind turbines, into Weimar.

- - - - - - - - - - - - - - -

⑩ Weimar

Historical epicentre of the German Enlightenment, best known as the town where intellectual heavyweights Goethe and Schiller did their thing, Weimar appeals to anyone with a passion for German history and culture. In summer, Weimar's many parks and gardens lend themselves to quiet contemplation of the town's cultural onslaught, or to taking a break from it. Must-sees include the museum at **Stadtschloss Weimar** (☏03643-545 400; www. klassik-stiftung.de; Burgplatz 4; adult/concession €5.50/4; ⊙10am-6pm Tue-Sun Apr-Oct, to 4pm Nov-Mar), the Unesco World Heritage **Herzogin Anna Amalia Bibliothek** (☏03643-545 400; www. klassik-stiftung.de; Platz der Demokratie 1; adult/concession €8/6.50; ⊙9.30am-2.30pm Tue-Sun), and, of course, the Goethe-Nationalmuseum (p76).

✕ ⮐ p53, p79

The Drive ⟫ Follow the B7 for 25km east into Jena.

- - - - - - - - - - - - - - -

⑪ Jena

Although signs of East German (GDR) aesthetics remain, Jena enjoys a picturesque setting on the Saale River, flanked by limestone hills and blessed with a climate mild enough for orchids and grapevines. Also an old university town (since 1558), Jena has an entirely different feel to Weimar and Erfurt. Close investigation will unearth fun, fringe, Berlinesque hang-outs and tasty cheap eats. Ascend the **JenTower** (☏03641-208 000; www.jentower. de; Leutragraben 1; viewing platforms €3.50; ⊙viewing platforms 10am-11pm) for fabulous views of the surrounding Saale River valley, take a trip into outer space at the **Zeiss Planetarium** (☏03641-885 488; www.planetarium-jena. de; Am Planetarium 5; adult/concession €11/9.50; ⊙box office 9.30am-1.30pm & 7-8pm Tue-Thu, 10.30am-noon & 6.30-8pm Fri, 1.30-8pm Sat, 12.30-6pm Sun), the world's oldest, or contemplate the life of a literary giant and his little garden in **Schiller's Gartenhaus** (Schiller's Garden House; ☏03641-931 188; www.uni-jena.de; Schillergässchen 2; adult/concession €3.50/2; ⊙11am-5pm Tue-Sun, closed Sun Nov-Mar).

✕ ⮐ p114

The Drive ⟫ Follow the B88 north for 34km through forests and fields, as it chases the sparkling Saale into Naumburg.

- - - - - - - - - - - - - - -

⑫ Naumburg

At the confluence of the Saale and Unstrut Rivers, Naumburg has a handsome **Altstadt**, striking Renaissance **Rathaus** and **Marientor** double gateway. Its enormous **Dom** (Cathedral of Sts Peter & Paul; ☏03445-230 1133; www. naumburger-dom.de; Domplatz 16-17; adult/concession €7.50/5.50; ⊙9am-6pm Mon-Sat, from 11am Sun Mar-Oct, shorter hours Nov-Feb), is a masterpiece of medieval architecture, featuring elements of the Romanesque and early Gothic design. Medieval stained-glass windows are augmented by ruby-red modern panes by Neo

DETOUR:
HALLE

Start: ⑬ **Leipzig**

Best known as the birthplace of Georg Friedrich Händel – learn all about him in the **Händel-Haus** (✆0345-500 900; www.handel-house.com; Grosse Nikolaistrasse 5; adult/concession €5/3.50; ◷10am-6pm Tue-Sun Apr-Oct, to 5pm Nov-Mar) – Halle is one of Germany's oldest cities, having celebrated its 1200th birthday in 2006. But the main reason to visit is to check out two impressive museums. The **Landesmuseum für Vorgeschichte** (State Museum of Pre-History; ✆0345-524 7363; www.lda-lsa.de; Richard Wagner Strasse 9; adult/concession €5/3; ◷9am-5pm Tue-Fri, 10am-6pm Sat & Sun) houses a phenomenal collection of major archaeological finds, one of the most significant in Europe. Permanent exhibits shed light on the early to late Stone Age and early Bronze Age, and include the oldest known fingerprint, the graves of Eulau and the Nebra Sky Disc. Art lovers will make a beeline to **Kunstmuseum Moritzburg** (Moritzburg Art Gallery; ✆0345-212 5911; www.kunstmuseum-moritzburg.de; Friedemann-Bach-Platz 5; adult/concession €12/9; ◷10am-6pm Thu-Tue), where the late-Gothic Moritzburg castle is a fantastic setting for a superb permanent collection, from the classics to the modern. When you're done, there are fine places to wine and dine. Halle is 40km northwest from Leipzig on the A14.

Rauch, one of the premier artists of the New Leipzig School. You may also want to pop into the **Nietzsche Haus** (✆03445-201 638; www.mv-naumburg.de/nietzschehaus; Weingarten 18; adult/concession €4/3; ◷2-5pm Tue-Fri, from 10am Sat & Sun), where the great philosopher spent most of his childhood.

The Drive 》 Head southeast on the B87 for 4km until the intersection with the B180. Continue heading southeast on the B180 for 10km until the junction with the A9 autobahn at exit 21a Naumburg. Head north on the A9 for 32km until exit 17 Leipzig West. Head east on the B181 for 13km into Leipzig.

- - - - - - - - - - - - - - - - - -

⑬ **Leipzig**

Leipzig's love affair with music stems from its connection to the lives and work of Bach, Mendelssohn and Wagner. Today, one of the world's top classical orchestras, the Gewandhausorchester, and the 800-year-old Thomanerchor boys' choir continue to delight audiences here. Along this theme, the **Bach-Museum** (✆0341-913 7202; www.bachmuseumleipzig.de; Thomaskirchhof 16; adult/concession/child under 16yr €8/6/free; ◷10am-6pm Tue-Sun) lets you treat your ears to any composition Bach wrote, while **Mendelssohn-Haus** (✆0341-127 0294; www.mendelssohn-stiftung.de; Goldschmidtstrasse 12; adult/concession incl audioguide €8/6; ◷10am-6pm) teaches you about Mendelssohn in the Biedermeier-furnished apartment where this remarkable musical prodigy lived until his sudden death, aged 38. At the fabulous **Museum für Musikinstrumente** (✆0341-973 0750; http://mfm.uni-leipzig.de; adult/concession €6/3, audioguide €1; ◷10am-6pm Tue-Sun), housed inside the complex of the **Museen im Grassi** (www.grassimuseum.de; Johannisplatz 5-11; combined ticket adult/concession €15/12; ◷10am-6pm Tue-Sun), you can discover music from five centuries through an interactive sound laboratory.

✗ 🛏 p71, p99, p115

The Drive 》 Take Torgauer Strasse northeast for 4.5km to the intersection with the A14 autobahn at exit 25 Leipzig Nordost. Head southeast on the A14 for 75km to the A4

GOETHE: LITERARY LION

Johann Wolfgang von Goethe (1749–1832) is the grandaddy of German literature and philosophy. He lived to 82, having written novels, essays, treatises, scientific articles, travelogues, plays and poetry. A consummate politician, Goethe was also a great 'Renaissance man', capable in many disciplines: during his life he served as town planner, architect, social reformer and scientist. Born in Frankfurt am Main and trained as a lawyer, Goethe became the driving force of the 1770s Sturm und Drang (Storm and Stress) literary movement. His work with Friedrich Schiller fostered the theatrical style known as Weimar Classicism. Goethe himself once described his work as 'fragments of a great confession'. His defining play in two parts, *Faust*, is a lyrical but highly charged retelling of the classic legend of a man selling his soul for knowledge. It's still regularly performed throughout Germany today.

interchange 76 Autobahn Dreieck Nossen. Merge here onto the A4 and head east for 20km to exit 78 Dresden Altstadt.

----

⑭ Dresden

Dresden's cultural heyday came under the 18th-century reign of Augustus the Strong, who supervised many of Dresden's iconic buildings. These include the **Zwinger** (☏0351-4914 2000; www.der-dresdner-zwinger. de; Theaterplatz 1; ticket for all museums adult/concession €12/9, courtyard free; ⊘6am-10pm Apr-Oct, to 8pm Nov-Mar), inspired by the palace at Versailles, which today houses three superb museums within its baroque walls, and the **Frauenkirche** (☏0351-6560 6100; www.frauenkirche -dresden.de; Neumarkt; audio-guide €2.50, cupola adult/

student €8/5; ⊘10am-noon & 1-6pm Mon-Fri, weekend hours vary), Dresden's most beloved symbol, rebuilt from a pile of rubble between 1994 and 2005. The original graced the skyline for two centuries until the devastating 1945 Allied firestorm of WWII levelled the church and most of the city. For something completely different, the **Deutsches Hygiene-Museum** (German Hygiene Museum; ☏0351-484 6400; www.dhmd.de; Lingnerplatz 1; adult/student/child under 16yr €9/4/free; ⊘10am-6pm Tue-Sun; ⊞) is, in fact, all about human beings. Living and dying, eating and drinking, sex and beauty are all addressed. There's a Children's Museum in the basement. If the kids have made it this far, why not head to the

Zoo (☏0351-478 060; www. zoo-dresden.de; Tiergartenstrasse 1; adult/child €13/5; ⊘8.30am-6.30pm Apr-Oct, to 4.30pm Nov-Mar)?

See p118 for a walking tour of Dresden.

✕ ⮑ p99, p71, p115

The Drive ⟫ Pick up the A4 autobahn at exit 78 Dresden Altstadt and follow it east for 102km to exit 94 Görlitz.

----

⑮ Görlitz

Congratulations, you made it! Görlitz, Germany's most eastern city, is a dreamy coalescence of fabulous architecture, cobbled streets and an intriguing history. Having miraculously escaped destruction during WWII, Görlitz offers the visitor nearly 4200 heritage buildings in styles from the Renaissance to 19th century. Be sure to pop in to the Barockhaus (p65), which will fascinate anyone with a taste for the odd with its curiously broad exhibits. For a history of the area, visit the **Schlesisches Museum zu Görlitz** (☏03581-879 10; www.schlesisches-museum. de; Brüderstrasse 8; adult/concession incl audioguide €6/4; ⊘10am-5pm Tue-Thu, to 6pm Fri-Sun), and drop by **Untermarkt** to see the **Rathaus** and **Peterskirche** (☏03581-428 7000; An der Peterskirche; ⊘10am-6pm Mon-Sat, 11.45am-6pm Sun), with its remarkable Sun Organ.

✕ ⮑ p71

Eating & Sleeping

Frankfurt ❸

✖ Zu den 12 Aposteln　German €€

(📞069-288 668; www.12aposteln-frankfurt.
de; Rosenbergerstrasse 1; mains €11-25;
🕐11.30am-1am; Ⓤ Konstablerwache) Glowing
with sepia-toned lamplight, the 12 Apostles has
ground-floor and cellar dining rooms serving
traditional German dishes: *Matjes* (herring)
with sour cream, apple and fried onion; roast
pork knuckle with pickled cabbage; Frankfurter
schnitzel with *Grüne Sosse* (green sauce); and
Käsespätzle (handmade cheese noodles with
onions). It brews its own light and dark beers
on the premises. Outside there's a tree-shaded
terrace.

🛏 Villa Orange　Boutique Hotel €€

(📞069-405 840; www.villa-orange.de;
Hebelstrasse 1; s/d from €140/170; 🅿 ❋ 🛜;
🚌12|18 Friedberger Platz) Offering a winning
combination of tranquillity, modern German
design and small-hotel comforts (such as
a quiet corner library), this century-old,
tangerine-coloured villa has 38 spacious rooms,
some with free-standing baths and four-poster
beds. Everything is organic – the sheets,
the soap and the bountiful buffet breakfast
(included) – with bikes also available to hire.

Erfurt ❾

✖ Fellini　Italian €€

(📞0361-642 1375; www.fellini-erfurt.de;
Fischmarkt 3; mains €7-28; 🕐11am-10pm
Mon-Sat) You can't beat the Fischmarkt location
of this smart Italian affair, where local suits
and casual tourists dine side by side. Expect
traditional Italian staples prepared well – the
pizza oven is wood fired, for example, and the
tagliatelle and tortelloni are homemade – and
good old-fashioned service.

🛏 Dorint Hotel am Dom Erfurt　Business Hotel €€€

(📞0361-644 50; www.hotel-erfurt.dorint.com;
Theaterplatz 2; d from €108; 🅿 ❋ 🛜) Situated
about 300m west of Domplatz (off Lauentor),
this luxurious business-oriented hotel has
160 rooms and suites that exude effortless
sophistication. Behind its vast glass-walled
atrium-lobby you'll also find the 'Gloriosa'
restaurant and an impeccable Zen-inspired
wellness area. Take tram 4 from Hauptbahnhof
to Theater.

Leipzig ⓭

🛏 Steigenberger Grandhotel Handelshof　Hotel €€€

(📞0341-350 5810; www.steigenberger.com;
Salzgässchen 6; r from €170; ❋ @ 🛜)
Behind the imposing historic facade of a 1909
municipal trading hall, this exclusive boutique-
luxury joint outclasses most of Leipzig's hotels
with its supercentral location, charmingly
efficient team and modern rooms with crisp
white-silver-purple colours, high ceilings and
marble bathrooms. The stylish bi-level spa is the
perfect bliss-out station.

Dresden ⓮

🛏 Gewandhaus Hotel　Boutique Hotel €€€

(📞0351-494 90; www.gewandhaus-hotel.de;
Ringstrasse 1; d from €125; 🅿 ❋ @ 🛜 🛏)
Revamped as a boutique hotel a few years ago,
the stunning Gewandhaus, an 18th-century
trading house of tailors and fabric merchants
that burned down in 1945, boasts sleek public
areas, beautiful and bright rooms, and a
breakfast that sets a high bar for the city.

Classic Trip

German Avenues Route

8

This quintessential German road trip, along the tree-lined avenues of the Harz Mountains and country highways of central Germany, leaves no marvel unturned.

TRIP HIGHLIGHTS

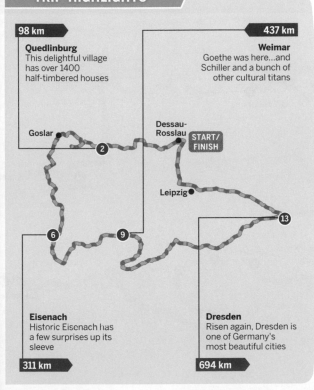

98 km

Quedlinburg
This delightful village has over 1400 half-timbered houses

437 km

Weimar
Goethe was here...and Schiller and a bunch of other cultural titans

Goslar

Dessau-Rosslau

START/FINISH

② Leipzig ⑬

⑥ ⑨

Eisenach
Historic Eisenach has a few surprises up its sleeve

311 km

Dresden
Risen again, Dresden is one of Germany's most beautiful cities

694 km

5–7 DAYS
1050KM / 652 MILES

GREAT FOR...

BEST TIME TO GO
Visit from May to July for fewer crowds and the best weather.

 ESSENTIAL PHOTO
Dresden by twilight on the banks of the Elbe.

 BEST FOR HISTORY
Few places pack as much punch as Eisenach's Wartburg.

Classic Trip

8 German Avenues Route

On this magic loop through the diverse natural beauty of the ancient states of Saxony-Anhalt, Lower Saxony, Thuringia and Saxony, you'll fall in love with the eye-catching villages of Quedlinburg and Goslar, perhaps take a steam train to the top of a mountain, see where Bach was born and Goethe died, keep watch from the Wartburg and ponder the histories written upon the culture-laden cities of Erfurt, Weimar, Dresden and Leipzig.

❶ Dessau-Rosslau

The former East German (GDR) town of Dessau-Rosslau, 130km south of Berlin, is best known for being the birthplace of the Bauhaus movement, but is also famed for the **Gartenreich Dessau-Wörlitz**, one of the finest garden ensembles in Germany. Begin at the main Bauhaus sites: the Bauhausgebäude (p50), erected in 1925–26 as a school of Bauhaus art, design and architecture, and the three Meisterhäuser (p50) where Bauhaus' leading lights lived. Juxtapose these with the 112-hectare Wörlitz Park & Schloss Wörlitz (p50), the pinnacle of the Garden Realm which is 20km east of town on the L133. Return to Dessau-Rosslau and head southwest on the B185 for 11km, for a peek at petite **Schloss & Park Mosigkau** (☎039404-521139; www.gartenreich.com; Knobelsdorffallee 3; palace €7.50; ⏱10am-5pm Tue-Sun May-Sep, Sat & Sun only Apr & Oct), a 'miniature Sanssouci'.

✕ 🛏 p53

The Drive 》 From Schloss & Park Mosigkau, take the B185 for 15km to the pretty village of Köthen, where Bach composed his Brandenburg concertos and The Well-Tempered Clavier. Continue on the B185 for 45km to the junction with the B6. Follow the B6 for 20km, to Quedlinburg.

TRIP HIGHLIGHT

❷ Quedlinburg

Situated on a fertile plain at the northern cusp of the Harz Mountains, little Quedlinburg, a Unesco World Heritage town, is one of the loveliest in the region. Learn about its centuries-old *Fachwerk* (half-timbered) houses (there are 1400 or so) in the **Fachwerkmuseum im Ständerbau** (☎03946-3828; Wordgasse 3; adult/concession €3/2; ⏱10am-5pm Fri-Wed Apr-Oct). Wander freely around its enchanting cobblestone streets and spectacular medieval marketplace, where you'll find a wonderful mix of original options for wining, dining and resting your head. Perched high on a 25m plateau above town, Quedlinburg's Renaissance palace houses today's **Schloss-museum** (☎03946-905 681; Schlossberg 1; adult/concession €9.50/7.50; ⏱10am-6pm Tue-Sun Apr-Oct, to 4pm Nov-Mar), with fascinating Ottonian-period exhibits dating from 919 to 1056. The **Lyonel Feininger Galerie** (☎03946-689 5930; www.feininger-galerie.de; Schlossberg 11; adult/concession €6/4; ⏱10am-6pm

Lübben

B87

A13

Riesa

Oschatz B6 Meissen

Döbeln

A4

Freiberg

Dresden

13

p118

4

Teplice

Annaberg-Buchholz

Most

Chomutov Ohre

Ohre

🔗 LINK YOUR TRIP

4 **Highlights of Saxony**

Pick up this scenic jaunt in Dresden to immerse yourself in Saxony's rich history and diverse architecture.

10 **German Fairy-Tale Road**

From Schmalkalden, head southwest for 110km to Steinau to link up with this whimsical journey.

Wed-Mon Apr-Oct, to 5pm Nov-Mar) exhibits the work of influential Bauhaus artist Lyonel Feininger (1871–1956). Feininger was born in New York and came to Germany at the age of 16, later fleeing the Nazis and returning to the US in 1937. Timing your visit for a weekday will make all the difference: Quedlinburg is a popular weekend destination.

 p114

The Drive » Head west on Westerhäuser Strasse (which becomes the B27) through another lovely village – Blankenburg – to the junction with the B81. Follow the B81 for 4km north: you'll see Blankenburg's handsome castle to your right. Turn left on the L85 and head west for 11.5km into Wernigerode.

----

③ Wernigerode

The winding streets of Wernigerode's attractive **Altstadt** (old town) are flanked by pretty half-timbered houses. This is the northern terminus of the steam-powered narrow-gauge heritage Harzquerbahn railway; the line to the summit of the Brocken also starts here. Dominating Wernigerode's town square, the spectacular towered **Rathaus** (town hall) began life as a theatre around 1277; it was given its mostly late-Gothic features in the 16th century. Take a stroll along **Breite Strasse**, essentially Wernigerode's main street, for both architectural and gastronomic reasons. A visit to the **Harzmusuem** (☏03943-654 454; www.harzmuseum.de; Klint 10; adult/concession €2/1.30; ◷10am-5pm Mon-Sat) will top up your knowledge on local geology, history and architecture. Round out a magical day with a castle visit to **Schloss Wernigerode** (☏03943-553 040; www.schloss-wernige rode.de; Am Schloss 1; adult/concession €7/6; ◷10am-6pm, closed Mon Nov-Apr), originally built in the 12th century but enlarged over the years to reflect late-Gothic and Renaissance tastes. You'll need to leave your car below; it's a 1.5km walk if you fancy it, but the easiest way to get there is by Bimmelbahn wagon from Marktstrasse.

The Drive » Head north on the B244 for 4km to the junction with the B6. Follow the B6 for 32km, over undulating hills, by meadows of golden canola and the odd wind turbine, and through picturesque villages into Goslar.

QUEDLINBURG'S HISTORIC BUILDINGS

With so many historic buildings, Quedlinburg is one town in which it's nice just to stroll the streets and soak up the atmosphere. The **Rathaus** (1320) dominates the **Markt**, and in front of this is a **Roland** statue from 1426. Just behind the Rathaus is the **Marktkirche St Benedikti** (1233), and nearby is the **Gildehaus zur Rose** (1612) at Breite Strasse 39. Running off Markt is the tiny **Schuhhof**, a shoemakers' courtyard, with shutters and stable-like 'gossip doors'. **Alter Klopstock** (1580), which is found at Stieg 28, has scrolled beams typical of Quedlinburg's 16th-century half-timbered houses.

From Stieg 28 (just north of Schuhhof), it's a short walk north along Pölle to **Zwischen den Städten**, a historic bridge connecting the old town and Neustadt, which developed alongside the town wall around 1200 when peasants fled a feudal power struggle on the land. Behind the Renaissance facade, tower and stone gables of the **Hagensches Freihaus** (1558) is the Wyndham Garden Quedlinburger Stadtschloss. Many houses in this part of town have high archways and courtyards dotted with pigeon towers. A couple of other places of special note are the **Hotel zur Goldenen Sonne** building (1671) at Steinweg 11 and **Zur Börse** (1683) at No 23.

HARZ MOUNTAIN RAILWAYS

Fans of old-time trains will be eager to get out from behind the wheel and into a *Wagen* (wagon) on any of the three narrow-gauge railways, a legacy of the GDR, that cross the Harz. This 140km integrated network is the largest in Europe, serving steam and diesel locomotives, and tackling gradients of up to 40% and curves as tight as 60m in radius.

The **Harzquerbahn** runs 60km on a north–south route between Wernigerode and Nordhausen. The serpentine 14km between Wernigerode and Drei Annen Hohne includes 72 bends; you'll get dropped off on the edge of Harz National Park.

From the junction at Drei Annen Hohne, the **Brockenbahn** begins the steep climb to Schierke and the Brocken. Trains to the Brocken (via Drei Annen Hohne) can be picked up from Wernigerode and Nordhausen; single/return tickets cost €29/45 from all stations. Many visitors take the train to Schierke and then follow a trail on foot to the Brocken summit (1141m).

The third service is the **Selketalbahn**, which begins in Quedlinburg and runs to Eisfelder Talmühle or Hasselfelde. At Eisfelder Tal, you can change trains for other lines. The picturesque Selketalbahn crosses the plain to Gernrode and follows Wellbach, a creek with a couple of good swimming holes, through deciduous forest to Mägdesprung, before joining the Selke Valley and climbing past Alexisbad to high plains around Friedrichshöhe, Stiege and beyond.

Check in with the folks at **Harzer Schmalspurbahnen** (📞03943-5580; www.hsb-wr. de; Bahnhofsplatz 6, Wernigerode) for fares and timetables.

4 Goslar

Gorgeous Goslar's beautiful medieval **Altstadt** attracts visitors by the busload. Founded by Heinrich I in 922, the town was important in its early days for silver mining. One of the nicest things to do here is wander through the historic streets around the **Markt**. Opposite the **Rathaus** is the **Glockenspiel**, a chiming clock depicting four scenes of mining in the area. It plays at 9am, noon, 3pm and 6pm.

A visit to the **Goslarer Museum** (📞05321-433 94; Konigstrasse 1; adult/concession €4/2; ⊘10am-5pm Tue-Sun) offers a good overview of local history.

The town's pride and joy is its reconstructed 11th-century Romanesque imperial palace, the **Kaiserpfalz** (📞05321-311 9693; Kaiserbleek 6; adult/concession €7.50/4.50; ⊘10am-5pm), seat of Saxon kings from 1005 to 1219. After centuries of decay, the building was resurrected in the 19th century and adorned with interior frescos of idealised historical scenes. About 3km south on Rammelsberger Strasse is the **Rammelsberg Museum & Besucherbergwerk** (Rammelsberg Museum & Visitors' Mine; 📞05321-7500; www.rammelsberg.de; Bergtal 19; adult/concession €16/11; ⊘9am-6pm Apr-Oct, to 5pm Nov-Mar), the shafts and buildings of a 1000-year-old mine that are now a must-see Unesco World Heritage site and museum.

🛏 p114

The Drive ⟫ Allow at least two hours for this scenic Harz Mountains section. Take the B241 as it twists and turns for 31km to the junction of the B243, just through the village of Osterode am Harz. Continue south on the foresty B243 for 30km: you'll cross the border of Lower Saxony into Thuringia, from where it's 49km of country roads, heading south on the L1014 and L1015 to Mühlhausen.

5 Mühlhausen

Mühlhausen flaunts medieval charisma.

ARCO IMAGES GMBH / ALAMY STOCK PHOTO ©

OFOKKE BAARSSEN / SHUTTERSTOCK ©

WHY THIS IS A CLASSIC TRIP
MARC DI DUCA, WRITER

This trip showcases Germany's evolution from medieval times to the industrialised, environmentally aware nation that's celebrated today. From just over an hour outside Berlin you can pick up this fantastic time warp around one of the longest-inhabited regions in the country, along tree-lined avenues, up mountains, down dales, through ancient forests and by sparkling rivers. I promise you won't be bored!

Above: Glockenspiel, Goslar (p105)
Right: Traditional *Fachwerk* (half-timbered) house, Quedlinburg (p103)
Left: Steam train (p105), Harz National Park

Encircled by nearly intact fortifications, its historic centre is a warren of cobbled alleyways linking proud churches and half-timbered houses. Admire its beauty from the 330m section of the **Town Fortification** (Am Frauentor; adult/concession €3/2; ☺10am-5pm mid-Apr–Oct; 👪), accessible through Inneres Frauentor, and the viewing platform in the **Rabenturm** (Raven's Tower). Originally the 12th-century fortification ran for 2.8km around the town, from which a remarkable 2km remain. In the early 16th century, the town became a focal point of the Reformation and a launch pad for the Peasants' War of 1525, led by local preacher Thomas Müntzer.

With reunification, Mühlhausen became united Germany's most central town, located a mere 5km north of the country's geographical centre in Niederdorla. Mühlhausen's **Rathaus** (📞03601-4520; Ratsstrasse 19; ☺9am-noon Mon, Tue, Thu & Fri, plus 1-6pm Tue & Thu) is an architecturally intriguing hotchpotch of Gothic, Renaissance and baroque styles. Inside, pay special attention to the **Great Hall** and the **Councillors' Chamber**.

The Drive >> Follow the L1016 south for 35km to Eisenach.

Classic Trip

TRIP HIGHLIGHT

❻ Eisenach

The modest appearance of hilly Eisenach, a small town on the edge of the Thuringian Forest, belies its association with two German heavyweights: Johann Sebastian Bach and Martin Luther. Luther went to school here and later returned to protective custody in the **Wartburg** (📞03691-2500; www.wartburg-eisenach.de; Auf der Wartburg 1; tour adult/concession €10/7; 🕐tours 8.30am-5pm Apr-Oct, 9am-3.30pm Nov-Mar, English tour 1.30pm), now itself protected by Unesco World Heritage status. When it comes to medieval castles and their importance in German history, you've hit the mother lode: allow at least two hours for exploration with your camera batteries fully charged. A century after Luther's incarceration, Bach, the grandest of all baroque musicians, was born in the **Bachhaus** (📞03691-793 40; www.bachhaus.de; Frauenplan 21; adult/concession €10/6; 🕐10am-6pm), a wattle-and-daub home, now one of Germany's best biographical museums. Admission includes a 20-minute concert played on antique

instruments. Music-lovers will also appreciate the **Reuter-Wagner Museum** (📞03691-743 293; Reuterweg 2; adult/concession €4/2; 🕐2-5pm Wed-Sun), honouring composer Richard Wagner in a villa once owned by writer Fritz Reuter. Eisenach also has a century-old automotive tradition – the world's first BMW rolled off the local assembly line in 1929. Since you're on a road trip why not check out **Automobile Welt Eisenach** (📞03691-772 12; www.awe-stiftung.de; Friedrich-Naumann-Strasse 10; adult/concession €6/3.50; 🕐10am-6pm Apr-Oct, 11am-5pm Nov-Mar, closed Mon) as well?

✕ 🛏 p79, p114

The Drive » Take the B19 south for 37km, admiring the tree-lined avenues, thick forests and lush fields, passing through the occasional sleepy village here and there, then take the L1026 east for 7km into Schmalkalden.

❼ Schmalkalden

As you drive into town, you'll pass the unmissable **Viba Nougat Welt** (📞03683-692 1600; www.viba-sweets.de; Nougat-Allee 1; 🕐10am-6pm; 🅿 🚻) where you'd be forgiven for being seduced into a sweet-toothed visit, but be sure to press on into Schmalkalden's **Altmarkt** as well, where in 1531 the Protestant princes established the Schmal-kaldic League to counter

the central powers of Catholic emperor Charles V, thus thrusting the little town into the heart of the Reformation. The town's handsome **Rathaus** (1419) once functioned as the meeting place of the Schmalkaldic League. The incongruous towers of the late-Gothic **Stadt-kirche St Georg** (1437–1509) overlook the square. You can almost hear the groans and creaks of its half-timbered houses, crowned by the hilltop, late-Renaissance **Schloss Wilhelmsburg** (📞03683-403 186; www.museumwilhelmsburg.de; Schlossberg 9; adult/concession €6/4; 🕐10am-6pm Apr-Oct, to 4pm Tue-Sun Nov-Mar; 🚻). Conceived by Landgrave Wilhelm IV of Hessen as a hunting lodge and summer residence in the 1580s, it has largely kept its original design, with lavish murals and stucco decorating most rooms.

The Drive » Head north on the L1026, as it skirts the dense Thuringian Forest, with stretches of road fully covered by ancient trees and epitomising the Avenues Route. After 22km you'll reach the village of Friedrichroda, with its pretty castle and mysterious caves, but tarry not. A further 8km north brings you to the A4 autobahn at exit 41b Gotha-Boxberg. Head east for 45km to exit 46 Erfurt West. From here, take the L3004 north for 11km into Erfurt.

❽ Erfurt

Thuringia's attractive capital has seen much

DETOUR: KZ-GEDENKSTÄTTE MITTELBAU DORA

Start: ⑤ Mühlhausen

During the final stages of WWII, when Hitler's grand plan turned to conducting war from underground bunkers, Mittelbau Dora was established as a satellite of the Buchenwald concentration camp after British bombers destroyed missile plants in Peenemünde. At least 20,000 prisoners were worked to their deaths here. After years of decay under the GDR, the **memorial site** (☎03631-495 820; www.buchenwald. de; Kohnsteinweg 20, Nordhausen; ☺10am-6pm Tue-Sun Mar-Sep, to 4pm Oct-Feb) today gives an insight into the horrors that unfolded here, and includes a modern museum that explains the background of the camp and the experiences of the prisoners.

From late 1943, thousands of mostly Russian, French and Polish POWs (many of whom had survived Auschwitz) toiled under horrific conditions. They dug a 20km labyrinth of tunnels in the chalk hills north of Nordhausen, within which were built the V1 and V2 rockets that rained destruction on London, Antwerp and other cities during the war's final stages. The US Army reached the gates in April 1945, cared for survivors and removed all missile equipment before turning the area over to Russia. Visitors are free to roam the grounds, crematorium and museum. The tunnels (roughly the diameter of an aircraft hangar) are only accessible on free 90-minute guided tours, running at 11am and 2pm Tuesday to Friday and at 11am, 1pm and 3pm on weekends. Within the dank walls you can see partially assembled rockets that have lain untouched for decades.

To get here, head north for 29km on the L1015 until you reach the A38 at exit 6 Leinefelde-Worbis, then follow it east for 26km to exit 10 Werther. Follow Kassleler Landstrasse and Strasse der Opfer des Faschismus for 8km until you reach a railway crossing. Turn left and follow the road into the memorial site.

since being founded in 742 by St Boniface as a bishopric on the Gera River. Known for its churches, steeples and synagogues, today's Erfurt is a vibrant city with an appearance that honours its medieval roots, while adding classy, contemporary flourishes. An overnight stay is recommended. Erfurt has a number of lovely squares to stroll between. Be sure to visit Domplatz and the monumentous Erfurter Dom (p96); **Anger**, a transport and shopping hub where old meets new; **Wenigemarkt**, the perfect place for a casual meal; and **Fischmarkt**, Erfurt's central square, where you'll find the neo-Gothic **Rathaus** and a collection of spectacular historical buildings. Museums abound, including the worthwhile **Angermuseum** (☎0361-655 1651; www.angermuseum.de; Anger 18; adult/concession €6/4; ☺10am-6pm Tue-Sun), with its strong collection of medieval art, and the fascinating **Alte Synagoge** (☎0361-655 1520; www. juedisches-leben.erfurt.de; Waagegasse 8; adult/concession €8/5; ☺10am-6pm Tue-Sun), one of Europe's oldest Jewish houses of worship.

✖ ⊨ p79, p99, p114

The Drive ⟫ Take the B7 for 22km east, through fields of canola and wind turbines, into Weimar.

- - - - - - - - - - - - - - - - - -

TRIP HIGHLIGHT

⑨ Weimar

Few German cities of Weimar's size can boast such a wealth of culture and history. Weimar's main claim to fame is that literary and philosophical titans Goethe and Schiller spent the

Classic Trip

bulk of their days here. If you're interested in these big daddies of German culture, you've come to the right place. You can't get much more authentic than **Goethe Gartenhaus** (📞03643-545 400; www.klassik-stiftung.de; Park an der Ilm; adult/concession €6.50/5; ⏱10am-6pm Tue-Sun Apr-Oct, to 4pm Nov-Mar), where the great man lived between 1776 and 1782. Learn all about him in the **Goethe-Nationalmuseum** (📞03643-545 400; www.klassik-stiftung.de; Frauenplan 1; adult/concession €12.50/9; ⏱9.30am-6pm Tue-Sun Apr-Oct, to 4pm Nov-Mar), then take a peek at the **Nietzsche Archiv** (📞03643-545 400; www.klassik-stiftung.de; Humboldtstrasse 36; adult/concession €3.50/2.50; ⏱11am-5pm Tue-Sun Apr-Oct), where philosopher Friedrich Nietzsche spent his final years in illness. Perhaps

the most spectacular and thought-provoking site is the Unesco World Heritage **Herzogin Anna Amalia Bibliothek** (📞03643-545 400; www.klassik-stiftung.de; Platz der Demokratie 1; adult/concession €8/6.50; ⏱9.30am-2.30pm Tue-Sun), which has been beautifully reconstructed after a fire in 2004 destroyed much of the building and its priceless contents. Some of the most precious tomes are housed in the magnificent **Rokokosaal** (Rococo Hall).

The Drive » Follow the B7 for 25km east into Jena.

🔟 Jena

Unlike its neighbours Erfurt and Weimar, Jena owes its beauty more to the Saale River and the surrounding limestone hills than to a wealth of architectural and heritage sites. That said, Jena too has an age-old history as well as a fun, modern vibe, courtesy of the 19,000 strong student body. The birthplace of precision optics – pioneered here by Carl Zeiss, Ernst Abbe and Otto Schott – it is Jena's pedigree as a city of science that sets it apart from other Thuringian towns. Today, several museums attest to this legacy, including the **Stadtmuseum & Kunstsammlung Jena** (City Museum & Art Collection; 📞03641-498 261; www.stadtmuseum-jena.de; Markt 7; adult/concession

---

TOP TIP:
WEIMARCARD

Pick up a great-value **WeimarCard** (€32.50 for two days) from the **tourist office** (📞03643-7450; www.weimar.de; Markt 10; ⏱9.30am-6pm Mon-Sat, to 2pm Sun Apr-Oct, 9.30am-5pm Mon-Fri, to 2pm Sat & Sun Nov-Mar) for free admission to most museums, discounted tours, free iGuides and free travel on local buses if you want to let someone else do the driving for a while.

Jena Historic Saalstrasse

€4/3; ⏱10am-5pm Tue, Wed & Fri, 3-10pm Thu, 11am-6pm Sat & Sun), where you can learn how the city evolved into a centre of philosophy and science, and the public Zeiss Planetarium (p96), the world's oldest. Goethe himself planted the ginkgo tree in the wonderful **Botanischer Garten** (☎03641-949 274; www.spezbot.uni-jena.de/botanischer-garten; Fürstengraben

26; adult/concession €4/2.50; ⏱10am-7pm Apr-Oct, to 6pm Nov-Mar), which boasts more than 12,000 plants from every climatic zone on earth.

✖ 🛏 p114

The Drive » Head south for 51km on the delightfully green B88, through thick forests and woodlands into Saalfeld.

⑪ Saalfeld

Gables, turrets and gates provide a cheerful welcome to Saalfeld, which has been sitting prim and pretty along the Saale River for 1100 years. Aside from the handsome medieval town centre, you might want to check out the **Feengrotten** (Fairy Grottoes; ☎03671-550 40; www.feengrotten.de;

Classic Trip

Feengrottenweg 2; adult/child €12/8, with Grottoneum & Fairy World €15/10; ☺10am-5pm May-Oct, 11am-3.30pm Nov-Apr; [P] [🚻]) if you're young at heart or travelling with kids. These former alum slate mines (1530–1850) were opened for tours in 1914 and rank among the world's most colourful grottoes, imbued with shades of brown, ochre, sienna, green and blue. Otherwise, take a stroll around the **Markt** then along Brudergasse, uphill to a 13th-century Franciscan monastery, now recycled as the **Stadtmuseum** (City Museum; ☎03671 598 471; www.museumimkloster.de; Münzplatz 5; adult/concession €5/3; ☺10am-5pm Tue-Sun). Its major allure is the celestial building itself, and the collection of local late-Gothic carved altarpieces.

The Drive » Follow the B281 for 57km until the intersection with the A4 autobahn at exit 56a Hermsdorfer Kreuz. Follow the A7 east for some faster roads for 86km into Chemnitz, at exit 69 Chemnitz Mitte.

- - - - - - - - - - - - - - - - - -

⑫ Chemnitz

Known from 1953 to 1990 as Karl-Marx-Stadt, Chemnitz, like most former East German cities, had to reinvent itself

after reunification. It's done so with some measure of success, at least in its revitalised city centre that boasts a pedestrianised glass-and-steel shopping-and-entertainment district. Although you're here primarily to stretch your legs en route to Dresden, there are some engaging museums that might pique your interest: lovers of modern art should not miss **Museum Gunzenhauser** (☎0371-488 7024; www.kunstsammlungen-chemnitz.de; Stollberger Strasse 2; adult/concession €8/5; ☺11am-6pm Tue, Thu-Sun, 2-9pm Wed) and its gallery of 20th-century expressionist works, housed in a 1930s former bank building in the austere New Objectivity style. **DAStietz** (☎0371-488-4101; www.dastietz.de; Moritzstrasse 20) is a beautifully renovated 1913 former department store and now a one-stop shop for art and culture, housing the city library, **Neue Sächsische Galerie** (☎0371-367 6680; www.neue-saechsische-galerie.de; adult/child €4/free; ☺11am-5pm Thu-Mon, to 7pm Tue), which presents contemporary Saxon art, and the **Museum für Naturkunde** (Natural History Museum; ☎0371-488 4551; www.naturkunde-chemnitz.de; adult/concession €4/2.50; ☺10am-5pm Mon, Tue, Thu & Fri, to 6pm Sat & Sun), whose most interesting exhibit, the **Versteinerter Wald** (petrified forest), can be

admired for free in the atrium; some of the stony trunks are 290 million years old.

The Drive » Take the A4 autobahn from exit 69 Chemnitz Mitte for 70km to exit 78 Dresden Altstadt.

- - - - - - - - - - - - - - - - - -

> TRIP HIGHLIGHT

⑬ Dresden

There are few city silhouettes more striking than once known fondly as the 'Florence of the North', Dresden. The classic view from the Elbe's northern bank takes in spires, towers and domes belonging to palaces, churches and stately buildings, and indeed it's hard to believe that the city was all but wiped off the map by Allied bombings in 1945. Dresden's beloved domed **Frauenkirche** (☎0351-6560 6100; www.frauenkirche-dresden.de; Neumarkt; audioguide €2.50, cupola adult/student €8/5; ☺10am-noon & 1-6pm Mon-Fri, weekend hours vary) collapsed after the WWII bombings, and was rebuilt from a pile of rubble between 1994 and 2005. Other must-sees include **Albertinum** (Galerie Neue Meister; ☎0351-4914 2000; www.skd.museum; enter from Brühlsche Terrasse or Georg-Treu-Platz 2; adult/concession/child under 17yr €12/9/free; ☺10am-6pm Tue-Sun), a Renaissance-era former arsenal transformed into the stunning home of the **Galerie Neue Meister** (New Masters Gallery), and one of Germany's most famous opera houses, the **Semperoper** (☏0351-320 7360; www.semperoper-erleben.de; Theaterplatz 2; tour adult/concession €11/7; ⊙hours vary), which opened in 1841 and hosted premieres of works by Strauss, von Weber and Wagner.

See p118 for a walking tour of Dresden.

✗ 🛏 p71, p99, p115

The Drive » Getting back onto the Avenues Route, take the B6 northwest for 60km to the little town of Oschatz, where there has been a settlement since neolithic times. Continue on the B6 through lowlands and fields for another 56km into Leipzig.

🄬 Leipzig

When it comes to art, the neo-realistic New Leipzig School has stirred up the international art world for well over a decade with such protagonists as Neo Rauch and Tilo Baumgärtel. Such contemporary art in all media is the speciality of the **Galerie**

LOCAL KNOWLEDGE: NOCH BESSER LEBEN

In Leipzig, this locally beloved **bar** (www.nochbesser leben.com; Merseburger Strasse 25; ⊙4.30pm-late) at the epicentre of the Plagwitz entertainment district is the perfect spot to meet a cool local crowd drinking an impressive selection of beer. With an upstairs band room, funky downstairs bar and bustling patio, it has a communal, friendly vibe for which only the German word *gemütlich* (approximately translated as cosy) will do.

für Zeitgenössische Kunst (☏0341-140 8126; www.gfzk-leipzig.de; Karl-Tauchnitz-Strasse 9-11; adult/concession per space €5/3, both spaces €8/4, Wed free; ⊙2-7pm Tue-Fri, noon-6pm Sat & Sun), presenting exhibits in a minimalist container-like space and a late 19th-century villa. The city's beloved **Nikolaikirche** (Church of St Nicholas; www.nikolaikirche.de; Nikolaikirchhof 3; ⊙10am-6pm Mon-Sat, to 4pm Sun) has Romanesque and Gothic roots, but since 1797 has sported a striking neoclassical interior with palm-like pillars and cream-coloured pews. The design is certainly gorgeous but the church is most famous for playing a key role in the nonviolent movement that led to the downfall of the East German government.

✗ 🛏 p71, p99, p115

The Drive » Head north on the B2 for 9km to the junction with the A14 autobahn at exit 23 Leipzig Mitte, then follow the A14 west for 14km to the A9 autobahn at exit 15 Schkeuditzer Kreuz. Head north on the A9 for 48km into Dessau-Rosslau.

Eating & Sleeping

Quedlinburg ❷

✗ Münzenberger Klause   German €€
(☎03946-2928; www.muenzenberger-klause.
de; Pölle 22; mains €9-21; ⊘11am-midnight
Tue-Sat) Serving traditional German fare with
flair, this atmospheric restaurant is loved by
locals and visitors alike. If you're seeking hearty
comfort food, look no further.

⌂ Romantik Hotel
am Brühl   Boutique Hotel €€€
(☎03946-961 80; www.hotelambruehl.de;
Billungstrasse 11; s/d from €120/135; P ✲ 🛜)
Well-appointed, spacious rooms and suites
are individually and classically styled in this
impressive boutique hotel on the outskirts of
the Altstadt. The apartments are delightful
and an excellent option for those travelling
with children or in a small group. A plentiful
breakfast buffet is included.

Goslar ❹

⌂ Hotel Alte
Münze   Boutique Hotel €€
(☎05321-225 46; www.hotel-muenze.de;
Münzstrasse 10-11; s/d from €95/115; P 🛜)
There's very little not to like about this boutique
hotel in the heart of the Altstadt, parts of which
are over 500 years old. Operating as a mint in
a previous incarnation, the hotel's hotchpotch
of rooms have been beautifully modernised
with spotless new bathrooms, flat-screen TVs
and wi-fi to complement the antiquey, creaky,
medieval vibe.

Eisenach ❻

✗ La Grappa
Pasquale Esposito   Italian €€
(☎03691-733 860; www.lagrappa-eisenach.de;
Frauenberg 8; mains €10-20; ⊘11.30am-2.30pm
& 5.30-11.30pm Tue-Sun, 11.30am-11.30pm Apr-
Sep; ✈) The sunny terracotta terrace of this

local favourite takes you straight back to the
homeland. Heavier meat dishes such as pork
fillet baked with cream, spinach and mozzarella
are balanced by a broad choice of fish, soups
and salads. Vegetarians have decent options on
the antipasti, pizza and pasta menus.

Erfurt ❽

✗ Schnitzler   German €€
(☎0361-644 7557; www.schnitzler-restaurant.
de; Domplatz 32; mains €10-22; ⊘11am-11pm;
🖶) It might be difficult for any self-proclaimed
schnitzel lover to pass by a restaurant that pays
such unabashed homage to the crumbed cutlet.
There's an enormous variety to choose from
(some using seasonal specialities such as wild
garlic, mushrooms and asparagus), the prices
are reasonable, and service comes with a smile.

⌂ Mercure Erfurt Altstadt   Hotel €€
(☎0361-594 90; www.accorhotels.com;
Meienbergstrasse 26-27; d from €90; P ✲ 🛜)
The best thing about this above-average hotel
is its prime location a few blocks from lovely
Wenigemarkt and the Anger transit hub. Rooms
are bright and comfortable, if not particularly
stylish, and online bargains can be found.
On-site parking costs €16 per night.

Jena ❿

✗ Landgrafen
Jena   Modern European €€€
(☎03641-507 071; www.landgrafen.com;
Landgrafenstieg 25; mains €9-24; ⊘3-11pm
Tue-Thu, 11.30am-11pm Fri & Sat, 11.30am-8pm
Sun; P 🖶) High in the hills with stunning
views over Jena, this smart multipurpose
restaurant serves genuinely interesting food
such as potato-wasabi soup with 'river-crab
tails'. There's a summer garden with bratwursts,
beers and a kids' playground, but the real appeal
lies with the stylish terrace (for casual eats) or
the dressy, upmarket dining room. Wines from
the Saale-Unstrut region are featured.

🛏 Hotel
Rasenmühle   Boutique Hotel €€

(📞03641-534 2130; www.hotel-rasenmuehle.de; Burgauer Weg 1a; s/d €60/95; P 🛜) While the rooms are smartly decorated and comfortable, the best thing about this little hotel is its leafy location in the midst of Paradies park. Most of the 11 rooms have views over the Saale River or parklands, there's free wi-fi and parking, and a communal kitchen is available to guests. At these prices, it's a winner.

Dresden ⓭

🍴 Raskolnikoff   International €€

(📞0351-804 5706; www.raskolnikoff.de; Böhmische Strasse 34; mains €10-15; ⏰11am-10.30pm) An artist squat in the 1980s, Raskolnikoff now brims with grown-up artsy-bohemian flair, especially in the sweet little garden at the back, complete with bizarre water feature. The seasonally calibrated menu showcases the fruits of the surrounding land in globally inspired dishes, including a variety of *pelmeni* (Russian dumplings), which proudly represent the Dostoyevsky character the establishment is named after.

🍴 Restaurant
Genuss-Atelier   German €€€

(📞0351-2502 8337; www.genuss-atelier.net; Bautzner Strasse 149; mains €16-31; ⏰5-11pm Wed-Fri, noon-3.30pm & 5-11pm Sat & Sun; 🚊11 to Waldschlösschen) Lighting up Dresden's culinary scene is this fantastic place that's well worth the trip on the 11 tram. The creative menu is streets ahead of most offerings elsewhere, although the best way to experience the 'Pleasure-Atelier' is to book a surprise menu (three/four/five courses €49/59/69) and let the chefs show off their craft. Reservations essential.

🛏 Hotel Schloss Eckberg   Hotel €€

(📞0351-809 90; www.schloss-eckberg.de; Bautzner Strasse 134; d Kavaliershaus/Schloss

from €90/135; P ❄ 🛜) This romantic castle set in its own riverside park east of the Neustadt is a breathtaking place to stay. Rooms in the Schloss itself are pricier and have oodles of historic flair, but staying in the modern Kavaliershaus lets you enjoy almost as many amenities and the same dreamy setting.

🛏 Pensione
la Campagnola   B&B €€

(📞0351-314 1023; www.la-campagnola -dresden.de; Friedrich-Wieck-Strasse 45; s/d €69/95; 🛜) If you don't mind a 20-minute tram ride to the centre, this 1697 half-timbered ferrymaster's house, facing Blue Wonder bridge in the riverside villa district of Loschwitz, is a charming option. Run by Italian restaurateurs, it has eight individually designed rooms with lots of retro touches. Breakfast at the downstairs restaurant is expectedly superb.

Leipzig ⓮

🍴 Cafe Puschkin   Cafe €

(📞0341-392 0105; www.cafepuschkin.de; Karl-Liebknecht-Strasse 74; mains €6-10; ⏰9am-2am) This charming old pub on the Südvorstadt neighbourhood's supercool Karli is a local institution. The selection of burgers, nachos and sausages won't blow you away, but it's good comfort food in a friendly and somewhat eccentric atmosphere. It's also a great breakfast spot following a night out.

🛏 Gwuni Mopera   B&B €€

(📞0341-6991 4463; www.gwuni-mopera. de; Sternwartenstrasse 4; s/d from €65/70, breakfast €8; 🛜) A tiny B&B hiding in the courtyard of a large Stalin-esque edifice on Rossplatz, Gwuni Mopera is a subtly atmospheric option with creaky wooden floors, retro-styled furniture and art on the walls. Bathrooms are shared, but guests are too few to fight over them. The African-sounding name is in fact an acronym that includes four nearby landmarks.

STRETCH YOUR LEGS
BERLIN

Start/Finish: Potsdamer Platz

Distance: 4.5km

Duration: Three hours

An Instagram-worthy cocktail of culture, architecture and history, this easy and entertaining walk checks off many of the famous Berlin landmarks you've seen in newscasts and history books, and even briefly follows the course of the infamous Berlin Wall.

Take this walk on Trip

Potsdamer Platz

Built on terrain once bifurcated by the Berlin Wall, the historic Potsdamer Platz quarter underwent a 1990s rebirth and is a showcase of urban renewal masterminded by international architects such as Renzo Piano and Helmut Jahn. Highlights include the glass-tented Sony Center, the **Panoramapunkt observation deck** (☏030-2593 7080; www.panoramapunkt.de; adult/concession €7.50/6, without wait €11.50/9; ☺10am-8pm Apr-Oct, to 6pm Nov-Mar) and Wall remnants.

The Walk ≫ There's a large parking garage below Potsdamer Platz; enter via Reichpietschufer, Linkstrasse, Ludwig-Beck-Strasse or Schellingstrasse. After seeing the Platz, follow the course of the Wall north on Ebertstrasse, along the eastern edge of the vast Tiergarten park.

Holocaust Memorial

This memorial consists of 2711 sarcophagi-like concrete columns rising sombrely from undulating ground. For context, visit the subterranean **Ort der Information** (Information Centre; ☏030-7407 2929; www.holocaust-mahnmal.de; Cora-Berliner-Strasse 1; audioguide €3; ☺10am-8pm Tue-Sun Apr-Sep, to 7pm Oct-Mar, last admission 45min before closing), whose exhibits will leave no one untouched.

The Walk ≫ Continue north on Ebertstrasse past the US Embassy to the Brandenburg Gate.

Brandenburg Gate & Pariser Platz

A symbol of division during the Cold War, the landmark Brandenburg Gate now epitomises German reunification. Modelled after Athens' Acropolis and completed in 1791, it stands sentinel over Pariser Platz, a harmoniously proportioned square framed by banks and embassies.

The Walk ≫ From Ebertstrasse, enter Tiergarten at Simsonweg. Walk past the memorial for the Sinti and Roma victims of Nazi Germany to Scheidemannstrasse, where the Reichstag will loom in front of you.

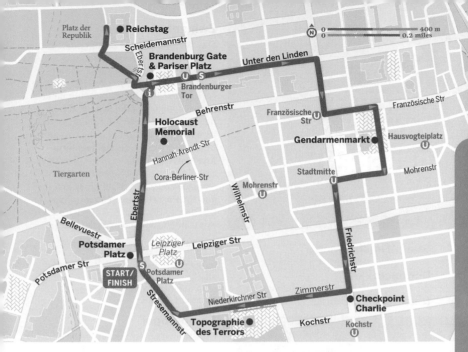

Reichstag

It's been burned, bombed, rebuilt, buttressed by the Wall, and finally turned into the modern home of the German parliament: the 1894 **Reichstag** (www.bundestag.de; Platz der Republik 1; lift 8am-midnight, last entry 9.45pm, Visitors Centre 8am-8pm Apr-Oct, to 6pm Nov-Mar;) is one of Berlin's most iconic buildings. For guaranteed access to its dome, make free reservations online. Bring ID.

The Walk » Backtrack to the Brandenburg Gate, cross Pariser Platz and walk east on Unter den Linden. Turn right on Friedrichstrasse and left on Französische Strasse.

Gendarmenmarkt

Berlin's most graceful square is bookended by two 18th-century cathedrals and punctuated by a grandly porticoed concert hall. Climb the tower of the French Cathedral for grand views.

The Walk » Consider stopping for coffee or a bite in one of the many cafes around the square, then walk west on Mohrenstrasse to Friedrichstrasse and continue south to Checkpoint Charlie.

Checkpoint Charlie

Checkpoint Charlie was the principal gateway for foreigners and diplomats between the two Berlins from 1961 to 1990. This potent symbol of the Cold War has largely degenerated into a tacky tourist trap, but the free open-air exhibit is one redeeming aspect.

The Walk » Take Zimmerstrasse west to Niederkirchner Strasse and the Topography of Terror museum.

Topographie des Terrors

On the site where once stood the Gestapo headquarters, this compelling **exhibit** (Topography of Terror; 030-2545 0950; www.topographie.de; Niederkirchner Strasse 8; 10am-8pm, grounds close at dusk or 8pm at the latest) chronicles the stages of terror and persecution, puts a face on the perpetrators, and details the impact they had on all of Europe.

The Walk » Follow Niederkirchner Strasse to Stresemannstrasse, turn right and you'll shortly be back at Potsdamer Platz.

STRETCH
YOUR LEGS
DRESDEN

Start/Finish: Zwinger

Distance: 2km

Duration: Four hours

This walk allows you to discover the sights of Dresden's beautifully restored Altstadt (old town). It takes you across and along the Elbe River, and past many of the churches, palaces and museums that make Saxony's capital such a beguiling and fascinating place.

Take this walk on Trips

Zwinger

Start by entering the **Zwinger** (☎0351-4914 2000; www.der-dresdner-zwinger.de; Theaterplatz 1; ticket for all museums adult/concession €12/9, courtyard free; ☺6am-10pm Apr-Oct, to 8pm Nov-Mar), a pleasure palace built for Augustus the Strong. It now houses three excellent museums within its baroque walls, though the two most interesting are the **Gemäldegalerie Alte Meister** (Old Masters Gallery; adult/concession €12/9, audioguide €3) and its amazing collection of religious art, and the **Porzellansammlung** (Porcelain Collection; adult/student €6/4.50), with its exquisite European and Asian china.

The Walk ≫ Park on or around Ostra Allee, where there's usually plenty of space (buy a parking ticket from the machines on weekdays). After Zwinger, head through the portal on the north side of its courtyard, and emerge onto Theaterplatz.

Semperoper

On Dresden's most famous square, Theaterplatz, you'll see the city's storied opera house, the **Semperoper** (☎0351-320 7360; www.semperoper-erleben.de; Theaterplatz 2; tour adult/concession €11/7; ☺hours vary) on one side, the Elbe in the distance and the impressive **Katholische Hofkirche** (Schlossplatz; ☺9am-5pm Mon-Thu, 1-5pm Fri, 10am-5pm Sat, noon-4pm Sun) to your right. This is Dresden's heart and its history is palpable. It's possible to visit the Semperoper on a tour if not going to a performance.

The Walk ≫ Walk across the square towards the Augustusbrücke and continue over the Elbe. Walk down the steps and along the green riverbank, taking in the wonderful views before crossing back to the Altstadt along the Carolabrücke.

Albertinum

The gorgeously renovated **Albertinum** (Galerie Neue Meister; ☎0351-4914 2000; www.skd.museum; enter from Brühlsche Terrasse or Georg-Treu-Platz 2; adult/concession/child under 17yr €12/9/free; ☺10am-6pm Tue-Sun) holds Dresden's best collection of modern art, in a stunning building that's well worth wandering into even if you don't intend

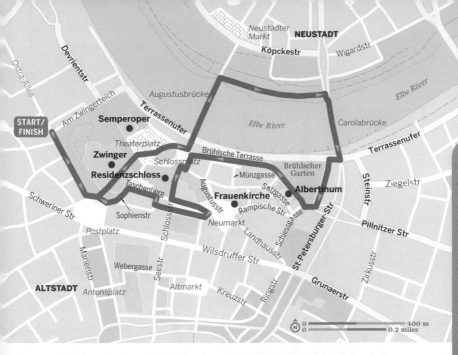

to visit the collection. Inside, Claude Monet's landscapes compete with the abstract visions of Marc Chagall. There's also a superb sculpture collection spread over the lower floors.

The Walk » Leaving the Albertinum, follow the walkway along the Brühlsche Terrasse for more epic river views, passing the stunning facade of the Dresden Fine Arts Academy on the way. At the bottom of the stairs, turn left onto Schlossplatz then head through the archway.

Residenzschloss

The fabulous palace home to the Electors of Saxony, the **Residenzschloss** (☎0351-4914 2000; www.skd. museum; Schlossplatz; adult/child €12/free, incl Historisches Grünes Gewölbe €21/free; ◷10am-6pm Wed-Mon) has been spectacularly restored and contains a wealth of fascinating museums. A must-see for any visitor is the incredible collection of jewels, diamonds, gold and silver in the **Historisches Grünes Gewölbe** (Historic Green Vault; ☎0351-4914 2000; www. skd.museum; Residenzschloss; €12; ◷10am-

6pm Wed-Mon) and the **Neues Grünes Gewölbe** (New Green Vault; adult/child under 17yr incl audioguide €12/free). Don't miss the exquisite wall murals both inside and outside the palace.

The Walk » From the palace walk the short distance to the Neumarkt, the main square of Dresden, which is dominated by the looming presence of the Frauenkirche.

Frauenkirche

Literally rising from the ashes of its WWII destruction, the magnificent **Frauenkirche** (☎0351-6560 6100; www. frauenkirche-dresden.de; Neumarkt; audioguide €2.50, cupola adult/student €8/5; ◷10am-noon & 1-6pm Mon-Fri, weekend hours vary) is the beloved symbol of Dresden. The original was part of the skyline for 200 years before the war, and was rebuilt from a pile of rubble between 1994 and 2005. A spitting image of the original, it's impressive both inside and out.

The Walk » From here, walk down Taschenberg and then up Ostra-Allee along the side of the Zwinger to get back to where you started.

119

Northwestern Germany

LEARN TO LOVE GERMAN WINE AMID GORGEOUS WINERIES on these trips, which take in the fabled vineyards of the Rhine and Moselle Valleys. You'll find more beauty outdoors as you tour the sheltered towns and pristine beaches of the North Sea.

Inside you'll find plenty to enjoy, from the churches and cultural must-sees of Cologne to the superb museums in the mighty cities of Germany's Ruhr Valley. History as far back as the Romans is found in ancient towns like Xanten.

History of a much more fanciful sort features in the German Fairy-Tale Road. The tales you loved as children have much more complex pasts, as visitors learn in the string of towns that include the dreamy Marburg and Bremen.

Cologne (p150, p158)
MATTHIAS HAKER PHOTOGRAPHY / GETTY IMAGES ©

Northwestern Germany

9 **North Sea Coast 5–7 Days**
A summer jaunt from Emden along the Wattenmeer coast to Sylt.

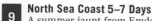 **German Fairy-Tale Road 5 Days**
10 Learn the fantasies and the horrors hidden in the stories of the Brothers Grimm.

11 **Cologne & the Ruhr Valley 4 Days**
From Romans to titans, iron to culture, this drive is about power.

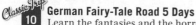 **Romantic Rhine 5–7 Days**
12 Fall under the spell of the castle-lined riverscape along the world-famous Rhine.

13 **Moselle Valley 2–4 Days**
Wind through the winery-filled Moselle from historic Trier to the river's end.

14 **German Wine Route 2–4 Days**
Bookended by twin gates, this picturesque route links up charming vine-draped villages.

✔ DON'T MISS

Cologne
The star of the region, Cologne makes its statement from the moment you spot the Dom's twin spires.
Trips **11** **12**

Wine Tasting
Learn to love Germany's often-excellent white wines. Sip exquisite vintages in cosy wineries amid the vineyards on
Trips **12** **13** **14**

Hambacher Schloss
Visit the hilltop castle where the German flag was raised for the first time.
Trip **14**

Sylt
Germany's favourite upscale-resort island has some of Europe's most beautiful beaches and some of Germany's most exclusive restaurants and clubs.
Trip **9**

Zollverein Coal Mine
Germany's industrial might reached its expressive pinnacle at this complex. Marvel at the beauty built into the mighty structures on
Trip **11**

North Sea Coast

9

This nautical whimsy whisks you from sleepy sea shanties and enchanting islands into the heart of high-culture Hanseatic city states and the embrace of Germany's premier seaside resort.

TRIP HIGHLIGHTS

613 km

Sylt
Pamper yourself silly at Germany's favourite seaside resort

9 FINISH

● Husum

383 km

Hamburg
Wealthy Hamburg has an age-old seafaring tradition

7

Bremerhaven ●

● Emden
START

6

263 km

Bremen
Cosmopolitan Bremen oozes style and culture

5–7 DAYS
613KM / 391 MILES

GREAT FOR...

BEST TIME TO GO
August to September: long days and thin crowds.

ESSENTIAL PHOTO
Capture the ethereal light of a late-night North Sea sunset.

BEST FOR OUTDOORS
Walk the Wadden Sea to an East Frisian Island.

Sylt (p132) Traditional Frisian house

North Sea Coast

From Emden, lightly dusted with the flavours of its Dutch neighbours, travel along the blustery, beautiful Wadden Sea and a take-your-pick selection of enchanting East Frisian Islands, to Bremerhaven, former seat of German emigration, onwards to the high-culture city states of Bremen and Hamburg, before retiring to Sylt, Germany's luxe island resort at the Danish border.

❶ Emden

You're almost in the Netherlands here: the flat landscape, dikes and windmills outside town and the melodic twang of the local Plattdütsch dialect combine to give this quiet seafaring city a Dutch flavour. Begin your trip with a visit to the **Bunkermuseum** (☑04921-322 25; www.bunkermuseum.de; Holzsägerstrasse 6; adult/child €4/2.50; ⊙10am-1pm & 3-5pm Tue-Fri, 10am-1pm Sat & Sun May-Oct), to remind yourself that life wasn't always this peaceful here, and check out the **Ostfriesisches Landesmuseum** (Regional History Museum; ☑04921-872 058; www.landesmuseum-emden. de; Brückstrasse 1, Rathaus; adult/child €8/free; ⊙10am-5pm Tue-Sun) for an overview of the people whose culture and wind-blown landscapes you're about to explore. Ferries operated by **AG-Ems** (☑01805-180 182; www.ag-ems.de) depart Emden for Borkum, the largest of the East Frisian Islands, popular with German and Dutch families who rent houses and come for their summer vacations.

The Drive » Follow Auricher Strasse north out of town for 3.5km to Landesstrasse and turn left, through the village of Hinte, then turn right onto the K229 for 8km to the village of Jennelt. Turn right onto the L4 for 750m then follow Greetsieler Strasse for about 5km into the delightful village of Greetsiel.

❷ Greetsiel

The tiny, photogenic port of Greetsiel was first documented as far back as 1388. There's little to do here but stretch your legs, take a walk around

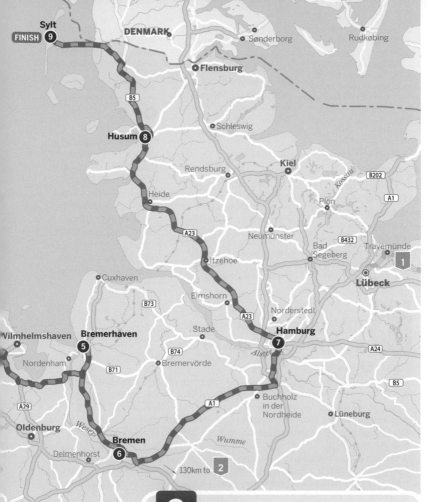

130km to **2**

LINK YOUR TRIP

1 Along the Baltic Coast

From Hamburg, drive northeast for 65km to Lübeck to join this aquatic excursion, and you'll have Germany's coasts covered.

2 Design for Life: Bauhaus to VW

It's 130km of autobahn action from Bremen southeast to Hanover, the final stop of our modern, architectural-themed jaunt.

the scenic harbour, check out a windmill or two and admire the handful of handsome buildings along the harbour wall. Why not pick up a souvenir while you're here?

The Drive » Turning back the way you came, pass the two windmills then turn left at the roundabout towards Norddeich on the L27: the raised bump the road follows on your left-hand side is a dike! Drive 14km across the moors until you reach the intersection with the K214 and turn left, following the road (and the dike) for 5km into Norddeich.

---

❸ Norddeich

There's only one real reason to hang about in the busy port of Norddeich: to take the **Reederei Frisia** (☎04931-9870; www.reederei-frisia.de) ferry to Norderney or Juist, which you might just

want to do. If an East Frisian island visit is on your itinerary, consider spending the night here before or after your trip. Watching the late-night midsummer sun setting from the dike wall is quite an experience.

🛏 p133

The Drive » Follow Ostermarscher Strasse, which becomes the L5, for 15km to the village of Nessmersiel. This is where you'll alight for walking trips on the Wadden Sea to Baltrum, if you've booked yourself a guide. Otherwise, continue 17km to Bensersiel (for ferries to Langeoog),

then onwards for 10km to Neuharlingersiel (ferries to Spiekeroog). It's 29km from here to Jever on the B461: follow the signs.

---

❹ Jever

The capital of the Friesland region is also known as 'Fräulein Maria', who peers out from attractions and shop windows in Jever. She was the last of the so-called Häuptlinge (chieftains) to rule the town in the Middle Ages, and although Russia's Catherine the Great got

DETOUR: EAST FRISIAN ISLANDS

Start: ❸ Norddeich

Lined up like diamonds in a tiara, from west to east, the seven East Frisian islands are: Borkum, Juist, Norderney, Baltrum, Langeoog, Spiekeroog and Wangerooge. Their long sandy beaches, open spaces and sea air make them a nature lovers' paradise and peaceful retreat. Like their North Frisian cousins Sylt, Amrum and Föhr, the islands are part of the Unesco World Heritage Wadden Sea (Wattenmeer) National Park.

When the tide recedes on the Wadden Sea, it exposes the mudflats connecting the mainland to the islands, enabling nature lovers to waddle their muddy way to Baltrum and its sister 'isles'. *Wattwandern*, as it is known, is a no-no without an experienced guide: tidal changes can quickly cut you off from the mainland. Tourist offices in Emden and Jever can hook you up.

If that's not your thing, a day trip or overnight stay on Norderney, Queen of East Frisia, might do the trick. Founded in 1797 by Friedrich Wilhelm II of Prussia, it fast became one of the most famous bathing destinations in Europe. The island's Art Deco **Kurtheater** and the neoclassical **Conversationshaus** (1840), which today houses the tourist office, are worth a visit. But if you need to be pampered, you'll love the sprawling, luxurious **Bade:haus** (☎04932-891 400; www.badehaus-norderney. de; Am Kurplatz 3; per 4hr €20.50; ⏰9.30am-9.30pm, women only from 5.30pm Wed) aquatic complex, day spa and sauna housed in the former Art Nouveau sea-water baths: reason enough for a day trip.

Tourist season runs from mid-May to September, but opening hours of tourist offices are irregular as are ferry schedules, which are subject to the tides. Same-day return trips are not always possible and advance planning is usually required.

her hands on Jever for a time in the 18th century, locals always preferred their home-grown queen. Having died unmarried and a virgin, Maria is the German equivalent of England's (in truth more worldly) Elizabeth I. Check out her story in Jever's **Schloss** (☎04461-969 350; www.schlossmu seum.de; Schlossplatz 1; adult/child €6/free, incl tower climb €7.50/4; ◷10am-6pm Tue-Sun, plus Mon mid-May–mid-Oct), then head to the **Friesisches Brauhaus zu Jever** (☎04461-137 11; www.jever.de; Elisabethufer 18; tours adult/child €9.50/3.50; ◷times vary) for a brewery tour and a cold pilsner.

The Drive ⟫ Head south on Mühlenstrasse then east on Silensteder Strasse until you reach the B210. Follow it south for 6km to the A29. Take the A29 south for 18km to Varel, then head east on the B437 for 38km. Pick up the A27 at exit 11 Stotel, heading north for 17km to exit 7, Bremerhaven Mitte.

- - - - - - - - - - - - - - - - -

❺ Bremerhaven

Bremerhaven's waterfront Havenwelten area, with its old ships and rusty docks juxtaposed against glistening contemporary architecture, is the product of a recent re-imagining of its harbour as a place to play and learn. Not only goods have been shipped out for decades from Bremerhaven, one of Europe's busiest ports, but people, too: almost

Jever Statue of Fräulein Maria

all German emigrants around the world headed off to their new lives from this very place. Hear their stories in the compelling **Deutsches Auswanderer-haus** (German Emigration Centre; ☎0471-902 200; www.dah-bremerhaven.de; Columbusstrasse 65; adult/child €15/9; ◷10am-6pm Mar-Oct, to 5pm Nov-Feb). Continuing on this global theme, the neighbouring **Klimahaus Bremerhaven 8° Ost** (Climate House; ☎0471-902 0300; www.klimahaus-bremer haven.de; Am Längengrad 8; adult/concession/family €17/12/49; ◷9am-7pm Mon-Fri, from 10am Sat & Sun Apr-Aug, 10am-6pm Sep-Mar) takes you on a fascinating journey around the world and its changing climes. If you've an inquisitive mind, both museums are reason enough to come to town.

The Drive ⟫ Heading back inland, follow the A7 autobahn for a speedy trip south, 60km into Bremen.

- - - - - - - - - - - - - - - - -

TRIP HIGHLIGHT

❻ Bremen

Bremen, one of Germany's three city states (along with Berlin and Hamburg), has a justified reputation for being among the country's most outward-looking and hospitable places, with a population that strikes a good balance between style, earthiness and good living. Bremen's vibrant districts have a host of fine restaurants, fun bars and a selection of excellent museums. Bremen's must-see **Altstadt** (old town) should be followed by a visit to the **Kunsthalle** (☎0421-329 080; www.kunsthalle-bremen. de; Am Wall 207; adult/concession €10/5; ◷10am-5pm Wed-Sun, to 9pm Tue;

2, 3 to Theater am Goetheplatz) for its collection of paintings and artworks: some are over 600 years old. To mix up the new with the old, take a look at the downtown **Übersee Museum** (Overseas Museum; ☏0421-160 380; www.uebersee-museum.de; Bahnhofplatz 13; adult/child/family €7.50/free/15; ☺9am-5pm Tue-Fri, from 10am Sat & Sun; 🚇Hauptbahnhof): exhibits on each of the world's continents offer insight into natural evolution with a dazzling collection of exotic artefacts. With over 300 engaging exhibits housed in a unique, shiny silver building resembling a clamshell, UFO or sperm whale, depending on your interpretation, Bremen's **Universum Science Center** (☏0421-334 60; www.universum-bremen. de; Wiener Strasse 1a; adult/child €16/11; ☺9am-6pm

Mon-Fri, from 10am Sat & Sun; 🚇6 to Universität-Süd) is one of a kind.

🍴 🛏 p133, p147

The Drive » Pick up the A1 just outside of town for a zippy 105km drive north to Hamburg and its famous port.

TRIP HIGHLIGHT

❼ Hamburg

Germany's second-largest city, and one of the world's busiest ports, has never been shy. A centre of international trade since the 19th century, it amassed great wealth and remains one of the country's richest cities, infused with a maritime spirit and an openness that has given rise to vibrant multicultural neighbourhoods. Hamburg has more cultural and historical attractions than one can squeeze into a day or

three. On **Deichstrasse** (ⓤRödingsmarkt) you can get a feel for the old canal and merchants' quarter. For bird's-eye views, take the glass lift to a 76.3m-high viewing platform in **Mahnmal St-Nikolai** (Memorial St Nicholas; ☏040-371 125; www.mahnmal-st-nikolai. de; Willy-Brandt-Strasse 60; adult/child €5/3; ☺10am-6pm May-Sep, to 5pm Oct-Apr; ⓤRödingsmarkt), now a WWII memorial site. Or head to the boisterous **Fischmarkt** (Grosse Elbstrasse 9; ☺5am-9.30am Sun Apr-Oct, from 7am Nov-Mar; 🚌112 to Fischmarkt, Ⓢ Reeperbahn) in St Pauli, running since 1703, where every Sunday in the wee hours some 70,000 locals and visitors converge. **Hamburger Kunsthalle** (☏040-428 131 200; www.hamburger-kunsthalle.de; Glockengiesserwall; adult/concessions €14/8, Thu

HAMBURG: A CITY SNAPSHOT

Hamburg's commercial character was forged in 1189, when local noble Count Adolf III persuaded Emperor Friedrich I (Barbarossa) to grant the city free trading rights and an exemption from customs duties. This transformed the former missionary settlement and 9th-century moated fortress of Hammaburg into an important port and member of the Hanseatic League.

The city prospered until 1842, when the Great Fire destroyed a third of its buildings. While it managed to recover in time to join the German Reich in 1871, the city was then involved in two devastating world wars. After WWI, most of Hamburg's merchant fleet (almost 1500 ships) was forfeited to the Allies. WWII saw more than half of Hamburg's housing, 80% of its port and 40% of its industry reduced to rubble; tens of thousands of civilians were killed.

In the post-WWII years, Hamburg harnessed its resilience to participate in Germany's economic miracle *(Wirtschaftswunder)*. Its harbour and media industries are now the backbone of its wealth. The majority of Germany's largest publications are produced here, including news magazines *Stern* and *Der Spiegel*.

Hamburg Miniatur Wunderland

evening €8/5; ⊙10am-6pm Tue, Wed & Fri-Sun, to 9pm Thu; ⓊHauptbahnhof-Nord) is one of Germany's most impressive art galleries, while the incredible scale of **Miniatur Wunderland** (☑040-300 6800; www.miniatur-wunderland. de; Kehrwieder 2; adult/child €15/7.50; ⊙hours vary; ⓊBaumwall) delights young and old.

✕ ⼞ p133

The Drive » Follow the A23 north for 105km until it becomes the B3. Continue across the moorish landscape for another 70km to Husum.

---

⑧ Husum

Warmly toned buildings huddle around Husum's photogenic Binnenhafen (inner harbour), colourful gabled houses line its narrow, cobbled lanes, and in late March and early April millions of purple crocuses bloom in the Schlosspark. The **Poppenspäler Museum** (☑04841-632 42; www. pole-poppenspaeler.de; König-Friedrich V-Allee 2; adult/child/family €2/1/5; ⊙11am-5pm Tue-Sun Mar-Oct, Sat & Sun Nov-Feb) has displays of enchanting handmade puppets, and even if you're not familiar with

the 19th-century author, the **Theodor-Storm-Haus** (Theodor Storm House; ☑04841-803 8630; www. storm-gesellschaft.de; Wasserreihe 31-35; adult/child €4/3; ⊙10am-5pm Tue-Fri, 11am-5pm Sat, 2-5pm Sun-Mon Apr-Oct, 2-5pm Tue, Sat & Sun Nov-Mar) holds appeal for its intimate depiction of a novelist's life in the rooms where he lived and worked.

The Drive » Follow the B5 north for 80km to the end of the road and about as far north in Germany as you can go. Congratulations, you made it! You can elect to leave your car on the mainland, or take the car ferry over to the island.

HELGOLAND

Helgoland's former rulers, the British, really got the better deal in 1891 when they swapped it for then-German-ruled Zanzibar. But Germans today are very fond of this lonesome North Sea outcrop of red-sandstone rock and its fresh air and warm weather, courtesy of the Gulf Stream. The 80m-tall Lange Anna (Long Anna) rock on the island's southwest edge is a compelling sight, standing alone in the ocean. There are also WWII bunkers and ruins to explore, and resurging numbers of Atlantic grey seals. Driving and cycling are not permitted on the tiny 4.2-sq-km island. By an old treaty, Helgoland is not part of the EU's VAT area, so many of the 1130 residents make their living selling duty-free cigarettes, booze and perfume to day-trippers who prowl the main drag, Lung Wai ('long way'). To swim, many head to neighbouring Düne, a blip in the ocean that is popular with nudists.

Helgoland makes an easy day trip, but if you want to stay, there are more than 1000 hotel beds. Get more information at www.helgoland.de. To get here from Hamburg take the **Helgoline** (☎ 0180-522 1445; www.helgoline.de; from Hamburg adult/ child from €73.80/36.90, from Cuxhaven €59.90/30; ☉ from Hamburg 9am, Cuxhaven 11.30am Apr-Oct) ferry or high-speed catamaran from piers 3/4 at the St Pauli Piers.

TRIP HIGHLIGHT

9 Sylt

The star of Germany's North Frisian Islands, glamorous Sylt has designer boutiques housed in quintessential reed-thatched cottages, gleaming luxury automobiles jamming the car parks, luxurious accommodation and some of the country's most acclaimed restaurants. Sylt's candy-striped lighthouses rise above wide expanses of shifting dunes, fields of gleaming canola and expanses of heath. On its west coast, fierce surf and strong winds gnaw at the shoreline. In the east, the retreating low-tidal shallows of the Wadden Sea shore expose vast mudflats. Aside from pampering yourself silly and burning a hole in your wallet, you'll want to visit 5000-year-old **Denghoog** (☎ 04651-328 05; ww.soelring-museen. de; Am Denghoog; adult/ child €5/2.50; ☉ 10am-5pm Mon-Fri, from 11am Sat & Sun May-Sep, 10am-4pm Mon-Fri, from 11am Sat & Sun Oct), a Stonehenge-esque archaeological site whose outer walls consist of 12 stones weighing around 40 tonnes, as well as the **Erlebniszentrum Naturgewalten** (Forces of Nature Centre; ☎ 04651-836 190; www.naturgewalten-sylt. de; Hafenstrasse 37; adult/ child €13.50/9; ☉ 10am-6pm), a state-of-the-art ecological museum dedicated to the North Sea.

✗ ⨂ p133

Eating & Sleeping

Norddeich ❸

🛏 Hotel Fährhaus   Hotel €€€

(🖉04931-988 77; www.hotel-faehrhaus.de; Hafenstrasse 1; s/d from €90/180; 🅿🛜🏊) This delightful hotel by the ferry terminal in Norddeich is a great place to spend the night before or after your visit to the island. Rooms are brightly furnished, there's an excellent restaurant (great for dinner and with a terrific breakfast spread) and even a rooftop infinity pool and sauna. Late-night summer sunsets are breathtaking.

Bremen ❻

🍴 Bremer Ratskeller   German €€

(🖉0421-321 676; www.ratskeller-bremen.de; Am Markt 11; mains €11-30; ⏰11am-midnight; 🛜) Ratskellers were traditionally built underneath the Rathaus (town hall) in every German town to keep the citizens and civil servants fed. Bremen's – in business since 1405! – is quite the experience, with high vaulted ceilings, private booths in little cubbies (the better to discuss town business), and good, heavy, no-fuss German food and beer. Service is attentive and friendly.

🛏 Radisson Blu   Hotel €€

(🖉0421-369 60; www.radissonblu.com/hotel-bremen; Böttcherstrasse 2; r from €90; 🅿❄🛜🏊) The 235 guest rooms and suites in this sprawling, full-service international hotel have been renovated to a high standard. In a premium location by the Markt, the hotel has annexed what was formerly the Haus Atlantis building. Its striking Himmelssaal room is now an event space – tours (€5) are available each Sunday at 11.30am.

Hamburg ❼

🍴 Fischbrötchenbude Brücke 10   Seafood €

(🖉040-3339 9339; www.bruecke-10.de; Landungsbrücken, Pier 10; sandwiches €4-10; ⏰10am-10pm, from 9am Sun; Ⓢ Landungsbrücken, Ⓤ Landungsbrücken) There are a gazillion fish-sandwich vendors in Hamburg, but we're going to stick our neck out and say that this vibrant, clean and contemporary outpost makes the best. Try a classic *Bismarck* (pickled herring) or *Matjes* (brined herring), or treat yourself to a bulging shrimp sandwich. Lovely tables outside.

🛏 Hotel Atlantic   Luxury Hotel €€€

(🖉040-288 80; www.kempinski.com; An der Alster 72-79; s/d from €150/175; ❄🛜🏊; Ⓤ Hauptbahnhof-Nord) Imagine yourself aboard a luxury ocean liner in this grand 252-room hotel, which opens onto Holzdamm. Built in 1909 for passengers departing for America, it has ornate stairwells, wide hallways and subtle maritime touches. It has all the services of a five-star hotel; many rooms have lake views, for which you pay a little extra.

Sylt ❾

🍴 Söl'ring Hof   European €€€

(🖉04651-836 200; www.soelring-hof.de; Am Sandwall 1, Rantum; mains from €45, 5-/9-course tasting menu €184/224; ⏰6.30-9.30pm May-Oct, shorter hours rest of year) You'd come here just for the location set among dunes. From the terrace you can hear the crash of the surf, muted by blowing grasses. But chef Johannes King's kitchen is the draw, with breathtaking takes on local, seasonal produce and seafood. Think caviar, oysters and pure indulgence.

🛏 Bundersand   Resort €€€

(🖉04651-460 70; www.budersand.de; Am Kai 3, Hörnum; r from €330; 🅿@🛜🏊) The 21st-century architecture is almost as stunning as the views at Sylt's most luxurious hotel. Many rooms have terraces with their own gardens where you can tickle your toes on grass while looking far out to the North Sea. The spa is legendary; use it to work out kinks generated on the beautiful private golf course.

Classic Trip

German Fairy-Tale Road

10

You might just live happily ever after! You'll certainly end this trip happy, having explored a beautiful swathe of Germany and learned the real stories behind Grimms' fairy tales.

TRIP HIGHLIGHTS

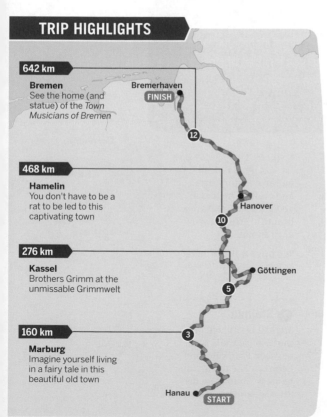

642 km

Bremen
See the home (and statue) of the *Town Musicians of Bremen*

Bremerhaven
FINISH

468 km

Hamelin
You don't have to be a rat to be led to this captivating town

Hanover

276 km

Kassel
Brothers Grimm at the unmissable Grimmwelt

Göttingen

160 km

Marburg
Imagine yourself living in a fairy tale in this beautiful old town

Hanau
START

5 DAYS
707KM / 439 MILES

GREAT FOR...

BEST TIME TO GO
Enjoy this trip May to September.

ESSENTIAL PHOTO
Bremen's *Town Musicians of Bremen* sculpture.

BEST FOR FAMILIES
Grimmwelt, Kassel's attraction dedicated to all things Grimm and fairy-tale-worthy.

Bremen *Bremen Town Musicians* by Gerhard Marcks (p144)

Classic Trip

10 German Fairy-Tale Road

Tirelessly roaming the villages and towns of 19th-century Germany, the Brothers Grimm collected 209 folk tales that had been passed down for countless generations. The stories they published often bear little resemblance to the sanitised versions spoon-fed to kids today; rather, they are morality tales with blood, gore, sex, the supernatural, magic and much more. See the locations of the stories and learn about the remarkable brothers on this trip, which includes a few non-Grimm fairy-tale sights as well.

❶ Hanau

A mere 20km east of Frankfurt on the Main River, Hanau is the birthplace of the Brothers Grimm (Jacob in 1785 and Wilhelm in 1786) and the perfect place to begin this trip. Not that their births are especially commemorated here...

Located within Philippsruhe Palace, dating from the early 18th century, the **Historisches Museum Schloss Philippsruhe** (☎06181-295 564; www.museen-hanau.de; Philippsruher Allee 45; adult/

concession €4/3; ⊙11am-6pm Tue-Sun; P) has displays on town history, arts and crafts. The parks and gardens (free) are a beautiful stroll in snow or in summer.

The Drive » Hop on the A66 for a quick 50km run through the rolling hills to Steinau.

❷ Steinau

Steinau is situated on the historic trade road between Frankfurt and Leipzig. (The town's full name is 'Steinau an der Strasse', an important

distinction when using your map app as there's another Steinau way up by the North Sea.)

The twin museums, **Brüder Grimm-Haus and Museum Steinau** (📞06663-7605; www.brueder -grimm-haus.de; Brüder Grimm-Strasse 80; adult/ concession €6/3.50; ⏱10am-5pm), inside the building where the Grimm family lived from 1791 to 1796, have exhibits on the brothers, their work and the history of Steinau.

The Drive » Head west on the L3196 for 18km to the B276, where you'll turn north. Weave through the valleys for 64km to the junction with the L3166 and follow the Marburg signs along the L3127, L3089, L3048 and L3125. Picnic spots abound along the route.

TRIP HIGHLIGHT

③ Marburg

Hilly, historic and de-lightful, university-town

LINK YOUR TRIP

2 **Design for Life: Bauhaus to VW**

Join this trip at Hanover to cover iconic German centres of design.

5 **Central Germany's Castles & Palaces**

At Kassel, detour through Germany's heartland to castles and lavish palaces all the way to Leipzig.

DETOUR: FULDA

Start: **2** Steinau

Although it's not quite on the Fairy-Tale Road, photogenic Fulda is well worth a side trip for those interested in sumptuous baroque architecture, historic churches and religious reliquaries. A Benedictine monastery was founded here in 744, and today Fulda has its own bishop.

Inside the baroque **Dom zu Fulda** (☎0661-874 57; www.bistum-fulda.de; Domplatz 1; ⊙10am-6pm Mon-Fri, to 3pm Sat, 1-6pm Sun Apr-Oct, to 5pm Mon-Fri Nov-Mar), built from 1704 to 1712, you'll find gilded furnishings, plenty of *putti* (infant figures), dramatic statues (eg to the left of the altar) and the tomb of St Boniface, who died a martyr in 754.

Fulda's history started in **Michaelskirche** (St Michael's Church; Michaelsberg 1; ⊙10am-6pm Apr-Oct, 10am-noon & 2-5pm Nov-Mar). A still-standing reminder of the abbey that made this town, this remarkable church was the monastic burial chapel. Beneath classic witch's-hat towers, a Carolingian rotunda and crypt recall Fulda's flourishing Middle Ages, when the abbey scriptorium churned out top-flight illuminated manuscripts.

Don't miss Fulda's spectacular **Stadtschloss** (☎0661-102 1814; adult/concession €3.50/2.50; ⊙10am-5pm Tue-Sun), built from 1706 to 1721 as the prince-abbots' residence. It now houses the city administration and function rooms. Visitors can enter the ornate **Historiche Räume** (Historic Rooms), including the grandiose banquet hall, and the octagonal **Schlossturm** (April to October) for great views of the town and magnificent **Schlossgarten** (palace gardens), where locals play *pétanque* (boules) and sunbathe in summer. The palace's fairy-tale qualities capture the era's extravagance. Don't miss the amazing **Speigelkabinett** (Chamber of Mirrors) and grandiose **Fürstensaal**, a banquet hall decorated with reliefs of tipsy-looking wine queens. Also, there are pretty views from the **Green Room** over the gardens to the Orangerie.

Fulda is 40km northeast of Steinau on the A66.

Marburg is 90km north of Frankfurt. It's a delight to wander the narrow lanes of the town's vibrant **Altstadt** (old town), sandwiched between a palace (above) and a spectacular Gothic church (below). On the south side of the focal Marktplatz is the historic **Rathaus** (town hall), dating to 1512. At the base of the Altstadt's Reitgasse is the neo-Gothic **Alte Universität** (1891), still a well-used

and well-loved part of Philipps-Universität – the world's oldest Protestant university. Founded in 1527, it once counted the Brothers Grimm among its students.

Perched at the highest point in town, a steep walk up from St-Marien-Kirche or the Marktplatz, is massive **Landgrafen-schloss** (☎06421-282 5871; www.uni-marburg.de/uni-museum; Schloss 1; museum adult/concession €5/3; ⊙museum 10am-6pm Apr-Oct,

to 4pm Nov-Mar; ⚑), built between 1248 and 1300. It offers panoramic views of bucolic hills, jumbled Marburg rooftops and the **Schlosspark**.

🍴 🛏 p146

The Drive » Head north on the B3; after 18km turn north on the L3073. Continue north for 37km through Gemunden and Frankenau to Edertal, where you'll find the park. Note how the forest gets thicker and darker as you go.

4 Kellerwald-Edersee National Park

Nationalpark Kellerwald-Edersee (www.nationalpark-kellerwald-edersee.de) encompasses one of the largest extant red-beech forests in Central Europe, the **Kellerwald**, and the **Edersee**, a serpentine artificial reservoir 55km northeast of Marburg and about the same distance southwest of Kassel. In 2011 this national park, along with Hainich National Park in Thuringia and a cluster of other parks and reserves with large beech forests, became a Unesco World Cultural Heritage site.

On a fairy-tale trip, it's fitting to wander into the deep woods, never forgetting that if your name is Grimm, nothing good is bound to happen. If you're lucky, you may see larger land animals like red deer; overhead, you might spot eagles and honey buzzards and, at night, various species of bat. (The brothers would surely approve.)

For information, head to the striking **visitors centre** (☎05635-992 781; www.nationalparkzentrum-kellerwald.de; Weg zur Wildnis 1, Vöhl-Herzhausen, off B252; exhibition entry €6.50/4; ☾10am-6pm Apr-Oct, to 4.30pm Tue-Sun Nov-Mar; ♿) at the western end of the Edersee.

The Drive » Drive east on the L3332, B485 and B253 for 28km until you reach the A49 autobahn and zip along northeast until you reach Kassel.

TRIP HIGHLIGHT

5 Kassel

Visitors to this culture-rich, sprawling hub on the Fulda River discover a pleasant, modern city.

Occupying a prime position atop the Weinberg bunker in the scenic **Weinbergpark** is the truly unmissable attraction on this trip, Kassel's **Grimmwelt** (☎0561-598 6190; www.grimmwelt.de; Weinbergstrasse 21; adult/concession €8/6; ☾10am-6pm Tue-Sun, to 8pm Fri; ♿). It could be described as an architect-designed walk-in sculpture housing the most significant collection of Brothers Grimm memorabilia on the planet. Visitors are guided around original exhibits, state-of-the-art installations and fun, hands-on activities, aided by entries from the Grimms' German dictionary: there was more to these brothers than just fairy tales, didn't you know?

Billed as 'a meditative space for funerary art', the **Museum für Sepulkralkultur** (Museum for Sepulchral Culture; ☎0561-918 930; www.sepulkralmuseum.de; Weinbergstrasse 25-27; adult/concession €6/4; ☾10am-5pm Tue-Sun, to 8pm Wed) aims to bury the taboo of discussing death.

✗ ⮰ p146

The Drive » The shortest leg of the trip takes you 6km west through Kassel's leafy suburbs. Take Wilhelmshöher Allee.

---

6 Wilhelmshöhe

Wilhelmshöhe is the classy end of Kassel. You can spend a full day exploring the spectacular baroque parkland, **Bergpark Wilhelmshöhe** (☎0561-3168 0751; www.museum-kassel.de; visitor centre Wilhelmshöher Allee 380; ☾9am-sunset, visitor centre 10am-5pm May-Sep, to 4pm Sat & Sun Oct-Apr; ℗♿), which takes its name from **Schloss Wilhelmshöhe** (☎0561-316 800; Schlosspark 1; adult/concession €6/4, Weissenstein wing incl tour €4/3, audioguide €3; ☾10am-5pm Tue-Sun, to 8pm Wed; ℗), the late 18th-century palace inside the expanse. Walk through the forest, enjoy a romantic picnic and explore the castles, fountains, grottoes, statues and water features: the **Herkules** (☎visitor centre 0561-3168 0781; Schlosspark Wilhelmshöhe 26, Herkules-Terrassen; adult/concession €6/4; ☾10am-5pm Tue-Sun mid-Mar–mid-Nov, daily May-Sep; ℗♿) statue and Löwenburg castle are also here.

The palace could star in any fairy tale. Home to Elector Wilhelm and later Kaiser Wilhelm

WHY THIS IS A CLASSIC TRIP
MARC DI DUCA, WRITER

Did they give us nightmares or fantasies? Or both? Who can forget hearing the wild stories of the Brothers Grimm as a child? Evil stepmothers, dashing princes, fair maidens, clever animals, mean old wolves and more. With every passing year, these stories become more sanitised. But the real fairy tales are far more compelling, as you'll learn on this trip.

Above: Altstadt houses, Marburg (p137)
Right: Brothers Grimm statue, Hanau (p136)
Left: Red deer stag (p139)

II, the opulent complex today houses one of Germany's best collections of Flemish and Dutch baroque paintings in the **Gemäldegalerie** (painting gallery), featuring works by Rembrandt, Rubens, Jordaens, Lucas Cranach the Elder, Dürer and many others.

✕ ⊨ p146

The Drive › Retrace your 6km drive on Wilhelmshöher Allee into Kassel and take the busy A7 right up to Göttingen.

❼ Göttingen

With over 30,000 students, this historic town nestled in a corner of Lower Saxony near the Hesse border offers a good taste of university-town life in Germany's north. Since 1734, the Georg-August Universität has sent more than 40 Nobel Prize winners into the world. As well as all those award-winning doctors and scientists, it also produced the fairy-tale-writing Brothers Grimm (as German language teachers).

Stroll around the pleasant **Markt** and nearby Barfüsserstrasse to admire the *Fachwerk* (half-timbered) houses. If you fancy, pop into a pub and make some new friends.

The city's symbol, the **Gänseliesel** (little goose girl) statue on Markt is hailed locally as the most kissed woman in

the world – not a flattering moniker, you might think, but enough to make her iconic.

 p147

The Drive » Take the L561 22km west to the B80, then head northwest for another 27km to Bad Karlshafen. Enjoy the curving panoramas as you follow the Weser River, which links several of the Fairy-Tale Road towns and cities.

➑ Bad Karlshafen

Bad Karlshafen's orderly streets and whitewashed baroque buildings were built in the 18th century for local earl Karl by French Huguenot refugees. The town was planned with an impressive harbour and a canal connecting the Weser and the Rhine to attract trade, but the earl died before his designs were completed. The only reminder of his grand plans is a tiny **Hafenbecken** (harbour basin) trafficked by white swans.

Take a stroll around the town centre, on the sinuous Weser's south bank, with the Hafenbecken and surrounding square, **Hafenplatz**, at its western end.

The interesting **Deutsches Huguenotten Museum** (German Huguenot Museum; ☎05672-1410; www.huguenot-museum-germany.com; Hafenplatz 9a; adult/concession €4/2; ☺10am-5pm Tue-Fri, 11am-6pm Sat & Sun mid-Mar–Oct, 10am-noon Mon-Fri Nov–mid-Mar) traces the history of the French Huguenot refugees in Germany, although it fails to mention how many were eaten by big bad wolves on the journey through the forest.

The Drive » Stay on the B83 for the 58km to Bodenwerder. You'll enjoy Weser vistas for much of the journey – which might lure you to stop for a picnic.

GRIMM FAIRY TALES

In the early 19th century, the Grimm brothers travelled extensively through central Germany documenting folklore. Their collection of tales, *Kinder- und Hausmärchen*, was first published in 1812 and quickly gained international recognition. It has 209 tales and includes such fairy-tale staples as follows:

» *Hansel and Gretel* – A mother tries to ditch her son and daughter, a witch tries to eat them and Gretel outsmarts her. Kids and father reunited and all are happy (the evil mother had died).

» *Cinderella* – The story that gave stepsisters a bad name. Still, when the prince fits the shoe onto our heroine, all is good with the world, although in the Grimm version, the stepsisters are blinded by vengeful doves.

» *Rapunzel* – An adopted girl with very long hair, a prince who goes blind and some evil older women are combined in this morality play that ends with love when the prince stumbles upon an outcast Rapunzel and his sight is restored. In the first edition of the Grimms' book, Rapunzel had children out of wedlock.

For entertaining synopses of all the Grimm fairy tales, see www.shmoop.com/grimms-fairy-tales. One thing you'll note is that the Grimm original versions are much bloodier, more violent and earthier than the ultra-sanitised, Disneyfied versions today.

Although best known for their fairy tales, it should be noted that the Brothers Grimm were serious academics who also wrote *German Grammar* and *History of the German Language*, enduring works that populate reference shelves to this day.

9 Bodenwerder

If Bodenwerder's most famous son were to have described his little hometown, he'd probably have painted it as a huge, thriving metropolis on the Weser. But then Baron Hieronymus von Münchhausen (1720–97) was one of history's most shameless liars (his whoppers were no mere fairy tales). He inspired the Terry Gilliam cult film, *The Adventures of Baron Munchausen*.

Bodenwerder's principal attraction, the **Münchhausen Museum** (☏05533-409 147; www.muenchhausenland.de; Münchhausenplatz 5; adult/child €3/2; ◷10am-5pm Apr-Oct, by arrangement Nov-Mar; Ⓟ), tackles the difficult task of conveying the chaos and fun associated with the 'liar baron' – a man who liked to regale dinner guests with his Crimean adventures, claiming he had, for example, tied his horse to a church steeple during a snow drift and ridden around a dining table without breaking one teacup. It holds paintings and displays of Münchhausen books in many languages.

The Drive » The B83 again takes you north 23km to Hamelin.

THE FAIRY-TALE ROAD

The 600km **Märchenstrasse** (Fairy-Tale Road; www.deutsche-maerchenstrasse.com) is one of Germany's most popular tourist routes, with over 60 stops along the way. It's made up of cities, towns and hamlets in four states (Hesse, Lower Saxony, North Rhine–Westphalia and Bremen), which can often be reached via a choice of roads rather than one single route. The towns are associated in one way or another with the works of Wilhelm and Jacob Grimm. Although most towns can be easily visited using public transport, a car lets you fully explore the route.

TRIP HIGHLIGHT

10 Hamelin

According to the Brothers Grimm's *Pied Piper of Hamelin*, in the 13th century *Der Rattenfänger* (Pied Piper) was employed by Hamelin's townsfolk to lure its rodents into the river. When they refused to pay him, he picked up his flute and led their kids away. Today the rats rule once again – fluffy and cute stuffed rats, wooden rats, and tiny brass rats adorning the sights around town.

Rodents aside, Hamelin (Hameln in German) is a pleasant town with half-timbered houses and opportunities for cycling along the Weser, on whose eastern bank lies Hamelin's circular **Altstadt**. The town's heart is its **Markt**.

Many of Hamelin's finest buildings were constructed in the Weser Renaissance style, which has strong Italian influences. Learn more at the town's revamped **Museum Hamelin** (☏05151-202 1217; www.museum-hameln.de; Osterstrasse 8-9; adult/concession €5/4; ◷11am-6pm Tue-Sun; ♿).

✕ ⊨ p147

The Drive » Drive 47km northwest on the B217.

11 Hanover

Known for its huge trade shows, Hanover has a past: from 1714, monarchs from the house of Hanover also ruled Great Britain and the British Empire for over a century.

Let your hair down at the spectacularly baroque **Herrenhäuser Gärten** (☏0511-1683 4000; www.herrenhaeuser-gaerten.de; Herrenhäuser Strasse 4; ◷9am-6pm Apr-Oct, to 4.30pm Nov-Mar, grotto to 5.30pm Apr-Oct, to 4pm Nov-Mar; Ⓤ4, 5 to Herrenhäuser Gärten), the grandiose Royal Gardens of

Classic Trip

Herrenhausen, which are considered one of the most important historic garden landscapes in Europe. Inspired by Versailles' gardens, they're a great place to slow down and smell the roses for a couple of hours, especially on a blue-sky day. With its fountains, neat flowerbeds, trimmed hedges and shaped lawns, the 300-year-old **Grosser Garten** (Great Garden) is the centrepiece of the experience.

The Drive » Take the A352 16km to the A7, then shoot northwest on that road and the A27 (127km).

TRIP HIGHLIGHT

⑫ Bremen

Bremen is well known for its fairy-tale character, a unique expressionist quarter and (it must be said, because Bremeners are avid football fans) one of Germany's most-exciting, if not overly successful, football teams.

With high, historic buildings rising up from this very compact square, Bremen's **Markt** is one of the most remarkable in northern Germany. The two towers of the 1200-year-old **Dom St Petri** (St Petri Cathedral; ☎0421-334 7142; www.stpetridom.de;

Sandstrasse 10-12; tower adult/child €2/1, museum free; ⏰10am-5pm Mon-Fri, to 2pm Sat, 2-5pm Sun Oct-May, Jun-Sep Mon-Fri & Sun to 6pm) dominate the north-eastern edge, beside the ornate and imposing **Rathaus**, which was erected in 1410. The Weser Renaissance balcony in the middle, crowned by three gables, was added between 1595 and 1618.

In front of the Rathaus is one of the hallmarks of Bremen, the city's 13m-high **Knight Roland statue** (1404). As elsewhere, Roland stands for a city's civic freedoms, especially the freedom to trade independently.

On the western side of the Rathaus you'll find the city's unmissable and famous symbol of the Grimm fairy tale: the *Bremen Town Musicians* (1951) by the sculptor Gerhard Marcks. The story tells of a donkey, a dog, a cat and a rooster who know their time is up with their cruel masters, and so set out for Bremen and the good life. On the way they encounter a forest cottage filled with robbers. They cleverly dispatch the crooks and, yes, live happily ever after. The statue depicts the dog, cat and rooster, one on top of the other, on the shoulders of the donkey. The donkey's nose and front legs are incredibly shiny having been

touched by many visitors for good luck.

✗ 🛏 p133, p147

The Drive » A quick shot up the autobahn (A27) for 65km will bring you to Bremerhaven and the North Sea.

----

⑬ Bremerhaven

Anyone who has had the fairy-tale dream of running away to sea will love

Bremen Knight Roland statue (p144)

Bremerhaven's waterfront – part trade machinery, part glistening glass buildings pointing to a more recent understanding of the harbour as a recreation spot.

Bremerhaven has long been a conduit that gathered the 'huddled masses' from the verdant but poor countryside and poured them into the world outside. Of the millions who landed in America, a large proportion sailed from here; an enticing exhibition at the **Deutsches Auswander- erhaus** (German Emigration Centre; ☎0471-902 200; www.dah-bremerhaven.de; Columbusstrasse 65; adult/child €15/9; ◷10am-6pm Mar-Oct, to 5pm Nov-Feb), the city's prime attraction, allows you to share their history. The museum stands exactly in the spot where 7.2 million emigrants set sail between 1830 and 1974. Your visit begins at the wharf where passengers gathered before boarding a steamer. You then visit passenger cabins from different periods (note the improving comfort levels) before going through the immigration process at New York's Ellis Island.

Classic Trip

Eating & Sleeping

Marburg ❸

✖ Bückingsgarten   German €€€

(☎06421-165 7771; www.bueckingsgarten
-marburg.de; Landgraf-Philipp-Strasse 6; mains
€18-26; ◷ noon-10pm) Choose from two
separate menus at this venerable restaurant,
opened by G Dietrich Bücking in 1807 and
now offering German standards alongside
international classics. Dine inside for the upscale
experience, or enjoy a stein and schnitzel in the
beer garden: both offer spectacular views from a
hilltop position adjacent to the castle.

✖ Café Barfuss   Cafe €

(☎06421-253 49; www.cafebarfuss.de;
Barfüsserstrasse 33; mains €4.50-9; ◷10am-
1am Mon-Thu, to 2am Fri-Sun; 🛜🍴) A local
institution, humble Barfuss is a no-fuss, offbeat
place with walls covered in coffee sacks and an
eclectic clientele of students, elderly couples
and sociable drinkers. The menu offers hearty,
healthy plates, including great cheap breakfasts
and plenty of vegetarian and pasta options.

🛏 Vila Vita Rosenpark   Hotel €€

(☎06421-600 50; www.rosenpark.com;
Anneliese Pohl Allee 7-17; s/d from €115/125;
🅿 ❄ @ 🛜 🏊) Marburg's swankiest digs
occupy a lovely spot on the Lahn River, a
short stroll from the station. If you're going to
splurge, superior double rooms and suites offer
better value at almost twice the size of singles.
There's an expansive wellness centre and two
restaurants on-site, and you can even order
your ideal pillow ahead, online!

🛏 Welcome Hotel Marburg   Hotel €€€

(☎06421-9180; www.welcome-hotels.com;
Pilgrimstein 29; s/d from €120/150; ❄ @ 🛜)
Just below the Altstadt, this central hotel has
151 bright, spacious rooms with large windows,
desks and armchairs. Though windows are
soundproofed, you may want to ask for a quieter
room at the rear of the building.

Kassel ❺

✖ Lohmann   German €

(☎0561-701 6875; www.lohmann-kassel.de;
Königstor 8; mains €9-23; ◷11.30am-2.30pm
Mon-Fri, 4.30-10pm Mon-Sat, noon-10pm Sun)
With roots that go back to 1888, this popular,
family-run *Kneipe* (pub) has an old-style birch-
and-maple-shaded beer garden with an outdoor
grill, while indoors is all beery chatter and the
happy tinkling of knives and forks. Schnitzel
(always pork) features heavily on the menu.

🛏 Pentahotel Kassel   Boutique Hotel €

(☎0561-933 9100; www.pentahotels.com;
Bertha-von-Suttner Strasse 15; r from €65;
🅿 ❄ 🛜) Spread over six floors, this slick hotel
has 137 compact, stylish rooms with ambient
lighting, arty design elements and free high-
speed wi-fi. There's a bar and restaurant on-site,
and you're nice and close to the wonders of
Bergpark Wilhelmshöhe and the convenience of
Kassel-Wilhelmshöhe station.

Wilhelmshöhe ❻

✖ Matterhorn Stübli   Swiss €€

(☎0561-399 33; www.matterhornstuebli.de;
Wilhelmshöher Allee 326; mains €15-26; ◷5.30-
11pm Tue-Sat, noon-2pm & 5.30-10pm Sun;
🍴) If you love cheese, fondue, schnitzel, or all
three, hotfoot it to this quaint Swiss restaurant.
If you like mushrooms as well, try the 'Original
Züri Geschnätzläts': veal escalopes served with
mushrooms and crispy rösti.

🛏 Kurpark Hotel
Bad Wilhelmshöhe   Hotel €€€

(☎0561-318 90; www.kurparkhotel-kassel.de;
Wilhelmshöher Allee 336; s/d from €115/145;
🅿 ❄ 🛜 🏊) In an excellent location near the
Unesco-listed Bergpark Wilhelmshöhe and
Kassel-Wilhelmshöhe train station, this stylish
hotel offers well-appointed rooms and common

areas, a restaurant and terrace, and an indoor pool, sauna and spa.

Göttingen ❼

✖ Zum Szultenburger
German €

(✆0551-431 33; Prinzenstrasse 7; mains €10-14; ⏰11am-3pm & 5-10pm Mon-Sat) This traditional German pub does things to the humble schnitzel that will make your mouth water, while the *Rindergulasch mit Spätzle* (beef goulash with hand-dropped noodles) is just the ticket in cold weather. It's cosy and cheap, the food is delicious, and the staff seem happy to be here, which makes all the difference. Cash only.

Hamelin ❿

✖ Rattenfängerhaus
German €€

(✆05151-3888; www.rattenfaengerhaus.com; Osterstrasse 28; mains €15-20; ⏰11am-3pm & 6-10pm Mon-Sat; 👪) One of Hamelin's finest ornamental Weser Renaissance–style buildings, the Rattenfängerhaus (Pied Piper House) has a facade dating to 1602, with older sections within. It's now home to an unashamedly tourist-centric restaurant, which has been serving 'rats' tails' flambéed at your table since 1966 (don't worry – it's all a pork-based ruse).

🛏 Komfort-Hotel Garni Christinenhof
Boutique Hotel €€€

(✆05151-950 80; www.christinenhof.de; Alte Marktstrasse 18; s/d incl breakfast €90/130; P🛈♿) Historic outside, modern within, this superwelcoming hotel has a tiny swimming pool in the vaulted cellar, a sauna, and compact (but pleasant and uncluttered) rooms. The owners take particular care with the generous buffet breakfast (entirely homemade) and parking is free of charge. Spread over two buildings, this is a great option in central Hamelin.

🛏 Schlosshotel Münchhausen
Luxury Hotel €€€

(✆05154-706 00; www.schlosshotel-muench hausen.com; Schwöbber 9, Aerzen; s/d tithe barn from €140/170, castle from €205/235, apt €170; P♿✳🛈) Palatial Schlosshotel Münchhausen, 12km southwest of Hamelin, occupies a baronial castle built in 1570. Stylish, contemporary rooms in the main wing have historic touches, the suites have tasteful period

furnishings and rooms in the tithe barn are entirely modern. Two restaurants, lavish spa facilities and two golf courses set in 8 hectares of gorgeous parkland round out the luxury.

Bremen ⓬

✖ Engel Weincafe
Cafe €

(✆0421-6964 2390; www.engelweincafe -bremen.de; Ostertorsteinweg 31; dishes €7-14; ⏰9am-1am Mon-Fri, from 10am Sat & Sun; 🛈🍽; 🚌2, 6 to Wulwesstrasse) Situated on a sunny corner in Das Viertel, this popular hang-out exudes the nostalgic vibe of the old-fashioned pharmacy it once was. The menu features breakfast, a hot lunch special, crispy *Flammkuchen* (Alsatian pizza, with crème fraîche), carpaccio, or just some cheese and a glass of wine from the international list.

✖ Kleiner Olymp
German €€

(✆0421-326 667; www.kleiner-olymp.de; Hinter der Holzpforte 20; mains €9-23; ⏰11am-11pm) This homely kitchen in Schnoor has a wonderful atmosphere, delicious (and not too heavy) North German cuisine and very reasonable prices. With a selection of mouthwatering soups and starters, fish and seafood feature predominantly on the menu: bouillabaisse, North Sea crabs and plaice cooked in a variety of ways.

🛏 Hotel Residence
Boutique Hotel €€

(✆0421-348 710; www.hotelresidence.de; Hohenlohestrasse 42; s/d from €75/115; P@🛈) This century-old terrace, now a charming hotel, also boasts some funky apartments. The main building has rooms facing the street, while the newer extension backs onto the railway line but is still reasonably quiet. Friendly staff and a sauna, bar and dining room complete the package. Rooms and apartments are furnished in differing styles. Buffet breakfast is €10.

🛏 Dorint Park Hotel Bremen
Hotel €€€

(✆0421-340 80; www.hotel-bremen.dorint.com; Im Bürgerpark; s/d from €80/160; P@🛈✳; 🚌6 to Am Stern) Although its exterior is certainly dated, this domed lakeside mansion surrounded by parkland impresses through its sheer extravagance and could be considered Bremen's only true five-star, grand hotel. It offers access to excellent spa, fitness and beauty facilities, a heated outdoor pool and views over the lake in a 'spa resort' ambience.

Cologne & the Ruhr Valley

11

Romans, steel and medieval treasures together forge an unbeatable trip through Germany's former industrial heartland, now the site of myriad and compelling reinventions.

TRIP HIGHLIGHTS

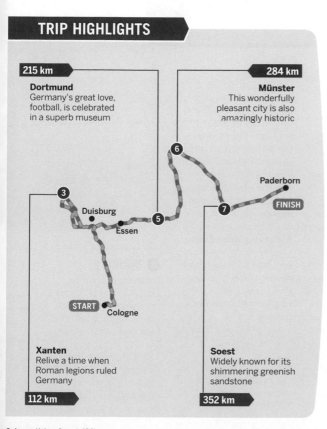

215 km

Dortmund
Germany's great love, football, is celebrated in a superb museum

284 km

Münster
This wonderfully pleasant city is also amazingly historic

Paderborn

Duisburg

Essen

Xanten
Relive a time when Roman legions ruled Germany

112 km

Cologne

Soest
Widely known for its shimmering greenish sandstone

352 km

4 DAYS
404KM / 251 MILES

GREAT FOR...

BEST TIME TO GO
Enjoy the food, drink and culture any time, but April to October is more fun outdoors.

ESSENTIAL PHOTO
The weirdly green stone of Soest shimmering in the sun.

BEST FOR FAMILIES
Xanten's Römer Museum brings the past alive for all ages.

11 Cologne & the Ruhr Valley

The Anabaptists were a religious cult that took over the then-pious city of Münster in 1535 – they didn't last but you can learn about their wild ideas at that city's impressive LWL-Museum für Kunst und Kultur. There are also many other fascinating stories here in one of Germany's most historic regions, which boasts dramatic chapters from Roman times till today.

----

① Cologne

Cologne is like a 3D textbook on history and architecture. Around town you'll stumble upon an ancient Roman wall, medieval churches like the magnificent **Dom** and more. But many don't realise that Germany's fourth-largest city was founded by the Romans in 38 BC and given the lofty name Colonia Claudia Ara Agrippinensium. Sculptures and ruins displayed outside the entrance of the **Römisch-Germanisches Museum** (Roman Germanic Museum; ☑0221-2212 4438; www.roemisch-germanisches-museum.de; Roncalliplatz 4; adult/child €3/1; ⊙10am-5pm Tue-Sun; ⓪5, 16, 18 Dom/Hauptbahnhof) are the overture to a full symphony of Roman artefacts found along the Rhine. Highlights include the giant Poblicius tomb (AD 30–40) and the magnificent 3rd-century **Dionysus mosaic**. Discover more of Cologne's past at the **Archäologische Zone** (www.miqua.lvr.de; Rathausplatz; ⓪5 Rathaus), whose deepest level has the Praetorium, with relics of a Roman governor's palace.

See p186 for a walking tour of Cologne.

 p155

The Drive » Travel at very un-Roman speeds north on the A3 autobahn 73km to Duisburg.

----

② Duisburg

Duisburg is home to Europe's largest inland port, whose immensity is best appreciated on a **boat tour** (Harbour Tour; ☑0203-713 9667; www.wf-duisburg.de; Schwanentor, Calaisplatz 3; adult/child €15/8; ⊙11am, 1.15pm & 3.30pm Apr-Oct; ⓪901 Rathaus,

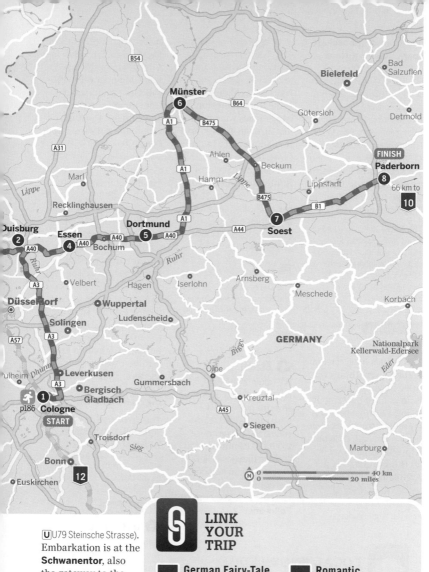

U U79 Steinsche Strasse).
Embarkation is at the
Schwanentor, also
the gateway to the
Innenhafen Duisburg
(inner harbour), an
urban quarter with
a mix of modern and
restored buildings.
Now a unique per-
formance space and
an all-ages adventure

LINK YOUR TRIP

10 German Fairy-Tale Road

Find out about Cinderella
and Co. by joining this route
at Bad Karlshafen, 66km
east of Paderborn on the
B64.

12 Romantic Rhine

At Cologne, follow the
riverscape along the world-
famous Rhine.

playground, **Landschaft-spark Duisburg-Nord**
(Landscape Park Duisburg-Nord; ☎0203-429 1942; www.landschaftspark.de; Emscher-strasse 71; admission free, activities vary; ⏰park 24hr, visitor centre 9am-6pm Mon-Fri, 11am-6pm Sat & Sun; P; 🚊903 Landschaftspark Nord) is a decommissioned iron works where molten iron used to flow 24/7 from its fiery furnaces.

The Drive ❯❯ Escape Duisburg on the A40, cross the Rhine and take exit 10 and the L287 north. At Rheinberg, join the B57 (Xantener Strasse). It's a straight shot northwest for 19km to Xanten.

TRIP HIGHLIGHT

❸ Xanten

Xanten has been the hub of the Lower Rhine ever since its founding as a Roman military camp in 12 BC. Within a century it grew into a respectable settlement called Colonia Ulpia Traiana. Revel in all things Roman at the **Archäologischer Park** (Archaeological Park; ☎02801-988 9213; www.apx.lvr.de; Am Rheintor; adult/concession/

under 18yr incl RömerMuseum €9/6/free; ⏰9am-6pm Mar-Oct, to 5pm Nov, 10am-4pm Dec-Feb; P; 🚊SL42 Am Rheintor). Its highlight is the **RömerMuseum**, which takes you on a journey through 400 years of Roman presence in the Lower Rhine region.

The crown jewel of Xanten's **Altstadt** (old town) is the **Dom St Viktor** (www.sankt-viktor-xanten.de), which has Roman-esque roots but is now largely Gothic.

🛏 p155

The Drive ❯❯ Leave Xanten driving south for 14km to the well-signposted A57. Continue south for 18km to the A40 and go east 33km to Essen.

❹ Essen

It's taken a few decades, but Germany's seventh-largest city has transitioned from industrial powerhouse to city of commerce and culture like few others. A grande dame among Germany's art repositories, the free **Museum Folkwang** (☎0201-884 5444; www.museum-folkwang.de;

Museumsplatz 1; ⏰10am-6pm Tue, Wed, Sat & Sun, to 8pm Thu & Fri; UPhilharmonie) has sparkling premises with galleries radiating out from inner courtyards and gardens. Don't miss a visit to the **Zollverein Coal Mine** (☎0201-830 3636; www.zollverein.de; Gelsenkirch-ener Strasse 181; ⏰grounds 6am-midnight, visitors centre 11am-6pm; 🚊107 Essen Zoll-verein), the Unesco-listed industrial complex whose star is the **Ruhr Museum** (☎0201-2468 1444; www.ruhrmuseum.de; Fritz-Schupp-Allee 15; adult/concession €8/5, audioguide €3; ⏰11am-6pm; 🚊107 Essen Zollverein). Engaging exhibits span the region's history. Just as the coal was transported on conveyor belts, a long escalator whisks you up to the foyer from where you descend into the building's dark bowels.

The Drive ❯❯ You are back on the A40 for the 38km to Dortmund. Evidence of the Ruhrgebiet's once-great industrial might are everywhere as you travel.

TRIP HIGHLIGHT

❺ Dortmund

Football (soccer) is a major Dortmund passion. Borussia Dortmund, the city's team in the Bundesliga (Germany's first league), has been national champion eight times, including for the 2011–12 season (they were runners-up as recently as 2018–19). It's appropriate that the city is home to

LOCAL KNOWLEDGE: WHAT'S A RUHRGEBIET?

Once known for its belching steelworks and filthy coal mines, the Ruhrgebiet – a sprawling postindustrial region of 53 cities and 5.3 million people – has worked hard in recent years to reinvent itself for the postindustrial future. It includes Duisburg, Essen and Dortmund, all stops on this route.

Xanten Old Roman pillars, Archäologischer Park

the **DFB-Museum** (German Football Museum; 📞0231-476 4660; www.fussballmuseum. de; Platz der Deutschen Einheit 1; adult/concession €17/14; 🕙10am-6pm Tue-Sun). Classic scenes of German football triumphs play across the facade of this vast new shrine to the nation's passion. Right outside the Hauptbahnhof, the museum has 6900 sq metres of exhibits dedicated to Germany's footballing prowess.

 p155

The Drive » Leave Dortmund on the B1 heading east for 13km. At the A1 autobahn, turn north to Münster.

TRIP HIGHLIGHT

⑥ Münster

One of the most appealing cities between Cologne and Hamburg, Münster has a beautiful centre with many architectural gems. The Altstadt is ringed with beautiful lakes and parks, buzzing with cyclists. The two massive towers of **Dom St Paul** (www.sankt-viktor-xanten. de) match the proportions of this 110m-long structure and the vast square it overlooks. It's a three-nave construction built in the 13th century.

Nearby, the **Historisches Rathaus** (Historic City Hall & Peace Hall; 📞0251-492 2724; Prinzipalmarkt 8-9; adult/child €2/1.50; 🕙Friedenssaal 10am-5pm Tue-Fri, to 4pm Sat & Sun) is a Gothic gem. In the **LWL-Museum für Kunst und Kultur** (Museum for Art& Culture; 📞0251-590 701; www.lwl-museum-kunst -kultur.de; Domplatz 10; adult/concession €9/4.50; 🕙10am-6pm Tue-Sat), explore a collection spanning the Middle Ages to the latest avant-garde creations, and learn about the Anabaptist religious cult.

🍴 🛏 p155

THE KRUPP DYNASTY

In the Ruhrgebiet, steel and Krupp are virtually synonyms. So are Krupp and Essen, for it's this bustling Ruhrgebiet city that is the ancestral seat of the Krupp family and the headquarters of one of the most powerful corporations in Europe. It all began rather modestly in 1811 when Friedrich Krupp and two partners founded a company to process 'English cast steel', but, despite minor successes, Krupp left a company mired in debt upon his death in 1826. Enter his son Alfred, then a tender 14, who would go on to become a seminal figure of the industrial age.

It was through the production of the world's finest steel that the 'Cannon King' galvanised a company that – by 1887 – employed more than 20,000 workers. It also provided womb-to-tomb benefits to its workers at a time when 'social welfare' had not yet entered the world's vocabulary. In an unbroken pattern of dazzling innovation, coupled with ruthless business practices, Krupp produced steel and machinery that was essential to the world economy.

Krupp will forever be associated, however, with the Third Reich. Not only did the corporation supply the hardware for the German war machine, it also provided much of the financial backing that Hitler needed to build up his political power base. Krupp plants were prime targets for Allied bombers. After the war, the firm slowly lost its way and in 1999 merged with arch-rival Thyssen.

An excellent source for an understanding of what the Krupp family has meant to Germany is William Manchester's brilliant chronicle *The Arms of Krupp* (1964).

The Drive ≫ The next stretch of driving will get you off the autobahn to wander past little villages amid verdant farmland. Take the L585 out of Münster; drive southeast over a series of roads for 42km to Beckum, and switch to the B475 for the final 26km.

---

⑦ Soest

One of northwest Germany's most appealing towns, Soest is a tranquil place with half-timbered houses and a clutch of treasure-filled churches that reflect the town's wealth during its Hanseatic League days. It's a maze of idyllic, crooked lanes that has been beautifully rebuilt and preserves much of its medieval character. Soest's one remarkable feature is its stone: a shimmering greenish local sandstone used in the town wall, churches and other public structures. Check out the late-Gothic **St Maria zur Wiese** (Wiesenkirche; ☎02921-132 51; www.wiesenkirche.de; Wiesenstrasse; ⊙11am-6pm Mon-Sat, noon-6pm Sun Apr-Sep, to 4pm Oct-Mar) and 10th-century Romanesque **St Patrokli** (☎02921-671 0660; www.sankt-patrokli.de; Propst-Nübel-Strasse 2; ⊙10am-5.45pm).

 p155

The Drive ≫ Drive 52km from Soest to Paderborn on the B1.

---

⑧ Paderborn

From the 8th century AD, Charlemagne used Paderborn as a power base to defeat the Saxons and convert them to Christianity, giving him the momentum needed to rise to greater things. Paderborn remains a pious place to this day – churches abound, and religious sculpture and motifs adorn facades, fountains and parks. Start at the massive (104m-long!) **Dom** (☎05251-125 1287; www.dom-paderborn.de; Markt 17; ⊙6.30am-6.30pm), a three-nave Gothic hall church.

p155

Eating & Sleeping

Cologne ➊

🍴 Feynsinn   International €€

(🕿0221-240 9210; www.cafe-feynsinn.de; Rathenauplatz 7; dinner mains €10-23; ⊘9am-1am Mon-Thu, to 2am Fri, 9.30am-1am Sat, 10am-1am Sun; �In9, 12, 15 Zülpicher Platz) This well-respected Zülpicher Viertel restaurant is an excellent pit stop at any time of the day. Come for extravagant breakfasts, light lunches and creative cakes or a dinner menu that weaves organic seasonal ingredients into sharp-flavoured dishes. Get a table overlooking the park.

Xanten ➌

🛏 Hotel van Bebber   Hotel €€

(🕿02801-6623; www.hotelvanbebber.de; Klever Strasse 12; s/d from €70-110; 🅿 ⊕ 🛜) Notables including Queen Victoria and Winston Churchill have slept in this old-school 35-room hotel. Rooms pair historical open beams and antiques with mod-cons. Deluxe rooms have views of the Dom, plus four-poster beds and big tubs. A generous (but optional) breakfast is €12 per person.

Dortmund ➎

🍴 Wenkers am Markt   German €€

(🕿0231-527 548; www.wenkers.de; Betenstrasse 1; mains €9-30; ⊘10am-10pm Mon-Sat, from noon Sun) A legendary place for quaffing before and after football matches, Wenkers has tables outside on a central square and serves German classics in gut-busting portions. It's been in the business since 1430.

Münster ➏

🍴 Holstein's Bistro   European €€

(🕿0251-449 44; www.butterhandlung-holstein. de; Horsteberg 1; mains €14-25; ⊘11.30am-7pm Tue-Fri, 11am-5pm Sat; 🍴) Münster's slow-food outpost has been raising the bar of inventive seasonal fare for almost 20 years. The menu reflects what's fresh, but there's usually a variety of soups, salads, pastas and more. Snare a table in the shadow of the Dom.

🍴 Altes Gasthaus Leve   German €€

(🕿0251-455 95; www.gasthaus-leve.de; Alter Steinweg 37; mains €4-29; ⊘noon-midnight Mon-Sat) Münster's oldest inn (since 1607) has painted tiles, oil paintings and copper etchings: a suitably rustic backdrop for hearty Westphalian and German fare. Besides seasonal specials, try stalwarts such as lima-bean stew and sweet-and-sour beef.

🛏 Hotel Busche am Dom   Hotel €€

(🕿0251-464 44; www.hotel-busche.de; Bogenstrasse 10; s/d from €70/105; ⊘reception 7am-10pm Mon-Fri, to 6pm Sat & Sun; @ 🛜; 🚍5, 6 Spiekerhof) Family-run with a fantastic location, this central hotel has 13 comfortable rooms in muted pastels. You'll hear the cathedral bells ringing on the hour. In good weather, enjoy the made-with-love buffet breakfast on the terrace.

Soest ➐

🍴 Brauhaus Zwiebel   German €€

(🕿02921-4424;www. brauhaus-zwiebel.de; Ulricherstrasse 24; mains €10-25; ⊘11am-midnight) A one-stop shop for myriad forms of pleasure in Soest, this long-running brewery produces excellent seasonal beers throughout the year. The food is predictably hearty, ample (yes, many dishes come with *Zwiebel* – onion) and enjoyed in the rustic half-timbered restaurant, the winter garden or the leafy beer garden in summer.

Paderborn ➑

🍴 Paderborner Brauhaus   German €€

(🕿05251-282 554; www.bono-gastronomie.de; Kisau 2; mains €10-25; ⊘5pm-1am Mon-Thu, to 2am Fri, 11.30am-2am Sat, to midnight Sun) When Paderborn locals arrange to meet at 'the' beer garden, they mean this sprawling gem sheltered by a grove of old trees hugging the little Pader River. The kitchen caters mostly to carnivores and includes some supertasty schnitzel and steaks tickled on the lava grill.

Classic Trip

Romantic Rhine

*After seeing powerhouse cities Düsseldorf,
Cologne and Bonn, epic scenery unfolds as the
Rhine Valley carves between towering cliffs,
clad in greenery and capped by castles, to
delightful Mainz.*

12

TRIP HIGHLIGHTS

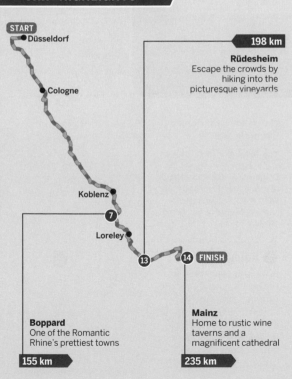

START
● Düsseldorf

● Cologne

Koblenz ●
7
Loreley ●
13   **14** FINISH

198 km

Rüdesheim
Escape the crowds by
hiking into the
picturesque vineyards

Boppard
One of the Romantic
Rhine's prettiest towns
155 km

Mainz
Home to rustic wine
taverns and a
magnificent cathedral
235 km

5–7 DAYS
235KM / 155 MILES

GREAT FOR...

BEST TIME TO GO
April to October offers
the best weather, but
July and August can
be crowded.

 ESSENTIAL PHOTO
Boat-shaped toll
castle Pfalzgrafstein
on a Rhine island.

 BEST FOR OUTDOORS
Hike through the vines
above Rüdesheim.

Bacharach (p165) A typical old German town on the Rhine

157

Classic Trip

12 Romantic Rhine

Boats gliding down the Rhine give passengers mesmerising views of the medieval villages, craggy hillsides, and castle after castle floating past. But on this trip you'll get up close to its mightiest sights, hike through its loftiest vineyards, and discover hidden treasures and romantic hideaways you'd never see from the water. (Though you'll have plenty of opportunities en route to board a cruise, too.)

① Düsseldorf

Survey the mighty Rhine from Düsseldorf's **Medienhafen**. This old harbour area continues to attract red-hot restaurants, bars, hotels and clubs. Crumbling warehouses have transformed into high-tech office buildings, rubbing shoulders with bold new structures designed by celebrated international architects, including Frank Gehry.

Of course, no visit to Düsseldorf is complete without exploring its **Altstadt** (old town), which claims to be the 'longest bar in the world'.

The Drive » It's a 44km drive south via the B1 and the A57 to Cologne. (Fear not: although this section travels through built-up areas and industrial estates, later stages become much more scenic.)

② Cologne

A walking tour (p186) is the best way to appreciate this engaging city (Germany's fourth-largest) on the Rhine. Must-sees include Cologne's world-famous **Dom** (Cologne Cathedral; ☎0221-9258 4720;

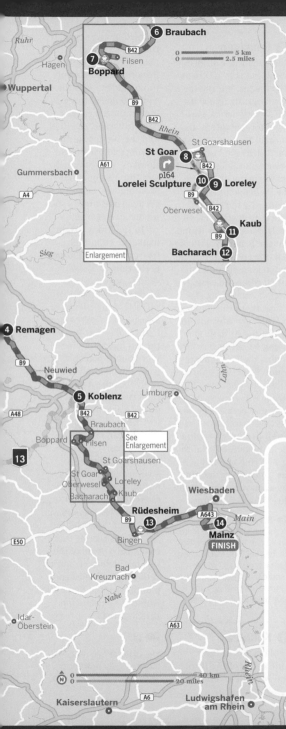

www.koelner-dom.de; Domkloster 4; tower adult/concession €5/2; ⏱6am-9pm May-Oct, to 7.30pm Nov-Apr, tower 9am-6pm May-Sep, to 5pm Mar, Apr & Oct, to 4pm Nov-Feb; 🚌5, 16, 18 Dom/Hauptbahnhof), whose twin spires dominate the skyline, as well as superb museums such as the Römisch-Germanisches Museum (p150); sculptures and ruins displayed outside its entrance are the overture to its symphony of Roman artefacts found along the Rhine.

✗ p155

The Drive » Drive south along the B51 on the Rhine's west bank before joining the A555 (29km all-up).

---

❸ Bonn

In a beautiful riverside setting, Ludwig van Beethoven's home town warrants a stop to visit the **Beethoven-Haus Bonn** (Beethoven House;

LINK YOUR TRIP

11 **Cologne & the Ruhr Valley**

At Cologne you can also pick up this absorbing route, visiting vibrant Ruhr cities such as Essen and Münster.

13 **Moselle Valley**

Koblenz sits at the confluence of the Rhine and the Moselle, source of more vineyard-ribboned views and irresistible wines.

☑0228-981 7525; www.
beethoven-haus-bonn.
de; Bonngasse 20; adult/
concession €9/6; ⊙10am-
6pm), where the great
composer was born in
1770. Other landmarks
include the soaring **Münster Basilica** (☑0228-985
880; www.bonner-muenster.
de; Münsterplatz), built on
the graves of the two
martyred Roman sol-
diers who later became
the city's patron saints.
It's currently closed for
reonovations, but the
cloister is still partially
accessible.

Bonn's old government
quarter dates from its
time as West Germany's
'temporary' capital,
between 1949 and 1991
(when a reunited German
government decided to
move to Berlin). For a
romp through recent
German history from
the end of WWII, pop by
the **Haus der Geschichte**
(Museum of History; ☑0228-
916 5400; www.hdg.de; Willy-
Brandt-Allee 14; ⊙9am-7pm
Tue-Fri, 10am-6pm Sat & Sun;
🅿; 🚌16, 63, 66 Heussallee/
Museumsmeile).

The Drive » Take the B9
southeast for 24km. Once
you leave the German state of
North Rhine-Westphalia and
enter Rhineland–Palatinate, the
road returns to the river's west
bank; on your right you'll see
the hilly wildlife park, Wildpark
Rolandseck.

④ Remagen

Remagen was founded by
the Romans in AD 16 as
Rigomagus, but the town
would hardly figure in
the history books were
it not for one fateful day
in early March 1945. As
the Allies raced across
France and Belgium to
rid Germany of Nazism,
the Wehrmacht tried
frantically to stave off
defeat by destroying all
bridges across the Rhine.
But the Brücke von Rema-
gen (the steel rail bridge)
lasted long enough for
Allied troops to cross the
river, contributing sig-
nificantly to the collapse
of Hitler's western front.
One of the bridge's sur-
viving basalt towers now
houses the **Friedensmu-
seum** (Peace Museum Bridge
at Remagen; ☑02642-218 63;
www.bruecke-remagen.de; An
der Alten Rheinbrücke 11; www.
bruecke-remagen.de 🅿), with
a well-presented exhibit
on Remagen's pivotal role
in WWII. Note that at
the time of writing, the
museum was temporarily
closed for renovations.

The Drive » Take the B9
southeast for 49km. The Rhine
winds back and forth away from
the road until you reach Koblenz.
Stay on the B9 until you've
crossed the Moselle to the town
centre, or risk getting lost in a
maze of concentric flyovers.

⑤ Koblenz

Koblenz sits at the
confluence of the Rhine
and Moselle rivers –
marked by the expansive
Deutsches Eck ('Ger-
man Corner'), adjoining
flower-filled parks and
promenades – and the
convergence of three
low mountain ranges
(the Hunsrück, the Eifel
and the Westerwald).
Its roots go back to the
Romans, who founded
a military stronghold
(Confluentes) here
because of the site's su-
preme strategic value.

On the Rhine's right
bank, the 118m-high
fortress **Festung Ehren-
breitstein** (☑0261-6675
4000; www.tor-zum-welterbe.
de; adult/child €7/3.50,
incl cable car €14.80/6.60,
audioguide €2; ⊙10am-6pm
Apr-Oct, to 5pm Nov-Mar)
proved indestructible
to all but Napoleonic
troops, who levelled it in
1801. To prove a point,
the Prussians rebuilt it as
one of Europe's mightiest
fortifications. It's accessible by car, on foot and
by cable car.

Inside Koblenz'
striking new glass
Forum Confluentes, the
Mittelrhein-Museum
(www.mittelrhein-museum.de;
Zentralplatz 1; adult/child €6/
free; ⊙10am-6pm Tue-Sun)
spans 2000 years of the
region's history, including
19th-century landscape
paintings of the Romantic
Rhine by German and
British artists.

🛏 p167

The Drive » Take the B49 to
the Rhine's east bank and travel
south on the B42; it's 13km to

CROSSING THE RHINE

No bridges span the Rhine between Koblenz and Mainz; the only way to cross the river along this stretch is by **Autofähre** (car ferry). Prices vary slightly but you can figure on paying about €4.50 per car, including driver; €1.50 per car passenger; €1.30 per pedestrian (€0.80 for a child); and €2 for bicycle and rider.

Bingen–Rüdesheim (www.bingen-ruedesheimer.de; ⊘5.30am-9.50pm Sun-Thu, to 12.50am Fri & Sat May-Oct, 5.30am-9.50pm Nov-Apr)

Boppard–Filsen (www.faehre-boppard.de; ⊘6.30am-10pm Jun-Aug, to 9pm Apr, May & Sep, to 8pm Oct-Mar)

Niederheimbach–Lorch (www.mittelrhein-faehre.de; ⊘6am-10.50pm Apr-Oct, to 6.50pm Nov-Mar)

Oberwesel–Kaub (www.faehre-kaub.de; ⊘6am-8pm Mon-Sat, 8am-8pm Sun Apr-Sep, 6am-7pm Mon-Sat, 8am-7pm Sun Oct-Mar)

St Goar–St Goarshausen (www.faehre-loreley.de; ⊘5.30am-10.30pm Mon-Fri, from 6.20am Sat, from 7.20am Sun May-Sep, shorter hours Oct-Apr)

Braubach. At this point of the drive, you leave the cityscapes behind and enter an older world of cobblestones, half-timbered villages, densely forested hillsides and ancient vineyards.

- - - - - - - - - - - - - - - - - -

6 Braubach

Framed by forest, vineyards and rose gardens, the 1300-year-old town of Braubach centres on its small, half-timbered **Marktplatz**. High above are the dramatic towers, turrets and crenellations of the 700-year-old **Marksburg** (☎02627-206; www.marksburg.de; Braubach; adult/child €7/5; ⊘10am-5pm mid-Mar–Oct, 11am-4pm Nov–mid-Mar), which is unique among the Rhine's fastnesses as it was never destroyed. The compulsory tour takes in the citadel, the Gothic hall and a grisly torture chamber.

The Drive » Hug the Rhine's east bank for 11km as it curves around to the car-ferry dock at Filsen. It's a five-minute crossing to charming Boppard.

- - - - - - - - - - - - - - - - - -

TRIP HIGHLIGHT

7 Boppard

Idyllically located on a horseshoe bend in the river, Boppard (pronounced 'bo-*part*') is one of the Romantic Rhine's prettiest towns, not least because its riverfront and historic centre are both on the same side of the railway tracks.

Boppard's riverfront promenade, the **Rheinallee**, has grassy areas for picnicking and a children's playground.

Many of the town's half-timbered buildings house cosy wine taverns, including its oldest, **Weinhaus Heilig Grab** (www.heiliggrab.de; Zelkesgasse 12; ⊘3pm-midnight Wed-Mon). In summer, sip local Rieslings under the chestnut trees, where live music plays on weekends.

Fantastic hiking trails fan out into the countryside, including the **Hunsrück Trails**, accessed by Germany's steepest scheduled railway route, the **Hunsrückbahn** (www.hunsrueckbahn.de; Hauptbahnhof; ⊘hourly 5am-11pm, from 6am Sat & Sun). Around the **Vierseenblick** (Four-Lakes-View), a panoramic outlook reached by **Sesselbahn** (Chairlift; ☎06742-2510; www.sesselbahn-boppard.de; Mühltal 12; adult/child one-way €5.50/3, return €8.50/4.50; ⊘10am-6pm mid-Apr–Sep, shorter hours Oct) creates the illusion that you're looking at four separate lakes rather than a single river.

The Drive » Take the B9 south for 15km, passing Burg

Classic Trip

WHY THIS IS A CLASSIC TRIP
MARC DI DUCA, WRITER

The romance along this stretch of the Rhine is timeless. Poets and painters including Lord Byron and William Turner are among those who have been inspired by this castle-crowned, forest-and-vineyard-cloaked valley. A fabled stop on the original European Grand Tour, the riverscape here is now a designated Unesco World Heritage site. It doesn't get more classic than that.

Above: Hunsrückbahn bridge (p161), Boppard
Right: Typical half-timbered house, Bacharach (p165)
Left: Statue of 'Die Lorelei', Loreley

Maus across the river near the village of Wellmich. Shortly afterwards, you'll spot Burg Rheinfels on the west bank above St Goar.

8 St Goar

Lording over the village of St Goar are the sprawling ruins of **Burg Rheinfels** (📞06741-7753; www.st-goar. de; Schlossberg 47; adult/child €5/2.50, guided mine tour €7/ free; ⏱9am-6pm Apr-Oct, to 5pm Mar & Nov, guided mine tours by reservation), once the Rhine's mightiest fortress. Built in 1245 by Count Dieter von Katzeneln-bogen as a base for his toll-collecting operations, its size and labyrinthine layout are astonishing. Kids (and adults) will love exploring the subterranean tunnels and galleries (bring a torch). From St Goar's northern edge, follow the Schlossberg road to the castle.

✕ 🛏 p167

The Drive » Take the five-minute car ferry across to the little village of St Goarshausen. From St Goarshausen's Marktplatz, follow the L338 as it twists steeply uphill through thick forest for 1.2km and turn right onto the K89 for 2.5km to reach Loreley.

9 Loreley

The most storied spot along the Romantic Rhine, Loreley is an enormous, almost vertical slab of slate; it owes its fame to a mythical maiden whose siren songs

are said to have lured sailors to their death in the river's treacherous currents. Heinrich Heine told the tale in his 1824 poem 'Die Lorelei'.

On the edge of the plateau 4km southeast of the village of St Goarshausen, visitor centre **Loreley Besucherzentrum** (☎06771-599 093; www.loreley-besucherzen

trum.de; Loreleyring 7; adult/child €2.50/1.50; ◎10am-5pm Mar-Oct) covers the Loreley myth and local flora, fauna, shipping and winemaking traditions. A 300m gravel path leads to a **viewpoint** at the tip of the Loreley outcrop, 190m above the river.

The Drive » Return to the B42 at the bottom of the hill; on your left, you'll see Burg Katz. Travel south for 2km to the car park by the breakwater for the next stop, the Lorelei Sculpture.

DETOUR: OBERWESEL

Start: **8** St Goar

It's a quick 7.8km south from St Goar along the B9 to the village of Oberwesel.

Every April, Oberwesel crowns not a *Weinkönigin* (wine queen), as in most Rhine towns, but a *Weinhexe* (wine witch) – a good witch, of course – who is said to protect the vineyards. Photos of all the *Weinhexen* crowned since 1946 are displayed in the cellar of Oberwesel's **Kulturhaus** (☎06744-714 726; www.kulturhaus-oberwesel.de; Rathausstrasse 23; adult/child €3/1; ◎10am-5pm Tue-Fri, from 2pm Sat & Sun Apr-Oct, 10am-2pm Tue-Fri Nov-Mar), along with 19th-century engravings of the Rhine and models of its riverboats.

Hidden sky-high up a vineyard-striped hillside, the flagstone terrace of **Günderode Haus** (☎06744-714 011; www.guenderodefilmhaus.de; Siebenjungfrauenblick; dishes €4-17; ◎11am-7pm Tue-Sat, 10am-6pm Sun Apr-Oct, shorter hours Nov-Mar) is incredible for a glass of wine, beer or brandy, with sweeping views over the Rhine. The adjacent 200-year-old half-timbered house was used as a film set for *Heimat 3* (2004); it now has a cinema room and hosts live music and literary events, as well as wine tastings. From Oberwesel, take the K93 east for 600m, turn right (north) onto the K95; after 1km, the car park's on your right.

---

⑩ Lorelei Sculpture

At the tip of a narrow breakwater jutting into the Rhine, a bronze sculpture of Loreley's famous maiden perches atop a rocky platform. From the car park, you can walk the 600m out to the sculpture, from where there are fantastic views of both riverbanks. Be aware that the rough path is made from jagged slate (wear sturdy shoes!) and the gentler sandy lower path is often underwater.

The Drive » Take the B42 south for 8km to the little village of Kaub, and park next to the ferry dock.

---

⑪ Kaub

Kaub is the gateway to one of the river's iconic sights. As if out of a fairy tale, 1326-built, boat-shaped toll castle **Pfalzgrafstein** (☎06774-745; www.burg-pfalzgrafenstein.de; adult/child €4/2.50, audioguide €1; ◎10am-6pm Tue-Sun Mar–Oct, to 5pm Sat & Sun Jan, Feb & Nov), with distinctive white-painted walls, red trim and slate turrets, perches on a narrow island in the middle of the Rhine. A once dangerous rapid here (since modified) forced boats to use the right-hand side of the river, where a chain forced ships to stop and pay a toll. The island makes a fabulously scenic picnic spot.

Alongside Kaub's car-ferry dock you can hop on a little **Fährboot** (www.faehre-kaub.de; adult/child €2/0.80; ⏱10am-6pm Tue-Sun Apr-Oct, to 5pm Mar, to 5pm Sat & Sun Nov, Jan & Feb) passenger ferry (it only runs from this side of the river).

The Drive » Take the car ferry across to the Rhine's west bank and head south on the B9 for 3km.

- - - - - - - - - - - - - - - - - - -

⓬ **Bacharach**

Tiny Bacharach conceals its considerable charms behind a **14th-century wall**. Enter one of the thick arched gateways under the train tracks and you'll find yourself in a medieval old town filled with half-timbered mansions. It's possible to walk almost all the way around the centre on top of the walls. The lookout tower on the upper section of the wall affords panoramic views.

Dating from 1421, **Zum Grünen Baum** (www.weingut-bastian-bacharach.de; Oberstrasse 63; ⏱6-10pm Apr-Oct, shorter hours Nov-Mar) serves some of Bacharach's best whites in rustic surrounds. Its nearby **Vinothèque** (☎06743-937 8530; www.weingut-bastian-bacharach.de; Koblenzer Strasse 1; ⏱11am-6pm Fri-Sun Apr-Oct, shorter hours Nov-Mar), by contrast, is state of the art. Owner Friedrich Bastian is a renowned opera singer, so music (and culinary)

CAT & MOUSE

Two rival castles stand either side of the village of St Goarshausen. Burg Peterseck was built by the archbishop of Trier to counter the toll practices of the powerful Katzenelnbogen family. The latter responded by building a much bigger castle high on the other side of town, Burg Neukatzenelnbogen, which was dubbed **Burg Katz**, meaning 'Cat Castle'. Highlighting the obvious imbalance of power between the Katzenelnbogens and the archbishop, Burg Peterseck was soon nicknamed **Burg Maus** ('Mouse Castle'). Both are closed to the public.

events take place year-round, including on Bastian's private river-island with its own vineyard.

🛏 p167

The Drive » Head south on the B9, passing Burg Reichenstein then Burg Rheinstein on your right. Then, on your left, in the river itself, you'll pass the Mäuseturm, a fortified tower used as a signal station until 1974. Drive through Bingen to the car-ferry dock at its eastern edge, and cross the river to Rüdesheim.

- - - - - - - - - - - - - - - - - - -

TRIP HIGHLIGHT

⓭ **Rüdesheim**

Depending on how you look at it, Rüdesheim's town centre – and especially its most famous feature, the tunnel-like medieval alley **Drosselgasse** – is either a touristy nightmare or a lot of kitschy, colourful fun. There's also wonderful walking in the greater area, which is part of the Rheingau wine region, famed for its superior Rieslings.

For a stunning Rhine panorama, head up the wine-producing slopes west of Rüdesheim to the **Niederwald Monument**. Erected between 1877 and 1883, this bombastic monument celebrates the Prussian victory in the Franco-Prussian War and the creation of the German Reich, both in 1871. To save climbing 203 vertical metres, glide above the vineyards aboard the 1400m-long **Seilbahn cable car** (Kabinenbahn; www.seilbahn-ruedesheim.de; Oberstrasse 37; adult/child one-way €5.50/3, return €8/4, with Sesselbahn €9/4.50; ⏱9.30am-7pm Jul & Aug, to 6pm Mon-Fri, to 7pm Sat & Sun Jun & Sep, shorter hours mid-Mar–May & Oct-Dec). A network of hiking trails extends from the monument.

🛏 p167

The Drive » Head east on the B42 for 23km and turn south on the A643 to cross the bridge over the Rhine. It's then 13km southeast to the centre of Mainz.

TRIP HIGHLIGHT

14 Mainz

The Rhine meets the Main at lively Mainz, which has a sizeable university, pretty pedestrian precincts and a *savoir vivre* dating from Napoleon's occupation (1797–1814). Strolling along the Rhine and sampling local wines in an **Altstadt** tavern are classic Mainz experiences. Try the 1791 **Weinstube Hottum** (Grebenstrasse 3; ⊙4pm-midnight) for wines purely from the Rheingau and Rheinhessen regions,

or vine-draped **Weingut Michel** (www.michel-wein.de; Jakobsbergstrasse 8; ⊙4pm-midnight Mon-Sat), which exclusively serves its own wines.

Highlights you won't want to miss include the fabulous **Mainzer Dom** (☏06131-253 412; www.mainz erdom.bistummainz.de; Markt 10; ⊙9am-6.30pm Mon-Fri, to 4pm Sat, 12.45-6.30pm Sun Mar-Oct, 9am-5pm Mon-Fri, to 3pm Sat, 12.45-3pm & 4-5pm Sun Nov-Feb), the ethereal windows of Chagall in **St-Stephan-Kirche** (www.st -stephan-mainz.bistummainz.de; Kleine Weissgasse 12; ⊙10am-5pm Mon-Sat, from noon Sun Mar-Oct, 10am-4.30pm Mon-Sat, from noon Sun Nov-Feb), and the first printed Bible in the **Gutenberg-Museum Mainz** (☏06131-

122 503; www.gutenberg-muse-um.de; Liebfrauenplatz 5; adult/child €5/2, audioguide €3.50; ⊙9am-5pm Tue-Sat, from 11am Sun). This museum commemorates native son Johannes Gutenberg who ushered in the information age here in the 15th century by perfecting movable type.

Also well worth a visit is the dungeonlike, brilliantly illuminated Roman archaeological site **Heiligtum der Isis und Mater Magna** (☏06131-600 7493; www.roemisches-mainz.de; Römerpassage 1; ⊙10am-6pm Mon-Sat). The easy-to-miss entrance is on the Römer Passage mall's ground floor, just inside the western entrance.

✖ p167

CRUISING THE RHINE

If you'd like to let someone else drive for a while and get a different perspective of the Rhine, it's easy to park up and hop on a cruise boat. From around Easter to October (winter services are very limited), passenger ships run by **Köln-Düsseldorfer** (KD; ☏0221-208 8318; www.k-d.com) link Rhine villages on a set timetable:

» You can travel to the next village or all the way between Mainz and Koblenz (one-way/return €50/55, downstream Mainz to Koblenz/upstream Koblenz to Mainz 5½/8 hours).

» Within the segment you've paid for (eg Boppard–Rüdesheim), you can get on and off as often as you like, but make sure to ask for a free stopover ticket each time you disembark.

» Children up to the age of four travel free, while those up to age 13 are charged a flat fee of €6 regardless of distance.

» Return tickets usually cost only slightly more than one-way.

» To bring a bicycle, there's a supplement of €3.

A few smaller companies also send passenger boats up and down the river:

Bingen-Rüdesheimer (www.bingen-ruedesheimer.de)

Loreley Linie (www.loreley-linie.com)

Rössler Linie (www.roesslerlinie.de)

Eating & Sleeping

Koblenz ❺

🛏 Hotel Stein — Boutique Hotel €€

(📞0261-963 530; www.hotel-stein.de;
Mayener Strasse 126; s/d from €85/110; 🅿 🛜)
Decorated in zesty colours such as tangerine
contrasted with dark timbers, Stein's 30
contemporary rooms are all soundproofed for
a peaceful night's sleep. The hotel is situated
across the Moselle River 2km north of Koblenz'
city centre. Michelin-starred restaurant
Schiller's (4-/5-/6-course menus €79/98/119,
with paired wines €107/133/161, 5-course veg
menu €89, with paired wines €124; 🕐6-10pm
Tue-Sat) is on the ground floor.

St Goar ❽

✕ Weinhotel Landsknecht — German €€

(📞06741-2011; www.hotel-landsknecht.de;
Aussiedlung Landsknecht 4; mains €12-25;
🕐 noon-2.30pm & 6-9pm Mar–mid-Dec; 🛜) The
dining room and terrace at this wonderful spot
1.5km north of St Goar feel like being aboard a
cruise boat, with close-up, uninterrupted river
views. Delicious home cooking spans pickled
salmon with quince mousse to schnitzel with
mushroom and Riesling sauce, and red-wine-
marinated plums with rosemary-and-vanilla
ice cream. Many of its **rooms** (single/double/
family from €70/90/140) also have Rhine
views.

🛏 Romantik Hotel Schloss Rheinfels — Historic Hotel €€

(📞06741-8020; www.schloss-rheinfels.de;
Schlossberg 47; s/d from €95/175; 🅿 🛜 ♿)
Part of the Burg Rheinfels (p163) castle
complex is occupied by a romantic hotel with
64 rooms and suites that range in size from tiny
to palatial. All have antique-style furnishings;
pricier rooms come with a river view. The
hotel has three restaurants: one rustic,
one semiformal and one gourmet. Cots and
babysitting services can be arranged.
Breakfast costs €18.

Bacharach ⓬

🛏 Rhein Hotel — Hotel €€

(📞06743-1243; www.rhein-hotel-bacharach.
de; Langstrasse 50; s/d from €45/95; 🅿 ❄ 🛜)
Right on the town's medieval ramparts in a
half-timbered building, this family-run hotel has
14 well-lit rooms with original artworks that are
named for the vineyards they overlook. Rooms
facing the river, and therefore the train tracks,
have double-glazing. Guests can borrow bikes
for free. Its **Stübers Restaurant** (mains €10-
21; 🕐5-10pm Mon-Sat, noon-2pm & 5.30-9pm
Sun early Mar-early Dec; 🍴) is top-notch.

Rüdesheim ⓭

🛏 Rüdesheimer Schloss — Boutique Hotel €€

(📞06722-905 00; www.ruedesheimer-schloss.
com; Steingasse 10; s/d/ste from €90/130/160;
🅿 🛜) Truly good places to sleep and eat are
thin on the ground in central Rüdesheim, but
this 18th-century building has 26 stunning
contemporary rooms designed by local and
regional artists. Its restaurant is excellent,
serving dishes like cheese-and-Riesling soup,
veal liver with truffled mash, and roast duck
stuffed with dates and figs. It also has a live
pianist and after-dinner dancing.

Mainz ⓮

✕ Zur Kanzel — European €€

(📞06131-237 137; www.zurkanzel.de;
Grebenstrasse 4; mains €9-25; 🕐5pm-1am
Mon-Fri, noon-4pm & 6pm-1am Sat) Germany
meets France in seasonally changing dishes
like grilled tuna with Riesling-and-sage sauce,
garlic-crusted rack of lamb with wilted spinach,
schnitzel with Frankfurt-style *Grüne Sosse*
(green sauce), and rump steak with herb butter,
as well as garlic snails. There's a lovely summer
courtyard. Cash only.

Moselle Valley

Follow the enchanting Moselle River as it flows, between vineyard-wrapped slopes ribboned with walking trails, from historic Trier through fairy-tale landscapes to park-and-flower-filled Koblenz.

13

TRIP HIGHLIGHTS

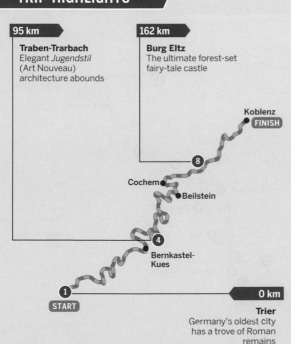

95 km

Traben-Trarbach
Elegant *Jugendstil*
(Art Nouveau)
architecture abounds

162 km

Burg Eltz
The ultimate forest-set
fairy-tale castle

Koblenz
FINISH

⑧

Cochem

Beilstein

④

Bernkastel-
Kues

①
START

0 km

Trier
Germany's oldest city
has a trove of Roman
remains

2–4 DAYS
195KM / 121 MILES

GREAT FOR...

BEST TIME TO GO
Wine festivals (www.
mosel-weinfeste.
de) abound between
late April and early
November.

 **ESSENTIAL
PHOTO**
Europe's steepest
vineyard – Calmont.

 **BEST FOR
WINE**
LOVERS
Bernkastel-Kues offers
opportunities to taste
the Moselle's famous
wines.

13 Moselle Valley

As you wind along the river's edge, and criss-cross over its narrow bridges, you'll pass huddled half-timbered villages, precariously perched hilltop castles (or their crumbling remains), and scores of snug, generations-old wineries serving hearty food and exquisite wines. Pack your hiking boots – from every stop along the route you can head up into the vines for sublime views over the valley.

TRIP HIGHLIGHT

❶ Trier

Before hitting the road, history buffs especially will want to explore Germany's oldest city, Trier, at the head of the Moselle Valley. A Unesco World Heritage site, this is where you'll find the country's finest ensemble of Roman remains, including the 2nd-century 'black gate' **Porta Nigra** (adult/child €4/2.50; ⏰9am-6pm Apr-Sep, to 5pm Mar & Oct, to 4pm Nov-Feb); a gladiatorial **Amphitheater**

(Olewiger Strasse; adult/child €4/2.50; ⊙9am-6pm Apr-Sep, to 5pm Mar & Oct, to 4pm Nov-Feb); thermal baths such as the labyrinthine **Kaisertherme** (Imperial Baths; Weberbachstrasse 41; adult/child €4/2.50; ⊙9am-6pm Apr-Sep, to 5pm Mar & Oct, to 4pm Nov-Feb); **Konstantin Basilika** (🖉0651-9949 1200; www.konstantin-basilika.de; Konstantinplatz 10; ⊙10am-6pm Mon-Sat, 1-6pm Sun Apr-Oct, 10am-noon & 2-4pm Tue-Sat, 1-3pm Sun Nov-Mar), constructed around AD 310 as Constantine's throne room (now a Protestant church); as well as Germany's oldest bishop's church, **Trierer Dom** (www.trierer-dom.de; Liebfrauenstrasse 12; ⊙6.30am-6pm Apr-Oct, to 5.30pm Nov-Mar),

LINK YOUR TRIP

12 **Romantic Rhine**
Swap one waterway for another: Koblenz sits at the confluence of the Moselle and Rhine rivers, where you can also pick up this route.

14 **German Wine Route**
For more vineyards (and more magnificent wines), drive 129km southeast from Koblenz to the German Wine Route's Bockenheim an der Weinstrasse.

which retains Roman sections.

Vineyards climbing the hillsides provide a taste of the road trip to come.

✕ 🛏 p175

The Drive » Cross Germany's oldest bridge, the Römerbrücke (whose 2nd-century stone pilings have held it up since legionnaires crossed on chariots) to the right (western) bank. Turn right onto the B51; after about 1km, the right-hand fork links up to the B53. Following the B53 along the river for 63km brings you to Bernkastel-Kues.

- - - - - - - - - - - - - - - - - - -

❷ Bernkastel-Kues

On the river's right (eastern) bank, higgledy-piggledy half-timbered houses with beautifully decorated gables cluster around Bernkastel's Marktplatz, including the Moselle's oldest half-timbered building, dating from 1416. Shaped like a bird's house, with a narrow base topped by a larger, wonkier upper level to allow carriages to pass through the narrow alley, it's now home to **Weinstube Spitzhäuschen** (🖉06531-7476; www.spitzhaeuschen.de; Karlstrasse 13; ⊙4-10pm Mon-Fri, from 3pm Sat & Sun Easter-Oct, 3-10pm Sat Nov-Dec, other times by appointment), where you can taste the Schmitz family's local wines. Looming above Bernkastel is the ruined 13th-century castle **Burg Landshut** (🖉06531-972

770; www.burglandshut.de; ⊙noon-9pm Thu-Tue).

Kues, on the left bank, is home to the 1458-founded **St-Nikolaus-Hospital** (www.cusanus.de; Cusanusstrasse 2; guided tour €7; ⊙9am-6pm Sun-Fri, to 3pm Sat, guided tour 10.30am Tue & 3pm Fri Apr-Oct), where, for more wine tasting, you'll find the **Mosel Vinothek** (🖉06531-4141; ⊙10am-6pm Apr-Oct, 11am-5pm Feb, Mar, Nov & Dec).

🛏 p175

The Drive » From the Bernkastel side of the river, head north, hugging the river as it bends west, for 7km to Zeltingen-Rachtig, then cross to the left (southern) bank: just on your right is one of the trip's biggest surprises.

- - - - - - - - - - - - - - - - - - -

❸ Kloster Machern

The Moselle might be better known for its wine but a former Cistercian monastery, founded in the 13th century, now houses this extraordinary **brewery** (🖉06532-951 50; www.brauhaus-kloster-machern.de; An der Zeltinger Brücke, Zeltingen-Rachtig; museum adult/child €3/1.50; ⊙museum 10am-6pm, bar 11am-1am, shop noon-5pm Easter-Oct, shorter hours Nov-Easter), with a bar made from a copper vat and dry hops hanging from the ceiling. There's a wicker-chair-filled terrace, and excellent local cuisine. Brews, including a *Dunkel* (dark), *Hell* (light) and *Hefe-Weizen* (wheat beer), are also sold at its shop. Also here is a museum exhibiting religious iconography, plus puppets, toys and model railways.

The Drive » Sticking to the left (eastern) bank, follow the river downstream as it twists, turns and twists again until you arrive at Traben, one of the twin towns making up Traben-Trarbach.

TRIP HIGHLIGHT

④ Traben-Trarbach

Traben, on the Moselle's left (northern) bank, lost its medieval appearance to three major fires but was compensated with beautiful *Jugendstil* (Art Nouveau) villas, many designed by Berlin architect Bruno Möhring.

Across the river in Trarbach, Möhring's works include the 1898-built, medieval-style bridge gate, the **Brückentor**, and a 1906 former winery that's now the unlikely home of 2000-plus wood, bronze and paper Buddha statues at the **Buddha Museum** (www.buddha-museum.de; Bruno-Möhring-Platz 1; adult/child €15/7.50; ⊙10am-6pm Tue-Sun).

Teetering above Trarbach are the ruins of 14th-century **Grevenburg**. Below the castle is **Weingut Louis Klein** (☏06541-6246; www.klein-wein.de; Enkircher Strasse 20;

90-min cellar tour incl tastings €8; ⊙10am-6pm Mon-Sat, to noon Sun, tours by reservation), which can also arrange vineyard tastings amid the vines.

🍴 🛏 p175

The Drive » From Trarbach, stay on the river's right (eastern) bank and follow the B53 north for 20km to the wine-producing town of Zell.

⑤ Zell

You'll know you've arrived in the charming town of Zell when you come to its roundabout. In the centre is a gigantic black cat, standing on top of a wine barrel raising a full glass and backed by vine-planted hills. So the story goes, in 1863, visiting merchants trying to find the best wine encountered a barrel guarded by a hissing, spitting *Schwarze Katz* (black cat). The merchants snapped up the now-renowned Zeller Schwarze Katz wine; you can taste and buy it at wine shops throughout the town.

The Drive » After heading 14km north on the left (western) bank, look up (and up!) as you leave the village of Bremm to spot Europe's, and allegedly the world's, steepest vineyard – Calmont, with a 65-degree gradient. Continuing downriver another 15km and crossing to the right (eastern) bank after Nehren takes you into Beilstein.

⑥ Beilstein

Beilstein's storybook-like half-timbered buildings centre on its 14th-century Marktplatz. Steep slopes lead to the baroque 17th-century Carmelite monastery church, **Karmeliterkirche St Josef** (www.st-josef-beilstein.de; Klostertreppe; ⊙8am-6pm). Its spectacular interior has a vaulted ceiling supported by soaring apricot-coloured columns. Also perched above the village is ruined **Burg Metternich** (☏02673-936 39; www.burg-metternich.de; adult/child €2.50/1; ⊙9am-6pm Apr-Nov). Built in 1129, the

Traben-Trarbach Grevenburg castle ruins

castle was destroyed by French troops in the Nine Years' War in 1689.

The Drive » Continue along the right (eastern) bank for 11km and cross the bridge to busy Cochem.

---

7 Cochem

Transport hub Cochem is the Moselle at its most touristy. Pastel-coloured, terrace-fronted restaurants line its waterfront. Behind them, Cochem's tangle of narrow, medieval alleyways are crammed with boutiques.

Rising above town is the dazzling **Reichsburg** (☏02671-255; www.reichsburg-cochem.de; Schlossstrasse 36; hourly tours in English adult/child €6/3; ⊙ tours 9am-5pm mid-Mar–Oct, shorter hours Nov–mid-Mar). This 11th-century castle fell victim to French troops in 1689, then stood ruined for centuries until it was restored to its current – if not always architecturally faithful – glory. Banquets here include a knighting ceremony.

🍴 p175

The Drive » Stay on the left (west) river bank and follow the B49 as it winds north, then east, for 17km to the village of Moselkern. At Moselkern, leave the river for 8km to reach Burg Eltz

---

TRIP HIGHLIGHT

8 Burg Eltz

At the head of the Eltz, a Moselle side valley, wonderful **Burg Eltz** (☏02672-950 500; www.burg-eltz.de; Burg-Eltz-Strasse 1, Wierschem; tour adult/child €10/6.50; ⊙9.30am-5.30pm Apr-Oct) is one of the most romantic medieval castles in Germany. Never destroyed, this vision of turrets, towers, oriels, gables and half-timber is still owned by the original family. From the Eltz car park, it's a shuttle bus ride or 1.3km walk to the castle.

173

The Drive ≫ Retrace your route to Moselkern, then follow the B416 along the left (north) bank. After 5.5km you'll pass tiny Hatzenport – vine-shaded riverfront winery Weinhaus Ibald, in the village centre, makes an idyllic stop. From Hatzenport, it's just another 5km (cross the bridge about halfway along) to Alken.

- - - - - - - - - - - - - - - - - -

🟎 Alken

Alken is one of the Moselle's oldest villages, tracing its roots to Celtic and Roman times. Built on Roman foundations from 1197, its hilltop castle, **Burg Thurant** (✆02605-2004; www.thurant. de; adult/child €4/2.50;

⊙10am-6pm May-Sep, to 5pm Mar, Apr & Oct–mid-Nov), has an intriguing history. From 1246 to 1248 it was fought over by the archbishops of Cologne and Trier, and divided in two parts (separated by a wall). Fascinating displays include medieval torture devices; the watchtower is accessible by ladder.

The Drive ≫ Along the Moselle's right (east) bank, the B49 squiggles for another 23km to Koblenz.

- - - - - - - - - - - - - - - - - -

🟎 Koblenz

Koblenz, with intriguing museums, flower-filled parks and a cable-car-accessed fortress, is a fitting last stop: at the broad **Deutsches Eck** ('German Corner'), the Moselle ends, emptying into the Rhine. Specialising in Rhine and Moselle wines by the glass and/or bottle, rustic **Alte Weinstube Zum Hubertus** (www.weinhaus-hubertus.de; Florinsmarkt 6; ⊙3.30-11pm Mon, Wed & Thu, noon-midnight Fri-Sun) occupies a half-timbered house dating from 1689, with an open fireplace, antique furniture, dark-wood panelling and a summer terrace.

Eating & Sleeping

Trier ❶

🍴 Alt Zalawen German €€

(🕿0651-286 45; www.altzalawen.de;
Zurlaubener Ufer 79; mains €6-18; ⏱3-10pm
Mon-Sat, from noon Sun; 🛜) The pick of
the cluster of bar-restaurants right on the
riverfront, with terraces extending to the path
running along the grassy bank, timber-panelled
Alt Zalawen is a picturesque spot for traditional
German specialities (schnitzels, sausages,
Spätzle – egg noodles) and local Trierer Viez
cider. If you're here in December, it's fêted for
its roast goose.

🛏 Becker's Design Hotel €€

(🕿0651-938 080; www.beckers-trier.de;
Olewiger Strasse 206; r from €110; 🅿 ❄ @ 🛜)
In the peaceful wine district of Olewig, across
the creek from the old monastery church, 3km
southeast of the centre, classy Becker's pairs
supremely tasteful rooms – ultramodern in
its hotel; rustically traditional in its Weinhaus
– with stellar **dining** (1-/3-course lunch menu
€18/28, 3-/4-course dinner menu €45/58, mains
€21-34; ⏱noon-2pm & 6-10pm Tue-Sun).

Bernkastel-Kues ❷

🛏 Christiana's
Wein & Art Hotel Boutique Hotel €€

(🕿06531-6627; www.wein-arthotel.de;
Lindenweg 18, Kues; s/d/ste from €65/85/125;
🅿 ❄ 🛜) Each of the 17 rooms at this sleek
hotel is named after a Moselle vineyard (with
corresponding wines in each minibar), and
features dramatic outsized photos of wine
glasses or barrels. Bathrooms are state of
the art; higher-priced rooms have spas and/
or balconies. Its steakhouse restaurant
overlooks the vines. Lock-up bike storage is
available.

Traben-Trarbach ❹

🍴 Alte Zunftscheune German €€

(🕿06541-9737; www.zunftscheune.de; Neue
Rathausstrasse 15, Traben; mains €11-23; ⏱5-
11pm Tue-Sat, 11.30am-3pm & 5-11pm Sun Easter-
Oct, 6-11pm Fri, 5-11pm Sat & Sun Nov-Easter;
🖉) Dine on delicious Moselle-style dishes such
as homemade black pudding and liver sausage,
pork medallions with Riesling cream sauce, or
grilled rump steak with asparagus and fried
potatoes, in a series of wonderfully atmospheric
rooms chock-full of rustic bric-a-brac, with
beautiful timber staircases. Its cellar still has
its original 1890s lighting. Reservations are
recommended. Cash only.

🛏 Hotel Bellevue Historic Hotel €€

(🕿06541-7030; www.bellevue-hotel.de; An der
Mosel 11, Traben; s/d/ste from €85/105/175;
🛜 ⛴) Topped by a Champagne-bottle-shaped
slate turret, this river-facing *Jugendstil* hotel
was built in 1903 by Bruno Möhring, with an oak
staircase in the lobby and beautiful stained-
glass windows in its gourmet restaurant,
Belle Epoque. Individually designed rooms are
overwhelmingly romantic. There's a minimum
two-night stay on weekends year-round and
minimum three-night stay at any time July to
October and December.

Cochem ❼

🍴 Alt Thorschenke German €€

(🕿02671-7059; www.thorschenke.de;
Brückenstrasse 3; mains €11-20; ⏱11am-9pm;
🛜) Wedged into the old medieval walls, away
from the busy riverfront restaurants, Alt
Thorschenke is a diamond find for regional
specialities, such as herring with apple and
onions, pork neck with mustard-cream sauce,
and several different types of schnitzel –
accompanied by wines from local producers.
Upstairs are 27 small but charming **rooms**
(doubles from €99), some with four-poster beds.

German Wine Route

14

Plunge into the Palatinate (Pfalz) region's vine-planted hills, rambling forests, chess-piece castles, wisteria-draped villages and thermal springs along one of Germany's oldest and loveliest touring routes.

TRIP HIGHLIGHTS

FINISH
● Bockenheim an der Weinstrasse

82 km
Bad Dürkheim
Curative spa waters and pretty parks

6

5

● Neustadt an der Weinstrasse
3

60 km
Hambacher Schloss
Historic hilltop castle with superb dining, too

70 km
Deidesheim
Cobbled streets filled with wineries and galleries

START ● Schweigen-Rechtenbach

● Wissembourg

2–4 DAYS
96KM / 59 MILES

GREAT FOR...

BEST TIME TO GO
Villages here are especially pretty during the spring bloom (March to mid-May).

ESSENTIAL PHOTO

Dürkheimer Riesenfass, the world's largest wine barrel.

BEST FOR FOODIES

Epicurean treats abound along the entire route.

14 German Wine Route

From the French border, you'll wind north along this venerable route through Germany's largest contiguous wine-growing area, which is blessed with a temperate climate that allows almonds, figs, lemons and kiwi fruit to thrive, and is scattered with half-timbered villages and castles. The route was inaugurated in 1935, and its western edge weaves through the hilly forest of the Pfälzerwald, a Unesco Biosphere Reserve with invigorating hiking and cycling trails.

❶ Schweigen-Rechtenbach

There's no missing the start of the German Wine Route, which is marked by a towering stone gate, the 1936-built **Deutsches Weintor** (German Wine Gate; Weinstrasse). Inside is one of Germany's largest wine cooperatives. At this vast **Vinothek** (☑06342-224; www.weintor. de; ◷10am-6pm Mar-Dec, from 1pm Mon-Thu, from 10am Fri Jan & Feb) you can pick up tourist information, stock up on bottles, or sample a variety of wines by the glass.

The Drive » From Schweigen-Rechtenbach, drive north for 16km along the Weinstrasse, which starts as the B38 and becomes the B48 at Bad Bergzabern. Just after pretty Klingenmünster (look out for its castle, Burg Landeck), the B48 swings west into the forested Pfälzerwald to Annweiler (28km all-up).

❷ Annweiler

At the westernmost edge of the Palatinate wine-growing region, up in the forested Pfälzerwald, Annweiler has a charming core of half-timbered buildings and cobbled squares bisected by a canal-like stream with giant wooden water-wheels.

It's 8.6km via the K2 to **Burg Trifels** (☑06346-8470; www.burgen-rlp.de; K2, Annweiler am Trifels; adult/child €4.50/2.50; ◷10am-6pm mid-Mar–Oct, to 5pm Sat & Sun Feb–mid-Mar & Nov), looming southeast of the town. Thought to be of Celtic origins, this enormous red-sandstone hilltop castle was first documented in 1081. Between 1125 and 1298 it was the repository of imperial treasures including, allegedly, a nail from Jesus' cross and a tooth from John the Baptist. Richard the Lionheart (Richard I of England) was imprisoned here from 1193 to 1194 for insulting Leopold V, Duke of Austria (after first having been incarcerated in Austria's Kuenringerburg from 1192 to 1193). Today, Burg Trifels' displays include a replica of the imperial crown jewels. Excavations a decade ago uncovered a probable Saxon-era wooden castle.

The Drive » Head east to Albersweiler to rejoin the Weinstrasse (here called the L507) and follow it northeast: Hambacher Schloss is west of the hamlet of Hambach along the one-way K9 to the car park at the top of the hill (27.5km in total).

TRIP HIGHLIGHT

❸ Hambacher Schloss

Atop a forested Pfälzerwald hill is the monumental **Hambacher Schloss** (☑06321-926 290; www.hambacher-schloss.de; Schlossstrasse, Wolfsburg; adult/child €5.50/2.50, incl tour €9/6, audioguide €3; ◷castle 10am-6pm Apr-Oct,

11am-5pm Nov-Mar, tours hourly 11am-4pm Apr-Oct, 11am, noon & 2pm Sat & Sun Nov-Mar). This 'cradle of German democracy' is where idealistic locals, Polish refugees and French citizens held massive protests for a free, democratic and united Germany on 27 May 1832, hoisting the black, red and gold German flag for the first time. An exhibition commemorates the event, known as the Hambacher Fest. Audioguides and tours are available in English.

Inside the castle, opening to a courtyard, **Restaurant 1832** (☏06321-959 7880; www.hambacherschloss. de; mains €16-23; ⊙11am-6pm Mar-Dec) is reason enough to make the trip up, with inspired modern German cuisine: liver dumpling soup; tagliatelle with roasted asparagus in fig sauce; fried calf's liver with glazed

LINK YOUR TRIP

13 **Moselle Valley**
More wines await in the beautiful Moselle Valley, a 129km drive northwest to Koblenz from Bockenheim an der Weinstrasse.

16 **German Castle Road**
From Bad Dürkheim, it's a straight 24km shot east to Mannheim.

grapes and potato-and-celery cake; and red mullet, shrimp and clams baked in parchment with cuttlefish risotto.

The Drive » Return via the one-way K14 to the Weinstrasse at Hambach and head north for 5.8km into Neustadt an der Weinstrasse. After crossing the railway tracks, turn left for 850m, then right on the B58; after 300m there's a large open-air car park on your left at the edge of the largely pedestrianised Altstadt.

---

④ Neustadt an der Weinstrasse

Vineyards fan out around Neustadt, a busy wine-producing town at the heart of the German Wine Route.

Neustadt's Altstadt teems with half-timbered houses, especially along Mittelgasse, Hinter-gasse, Metzgergasse and Kunigundenstrasse. It's anchored by the cobbled Marktplatz, which is flanked by the baroque Rathaus (town hall), as well as the Gothic **Stiftskirche** (☑06321-841 79; www.stiftskirche-neustadt. de; Marktplatz 2; adult/child church tours €3/1, tower tours €3/1; ⊕11am-3pm Mon-Sat, from noon Sun, church tour 4pm Fri, tower tour noon Sat). Built from red sandstone, this church, dating from the 14th century, has been shared by Protestant and Catholic congregations since 1708. Recent renovations revealed frescos from 1410 that depict a snapshot of life at the time, with bakers, craftspeople and market traders. Every Saturday at noon guided tours take you into the tower, reached by 184 steps (book ahead).

✕ 🛏 p183

The Drive » Follow the B38 northeast to the roundabout and continue straight ahead onto the L516, which becomes the Weinstrasse; after 8.2km, you'll arrive in Deidesheim.

TRIP HIGHLIGHT

⑤ Deidesheim

Draped in pale purple-flowering wisteria in the springtime, diminutive Deidesheim is centred on its charming Marktplatz. This is one of the German Wine Route's most picturesque – and upmarket – villages, with plenty of opportunities for wine tasting, relaxed strolling and sublime dining.

Deidesheim is a 'Cittaslow' town, an extension

DETOUR: WISSEMBOURG, FRANCE

Start: ① Schweigen-Rechtenbach

From Schweigen-Rechtenbach, it's an easy 5km detour south over the French border to Wissembourg along the B38 (which becomes the D264 when you enter France).

The chic little town's compact centre is awash with centuries-old architectural treasures along with *boulangeries* (bakeries), *fromageries* (cheese shops) and, yes, *caves viticoles* (wine cellars).

Plaques mark 25 key sights around town that you can follow on a walking circuit. Highlights include the 1448-built **Maison du Sel** (Salt House), first a hospital, then a salt warehouse and later a slaughterhouse; the magnificent **Église Sts-Pierre-et-Paul**, incorporating a square tower from an 11th-century abbey church and dazzling stained-glass windows; and the **Couvent des Augustins**, a 1279-founded convent converted into private residences during the French Revolution.

On Wissembourg's main square, Place de la République, the tourist office sells maps outlining the walking route and has details of local hiking and cycling. Alternatively, visit www.ot-wissembourg.fr for information.

German Wine Route Cycling through vineyards

of the Slow Food movement that aims to rebalance modern life's hectic pace not only through 'ecogastronomy' but also local arts, crafts, nature, cultural traditions and heritage. Galleries and artisans' studios (such as jewellery makers and potters) can be visited along the **Kunst und Kultur** (Art and Culture) Circuit; look for dark-blue-on-yellow 'K' signs.

The town is home to 10 **winemakers** (some closed Sunday) that welcome visitors – look for signs reading *Weingut* (winery), *Verkauf* (sale) and *Weinprobe* (wine

tasting) and ring the bell. Many can be found along the small streets west of **Pfarrkirche St Ulrich** (www.pfarrei-deidesheim.de; Marktplatz; ⊗8am-5pm).

A Marktplatz landmark with a canopied outdoor staircase, the **Altes Rathaus** (old town hall) dates from the 16th century. Inside is the three-storey **Museum für Weinkultur** (Museum of Wine Culture; ☎06326-981 561; Marktplatz 9; ⊗3-6pm Wed-Fri, 2-5pm Sat Apr-Dec), featuring displays on winemakers' traditional lifestyle and naive-art portrayals of the German Wine Route.

Shutterbugs will love the recently revamped **Deutsches Museum für Foto-, Film- und Fernsehtechnik** (German Photography, Film & TV Museum; ☎06326-6568; www.3f-museum.de; Weinstrasse 33; adult/child €4/2.50; ⊗10am-4pm Thu, 2-6pm Fri & Sat, 11am-6pm Sun), tucked down an alleyway across from the Rathaus, with an impressive collection of historic photographic and movie-making equipment.

Signposted walking and cycling routes lead you through vineyards and the Pfälzerwald.

🛏 p183

The Drive ≫ It's a glorious 6.8km drive north from Deidesheim along the Weinstrasse (L516) through gently rolling hills ribboned with vineyards to Bad Dürkheim.

----

⑥ Bad Dürkheim

Adorned with splashing fountains, the spa town of Bad Dürkheim is famous for its thermal springs, lovely parks like the azalea-and-wisteria-filled **Kurgarten** (Mannheimer Strasse), and what's claimed to be the world's largest wine festival, the **Dürkheimer Wurstmarkt** (www.duerkheimer-wurstmarkt.de; ☺ mid-Sep). It also has one of the world's largest wine barrels, the gigantic **Dürkheimer Riesenfass**. It has a diameter of 13.5m and a volume of 1,700,000L, and contains the Restaurant Dürkheimer Fass.

Test the waters at the modern **Kurzentrum** spa. In its lobby, you can taste the salty water (said to be good for your digestion) from a fountain.

Weinwanderwege (vineyard trails) from St Michaelskapelle, a chapel atop a little vine-clad hill, lead to Honigsäckel and the Hochmess vineyards (a 6km circuit).

 p183

The Drive ≫ At Bad Dürkheim, the Weinstrasse becomes the L271; follow it north via the village of Ungstein for 19km to Bockenheim an der Weinstrasse.

----

⑦ Bockenheim an der Weinstrasse

The village of Bockenheim an der Weinstrasse, not to be confused with the Frankfurt district of Bockenheim, marks the end of the German Wine Route.

Spanning the road at the village's northern edge in Roman *castrum* style is the modern, brick-and-tile **Haus der Deutsche Weinstrasse** (House of the German Wine Route; Weinstrasse 91b), built in 1995 as a counterpart to the Deutsches Weintor at the route's starting point in Schweigen-Rechtenbach. There's a cafe inside, but better dining options are elsewhere.

 p183

Eating & Sleeping

Neustadt an der Weinstrasse ④

✕ Urgestein   German €€€

(☎06321-489 060; www.restaurant-urgestein.
de; Rathausstrasse 6; 5-/6-course menus
€100/120, with paired wines €140/160; ⊙6-
10pm Tue-Sat) For a gastronomic extravaganza,
book a table at Benjamin Peifer's Michelin-
starred, vaulted brick cellar restaurant within
a half-timbered house in the town centre. Over
300 wines complement exquisite dishes like
pickled trout with sauerkraut and horseradish,
followed by steamed liver dumplings with
Riesling foam, hay-roasted pigeon with foie gras
mousse, and nougat ganache with hazelnut
yoghurt.

⌂ Gästehaus-Weingut
Helbighof   Guesthouse €€

(☎06321-327 81; www.helbighof.de; Andergasse
40; d from €90; P 🛜) Beneath the Hambacher
Schloss amid sprawling vineyards, this
charming family-run winery has just five
guest rooms, so book well ahead. The pick is
room 3, with balconies on two sides. Its superb
wines are sold at an honour bar; a sun terrace
overlooks the vines. Turn right after Andergasse
36, then immediately left to reach the driveway.
Cash only.

Deidesheim ⑤

⌂ Deidesheimer
Hof   Boutique Hotel €€€

(☎06326-968 70; www.deidesheimerhof.de; Am
Marktplatz; s/d from €125/165; P ❄ 🛜) In a
storybook gabled building dating from the 16th
century, this renowned hotel has 28 individually

decorated, ultra-spacious rooms (the smallest
are 25 sq metres), and two fine restaurants: one
is a Michelin-starred affair.

Bad Dürkheim ⑥

✕ Restaurant
Dürkheimer Fass   German €€

(☎06322-2143; www.duerkheimer-fass.de; St
Michaels-Allee 1; mains €15-27; ⊙11am-11pm
Thu-Tue Apr-Oct, slightly shorter hours Nov-Mar;
🚼) This convivial spot occupies the landmark
Dürkheimer Riesenfass, the world's largest wine
barrel, which has had a restaurant inside since
a master cooper built it out of 200 pine trees
in 1934. Dishes range from *Leberk Nödel* (liver
dumplings) to *Jägerschnitzel* (schnitzel with
forest-mushroom sauce) and *Zander* (perch
fillet) with *Grüne Sosse* (green sauce). There's
a summer beer garden.

Bockenheim an der
Weinstrasse ⑦

✕ Bockenheimer
Weinstube   German €€

(☎06359-409 0050; www.bockenheimer
weinstube.de; Weinstrasse 91; mains €9-25;
⊙5-10pm Wed-Sat, from 11.30am Sun Apr-Oct,
shorter hours Nov-Mar) You can just drop by to
try local wines by the glass, but top-notch local
specialities at this rustic *Weinstube* (wine bar)
include *Saumagen* (pig's stomach) stuffed with
whole chestnuts, *Bratwurst* with sauerkraut,
and *Flammkuchen* (Alsatian pizza). When the
sun is shining, the sweetest seats are in the
vine-draped, flower-filled summer courtyard.

STRETCH YOUR LEGS
FRANKFURT

Start/Finish: Alte Oper

Distance: 4.4km

Duration: Four hours

This walk chronicles Frankfurt's history through its architecture, taking in its medieval core and magnificent cathedral, its famed museum embankment along the sweeping Main River, and its glittering contemporary skyscrapers.

Take this walk on Trip

Alte Oper

Leave your car in the parking station opposite Frankfurt's 'old opera house', the 1880-inaugurated, Italian Renaissance–style **Alte Oper** (www.alteoper.de; Opernplatz 1; [U]Alte Oper), and check out the statues of Goethe and Mozart gracing its facade. Except for the mosaics in the lobby, the interior – only open during concerts – is modern.

The Walk » Head east for 400m on Grosse Bockenheimer Strasse, along the stretch locally known as 'Fressgass' (Eat Street) for its gourmet shops and restaurants, then north for 50m along Börsenstrasse to Börsenplatz.

Frankfurt Stock Exchange

Built in 1843, Frankfurt's neoclassical **Börse** (www.deutsche-boerse.com; Börsenplatz 4; [U]Hauptwache), one of the world's largest stock exchanges, has allegorical statues of the five continents adorning its porch. In the square out front, the **Bulle und Bär** sculpture depicts a showdown between a bull and a bear.

The Walk » Turn right onto Schillerstrasse for 100m, crossing Fressgass; Café Hauptwache is on your right, opposite mustard-coloured church St-Katharinen-Kirche.

Café Hauptwache

One of the most beautiful buildings in Frankfurt to have escaped WWII's destruction is this 1730-built baroque guardhouse, now dwarfed by skyscrapers. A **restaurant** (www.cafe-hauptwache.de; An der Hauptwache 15; mains €10-20; ◎10am-9pm Mon-Sat, to 8pm Sun; [U]Hauptwache) since 1904, it's enveloped by summer terraces that are perfect for a glass of Frankfurt's famous *Apfelwein* (apple wine).

The Walk » Follow Frankfurt's main pedestrianised shopping street Zeil east for 300m; turn right and follow Hasengasse for 450m to the Kaiserdom.

Kaiserdom

Frankfurt's historic centre was heavily bombed during WWII, but its 13th-century **Kaiserdom** (www.dom-frankfurt.de; Domplatz 1; tower adult/child €3/1.50;

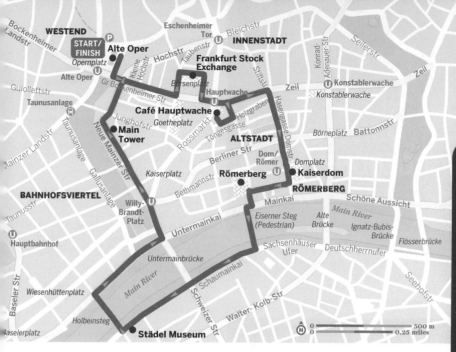

church 9am-8pm Sun-Thu, from 1pm Fri, tower 9am-6pm Apr-Oct, 10am-5pm Nov-Apr; Ⓤ Dom|Römer), topped by a 95m-high Gothic tower (which you can climb via 324 steps), was salvaged and restored.

The Walk ≫ It's just 200m west to Römerberg.

Römerberg

The city's old **central square** (Ⓤ Dom|Römer), reconstructed after WWII, highlights how beautiful its medieval core once was. Its ornately gabled buildings include the **Römer** (old town hall), and its single-spired Protestant **Alte Nikolaikirche** (www.alte-nikolai kirche.de; ⊙ 10am-8pm Apr-Sep, to 6pm Oct-Mar) was one of the few structures to survive the war almost intact.

The Walk ≫ Head 100m south to the river, cross the iron Eiserner Steg bridge, and follow Schaumainkai west along the Museumsufer (Museum Embankment) for 750m.

Städel Museum

If you only get to one Frankfurt museum, make it the **Städel** (✆ 069-605 098; www.staedelmuseum.de; Schaumainkai 63; adult/concession €14/12; ⊙ 10am-7pm Tue, Wed, Sat & Sun, to 9pm Thu & Fri; 🚆 15|16 Otto-Hahn-Platz). Founded in 1815, this world-renowned art gallery has an outstanding collection.

The Walk ≫ Cross pedestrian Holbeinsteg back to the north bank and follow the riverfront promenade east for 450m, then north for 560m along Neue Mainzerstrasse to Main Tower.

Main Tower

Survey the ground you've covered by taking a 45-second lift ride to the observation platform of the 200m-high **Main Tower** (www.maintower.de; Neue Mainzer Strasse 52-58; adult/child €7.50/5; ⊙ 10am-9pm Sun-Thu, to 11pm Fri & Sat Apr-Oct, 10am-7pm Sun-Thu, to 9pm Fri & Sat Nov-Mar; Ⓤ Alte Oper), one of the tallest and most distinctive high-rises in 'Mainhattan'.

The Walk ≫ From Main Tower, walking 400m north along Neue Mainzerstrasse brings you back to the Alte Oper.

STRETCH YOUR LEGS
COLOGNE

Start/Finish: Kölner Dom

Distance: 2km

Duration: Three hours

Cologne's history is everywhere, as you'll see on this walk, which circles through the heart of the bustling city. You can view Roman or medieval ruins, and you'll always be near somewhere to pause for refreshments.

Take this walk on Trips

Kölner Dom

Cologne's geographical and spiritual heart – and its single-biggest tourist draw – is the magnificent **Kölner Dom** (www.koelner-dom.de), with its soaring twin spires, art and treasures. Climb its south tower (533 steps) to the base of the steeple that dwarfed all European buildings until Eiffel built a certain tower in Paris. The underground Domforum visitor centre is good for info and tickets.

The Walk » There are numerous large parking facilities around the Dom and the neighbouring Hauptbahnhof (follow the signs). After Kölner Dom, walk south across the Roncalliplatz to Am Hof, turn east past some good beer halls, then go south again on Bechergasse to Rathausplatz.

Altes Rathaus

Dating to the 15th century and much restored, the **old city hall** (Rathausplatz; ☺8am-4pm Mon, Wed & Thu, to 6pm Tue, to noon Fri; ⊕5 Rathaus) has fine bells that ring daily at noon and 5pm. The Gothic tower is festooned with statues of old city notables.

The Walk » Head to the west side of the Rathaus.

Archäologische Zone

Cologne used the construction of the U-Bahn line to also build this grand **archaeological museum** (www.miqua.lvr.de) under the Rathausplatz. At the deepest level is the Praetorium, with relics of a Roman governor's palace. One level up are relics from the Middle Ages Jewish community.

The Walk » Cross the Marsplatz on the south side of the square to the museum.

Wallraf-Richartz-Museum

A famous collection of European paintings from the 13th to the 19th centuries, the **Wallraf-Richartz-Museum** (www.wall raf.museum; Obenmarspforten; adult/concession €8/4.50; ☺10am-6pm Tue-Sun; ⊕1, 7, 9 Heumarkt, ⊕5 Rathaus) occupies a postmodern cube designed by OM Ungers. Works are shown chronologically, with the oldest on the 1st floor. Stand-outs include

11 12

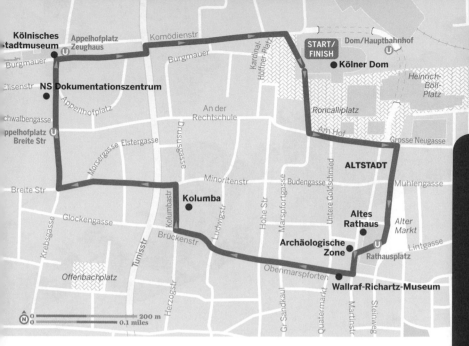

brilliant examples from the Cologne School, known for its distinctive use of colour.

The Walk » Go west past oodles of shops on Obenmarspforten for four streets, then turn north on Kolumbastrasse.

Kolumba

Art, history, architecture and spirituality form a harmonious tapestry in this spectacular collection of religious treasures of Cologne's archdiocese. Called **Kolumba** (www.kolumba.de; Kolumbastrasse 4; adult/child €5/free; ⊙noon-5pm Wed-Mon; 🚋5 Rathaus), the building encases the ruins of the late-Gothic church of St Kolumba and layers of foundations dating to Roman times. Don't miss the 12th-century carved ivory crucifix.

The Walk » Walk west on commercial Breite Strasse, then turn north on Dumont-Strasse.

NS Dokumentationszentrum

Cologne's Third Reich history is poignantly documented in the **NS Documentation Centre** (NS-DOK; www.museenkoeln. de/ns-dokumentationszentrum; Appellhofplatz 23-25; adult/concession €4.50/2; ⊙10am-6pm Tue-Fri, 11am-6pm Sat & Sun; 🚋3, 4, 5, 16, 18 Appellhofplatz). In the basement of this mundane-looking building was the local Gestapo prison where scores of people were interrogated, tortured and killed.

The Walk » It's just a short jaunt north again along low-key Dumont-Strasse.

Kölnisches Stadtmuseum

The **Kölnisches Stadtmuseum** (Cologne City Museum; www.koelnisches-stadtmuseum. de; Zeughausstrasse 1-3; adult/concession €5/3; ⊙10am-8pm Tue, to 5pm Wed-Sun; 🚋3, 4, 5, 16, 18 Appellhofplatz), in the former medieval armoury, explores Cologne history. There are exhibits on Carnival, *Kölsch* (the local beer), eau de cologne and other things that make the city unique. An amazing **model** re-creates the city of 1571; it's huge yet minutely detailed.

The Walk » Return to the Dom along Komödienstrasse, with the cathedral towers looming ever closer. Stop for a much-deserved refreshment at Café Reichard, facing the Dom.

Southern Germany

DREAMY CASTLES AND ROMANTIC ALPINE MEADOWS, GLASS ART AND GLASSY MOUNTAIN LAKES, DARK TOURISM AND ENIGMATIC FORESTS – southern Germany has the lot and tons more besides.

Variety is the watchword in Bavaria and Baden-Württemberg (the states that make up Germany's south); this chapter's routes offer a Zeppelin ride above Lake Constance, ascending Germany's highest mountain by train and passing through the Bavarian Forest, all in a matter of days.

But all the routes have something in common – the affluent south is infused with that feeling of *Gemütlichkeit,* a state of cosiness and good cheer you'll discover in every traditional tavern from Franconia to the Alps.

Würzburg Main staircase, Würzburg Residenz (p214)
IGOR PLOTNIKOV / SHUTTERSTOCK ©

189

Southern Germany

15 **Bergstrasse 2–4 Days**
A diverse route following an old Roman trade route.

Classic Trip
16 **German Castle Road 7 Days**
Castles, palaces and fortresses galore along this route from Mannheim to Bayreuth.

Classic Trip
17 **The Romantic Road 10 Days**
A ribbon of historical quaintness running through Bavaria's western reaches.

18 **Glass Route 7 Days**
A glass-themed drive through eastern Bavaria's under-visited and thickly forested border regions.

Classic Trip
19 **German Alpine Road 7 Days**
Take the high road through Germany's slice of Europe's top peaks.

20 **Lake Constance 7 Days**
A circular tri-state route around one of Europe's most attractive lakes.

Königssee

Take an ecofriendly electric-boat tour across the tranquil expanse of Germany's most picturesque lake. Trip 19

Würzburg Residenz

Ogle the world's largest fresco at Würzburg's magnificent Unesco-listed palace. Trip 17

Rothenburg ob der Tauber

Circle this town's medieval walls before celebrating Christmas in July with a tasty snowball! Trips 16 17

Neuschwanstein Castle

The world's most famous castle, striking a fairy-tale pose against Alpine forests, inspired Disney's citadel. Trip 17

Zugspitze

This is Germany's highest mountain, but you needn't worry about a tiring ascent – take the train! Trip 19

21 Fantastic Road 4–6 Days
Fascinating ring through Baden-Württemberg and a chunk of the Black Forest.

22 Schwarzwaldhochstrasse 2–4 Days
High-altitude motoring through the magnificent landscapes of the Black Forest.

191

Bergstrasse

15

As you drive Germany's beautiful Bergstrasse ('mountain road'), you'll realise it could just as easily be called Burgstrasse ('castle road') for the lofty castles lining this short but attraction-packed route.

TRIP HIGHLIGHTS

START
Darmstadt

2 **13 km**
Grube Messel
Archaeological discoveries here date back 49 million years

3

Lorsch Abbey

33 km
Burg Frankenstein
The castle that inspired author Mary Shelley

5 **91 km**
Heidelberg
Renowned for its red-sandstone castle

HockenheimRing

Wiesloch
FINISH

2–4 DAYS
125KM / 77 MILES

GREAT FOR...

BEST TIME TO GO
Any time of year works but you'll enjoy the best weather between April and October.

 ESSENTIAL PHOTO
Wiesloch's statue of Bertha Benz, the world's first road-tripper.

 BEST FOR DRIVERS
The HockenheimRing Formula One Grand Prix track.

15 Bergstrasse

This Roman trade route along the edge of the Odenwald mountain range might be just 125km, but the diversity you'll encounter is astonishing: *Jugendstil* (art nouveau) architecture, archaeological discoveries, the castle that inspired Mary Shelley's *Frankenstein*, a monumental medieval abbey, romantic Heidelberg, Wiesloch (where trailblazer Bertha Benz made motoring history), and Germany's most famous racetrack.

The Drive >> From Darmstadt's Schloss, head east on Alexanderstrasse, which becomes the L3094. Follow it for 10km through beautiful forest; Grube Messel is signposted 300m off on your left.

TRIP HIGHLIGHT

❷ Grube Messel

A Unesco World Heritage site, this one-time coal-and-shale-oil quarry 10km northeast of Darmstadt, known as **Grube Messel** (Messel Pit; ☑0615-971 7590; www.grube-messel. de; Rossdörfer Strasse 108, Messel; visitor centre adult/child €10/8, 1hr tour €7; ◷10am-5pm, tours by reservation), is an archaeological wonder, with superbly preserved animal and plant remains from the Eocene era (around 49 million years ago). Fossils of ancient horses found here illustrate the evolutionary path towards the modern beast.

A pretty half-timbered house 3km south of the visitor centre is a fossil-filled **museum** (☑0615-951 19; www.messelmuseum. de; Langgasse 2, Messel; ◷11am-5pm daily Apr-Oct, Sat & Sun Nov-Mar). Better yet, you can visit the pit itself with a German-speaking guide or pre-arrange an English-speaking tour (extra €20 per group).

Other intriguing finds from the site are displayed at the **Hessisches Landesmuseum** (☑06151-165 7000; www.hlmd. de; Friedensplatz 1; adult/child

❶ Darmstadt

Famed for its technical university and the creation of superheavy element Darmstadtium (Ds; atomic number: 110), Darmstadt is a designated *Wissenschaftsstadt* (City of Science). Part of the university is housed in Darmstadt's spectacular **Schloss**, along with a **museum** (☑06151-240 35; www.schlossmuseum-darm stadt.de; Marktplatz 15; adult/child €4/2.50; ◷10am-5pm Fri-Sun, tours every 90min).

The best place to see the city's renowned *Jugendstil* (Art Nouveau) architecture is **Mathildenhöhe** (☑06151-132 778; www.mathildenhoehe. eu; Olbrichweg 13; museum adult/child €5/3; ◷11am-6pm Tue-Sun Apr-Sep, to 5pm Oct-Mar), the former *Künstlerkolonie* (artists colony), established in 1899 by Grand Duke Ernst Ludwig. Surrounded by a fountain-filled hilltop park, the museum showcases *Jugendstil* furniture, tableware, textiles, ceramics and jewellery.

Or simply splash about at the exquisite 1909 indoor-outdoor *Jugendstil* pool-and-spa complex, **Jugendstilbad** (www.jugendstilbad.de; Mercksplatz 1; pools 2hr/4hr/all day €6.30/8.60/10.90, incl spa €9.80/12.60/15, €1 more at weekends; ◷10am-10pm).

✕ ⌂ p199

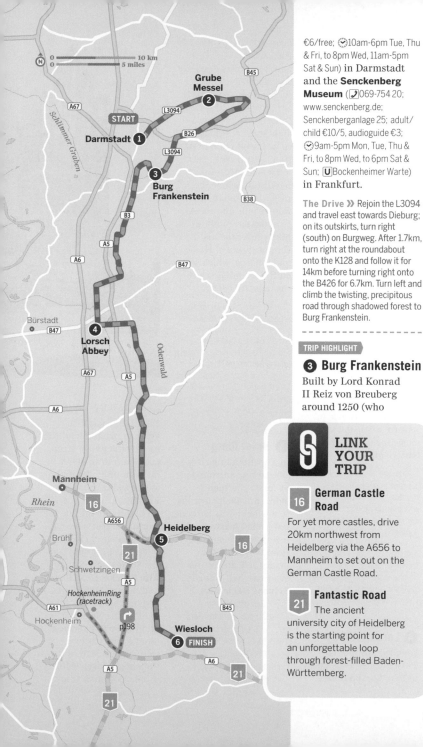

€6/free; ⊙10am-6pm Tue, Thu & Fri, to 8pm Wed, 11am-5pm Sat & Sun) in Darmstadt and the **Senckenberg Museum** (☏069-754 20; www.senckenberg.de; Senckenberganlage 25; adult/ child €10/5, audioguide €3; ⊙9am-5pm Mon, Tue, Thu & Fri, to 8pm Wed, to 6pm Sat & Sun; Ⓤ Bockenheimer Warte) in Frankfurt.

The Drive » Rejoin the L3094 and travel east towards Dieburg; on its outskirts, turn right (south) on Burgweg. After 1.7km, turn right at the roundabout onto the K128 and follow it for 14km before turning right onto the B426 for 6.7km. Turn left and climb the twisting, precipitous road through shadowed forest to Burg Frankenstein.

- - - - - - - - - - - - - - - - - - -

TRIP HIGHLIGHT

❸ Burg Frankenstein

Built by Lord Konrad II Reiz von Breuberg around 1250 (who

⛓ LINK YOUR TRIP

16 German Castle Road

For yet more castles, drive 20km northwest from Heidelberg via the A656 to Mannheim to set out on the German Castle Road.

21 Fantastic Road

The ancient university city of Heidelberg is the starting point for an unforgettable loop through forest-filled Baden-Württemberg.

thereafter added *'von und zu Frankenstein'* to his name), hulking, partly ruined hilltop castle **Burg Frankenstein** ([📞]06151-501 501; www. frankenstein-restaurant. de; Ralphweg, Mühltal; entry by donation; [🕐]9am-sunset except during events) was visited by Mary Shelley on her German travels in 1814, inspiring the title of her Gothic novel and its protagonist, Dr Franken-stein. Tours of the castle are in German; you're free to walk around the castle and grounds, or to just stop in for a drink on its restaurant's panor-amic terrace.

If you time it right, you can also catch atmospheric events here, including one of Europe's largest – and spooki-est – Halloween parties, as well as medieval banquets, costumed ad-venture castle days, live music including jazz, and theatre nights.

The Drive » Twist back downhill and take the B426 west for 1.4km before turning left (south) onto the B3. After Zwingenberg you'll see Schloss Auerbach looming on your left above the town of Auerbach. Turn west on the B47 for 2.7km then right onto Bensheimer Strasse in the charming village of Lorsch and follow the signs to Lorsch Abbey (29km all-up).

---

④ Lorsch Abbey

Founded around AD 760 and Unesco-listed in 1991, **Lorsch Abbey**

(Kloster Lorsch; [📞]06251-869 200; www.kloster-lorsch.de; Nibelungenstrasse 35, Lorsch; adult/child €6/4; [🕐]10am-5pm Tue-Sun, English tours hourly 11am-4pm Tue-Sun Mar-Oct, Sat & Sun Nov-Feb) was a significant religious site in its Carolingian heyday (8th to 10th centuries). Preserved medieval buildings include the rare, Carolingian-era Königshalle and the Al-tenmünster; museum ex-hibits cover the history of the abbey, life in Hesse, and tobacco, which was cultivated in Lorsch in the late 17th century.

The Drive » Return to the B3 and take it south for 32km to Heidelberg. En route, look out for castles, including Starkenburg (housing a hostel) on your left above Heppenheim village, and Wachenburg (home to a restaurant) on your left above the town of Weinheim.

TRIP HIGHLIGHT

⑤ Heidelberg

In a spellbinding river-side setting surrounded by forest, Germany's oldest university town is renowned for its baroque, red-roofed **Altstadt** (old town), which emerged from WWII almost unscathed, and for its evocative half-ruined **Schloss Heidelberg**

([📞]06221-658 880; www. schloss-heidelberg.de; Schloss-hof 1; adult/child incl Bergbahn €8/4, tours €5/2.50, audio-guide €5; [🕐]grounds 24hr, castle 8am-6pm, English tours hourly 11.15am-4.15pm Mon-

Fri, from 10.15am Sat & Sun Apr-Oct, fewer tours Nov-Mar). You can reach the hilltop castle either via a steep, cobbled trail in about 10 minutes or by Bergbahn (cogwheel train) from Kornmarkt station. Cas-tle highlights include the world's largest wine cask and fabulous views.

For the best views *of* the Schloss, cross the **Alte Brücke**, Heidelberg's 200m-long, 1786-built 'old bridge', to the right bank of the Neckar River and the **Schlangenweg** (Snake Path), whose switchbacks lead to the **Philosophenweg** (Phil-osophers' Walk). Don't

Darmstadt Wedding Tower (left) and the Russian Orthodox church (right) at Mathildenhöhe (p194)

drive up here, as the road is narrow and there's nowhere to turn around at the top.

Heidelberg's charms draw 11.8 million visitors a year. They follow in the footsteps of the late 18th- and early 19th-century Romantics, most notably the poet Goethe. Heidelberg also inspired Britain's William Turner to paint some of his greatest landscapes. In 1878, Mark Twain began his European travels in Heidelberg, recounting his observations in *A Tramp Abroad* (1880). Heidelberg's rich literary history, along with its thriving contemporary scene, saw it named a Unesco City of Literature in 2014.

The longer you spend here, the more heart-stopping panoramas and hidden treasures you'll discover.

✕ 🛏 p199

The Drive » It's just 14km south from Heidelberg along the B3 to Wiesloch, at the foot of the Kraichgau hills.

- - - - - - - - - - - - - - - -

❻ Wiesloch

Cute little Wiesloch was pivotal in the evolution of road trips: this is where Bertha Benz

– business partner and wife of automobile inventor Karl Benz – refuelled on the first-ever long-distance drive in 1888. Bertha stopped at Wiesloch's pharmacy, the **Stadt-Apotheke** (☎06222-588120; www. stadtapotheke-wiesloch.de; Hauptstrasse 96; ⏲8.30am-1pm & 2-6.30pm Mon-Fri, 9am-2pm Sat), which provided her with Ligroin (petroleum ether), making it the world's first filling station. Still a pharmacy today, its small **history museum** only opens a handful of days a year. Outside on the cobbled square there's

DETOUR: HOCKENHEIMRING

Start: ⑤ Heidelberg

One detour no dedicated road-tripper will want to miss is to the hallowed **HockenheimRing** (☎06205-950 222; www.hockenheimring.de; Am Motodrom, Hockenheim; Insider Tour adult/child €12/6.50; ⊙Insider Tour 11am except race days). Signposted 22km southwest of Heidelberg just east of the A6, it has three circuits and stands that accommodate up to 120,000 fans, and hosts some of Germany's most famous car races, including the Formula One German Grand Prix (in even-numbered years).

Start by taking a look behind the scenes on an **Insider Tour**, available in English and German. Tickets are sold at the **Motor Sport Museum** (☎06205-950 222; www.hockenheimring.de; Am Motodrom, Hockenheim; adult/child €6/3; ⊙10am-5pm Apr-Oct, 10am-5pm Sun Nov-Mar, longer hours on race days).

While you're here, make time to check out the museum's fantastic collection of historic motorcycles, some a century old, and its ensemble of historic race cars. Upstairs, look out for the reconstruction of the world's first motorcycle, built from wood by Maybach and Daimler in 1885.

If roaring along on a speed-limit-less autobahn doesn't get your adrenaline pumping any more, you can take to the Hockenheim track yourself when it isn't being used for a race:

Renntaxi (per person €249) Three laps on the Grand Prix course with a professional driver in a superfast racing car, such as a Porsche GT3, a Mercedes SLK 350 or an Audi R8 V10.

Race'n'Roll (€469) Drive a race car yourself.

Touristenfahrten (€18 per 15min) Drive your own car around the track.

a bronze-and-steel **statue** of Bertha driving her three-wheeled contraption.

Bertha set out with her two teenage sons, without her husband's knowledge, to highlight the possibilities of the machine no one had wanted to buy. Repairs en route included clearing a clogged fuel line with her hat pin, and fixing a broken ignition with her garter. Her circuit – from Mannheim to Pforzheim and back, which she took at an average speed of 16km/h – is now the 194km **Bertha Benz Memorial Route** (www.bertha-benz.de).

Eating & Sleeping

Darmstadt ❶

✕ Elisabeth   Cafe €

(☎06151-278 7858; www.suppkult.de;
Schulstrasse 14; dishes €5-7; ⏱11am-4pm
Mon-Sat; ✍) Hidden down a passageway in a
picnic-table-filled courtyard, this wonderful
spot specialises in homemade soups (which
change daily): pork meatballs and split green
peas; curried apple and potato; lentil, carrot
and leek; and roast tomato with sheep's cheese,
all served with home-baked sourdough or rye
bread. Salads are also available as meals. Finish
off with fabulous cakes.

⛏ Hotel Jagdschloss
Kranichstein   Historic Hotel €€

(☎06151-130 670; www.hotel-jagdschloss
-kranichstein.de; Kranichstein Strasse 261; r from
€94; ℗ @ 🛜) Set on 4.2 hectares of forest
and parkland 5km northeast of Darmstadt, this
1580-built hunting lodge is now a magnificent
hotel, with contemporary countrified rooms
throughout the estate's buildings. Breakfast
starts from €17; epicurean options include a
game-specialist restaurant, bar-bistro, and
Bierstube in the armory, opening to a beer
garden, plus gourmet hampers for summer
picnicking in the grounds.

Heidelberg ❺

✕ 'S' Kastanie   European €€€

(☎06221-728 0343; www.restaurant-s-kastanie.
de; Elisabethenweg 1; 3-/4-/5-course dinner
menus €31/47/58, mains €16-34; ⏱6-11pm
Wed-Fri, from 5pm Sat, 11.30am-9pm Sun; ✍)
A panoramic terrace provides sweeping views
of the river at this gorgeous 1904-built former
hunting lodge, with stained glass and timber

panelling, set in the forest near the castle. Chef
Sven Schönig's stunning creations include a
sweet potato and goats' cheese tower with
papaya, and goose-stuffed ravioli.

✕ Schnitzelbank   German €€

(☎06221-211 89; www.schnitzelbank-heidelberg.
de; Bauamtsgasse 7; mains €15-22; ⏱5pm-1am
Mon-Fri, from 11.30am Sat & Sun) Small and
often jam-packed, this cosy wine tavern has
you sampling the local tipples (all wines are
regional) and cuisine while crouched on wooden
workbenches from the time when this was still
a cooperage. It's these benches that give the
place its name, incidentally, not the veal and
pork schnitzel on the menu. Other specialities
include *Schäufele* (stuffed pig's stomach).

⛏ Hotel Villa
Marstall   Historic Hotel €€

(☎06221-655 570; www.villamarstall.de;
Lauerstrasse 1; s/d from €115/135; ⏱reception
7am-10pm Mon-Sat, 8am-6pm Sun; ❄🛜) A
19th-century neoclassical mansion directly
overlooking the Neckar River, Villa Marstall
is a jewel with cherrywood floors, solid-
timber furniture and amenities including a
lift. Exquisite rooms are decorated in whites,
creams and bronzes, and come with in-room
fridges (perfect for chilling a bottle of regional
wine). A sumptuous breakfast buffet (€10) is
served in the red-sandstone vaulted cellar.

⛏ Kulturbrauerei
Hotel   Hotel €€

(☎06221-502 980; www.heidelberger
-kulturbrauerei.de; Leyergasse 6; r from €99; 🛜)
This stylish Altstadt hotel above the eponymous
microbrewery (⏱7am-11pm) has romantic
cream-coloured rooms with polished parquet
floors, classical furniture and large windows.
Breakfast is €12 for guests.

Classic Trip

German Castle Road

16

On this trip you'll follow a ribbon of fairy-tale castles that winds its way across Germany's south, along with the wonderful historic towns that host them.

TRIP HIGHLIGHTS

29 km

Heidelberg
Romantic castle ruins lording over Heidelberg's old town

319 km

Nuremberg
Bavaria's second city is packed with history

FINISH
Bayreuth

Mannheim **2**
START

5

6

Schwäbisch Hall

Rothenburg ob der Tauber
A romantically walled, perfectly preserved medieval town

208 km

7 DAYS
600KM / 373 MILES

GREAT FOR...

BEST TIME TO GO
To get the best out of this trip, travel between Easter and October.

 ESSENTIAL PHOTO

The view from Nuremberg's Sinwell Tower.

 BEST FOR HISTORY

Nuremberg is a treasure trove of European history.

Classic Trip

16 German Castle Road

This romantic trip will take you castle-hopping across 600km of southern Germany and through 1000 years of the country's history. From Germany's biggest baroque pile in Mannheim to Bayreuth's Altes Schloss, it's a castle a day on this route. When palace fatigue sets in, there's nothing easier than escaping to a contemporary art gallery, fascinating museum, or traditional tavern to sample the local sausages and unsurpassed beer.

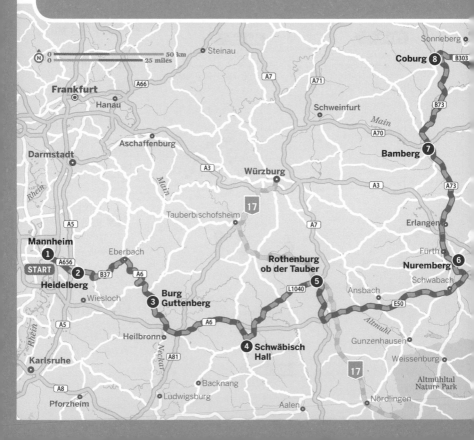

❶ Mannheim

The Castle Road kicks off in style at the gates of **Barockschloss Mannheim** (☎06221-658 880; www.schloss-mannheim.de; cnr Bismarckstrasse & Breite Strasse; adult/child incl audioguide €7/3.50, incl guided tour €10/5; ⏰10am-5pm Tue-Sun). The city's most famous sight is Germany's largest baroque palace. Now occupied by the city's university, the 450m-long structure was built over the course of 40 years in the mid-1700s but was almost completely destroyed during WWII. Off the main courtyard are the **Schloss Museum**, where you can see the impressively rococo Kabinettsbibliothek, saved from wartime destruction (having been stored offsite), and several baroque halls – each a feast of stucco, marble, porcelain and chandeliers – rebuilt after the war.

The **Schlosskirche** (Bismarckstrasse 14; ⏰10am-5pm) was constructed between 1720 and 1731, and rebuilt post-WWII. Mozart performed here in 1777. It belongs to the Alt-Katholiken (Old Catholics), a movement that split with Rome over papal infallibility in the 1870s and is now part of the Anglican Communion.

🗡️ 🛏️ p210

The Drive » To reach Heidelberg from Mannheim, take the B36 then the A656 heading southeast. Traffic can be heavy on these roads. Heidelberg is just 19km from Mannheim, meaning it can also be tackled as a day trip by public transport; Mannheim's S-Bahn and regional trains make the run every few minutes.

TRIP HIGHLIGHT

❷ Heidelberg

Towering over the **Altstadt** (old town), the ruins of Renaissance **Schloss Heidelberg** (☎06221-658 880; www.schloss-heidelberg.de; Schlosshof 1; adult/child incl Bergbahn €8/4, tours €5/2.50, audioguide €5; ⏰grounds 24hr, castle 8am-6pm, English tours hourly 11.15am-4.15pm Mon-Fri, from 10.15am Sat & Sun Apr-Oct, fewer tours Nov-Mar) cut a romantic figure, especially across the Neckar River when illuminated at night. It's a steep climb, but once you arrive up top, you'll be struck by the far-reaching views over the Neckar and the Altstadt rooftops. The only way to see the interior is by tour, which can be safely skipped. After 6pm you can stroll the grounds for free.

Another sight in town that tourists gravitate to is the **Marktplatz**, the focal point of Altstadt street life. The trickling **Hercules fountain** in the middle – that's him up

LINK YOUR TRIP

17 **The Romantic Road** The Castle Road and the Romantic Road meet in Rothenburg ob der Tauber.

18 **Glass Route** Bayreuth is 60km northwest of Weiden, the northern end of the Glass Route.

on top of the pillar – is where petty criminals were chained and left to face the mob in the Middle Ages.

 p199

The Drive » To reach the next stop at Burg Guttenberg, the quickest route is to take the A6 autobahn, a journey of 62km which you should cover in a snappy 45 minutes. However, a much more picturesque but considerably slower way to go is to follow country roads along the Neckar Valley where several dramatic castle ruins wait to be discovered.

❸ Burg Guttenberg

Rising high above the Neckar Valley, lonely **Burg Guttenberg** (www. burg-guttenberg.de; Burgstrasse, Hassmersheim; adult/ concession €5/4; ⊙10am-6pm Apr-Oct) is one of the most dramatic castles on this part of the route and a fine example of an intact 14th-century castle. In addition to the gobsmacking views of the surrounding vineyards and forests, the award-winning exhibition inside acquaints visitors with the life of medieval knights. The castle has a tavern with great views.

The Drive » From Burg Guttenberg continue south along the attractive Neckar Valley until you reach the town of Neckarsulm. From there, take the A6 autobahn as far as exit 43 for Schwäbisch Hall. The whole journey is 72km and should take little more than an hour.

----

❹ Schwäbisch Hall

Out on its rural lonesome near the Bavarian border, Schwäbisch Hall is an unsung gem. It's a medieval time capsule of higgledy-piggledy lanes, soaring half-timbered houses built high on the riches of salt, and covered bridges that criss-cross the Kocher River – story book stuff.

Buzzy cafes and first-rate museums add to the appeal of this town, known for its rare black-spotted pigs, which can be seen at the **Hohenloher Freilandmuseum** (☎0791-971 010; www.wackershofen. de; Wackershofen; adult/ concession €8/6; ⊙9am-6pm May-Sep, 10am-5pm Tue-Sun rest of year), an open-air farming museum that will be a sure-fire hit with the kids. It's 6km northwest of Schwäbisch Hall and served by bus 7. However, Schwäbisch Hall's top attraction is the **Kunsthalle Würth** (www.kunst.wuerth.com; Lange Strasse 35; ⊙10am-6pm daily, guided tours 11.30am & 2pm Sun), a contemporary gallery housed in a striking limestone building that preserves part of a century-old brewery. Stellar temporary exhibitions have recently spotlighted Viennese art and Henri Matisse. Guided tours are in German only but audioguides in English are available.

 p210

The Drive » The best way to reach the next halt – at Rothenburg ob der Tauber, 55km away to the northeast – is to take the L2218 country road back to the A6 motorway. After a short stretch of superfast autobahn driving, take exit 45 and the L1040 that will take you all the way to your destination. You are now in Bavaria.

TRIP HIGHLIGHT

❺ Rothenburg ob der Tauber

A medieval gem, Rothenburg ob der Tauber is also a top stop along the Romantic Road (Trip 17). With its web of cobbled lanes, crooked medieval houses and towered walls, the town is a fairy tale in bricks and plaster.

A striking feature here is the **Stadtmauer** (Town Walls), which forms a 2.5km uninterrupted ring around the historical core.

At the **Käthe Wohlfahrt Weihnachtsdorf** (www.wohlfahrt.com; Herrngasse 1; ⊙10am-6.30pm Mon-Fri, to 7pm Sat, from 10am-6pm Sun) you can buy a mind-boggling assortment of high-quality Yuletide decorations, so you can celebrate Christmas every day of the year if you want. Next door is the **Deutsches Weihnachtsmuseum**

(Christmas Museum; ☏09861-409 365; www.weihnachts museum.de; Herrngasse 1; adult/child/family €4/2.50/7; ⊙10am-5pm Easter-Christmas, shorter hours Jan-Easter) – also an odd experience in July.

Rothenburg's most popular museum is the **Mittelalterliches Kriminalmuseum** (Medieval Crime & Punishment Museum; www.kriminalmuseum.eu; Burggasse 3; adult/concession €7/4; ⊙10am-6pm Apr-Oct, 1-4pm Nov-Mar), **where you can view medieval implements of torture and punishment.**

✖ ⮕ p224

The Drive » There are several ways of getting to your next stop, the city of Nuremberg. The simplest is to head south to the autobahn, which will see you get through the 111km in around 1½ hours. Slower routes go via Ansbach, which also has a magnificent Residenz (palace).

- - - - - - - - - - - - - - - -

TRIP HIGHLIGHT

❻ Nuremberg

Bavaria's second city is a lively, energetic and moodily historic place. For centuries, it was the undeclared capital of the Holy Roman Empire and

---

NUREMBERG FOR KIDS

No city in Germany's south has more for kids to see and do than Nuremberg. In fact keeping the little 'uns entertained in the Franconian capital is child's play.

Museums

Children & Young People's Museum (☏0911-600 040; www.kindermuseum-nuernberg. de; Michael-Ende-Strasse 17; adult/family €7.50/19.50; ⊙2-5.30pm Sat, 10am-5.30pm Sun Sep-Jun) Educational exhibitions and lots of hands-on fun – just a pity it's not open more often.

School Museum (☏0911-530 2574; Äussere Sulzbacher Strasse 62; adult/child €6/1.50; ⊙9am-5pm Tue-Fri, 10am-6pm Sat & Sun) Re-created classroom plus school-related exhibits from the 17th century to the Third Reich.

Deutsche Bahn Museum (☏0800-3268 7386; www.dbmuseum.de; Lessingstrasse 6; adult/ child €6/3; ⊙9am-5pm Tue-Fri, 10am-6pm Sat & Sun) Feeds the kids' obsession for choo-choo trains.

Play

Playground of the Senses (www.erfahrungsfeld.nuernberg.de; Wöhrder Wiese; adult/child €8.50/7; ⊙9am-6pm Mon-Fri, 1-6pm Sat, 10am-6pm Sun May–mid-Sep) Some 80 hands-on 'stations' designed to educate children in the laws of nature, physics and the human body. Take the U2 or U3 to Wöhrder Wiese.

Toys

Playmobil (☏0911-9666 1700; www.playmobil-funpark.de; Brandstätterstrasse 2-10; €12.90; ⊙10am-6pm mid-Feb–Mar, 9am-6pm Apr, 9am-7pm May–mid-Sep) This theme park has life-size versions of the popular toys. It's located 9km west of the city centre in Zirndorf; take the S4 to Anwanden, then change to bus 151. Free admission if it's your birthday.

Käthe Wohlfahrt Christmas shop (www.wohlfahrt.com; Königstrasse 8; ⊙10am-7pm Mon-Sat) The Nuremberg branch of this year-round Christmas shop.

Spielzeugmuseum (Toy Museum; Karlstrasse 13-15; adult/child €6/1.50; ⊙10am-5pm Tue-Fri, to 6pm Sat & Sun) Some 1400 sq metres of Matchbox, Barbie, Playmobil and Lego, plus a great play area.

Classic Trip

WHY THIS IS A CLASSIC TRIP
MARC DI DUCA, WRITER

Think of Central Europe and castles – medieval, Renaissance and in all manner of 'neo' styles – probably come to mind. This route satisfies the longing many history fans have to take a peek at the way dukes, royals, prince-bishops and assorted other gentry once lived, a world away from the crooked medieval streets of the towns that surround them.

Above: Historic street, Rothenburg ob der Tauber (p216)
Right: Bamberger Reiter statue (p208), Bamberg
Left: Playmobil (p205), Nuremberg

ELIZABETH BEARD / GETTY IMAGES ©

the preferred residence of most German kings, who kept their crown jewels at the **Kaiserburg** (Imperial Castle; ☎0911-244 6590; www.kaiserburg-nuernberg.de; Auf der Burg; adult/child incl Sinwell Tower €7/free, Palas & Museum €5.50/free; ☉9am-6pm Apr-Sep, 10am-4pm Oct-Mar). This enormous castle complex above the Altstadt poignantly reflects Nuremberg's medieval might. The main attraction is a tour of the newly renovated residential wing to see the lavish Knights' and Imperial Hall, a Romanesque double chapel, and an exhibit on the Holy Roman Empire. This segues to the Kaiserburg Museum, which focuses on the castle's military and building history. Elsewhere, enjoy panoramic views from the Sinwell Tower or peer 48m down into the Deep Well.

Nuremberg's other stellar sight is the **Germanisches Nationalmuseum** (German National Museum; ☎0911-133 10; www.gnm.de; Kartäusergasse 1; adult/child €8/5; ☉10am-6pm Tue & Thu-Sun, to 9pm Wed), the German-speaking world's biggest and most important museum of Teutonic culture.

✕ ⮑ p210

The Drive » From busy Nuremberg head north along the A73 via Forchheim, a trip of about 61km. To the east of the road extends the so-called Fränkische Schweiz (Franconian

Classic Trip

Switzerland), a soothing area of wooded hills, lazy rivers and village breweries producing Franconia's countless types of tasty *Landbier* (regional beer).

- - - - - - - - - - - - - - - - -

❼ Bamberg

A disarmingly beautiful architectural masterpiece with an almost complete absence of modern eyesores, Bamberg's entire **Altstadt** is a Unesco World Heritage site and one of Bavaria's unmissables. Generally regarded as one of Germany's most attractive settlements, the town is bisected by rivers and canals and was built on seven hills, earning it the inevitable nickname of 'Franconian Rome'. Make your way across its bridges and along the narrow medieval streets to the gaggle of hilltop sights, beginning with the **Neue Residenz** (New Residence; 📞0951-519 390; Domplatz 8; adult/child €4.50/free; 🕐9am-6pm Apr-Sep,

10am-4pm Oct-Mar). This splendid episcopal palace gives you an eyeful of the lavish lifestyle of Bamberg's prince-bishops who, between 1703 and 1802, occupied its 40-odd rooms. Nearby rises the **Bamberger Dom** (www. erzbistum-bamberg.de; Dom-platz; 🕐9.30am-6pm Apr-Oct, to 5pm Nov-Mar), a cathedral packed with artistic treasures, most famously the life-size equestrian statue of the **Bamberger Reiter** (Bamberg Horseman), whose true identity remains a mystery.

The Drive ›› The B73 is your road today as you head 53km north to Coburg. Along the way you pass through Lichtenfels, a small town renowned for its basket-weaving traditions and its commanding baroque basilica visible for miles around.

- - - - - - - - - - - - - - - - -

❽ Coburg

Coburg is most famous for its associations with the British royal family – Prince Albert of Saxe-Coburg-Gotha famously married his cousin Queen Victoria in 1840. Albert spent his childhood at **Schloss**

Ehrenburg (www.schloesser -coburg.de; Schlossplatz; adult/child €4.50/free; 🕐tours at least hourly 9am-6pm Tue-Sun Apr-Sep, 10am-4pm Tue-Sun Oct-Mar), a lavish palace and erstwhile residence of the Coburg dukes. Queen Victoria stayed here in a room with Germany's first flushing toilet (1860). The splendid **Riesensaal** (Hall of Giants) has a baroque ceiling supported by 28 statues of Atlas. Prince Albert's statue can be found on Coburg's **Marktplatz**.

However, Coburg's blockbuster attraction is **Veste Coburg** (www. kunstsammlungen-coburg. de; adult/concession €8/6; 🕐9.30am-5pm daily Apr-Oct, 1-4pm Tue-Sun Nov-Mar), a storybook medieval fortress towering over the old centre. With its triple ring of fortified walls, it's one of the most impressive fortresses in Germany. It houses the vast collection of the **Kunstsammlungen**, with works by star painters such as Rembrandt, Dürer and Cranach the Elder. The elaborate **Jagdintarsien-Zimmer** (Hunting Marquetry Room) is a superlative example of carved woodwork.

Also famous in Coburg are its sausages. Around 30cm long, they are grilled over the embers of pine cones, giving them a sappy, smoky flavour. The tasty result is then served

TOP TIP: NÜRNBERG CARD

Costing just €28, the Nürnberg Card allows admission to all the city's museums (there are 40 to choose from) and access to the excellent public transport system. It's available from tourist offices in Nuremberg or via www.tourismus.nuernberg.de.

CONTINUING INTO THE CZECH REPUBLIC

In 1994 the Castle Road was extended into the Czech Republic, a country as rich in castle architecture as southern Germany. The route crosses the border between Bavaria and the Czech Republic at Cheb. Be aware that cars hired in Germany cannot normally be taken into the Czech Republic without additional insurance.

Castle highlights of the Czech section of the route include idyllic **Loket**, with its perfectly preserved medieval town; **Bečov nad Teplou**, with its famous reliquary; **Křivoklát Castle**, set dramatically against the forests of Central Bohemia; 14th-century **Karlštejn Castle**, built to house the imperial crown jewels of the Holy Roman Empire; and of course **Prague Castle**, the daddy of all Central European royal residences, where a millennium of history is presented in fascinating exhibitions.

in a tiny bread bun with a dollop of mustard. The best places to try them are the unpresuming kiosks on Marktplatz.

🛏 p211

The Drive » The most attractive way to cover the 74km between Coburg and Bayreuth is to take the B303 and then the B85 via Kulmbach, where the hilltop Plassenburg is worth stopping to explore.

- - - - - - - - - - - - - - - - -

❾ Bayreuth

Bayreuth is best known for its Wagner connections, but its glory days began in 1735 when Wilhelmine, sister of King Frederick the Great of Prussia, was forced to marry stuffy Margrave Friedrich. Bored with the local scene, the cultured Anglo-oriented Wilhelmine invited the finest artists, poets, composers and architects in Europe to court. The period bequeathed some eye-catching buildings, still on display for all to see. The **Altes Schloss** (adult/child €4.50/free; ⏰9am-6pm Apr-Sep) was Wilhelmine's summer residence. Visits to the palace are by guided tour only and take in the **Chinese Mirror Room** where Countess Wilhelmine penned her memoirs. The **Neues**

Schloss (📞0921-759 690; Ludwigstrasse 21; adult/child €5.50/free; ⏰9am-6pm Apr-Sep, 10am-4pm Oct-Mar) lies a short distance south of the main shopping street, **Maxmilianstrasse**. A riot of rococo style, the Margrave's residence post-1753 features a vast collection of 18th-century Bayreuth porcelain. The **Spiegelscherbenkabinett** (Broken Mirror Cabinet), which is lined with irregular shards of broken mirror, is supposedly Margravine Wilhelmine's response to the vanity of her era.

✕ 🛏 p211

Classic Trip

Eating & Sleeping

Mannheim ❶

✕ Café Prag   Cafe €

(E4, 17; dishes €2-8; ⏰10am-6pm Mon-Sat, from 1pm Sun) A former tailor's shop and cigar store, built in 1902, is now an arty cafe with *Jugendstil* (Art Nouveau) woodwork, cranberry-red walls and a prewar Central European feel. Smooth jazz on the stereo makes a perfect backdrop for enjoying an espresso with a croissant or rhubarb cake, or focaccia with toppings like pastrami and horseradish or avocado and alfalfa. Cash only.

🛏 Maritim Hotel   Luxury Hotel €€

(☎0621-158 80; www.maritim.de; Friedrichsplatz 2; s/d from €130/145; P ✳ @ 🛜 🏊) Built in 1901 in the sumptuous style of the Renaissance, this grand hotel overlooks Friedrichsplatz. Its 173 rooms are more austere than the exterior would suggest, but they're spacious, and many have balconies or terraces. Amenities include a swimming pool, sauna and steam bath, two upmarket restaurants and a piano bar with music most nights.

Schwäbisch Hall ❹

✕ Rebers Pflug   International €€€

(☎0791-931 230; www.rebers-pflug.de; Weckriedener Strasse 2; mains €19-44, 3- to 7-course menu €62-120; ⏰6-9pm Mon-Sat, noon-1pm Sat; 🅿) Hans-Harald Reber presides over the stove at this 19th-century country house, one of Schwäbisch Hall's Michelin-starred haunts. He puts an imaginative spin on seasonal, regional numbers such as local venison with chanterelles and parsley-root *Spätzle* (egg noodles), and suckling pig cooked two ways with plum jus and sweet-potato cream. Vegetarians are also well catered for.

🛏 Hotel Scholl   Hotel €€

(☎0791-975 50; www.hotel-scholl.de; Klosterstrasse 2-4; d €78-160; 🛜) A charming pick behind Am Markt, this family-run hotel has rustic-chic rooms with parquet floors and granite or marble bathrooms. Most striking of all is the attic penthouse with its beams, free-standing shower and far-reaching views over town. Breakfast is a fine spread of cold cuts, fruit and cereals.

Nuremberg ❻

✕ Albrecht Dürer Stube   Franconian €€

(☎0911-227 209; www.albrecht-duerer-stube. de; cnr Albrecht-Dürer-Strasse & Agnesgasse; mains €7-16; ⏰5.30pm-midnight Mon-Sat, plus 11.30am-2.30pm Fri & Sun) This unpretentious and intimate restaurant has a Dürer-inspired dining room, prettily laid tables, a ceramic stove keeping things toasty and a menu of Nuremberg sausages, steaks, sea fish, seasonal specials, Franconian wine and *Landbier*. There aren't many tables so booking ahead at weekends is recommended.

✕ Bratwursthäusle   Franconian €€

(www.die-nuernberger-bratwurst.de; Rathausplatz 1; meals €8-16; ⏰11am-10pm) Seared over a flaming beech-wood grill, the little links sold at this rustic inn next to the Sebalduskirche arguably set the standard across the land. You can dine in the timbered restaurant or on the terrace with views of the Hauptmarkt. Service can be flustered at busy times and it's cash only when the bill comes.

🛏 Agneshof   Hotel €€

(☎0911-214 440; www.agneshof-nuernberg. de; Agnesgasse 10; s/d from €80/100; P 🛜) Tranquilly located in the antiques quarter near the Sebalduskirche, the Agneshof's public areas have a sophisticated, artsy touch. The 74 box-ticking rooms have whitewashed walls and standard hotel furniture; some at the top have views of the Kaiserburg. There's a state-of-the-art wellness centre, and a pretty summer courtyard garden strewn with deckchairs.

🛏 Hotel Deutscher Kaiser
Hotel €€

(📞0911-242 660; www.deutscher-kaiser-hotel.de; Königstrasse 55; s/d from €90/110; 🛜) Aristocratic in its design and service, this centrally located treat of a historic hotel has been in the same family since the turn of the 20th century. Climb the castle-like granite stairs to find rooms of understated simplicity, flaunting oversize beds, Italian porcelain, silk lampshades and real period furniture (*Biedermeier* and *Jugendstil*).

Coburg ⑧

🛏 Hotelpension Bärenturm
Guesthouse €€

(📞09561-318 401; www.baerenturm-hotelpension.de; Untere Anlage 2; s/d from €75/90; P🛜) For those who prefer their complimentary pillow pack of gummy bears served with a touch of history, Coburg's most characterful digs started life as a defensive tower that was expanded in the early 19th century to house Prince Albert's private tutor.

Each of the 15 rooms is a gem boasting squeaky parquet floors, antique-style furniture and regally high ceilings.

Bayreuth ⑨

✕ Oskar
Franconian, Bavarian €€

(📞0921-5160553; www.oskar-bayreuth.de; Maximilianstrasse 33; mains €6-16; ⊘8am-1am Mon-Sat, from 9am Sun; 🛜) At the heart of the pedestrianised shopping boulevard, this multitasking, open-all-hours bar-cafe-restaurant is Bayreuth's busiest eatery. It's good for a busting Bavarian breakfast, a light lunch in the covered garden cafe, a full-on dinner feast in the dark-wood restaurant, or a *Landbier* and a couple of tasty Bayreuth bratwursts anytime you feel.

🛏 Hotel Goldener Anker
Hotel €€€

(📞0921-787 7740; www.anker-bayreuth.de; Opernstrasse 6; s €100-140, d €170-235; P⊖🛜) Bayreuth's top address since 1753 stands just a few metres from the opera house and oozes refined elegance, with many of the rooms decorated in traditional style with heavy curtains, dark woods and antique touches. There's a swanky restaurant at ground level, the service is impeccable and there is fresh fruit waiting for you on arrival.

The Romantic Road

17

On this trip you'll experience story book Germany – medieval walled towns, gabled townhouses, cobbled squares and crooked streets, all preserved as if time has come to a standstill.

TRIP HIGHLIGHTS

0 km

Würzburg
Bavaria's finest baroque palaces and delicate wines

1 START

4

99 km

Rothenburg ob der Tauber
Wander the streets of this medieval marvel

5

● Nördlingen

149 km

Dinkelsbühl
The Romantic Road's quaintest town

Augsburg ●

350 km

Neuschwanstein & Hohenschwangau Castles
Two of Germany's top castles rise amid Alpine wonder

● Schongau

14 FINISH

---

10 DAYS
350KM / 217 MILES

GREAT FOR...

BEST TIME TO GO
Any time of year.

 ESSENTIAL PHOTO

The half-timbered buildings of Rothenburg ob der Tauber's Plönlein.

✓ BEST TWO DAYS

The stretch between stops 4 and 6 takes in the most romantic towns of the Romantic Road.

Classic Trip

17 The Romantic Road

From the vineyards of Würzburg to the foot of the Alps, the Romantic Road (Romantische Strasse) is by far the most popular of Germany's touring routes. This well-trodden trail cuts through a cultural and historical cross-section of southern Germany, coming to a climax at the gates of King Ludwig II's crazy castles. The route links some of Germany's most picturesque towns, many appearing untouched since medieval times.

TRIP HIGHLIGHT

❶ Würzburg

This scenic town in Bavaria's northeast corner straddles the Main River and is renowned for its art, architecture and delicate wines. A large student population keeps things lively and hip nightlife pulsates through its cobbled streets.

Top billing goes to the **Würzburg Residenz** (www.residenz-wuerzburg. de; Balthasar-Neumann-Promenade; adult/child €7.50/ free; ⏰9am-6pm Apr-Oct, 10am-4.30pm Nov-Mar, 45min English tours 11am & 3pm, plus 1.30pm & 4.30pm Apr-Oct), a vast Unesco-listed palace built by 18th-century architect Balthasar Neumann as the home of the local prince-bishops. It's one of Germany's most important and beautiful baroque palaces. The wonderful zigzagging Treppenhaus (Staircase) is capped by the world's largest fresco, a masterpiece by Giovanni Battista Tiepolo depicting allegories of the four then-known continents

(Europe, Africa, America and Asia). The **Dom St Kilian** (www.dom-wuerzburg. de; Domstrasse 40; ⏱8am-7pm Mon-Sat, to 8pm Sun) is a highly unusual cathedral with a Romanesque core and baroque Schön-bornkapelle, also by Neumann.

✕ ⤶ p224

The Drive » Take the B19 south to join the A3 motorway; follow this to meet the B81, which goes all the way to Tauberbischofsheim (37km).

2
Tauberbischofsheim
The main town of the pretty Tauber Valley, this small settlement has a picturesque market-place dominated by a neo-Gothic town hall and lined with typical half-timbered houses. Follow the remains of medieval town walls to the Kurmainzisches

§ LINK YOUR TRIP

16 German Castle Road

The Romantic and the German Castle Roads intersect in Rothenburg ob der Tauber.

19 German Alpine Road

The German Alpine and the Romantic Roads meet in Füssen.

Classic Trip

Schloss, housing the **Tauberfränkisches Land-schaftsmuseum** (www.tauberfraenkisches-land schaftsmuseum.de; Schloss-platz; €3; ⏱2-4.30pm Tue-Sat, 10am-noon & 2-4.30pm Sun Easter-Oct), where you can learn about Tauber-bischofsheim's past.

The Drive » The 34km dash to Weikersheim passes through Lauda-Königshofen, a pretty stop in the Tauber Valley.

- - - - - - - - - - - - - - - -

❸ Weikersheim

Top billing in under-visited Weikersheim is **Schloss Weikersheim** (www.schloss-weikersheim. de; Marktplatz 11; adult/child €6.50/3.30; ⏱9am-6pm Apr-Oct, 10am-5pm Nov-Mar), the Romantic Road's finest palace. Renaissance to the core, it's surrounded by beautiful formal gardens inspired by Versailles. Highlights include the enormous Knights Hall dating from around 1600 and over 40m long. The rich decor includes a huge painted ceiling, each panel depicting a hunting scene, and the amazingly ornate fireplace. The unforgettable rococo mirror cabinet, with its gilt-and-red decor, is also part of the guided tour, after which you

---

ROTHENBURG'S SNOWBALLS

Where can you get your hands on a snowball in July? Why, in Rothenburg ob der Tauber, of course! The town's speciality are *Schneeballen* (snowballs), ribbons of dough shaped into balls, deep-fried then coated in icing sugar, chocolate and other dentist's foes. Some 24 types are made at **Diller's Schneeballen** (www.schneeballen.eu; Hofbronnengasse 16; ⏱10am-6pm); a smaller range can be enjoyed all over town.

---

can wander the elegantly laid-out gardens.

The Drive » The short 28km journey between Weikersheim and Rothenburg ob der Tauber follows minor country roads all the way. You could also detour via Creglingen, a minor stop on the Romantic Road.

- - - - - - - - - - - - - - - -

TRIP HIGHLIGHT

❹ Rothenburg ob der Tauber

A well-preserved historical town, Rothenburg ob der Tauber is the Romantic Road's most popular stop. Once you're finished with the main sights, there are some less obvious attractions here.

You'll often see the **Plönlein** in brochures and tourist bumf, a gathering of forks in the cobbled road (Obere Schmiedgasse) occupied by possibly the quaintest, most crooked half-timbered house you'll ever see.

Hidden down an alley is the **Alt-Rothenburger Handwerkerhaus** (www.alt -rothenburger-handwerkerhaus.

de; Alter Stadtgraben 26; adult/child €3/1.50; ⏱11am-5pm Mon-Fri, from 10am Sat & Sun Easter-Oct, 2-4pm daily Dec), where numerous artisans – coopers, weavers, cobblers and potters – have their workshops, and mostly have had for their house's 700-plus-years' existence. It's half museum, half active workplace; you can easily spend an hour or so watching the artisans at work.

✗ p224

The Drive » The quickest way to Dinkelsbühl is the A7 motorway (50km). For a slower and longer experience, follow the official Romantic Road route along country roads via Schillingsfürst, another quaint halt.

- - - - - - - - - - - - - - - -

TRIP HIGHLIGHT

❺ Dinkelsbühl

Immaculately preserved Dinkelsbühl is arguably the Romantic Road's most authentically medieval halt. Like Rothenburg, it is ringed by medieval walls, boasting 18 towers and four gates. The joy of Dinkelsbühl is aimless wandering through the crooked lanes, but for a history lowdown visit the **Haus der Geschichte** (House of History; www.hausder geschichte-dinkelsbuehl.de; Altrathausplatz 14; adult/child €4/2; ⊘9am-6pm Mon-Fri, 10am-5pm Sat & Sun May-Oct, 10am-5pm Nov-Apr), in the same building as the tourist office.

✕ ⌂ p224

The Drive » Just 32km separate Dinkelsbühl from Nördlingen along the B25, accompanied by the Wörnitz River for the first part of the journey. A few kilometres short of Nördlingen is Wallerstein, a small market town with the beautiful Church of St Alban, also a Romantic Road stop.

---

6 Nördlingen

Charmingly medieval, Nördlingen lies within the Ries Basin, a massive impact crater gouged out by a meteorite more than 15 million years ago. The crater – some 25km in diameter – is one of Earth's best preserved, and has been declared a special 'geopark'. Nördlingen's 14th-century walls, all original, mimic the crater's rim and are almost perfectly circular: **Rieskrater Museum** (Eugene-Shoemaker-Platz 1; adult/child €4.50/2.50, ticket also valid for Stadtmuseum; ⊘10am-4.30pm Tue-Sun, closed noon-1.30pm Nov-Mar) tells the story. Next door

TOP TIP: GUEST CARDS

Overnight anywhere in the Alps and your hotel should issue a free *Gästekarte*, which gives free bus travel plus many other discounts on admission and activities.

is the **Stadtmuseum** (Vordere Gerbergasse 1; adult/child €4.50/2.50, ticket also valid for Rieskrater Museum; ⊘1.30-4.30pm Tue-Sun Apr-early Nov), giving an interesting rundown of Nördlingen's story so far.

On a completely different note, the **Bayerisches Eisenbahnmuseum** (www.bayerisches-eisenbahnmuseum.de; Am Hohen Weg 6a; adult/child €6/3; ⊘noon-4pm Tue-Sat, 10am-5pm Sun May-Sep, 10am-5pm Sat & Sun Mar, Apr & Oct) near the train station is a retirement home for locos that have puffed their last. The museum runs steam trains up to Dinkelsbühl, Feuchtwangen and Gunzenhausen several times a year; the website has details.

✕ ⌂ p225

The Drive » The 19km drive to Harburg is along the arrow-straight B25.

---

7 Harburg

Looming over the Wörnitz River, the medieval covered parapets, towers, turrets, keep and red-tiled roofs of 12th-century **Schloss Harburg** (www.burg-harburg.de; Burgstrasse 1; courtyard admission €3, tour €4; ⊘10am-5pm mid-Mar–Oct) are so perfectly preserved they almost seem like a film set. Tours tell the Schloss's long tale and evoke the ghosts said to use the castle as a hang-out.

From the castle, the walk to Harburg's cute, half-timbered **Altstadt** (old town) takes 10 minutes, slightly more the other way (uphill). A fabulous village-and-castle panorama can be admired from the 1702 stone bridge spanning the Wörnitz.

The Drive » Follow the B25 12km to Donauwörth.

WILLY WONKA'S NÖRDLINGEN

If you've seen the 1971 movie *Willy Wonka & the Chocolate Factory*, you've already looked down upon Nördlingen from a glass lift – aerial shots of the town were used in the film's final sequences.

Classic Trip

WHY THIS IS A CLASSIC TRIP
MARC DI DUCA, WRITER

This 350km-long ribbon of historical quaintness is the Germany you came to see, but things can get crowded in the summer months, taking away a bit of the romance. Do the trip in winter when Bavaria's chocolate-box towns look even prettier under a layer of snow.

Above: King Ludwig II's robe at the Museum of the Bavarian Kings (p221), Hohenschwangau
Right: Historic town of Rothenburg ob der Tauber (p216)
Left; *Schneeballen* (snowballs; p216), Rothenburg ob der Tauber

LAMIAFOTOGRAFIA / SHUTTERSTOCK ©

⑧ Donauwörth

Sitting pretty at the confluence of the Danube and Wörnitz rivers, the small town of Donauwörth had its heyday as a Free Imperial City in the 14th century. WWII destroyed 75% of the medieval old town but three gates and five town-wall towers still guard it today. The main street is Reichstrasse, which is where you'll discover the **Liebfraukirche**, a 15th-century Gothic church with original frescos and a sloping floor that drops 120cm. Swabia's largest church bell (6550kg) swings in the belfry. The town's other major attraction is the **Käthe-Kruse-Puppenmuseum** (www.kaethe-kruse.de; Pflegstrasse 21a; adult/child €2.50/1.50; ⊙11am-6pm Tue-Sun May-Sep, 2-5pm Thu-Sun Oct-Apr). In a former monastery, it's a nostalgia-inducing place of old dolls and dollhouses from world-renowned designer Käthe Kruse (1883–1968).

The Drive » Augsburg is 47km away via the B2 and the A8 motorway. The scenic route via back roads east of the A8 passes close to the pretty town of Rain, another minor halt on the Romantic Road.

⑨ Augsburg

Augsburg is the Romantic Road's largest city and one of Germany's oldest, founded by the stepchildren of Roman

219

Classic Trip

emperor Augustus over 2000 years ago. This attractive city of spires and cobbles is an engaging stop, though less quaint than others along the route.

Augsburg's top sight is the **Fuggerei** (www. fugger.de; Jakober Strasse; adult/concession €6.50/3; ☺8am-8pm Apr-Sep, 9am-6pm Oct-Mar), Europe's oldest Catholic welfare settlement, founded by banker and merchant Jakob Fugger in 1521. Around 200 people inhabit the complex today; see how the residents of yesterday lived by visiting the **Fuggereimuseum** (Mittlere Gasse 14; admission incl with entry to the Fuggerei;

☺9am-8pm Mar-Oct, to 6pm Nov-Apr).

Two famous Germans have close associations with Augsburg. Protestant Reformation leader Martin Luther stayed here in 1518 – his story is told at **St Anna Kirche** (Im Annahof 2, off Annastrasse; ☺noon-6pm Mon, 10am-12.30pm & 3-6pm Tue-Sat, 10am-12.30pm & 3-5pm Sun May-Oct, slightly shorter hours Nov-Apr). The birthplace of poet and playwright Bertolt Brecht is now a museum, the **Brechthaus** (☎0821-324 2779; www. brechthaus-augsburg.de; Auf dem Rain 7; adult/concession €3.50/2.50; ☺10am-5pm Tue-Sun).

✕ ▭ p225

The Drive » Drive 41km to Landsberg am Lech along the B17. The route mostly follows the valley of the Lech River. Look out for signs to the saucily named town of Kissing!

---

❿ Landsberg am Lech

A walled town on the Lech, lovely Landsberg has a less commercial ambience than others on the route. Just like the Wieskirche further south, the small baroque **Johanniskirche** (Vorderer Anger 215) was created by architect Dominikus Zimmermann, who lived in Landsberg and served as its mayor. **Neues Stadtmuseum** (www.museum -landsberg.de; Von-Helfenstein-Gasse 426; adult/child €3/1.50; ☺2-5pm Tue-Fri, from 11am Sat & Sun May-Jan, closed Feb-Apr) tells Landsberg's tale from prehistory to the 20th century.

The Drive » The 28km drive along the B17 to Schongau should take 30 minutes. En route you pass through Hohenfurch, a pretty little town regarded as the gateway to the Pfaffenwinkel, a foothill region of the Alps.

DETOUR: EICHSTÄTT & THE ALTMÜHLTAL NATURE PARK

Start: ❽ Donauwörth

A short 55km off the Romantic Road from Donauwörth lies the town of Eichstätt, the main jumping-off point for the serenely picturesque 2900-sq-km Altmühltal Nature Park, which follows the wooded valley of the Altmühl River. Canoeing is a top activity here, as is cycling and camping. The park is an ideal break from the road and a relaxing place to spend a few days in unspoilt natural surroundings. Eichstätt itself has a wealth of architecture, including the richly adorned medieval **Dom** (www. bistum-eichstaett.de/dom; Domplatz; ☺7.15am-7.30pm), with its museum, the baroque **Fürstbischöfliche Residenz** (Residenzplatz 1; tour €1; ☺7.30am-noon Mon-Fri, 2-4pm Mon-Wed, 2-5.30pm Thu), where local prince-bishops once lived it up, and the **Willibaldsburg** (☎08421-4730; Burgstrasse 19; adult/child €2.50/free; ☺9am-6pm Tue-Sun Apr-Oct, 10am-4pm Tue-Sun Nov-Mar), a 14th-century castle that houses a couple of museums.

⑪ Schongau

One of the lesser-visited stops on the Romantic Road, attractive Schongau is known for its largely intact medieval defences. The Gothic **Ballenhaus** (Marienplatz 2) served as the town hall until 1902 and has a distinctive stepped gable; it now houses a cafe. Other attractions include the **Church of Maria Himmelfahrt** (Kirchenstrasse 23), with a choir by baroque architect, Dominikus Zimmermann.

The Drive ≫ Take the B17 south until you reach Steingaden. From there country roads lead east and then south to Wies. This is where Bavaria starts to take on the look of the Alps, with flower-filled meadows in summer and views of the high peaks when the weather is clear.

⑫ Wieskirche

Located in the village of Wies, the **Wieskirche** (☎08862-932 930; ⏰8am-8pm Apr-Oct, to 5pm Nov-Mar)

LANDSBERG'S DARK LITERARY CONNECTIONS

Landsberg am Lech can claim to be the town where one of the German language's best-selling books was written. Was it by Goethe, Remarque, Brecht? No, unfortunately, it was by Adolf Hitler. It was during his 264 days of incarceration in a Landsberg jail, following the 1923 beer-hall putsch, that Hitler penned his hate-filled *Mein Kampf,* a book that sold an estimated seven million copies when published. The jail later held Nazi war criminals and is still in use.

is one of Bavaria's best-known baroque churches and a Unesco-listed site, the monumental work of legendary artist-brothers, Dominikus and Johann Baptist Zimmermann. In 1730, a Steingaden farmer claimed he'd witnessed his Christ statue shedding tears. Pilgrims poured into the town in such numbers over the next decade that the local abbot commissioned a new church to house the weepy work. Inside the almost-circular structure, eight snow-white pillars are topped by gold capitals

and swirling decorations. The unsupported dome must have seemed like God's work in the mid-17th century, its surface adorned with a pastel ceiling fresco celebrating Christ's resurrection.

The Drive ≫ Backtrack to Steingaden and rejoin the B17 to reach Füssen (27km). The entire journey is through the Alps' increasingly undulating foothills, with gorgeous views of the ever-nearing peaks along the way.

⑬ Füssen

Nestled at the foot of the Alps, tourist-busy Füssen

MUSEUM OF THE BAVARIAN KINGS

Palace-fatigued visitors often overlook the worthwhile **Museum der Bayerischen Könige** (Museum of the Bavarian Kings; www.museumderbayerischenkoenige.de; Alpseestrasse 27; adult/child €11/free; ⏰9am-5pm), installed in a former lakeside hotel 400m from the castle ticket office (towards Alpsee Lake) in Hohenschwangau. The big-window views across the beautiful lake (a great picnic spot) to the Alps are almost as amazing as the Wittelsbach bling on show, including Ludwig II's famous blue-and-gold robe. The architecturally stunning museum is packed with historical background on Bavaria's first family and is well worth the extra legwork. A detailed audioguide is included in the ticket.

Classic Trip

is all about the nearby castles of Neuschwanstein and Hohenschwangau, but there are other reasons to linger. The town's **historical centre** is worth half a day's exploration and, from here, you can easily escape the crowds into a landscape of gentle **hiking trails** and Alpine vistas. Or, take an hour or two in Füssen's very own castle, the **Hohes Schloss** (Magnusplatz 10; adult/child €6/free; ⏰ galleries 11am-5pm Tue-Sun Apr-Oct, 1-4pm Fri-Sun Nov-Mar), today home to an art gallery.

 ⬛ p225

The Drive ⟫ To drive to King Ludwig II's castles, take the B17 across the river until you see signs for Hohenschwangau. Parking is at a premium in summer. However, as the castles are a mere 4km from Füssen's centre, it's probably not worth driving at all. RVO buses 78 and 73 (www.rvo-bus.de) run there from Füssen Bahnhof (at least hourly, tickets from the driver).

TRIP HIGHLIGHT

⑭ Neuschwanstein & Hohenschwangau Castles

The undisputed highlights of any trip to Bavaria, these two castles make a fitting climax to the Romantic Road.

Schloss Neuschwanstein (☎ tickets 08362-930 830; www.neuschwanstein.de; Neuschwansteinstrasse 20; adult/child €13/free, incl Hohenschwangau €25/free; ⏰ 9am-6pm Apr–mid-Oct, 10am-4pm mid-Oct–Mar) was the model for Disney's *Sleeping Beauty* castle. King Ludwig II planned this fairy-tale pile himself, with the help of a stage designer rather than an architect. He envisioned it as a giant stage on which to re-create the world of Germanic mythology, inspired by the operatic works of his friend Richard Wagner.

It was at nearby **Schloss Hohenschwangau** (☎ 08362-930 830; www.hohenschwangau.de; Alpseestrasse 30; adult/child €13/free, incl Neuschwanstein €25/free; ⏰ 8am-5pm Apr–mid-Oct, 9am-3pm mid-Oct–Mar) that King Ludwig II grew up and

✓ TOP TIP:
VISITING NEUSCHWANSTEIN & HOHENSCHWANGAU CASTLES

The castles can only be visited on guided tours (35 minutes). Buy timed tickets from the **Ticket Centre** (☎ 08362-930 830; www.hohenschwangau.de; Alpseestrasse 12; ⏰ 7.30am-5pm Apr–mid-Oct, 8.30am-3pm mid-Oct–Mar) at the foot of the castles. In summer, arrive as early as 8am to ensure you get in that day.

Schloss Neuschwanstein Throne room ceiling detail

later enjoyed summers until his death in 1886. His father, Maximilian II, built this palace in a neo-Gothic style atop 12th-century ruins. Less showy than Neuschwanstein, it has a distinctly lived-in feel, where every piece of furniture is a used original. It was at Hohenschwangau where Ludwig first met Wagner.

Classic Trip

Eating & Sleeping

Würzburg ❶

✗ Bürgerspital
Weinstube   Franconian €€

(☎0931-352 880; www.buergerspital-wein
stuben.de; Theaterstrasse 19; mains €13-27;
⏱10am-midnight) If you are going to eat out
just once in Würzburg, the aromatic and cosy
nooks of this labyrinthine medieval place
probably provide the top local experience.
Choose from a broad selection of Franconian
wines (some of Germany's best) and wonderful
regional dishes and snacks, including
Mostsuppe (a tasty wine soup).

Hotel Rebstock   Hotel €€€

(☎0931-309 30; www.rebstock.com;
Neubaustrasse 7; r €160-430; ❄🛜)
Würzburg's top digs, in a squarely renovated
rococo town house, has 70 unique, stylishly
finished rooms with the gamut of amenities,
impeccable service and an Altstadt location.
A pillow selection and supercomfy 'gel' beds
should ease you into slumberland, perhaps after
a fine meal in the dramatic bistro or the gourmet
restaurant.

Rothenburg ob der Tauber ❹

✗ Mittermeier   International €€€

(☎09861-945 430; www.villamittermeier.de;
Vorm Würzburger Tor 7; 4-8 course menu €50-
100; ⏱6-10.30pm Tue-Sat; 🅿🛜) Supporters
of the Slow Food movement and deserved
holders of a Michelin Bib Gourmand, this hotel
restaurant pairs punctilious artisanship with
top-notch ingredients, sourced regionally
whenever possible. There are five different
dining areas including a black-and-white tiled
'temple', an alfresco terrace and a barrel-
shaped wine cellar. The wine list is one of the
best in Franconia.

✗ Zur Höll   Franconian €€

(☎09861-4229; www.hoell.rothenburg.de;
Burggasse 8; mains €7-20; ⏱5-11pm Mon-Sat)
This medieval wine tavern is in the town's oldest
original buildings, with sections dating back to
the year 900. The menu of regional specialities
is limited but refined, though it's the superb
selection of Franconian wines that people really
come for.

Dinkelsbühl ❺

✗ Haus
Appelberg   Franconian, International €€

(☎09851-582 838; www.haus-appelberg.
de; Nördlinger Strasse 40; dishes €7-115;
⏱6pm-midnight Mon-Sat; 🛜) At this 40-cover
wine restaurant, owners double as cooks to
keep tables supplied with traditional dishes
such as local fish, Franconian sausages and
Maultaschen (pork-and-spinach ravioli). On
warm days swap the rustic interior for the
secluded terrace, a fine spot for some evening
idling over a Franconian white.

🛏 Dinkelsbühler
Kunst-Stuben   Guesthouse €€

(☎09851-6750; www.kunst-stuben.de;
Segringer Strasse 52; r €100-170; ➡@🛜)
Personal attention and charm by the bucketload
make this guesthouse, situated near the
westernmost gate (Segringer Tor), one of the
best on the entire Romantic Road. Furniture
(including the four-posters) is all handmade by
Voglauer, the cosy library is perfect for curling
up with a good read, and the suite is a matchless
deal for travelling families. The artist owner will
show his Asia travel films if enough guests are
interested.

Nördlingen ⑥

✕ La Fontana — Italian €

(www.lafontana.eu; Bei den Kornschrannen 2; mains €6-18; ⊙9.30am-11pm Mon-Sat, from 10am Sun Apr-Sep, closed Mon Oct-Mar; 🛜) Nördlingen's most popular restaurant is this large Italian pizza-pasta place occupying the terracotta Kornschrannen as well as tumbling tables out onto Schrannenstrasse. The menu is long, the service swift and when the sun is shining there's no lovelier spot to fill the hole.

🛏 Kaiserhof Hotel Sonne — Hotel €€

(📞09081-5067; www.kaiserhof-hotel-sonne.de; Marktplatz 3; s €55-75, d €80-120; 🅿🛜) Right on the main square, Nördlingen's top digs once hosted crowned heads and their entourages, but has quietly gone to seed in recent years. However, rooms are still packed with character, mixing modern comforts with traditional charm, and the atmospheric regional restaurant downstairs is still worth a shot.

Augsburg ⑨

✕ August — International €€€

(📞0821-352 79; Johannes-Haag-Strasse 14; dinner €169; ⊙from 7pm Wed-Sat) Most Augsburgers have little inkling their city possesses two Michelin stars, both of which belong to chef Christian Grünwald. Treat yourself to some of Bavaria's most innovative cooking in the minimalist dining room, though with just 16 covers, reservations are essential.

✕ Bauerntanz — German €€

(www.bauerntanz-augsburg.de; Bauerntanzgässchen 1; mains €8-20; ⊙11am-11.30pm) Belly-satisfying helpings of creative Swabian and Bavarian food – *Spätzle* (veal medallions) and more *Spätzle* – are plated up by friendly staff at this prim Alpine tavern with lace curtains, hefty timber interior and chequered fabrics. When the sun makes an appearance, everyone bails for the outdoor seating.

🛏 Dom Hotel — Hotel €€

(📞0821-343 930; www.domhotel-augsburg. de; Frauentorstrasse 8; s €80-150, d €100-180; 🅿😄🛜🎫) Augsburg's top choice packs a 500-year-old former bishop's guesthouse (Martin Luther and Kaiser Maximilian I stayed here) with 57 rooms, all different but sharing a stylishly understated air and pristine upkeep; some have cathedral views. However, the big pluses here are the large swimming pool, fitness centre and solarium. Parking is an extra €6.

Füssen ⑬

✕ Zum Franziskaner — Bavarian €€

(Kemptener Strasse 1; mains €7-18; ⊙11.30am-10pm) This traditional restaurant specialises in *Schweinshaxe* (pork knuckle) and schnitzel, prepared in more varieties than you can shake a haunch at. There's some choice for non-carnivores such as *Käsespätzle* (rolled cheese noodles) and salads, and when the sun shines the outdoor seating shares the pavement with the 'foot-washing' statue.

✕ Zum Hechten — Bavarian €€

(Ritterstrasse 6; mains €8-19; ⊙10am-10pm) Füssen's best hotel restaurant keeps things regional with a menu of Allgäu staples like schnitzel and noodles, Bavarian pork-themed favourites, and local specialities such as venison goulash from the Ammertal. Post-meal, relax in the wood-panelled dining room caressing a König Ludwig Dunkel, one of Germany's best dark beers brewed by the current head of the Wittelsbach family.

🛏 Hotel Sonne — Design Hotel €€

(📞08362-9080; Prinzregentenplatz 1; s/d from €100/120; 🅿🛜) Although traditional looking from outside, this Altstadt favourite offers an unexpected design-hotel experience within. Themed rooms feature everything from swooping bed canopies to big-print wallpaper, huge pieces of wall art to sumptuous fabrics. The public spaces are littered with pieces of art, period costumes and design features – the overall effect is impressive and unusual for this part of Germany.

Glass Route

18

Strung along Bavaria's eastern flank like a necklace of gleaming beads, this glass-themed route takes in museums, workshops and theme parks, all set in wonderfully forested landscapes.

TRIP HIGHLIGHTS

7 DAYS
270KM / 167 MILES

GREAT FOR...

BEST TIME TO GO
Easter to October when all sights are open.

ESSENTIAL PHOTO
The confluence of three rivers in Passau.

BEST FOR SHOPPING
JOSKA Bodenmais for authentic local glassware.

60 km

Frauenau
For the region's dazzlingly modern Glasmuseum

FINISH
Weiden

93 km

JOSKA Bodenmais
A glass-themed entertainment park

6

3

Gläserne Wald

Tittling

1 **START**

0 km

Passau
Historical city at the confluence of three rivers

Gläserne Wald (*Glass Forest* by Rudolf Schmid; p230)

227

18 Glass Route

Think Bavaria, think Alpine meadows, tankards of beer and fast cars – but few may know that the eastern part of the region along the Czech border has a long tradition of making glass. However, viewing the region's glazed and glittering creations is just one of the delights of this low-key route – you'll also be passing through the semiwilderness of the mysterious and undervisited Bavarian Forest National Park.

TRIP HIGHLIGHT

❶ Passau

Passau is a delightful town, its **Altstadt** (old town) is stacked atop a narrow peninsula that jabs its sharp end into the confluence of three rivers: the Danube, the Inn and the Ilz. The glass highlight here is the **Passauer Glasmuseum** (☎0851-350 71; www. glasmuseum.de; Schrottgasse 2; adult/child €7/5; ☉9am-5pm) within the Hotel Wilder Mann. This warren-like museum is

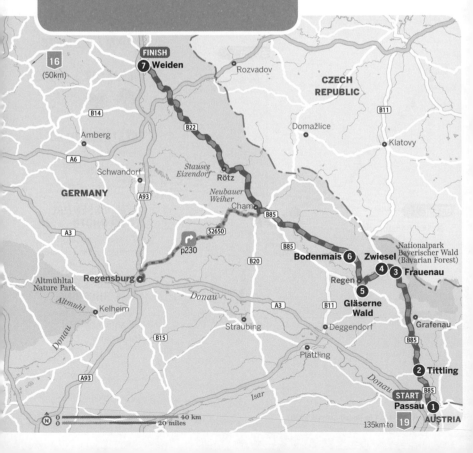

filled with some 30,000 priceless pieces of glass and crystal from the baroque, classical, Art Nouveau and Art Deco periods. Much of what you see hails from Bohemia's glassworks, but there are also works by Tiffany and famous Viennese producers.

Passau's other unmissable sight is the **Dom St Stephan** (Domplatz; ⏲6.30am-7pm), a late 17th-century confection by a team of Italians, notably architect Carlo Lurago and stucco master Giovanni Battista Carlone. The interior is a top-heavy baroque affair with a mob of saints and cherubs gazing down at the congregation from

LINK YOUR TRIP

 German Castle Road

Weiden, the northern terminus of this route, is just 60km southeast from Bayreuth to link up with the castle route.

 German Alpine Road

Passau, at this route's southern end, is a 145km drive north from Berchtesgaden on the Alpine Road. (The route passes through Austria so you'll need an Austrian motorway vignette.)

countless cornices and capitals.

 p233

The Drive » A mere 22km on the B85 separates Passau from Tittling, an easy drive across rolling farmland.

❷ Tittling

Tiny Tittling on the southern edge of the Bavarian Forest is home to a big attraction – the **Museumsdorf Bayerischer Wald** (📞08504-8482; www.museumsdorf. com; Am Dreiburgensee; adult/child €7/5; ⏲9am-5pm Apr-Oct), the largest open-air museum in Europe. This 20-hectare site hosts 150 typical Bavarian Forest timber cottages and farmsteads, as well as mills, schools and stables, all from the 17th to 19th centuries. Exhibitions range from clothing and furniture to pottery and farming implements. You certainly get a lot for the admission price – you could spend hours ducking in and out of the various buildings. If you are feeling peckish at the end of your tour, drop into the on-site **Gasthaus Mühlhiasl** for some belly-filling east Bavarian fare.

The Drive » This section of the route takes you deep into the dark hills of the Bavarian Forest as you head north for 38km on minor road 2132 then

the B85. Along the way you'll pass by Grafenau (p233), which has one of the best places to stay in the Bavarian Forest.

TRIP HIGHLIGHT

❸ Frauenau

For as long as the region has been producing glass, Frauenau has been a key location and still boasts three glass factories. So when it came to deciding where to put the region's dazzlingly modern **Glasmuseum** (📞09926-941 020; www.glasmuseum-frauenau. de; Am Museumspark 1; adult/child €5/free, Sun €1; ⏲9am-5pm Tue-Sun), Frauenau won the day. The superb exhibition covers four millennia of glass-making history, starting with the ancient Egyptians and ending with modern glass art from around the world. Demonstrations and workshops for kids are regular features, as are superb temporary exhibitions. It goes without saying that the museum is an essential stop on any trip along the Glasstrasse.

The Drive » From Frauenau it's a short 8km jaunt to your next stop in Zwiesel. Most base themselves in Zwiesel and make day trips out to Frauenau. The two towns, and several others, are linked by the Waldbahn, a private railway line serving the communities of the Bavarian Forest.

➍ Zwiesel

Zwiesel is the main settlement in the Bavarian Forest National Park and the traditional centre of glass production in the region. The **Zwieseler Glasfachschule** (Zwiesel Glassmaker's School) is where many of the artisans of eastern Bavaria learn their trade. The town's main place of interest is the **Waldmuseum** (📞09922-503 706; www.waldmuseum.zwiesel. de; Kirchplatz 3; adult/child €6/1; ⏱10am-4pm Thu-Mon), housed in a former brewery. This 'Forest Museum' has exhibitions on local customs, flora and fauna, life in the forest and, of course, glass-making.

🛏 p233

The Drive » This 16km drive takes you through more wooded hills on country roads to the next stop at the castle of Weissenstein (for the Gläserne Wald), 5km south of the town of Regen.

➎ Gläserne Wald

One of the more unusual sights along the Glass Route is the **Gläserne Wald** (Glass Forest; www. glaeserner-wald.de; Weissenstein) near the town of Regen. Here glass artist Rudolf Schmid has created a forest of glass trees, some as much as 8m tall. The trees, in a number of transparent shades, are set in a flowery meadow next to Weissenstein Castle and are an intriguing sight;

DETOUR: REGENSBURG

Start: ➏ **JOSKA Bodenmais**

It would be a pity to pass through eastern Bavaria without calling in at one of the state's most engaging cities, Regensburg. A Roman settlement completed under Emperor Marcus Aurelius, the city was the first capital of Bavaria, the residence of dukes, kings and bishops, and for 600 years a Free Imperial City. Two millennia of history bequeathed the city some of the region's finest architectural vestiges, a fact recognised by Unesco in 2006.

One of Regensburg's top attractions is the **Schloss Thurn und Taxis** (www. thurnundtaxis.de; Emmeramsplatz 5; tours adult/child €13.50/11; ⏱tours hourly 10.30am-4.30pm late Mar-early Nov, to 3.30pm Sat & Sun early Nov-late Mar). In the 15th century, Franz von Taxis (1459–1517) set up the first European postal system, which remained a monopoly until the 19th century. In recognition of his services, the family was given the former Benedictine monastery St Emmeram, henceforth known as Schloss Thurn und Taxis. It soon became one of the most modern palaces in Europe, and featured such luxuries as flushing toilets, central heating and electricity. Tours include the **Basilika St Emmeram**.

A chunk of Regensburg's Roman heritage has survived in the shape of the Roman Wall in a street called Unter den Schwibbögen. Dating from AD 179 the rough-hewn Porta Praetoria arch is the tallest Roman structure in Bavaria and formed part of the city's defences for centuries. A short walk away is the **Steinerne Brücke** (Stone Bridge), a 900-year-old bridge that was at one time the only fortified crossing of the Danube. Neglected and damaged for centuries (especially by the buses that once used it), the bridge has recently been restored. At the old-town end of the bridge, the **World Heritage Visitors Centre** (www.regensburg-welterbe.de; Weisse-Lamm-Gasse 1; ⏱10am-7pm) focuses on the city's Unesco sites using interesting interactive multimedia exhibits.

Passau Glasswear at Passauer Glasmuseum (p228)

BAVARIAN FOREST NATIONAL PARK

A paradise for outdoor fiends, the Bavarian Forest National Park extends around 243 sq km along the Czech border, from Bayerisch Eisenstein in the north to Finsterau in the south. Its thick forest, most of it mountain spruce, is criss-crossed by hundreds of kilometres of marked hiking, cycling and cross-country skiing trails; some now link up with a similar network across the border. The region is home to deer, wild boar, fox, otter and countless bird species.

Around 1km northeast of the village of Neuschönau (a short detour north of your route from the village of Grafenau) stands the **Hans-Eisenmann-Haus** (☏08558-961 50; www.nationalpark-bayerischer-wald.de; Böhmstrasse 35; ⏰9am-6pm May-Oct, to 5pm Jan-Apr), the national park's main visitor centre. The free exhibition has hands-on displays to shed light on topics such as pollution and tree growth, plus a children's discovery room, a shop and a library.

SOUTHERN GERMANY 18 GLASS ROUTE

many more are set to be added in coming years.

The Drive » Some 16km divide the Glass Forest from the next halt in Bodenmais, following roads 2135 and 2132 through the thickly forested landscape.

TRIP HIGHLIGHT

⑥ JOSKA Bodenmais

The glass highlight of the small town of Bodenmais is **JOSKA Bodenmais** (☏09924-7790; www.joska.com; Am Moosbach 1; ⏰9.30am-6pm Mon-Fri, to 5pm Sat year-round, 10am-5pm Sun May-Oct), a crystal theme park complete with crystal shops, public artworks, a beer garden, a year-round Christmas market, a crystal gallery and a workshop where visitors can try their hand at glass-blowing.

The Drive » The biggest distance of the route; it's around 117km to Weiden, sticking to the 2132 and B22. You quickly leave the Bohemian forest and enter a hilly landscape of huge agricultural fields, passing through the towns of Cham and Rötz on the way.

⑦ Weiden

Boasting several sheet-glass factories, the large town of Weiden often hosts glass-art exhibitions (ask the tourist office for details), many of them in cooperation with partners across the border in the Czech Republic, which itself has a huge glass- and crystal-producing tradition. Otherwise the town is a pleasantly low-key place to end your exploration of Bavaria's glassy traditions.

✕ ⮞ p233

Eating & Sleeping

Passau

✕ Heilig-Geist-Stifts-Schenke
Bavarian €€

(📞0851-2607; www.stiftskeller-passau.de; Heilig-Geist-Gasse 4; mains €12-22; ⏱11am-11pm, closed Wed & Thu; 🛜) Not only does this historical inn have a succession of walnut-panelled ceramic-stove-heated rooms, a candlelit cellar (from 6pm) and a vine-draped garden, but the food is equally inspired. Amid the river fish, steaks and seasonal dishes there are quite gourmet affairs such as beef fillet in flambéed cognac sauce. Help it all along with one of the many Austrian and German wines in stock.

🛏 Hotel Schloss Ort
Boutique Hotel €€

(📞0851-340 72; www.hotel-schloss-ort.de; Im Ort 11; s/d from €70/90; P🛜) The most characterful place to sleep in Passau, this 800-year-old medieval palace by the Inn River conceals a soothingly tranquil boutique hotel, stylishly done out with polished timber floors, crisp white cotton sheets and wrought-iron bedsteads. Many of the 18 rooms enjoy river views and breakfast is served in the vaulted restaurant.

🛏 Hotel Wilder Mann
Hotel €€

(📞0851-350 71; www.wilder-mann.com; Höllgasse 1; s/d from €70/100; P🛜) Sharing space with the Glasmuseum (p228), this historic hotel boasts former guests ranging from Empress Elisabeth (Sisi) of Austria to Yoko Ono. In the rooms, folksy painted furniture sits incongruously with 20th-century telephones and 21st-century TVs. The building is a warren of staircases, passageways and linking doors, so make sure you remember where your room is.

Grafenau

🛏 Das Reiners
Hotel €€

(📞08552-964 90; www.dasreiners.de; Grüb 20; r from €100; P🛜🏊) This elegant hotel in Grafenau is good value for the weary traveller. The stylish rooms are spacious and most have balconies. Guests are treated to a pool and sauna, and scrumptious buffet meals. Half-board and other deals are available.

Zwiesel ❹

🛏 Hotel Zur Waldbahn
Hotel €€

(📞09922-8570; www.zurwaldbahn.de; Bahnhofplatz 2; s €65-70, d €90-115; P🛜) Many of the rooms at this characteristic inn, opposite Zwiesel train station, run by three generations of the same family, open to balconies with views over the town. The breakfast buffet is an especially generous spread and even includes homemade jams. The restaurant serves traditional local fare and is probably the best in town.

Weiden ❼

✕ Die Villa
International €€

(www.facebook.com/dievillaweiden; Hinterm Zwinger 14; mains €8-18; ⏱11.30am-3pm & 5-11.30pm Wed-Sat; 🍴) This cafe-restaurant on the southern edge of the old town serves up an eclectic menu of vegetarian curries, Greek veal steaks, saltimbocca and tofu-based dishes in an elegant villa setting.

🛏 Altstadthotel Brauwirt
Hotel €€

(📞0961-388 1800; www.altstadthotel-braeuwirt.de; Türlgasse 10-14; s/d €75/110; 🛜) Inn of choice in Weiden, with a bull's-eye location in the centre, one of the town's best restaurants, a house brewery, 25 very well appointed, spacious business-class rooms and a sauna with fitness facilities. Breakfast is an extra €10 per person.

Classic Trip

German Alpine Road

This exciting drive winds through the foothills of the Bavarian Alps, taking in romantic castles, lakes of drinkably pure water and high peaks whose snow mantle remains year-round.

19

TRIP HIGHLIGHTS

176 km

Schloss Linderhof
Pocket-size Ludwig II castle in a remote location

450 km

Königssee
Electric-boat trips on Germany's most picturesque lake

Schloss Herrenchiemsee

Bad Tölz

START
Lindau

④
⑤

⑪
FINISH

Garmisch-Partenkirchen
Take the train to the top of the Zugspitze, Germany's highest peak

198 km

7 DAYS
450KM / 280 MILES

GREAT FOR...

BEST TIME TO GO
From Easter to October you'll encounter warmer weather and better road conditions.

ESSENTIAL PHOTO
Pretty Schloss Linderhof makes for a beautiful shot.

BEST FOR OUTDOORS
Vista-rich hiking trails ring the Königssee.

19 German Alpine Road

The Alpenstrasse, as it's known in German, was the country's first touring road, dating from 1858. Since then generations of horse riders, motorbikers, cyclists and campervanners have been discovering the magnificence of the Bavarian Alps. A bonus of this route is its variety – one day you can be exploring one of King Ludwig II's castles, the next picnicking on an Alpine meadow, and the day after that taking a boat trip across a glassy Alpine lake.

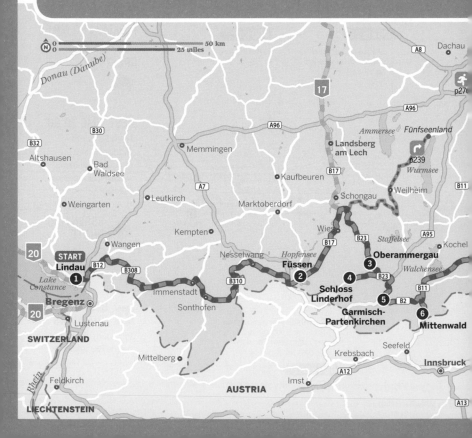

---

❶ Lindau

Brochures rhapsodise about Lindau being Germany's 'Garden of Eden' and the 'Bavarian Riviera'. Paradise and southern France it ain't but it is, well, pretty special. Cradled in the southern crook of Lake Constance and almost dipping its toes into Austria, this is a good-looking, outgoing little town, with a candy-coloured postcard of an Altstadt (old town), Alpine views (on clear days) and lakefront cafes that use every sunray to

the max. It's the lake that really is the main draw here, and the harbourside **Seepromenade**, with its palms, bobbing boats and folk sunning themselves in pavement cafes, is an unmissable part of the experience. Out at the harbour gates, look-

ing across the Alps, is Lindau's signature 33m-high **Neuer Leuchtturm** (New Lighthouse; Hafenplatz; adult/concession €2.10/0.80; ◷11am-6pm), which can be climbed for cracking views out over Lindau and the lake.

LINK YOUR TRIP

17 The Romantic Road

The Romantic and German Alpine Roads come together in Füssen.

20 Lake Constance

Lindau starts both the Lake Constance and German Alpine Road routes.

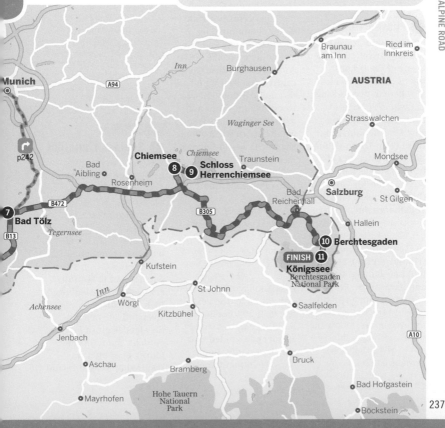

Classic Trip

Lindau's biggest architectural stunner is the 15th-century step-gabled **Altes Rathaus** (Old Town Hall; Bismarckplatz 4), a frescoed frenzy of cherubs, merry minstrels and galleons.

✗ ▭ p245, p253

The Drive » The most scenic way to go from Lindau to Füssen is to follow the B308 then the B310 via Immenstadt and Pfonten. This 104km route takes in many minor stops along the Deutsche Alpenstrasse.

----

② Füssen

Bustling with tourist traffic year-round, Füssen is one of the liveliest towns in the Alps. Most stay here to access King Ludwig II's castles at nearby Hohenschwangau; see The Romantic Road (Trip 17) for details. But there are other attractions... For fabulous views of the Alps and the Forggensee, take the **Tegelbergbahn** (www.tegelbergbahn.de; one-way/return €14.50/22; ☺9am-5pm) to the top of the Tegelberg (1730m), a prime launch point for hang-gliders and parasailers. From here it's a wonderful hike down to the castles (two to three hours; follow the signs to Königsschlösser).

The river that flows through Füssen is the

Lech – walk a kilometre south from the bridge across the river to the Lechfall where the chilly water squeezes through a tight gorge. There are forest trails to the castles from here, too.

✗ ▭ p225

The Drive » A hefty chunk of the Alps stands between Füssen and Oberammergau, making for a photogenic if roundabout route. Take the B17 as far as Steingaden, then the minor St2058 to the Ammer River, where you head south along the B23.

----

③ Oberammergau

Quietly quaint Oberammergau occupies a wide valley surrounded by the dark forests and snow-dusted peaks of the Ammergauer Alps. The centre is packed with traditional painted houses, woodcarving shops and awestruck tourists who come here to learn about the town's world-famous Passion Play.

The top attraction here is the **Passionstheater** (☎08822-941 36; www.passionstheater.de; Othmar-Weis-Strasse 1; adult/child tour €6/2, combined tour & Oberammergau Museum entry €8/3; ☺10am-5pm Tue-Sun Easter-Oct), where the Passion Play is performed every decade (the next one is in 2020). The building can be visited as part of a guided tour, which provides ample background on the play's

history and lets you peek at the costumes and sets. Also unmissable is the **Oberammergau Museum** (☎08822-941 36; www.oberammergaumuseum.de; Dorfstrasse 8; adult/child €3.50/1.50, combined museum entry & Passiontheater tour adult/concession €6/5; ☺10am-5pm Tue-Sun Apr-Oct), one of the best places to view exquisite examples of Oberammergau's famously intricate woodcarving art. Local craftspeople can produce anything from an entire nativity scene in a single walnut shell to a life-size Virgin Mary.

The Drive » The next stop at Schloss Linderhof is a short, snappy transfer along a picturesque valley. The monastery at Ettal is just a few kilometres off this route and worth a stop to sample the monks' Ettaler Klosterlikör, a sugary herbal digestif.

TRIP HIGHLIGHT

④ Schloss Linderhof

A trove of weird treasures, **Schloss Linderhof** (www.schlosslinderhof.de; adult/child €8.50/free; ☺9am-6pm Apr–mid-Oct, 10am-4.30pm mid-Oct–Mar) was Ludwig II's smallest but most sumptuous palace, and the only one he lived to see fully completed. Finished in 1878, the palace hugs a steep hillside in a fantasy landscape of French gardens, fountains and follies. Linderhof was inspired by Versailles and

DETOUR: FÜNFSEENLAND

Start: ❸ Oberammergau

Once a royal retreat and still a popular place of residence with the rich and famous, the Fünfseenland (Five Lakes District) is set in a glacial plain to the southwest of Munich.

The most popular of the five lakes is the **Starnberger** See, also the largest at 21km long. Those on the King Ludwig II trail should make a beeline for the tiny village of Berg on the eastern shore. It was here that the 'mad king' famously (and mysteriously) drowned along with his doctor in just a few feet of water. The spot where his body was found is marked with a large solemn cross backed by a Votivkapelle (Memorial Chapel). Berg is 5km from the town of Starnberg and can be reached on foot in around an hour.

The other lakes – **Ammersee**, **Pilsensee**, **Wörthsee** and **Wesslinger See** – are smaller and offer more secluded charm. Swimming, boating and windsurfing are popular activities on all lakes, and the district is also criss-crossed by a whopping 493km network of bike paths and 185km of hiking trails.

One unmissable sight by the Ammersee is the gorgeous hilltop monastery of **Kloster Andechs**, founded in the 10th century. Long a place of pilgrimage, today visitors come here primarily to slurp the Benedictines' fabled ales. After inspecting the church, which contains the remains of Carl Orff, the composer of *Carmina Burana*, plunge into the nearby **Bräustüberl**, the monks' beer hall and garden. There are seven varieties of beer on offer, from the rich and velvety *Doppelbock* dark to the fruity unfiltered *Weissbier* (wheat beer).

Andechs and Starnberg are around an hour by car from Oberammergau.

dedicated to Louis XIV, the French 'Sun King'.

Linderhof's myth-laden, jewel-encrusted rooms are a monument to the king's excesses. The **private bedroom** is the largest, heavily orna-mented and anchored by an enormous 108-candle crystal chandelier weigh-ing 500kg. An **artificial waterfall**, built to cool the room in summer, cascades just outside the window.

Created by the famous court gardener Carl von Effner, the gardens and outbuildings (open April to October) are as fascin-ating as the castle itself. The highlight is the **S**, where Ludwig would preside over nightly entertainment from a peacock throne.

The Drive ⟫ Backtrack along the valley to the B23 which joins the B2 at Oberau. The journey to Garmisch-Partenkirchen is 26km and should take no more than 30 minutes.

- - - - - - - - - - - - - - - - -

TRIP HIGHLIGHT

❺ Garmisch-Partenkirchen

An incredibly popular hang-out for out-doorsy types, skiing fans and day-trippers from Munich, the double-barrelled resort of Garmisch-Partenkirchen (G-P) is blessed with a fa-bled setting a snowball's throw from the Alps. The area offers some of the best skiing in the land, including runs on Germany's highest peak, the 2964km **Zugspitze** (www.zugspitze.de; return adult/child €58/32; ⊙ train 8.15am-2.15pm).

No visit to G-P would be complete without a Zugspitze **train trip**. The round trip starts in Garmisch aboard a *Zahnradbahn* (cogwheel train) that chugs along

Classic Trip

WHY THIS IS A CLASSIC TRIP
MARC DI DUCA, AUTHOR

It's no wonder this was chosen by Bavaria's nobility as the original touring route – a more varied and picturesque string of places you couldn't hope to find anywhere else in Germany. Towering 2000m-high peaks, quaint Bavarian taverns, rivers flowing jade-green with snowmelt and some of Germany's most intriguing castles – the magic of the German Alps meets you at every corner.

Above: Peacock throne, Schloss Linderhof (p238)
Right: Cable car, Garmisch-Partenkirchen (p239)
Left: Altes Rathaus (Old Town Hall), Lindau (p238)

the mountain base to the Eibsee, an idyllic forest lake. From here, the Eibsee-Seilbahn, a supersteep cable car, swings to the top. When you're done admiring the views, the Gletscherbahn cable car brings you to the Zugspitze glacier at 2600m, from where the cogwheel train heads back to Garmisch.

Easily accessible from town, the narrow and dramatically beautiful 700m-long **Partnachklamm** (www. partnachklamm.eu; adult/child €6/3; 8am-6pm May & Oct, 6am-10pm Jun-Sep, 9am-6pm Nov-Apr) is a hikeable gorge with walls rising up to 80m.

✕ 🛏 p245

The Drive ⟩⟩ Just 18km separate Garmisch-Partenkirchen from Mittenwald, along the B2. Most tackle it as a day trip and trains run hourly between the two.

- - - - - - - - - - - - - - - -

❻ Mittenwald

Nestled in a cul-de-sac under snow-capped peaks, sleepily alluring Mittenwald is the most natural spot imaginable for a resort. This drowsy village is known far and wide for its master violin makers, and its citizens seem almost bemused by its popularity. The air is ridiculously clean, and on the main street the loudest noise is a babbling brook.

Skiing on the **Karwendel** ski field is the main attraction, but there is one fascinating off-piste sight – the **Geigenbaumuseum** (www.geigenbaumuseum-mittenwald.de; Ballenhausgasse 3; adult/child €5.50/2; ⏱10am-5pm Tue-Sun Feb–mid-Mar & mid-May–mid-Oct, shorter hours rest of year), a collection of over 200 locally crafted violins and the tools used to fashion them. It's also the venue for occasional concerts.

The Drive » The 57km scenic route between Mittenwald and Bad Tölz follows the B11 north to the stunningly beautiful Walchensee. Take the 2072 along the lakeshore, then through some marvellous Alpine terrain to the B13, Lengries and onto Bad Tölz.

---

❼ Bad Tölz

A pretty spa town straddling the Isar River, Bad Tölz is a delightful spot known for its attractive, frescoed houses. It's also the gateway to the Tölzer Land region and its emerald-green lakes, the **Walchensee** and the **Kochelsee**. The town is worth a couple of hours' wander, perhaps followed by a climb up the **Kalvarienberg** (Cavalry Church), the destination for the town's famous **Leonhardifahrt** (Leonhardi pilgrimage; www.toelzer-leonhardifahrt.bayern; ⏱6 Nov).

The Drive » Some 72km divide Bad Tölz from the shores of the Chiemsee. The quickest route is along the B72 and the A8, but there are other more picturesque options.

---

❽ Chiemsee

Most foreign visitors arrive at the shores of the **Bavarian Sea** – as Chiemsee is affectionately known – in search of King Ludwig II's Schloss Herrenchiemsee. This is Bavaria's biggest lake (if you don't count Lake Constance, which is only partially in the state), and its natural beauty and water sports

DETOUR: MUNICH

Start: ❼ Bad Tölz

Just over 50km north of Bad Tölz, Munich is one of Germany's top cities and a magnet for tourists from all over the globe. You could explore this affluent, stylish city for weeks and not see everything, but a few days can give you a taste of what Bavaria's capital is all about. Take in the city-centre highlights on our walking tour (p270).

Most people start their exploration at the **Marienplatz**, a popular gathering spot that packs a lot of personality into a compact frame. It's anchored by the Mariensäule (Mary's Column). From here it's a short walk to the city's top attraction, the **Residenz**. All the trappings of the lifestyles of Bavaria's Wittelsbach rulers are on display at the Residenzmuseum, which takes up around half of the palace.

Not far from the Residenz is the **Hofbräuhaus** (☎089-290 136 100; www.hofbraeuhaus.de; Am Platzl 9; ⏱9am-midnight), Munich's most famous beer hall, although there are many others that are just as characterful. Of the city centre's churches, two stand out: the landmark **Frauenkirche** and the late-baroque **Asamkirche**.

Munich has often been dubbed the 'city of art and beer' and when you've tried the beer, next comes the **Kunstareal** (www.kunstareal.de), a whole district of world-class art museums including the Alte Pinakothek, the Museum Brandhorst, the Neue Pinakothek and the Pinakothek der Moderne.

make the area popular with Munich folk – many of the city's affluent residents own weekend retreats by the shimmering waters.

The towns of **Prien am Chiemsee** and, about 5km south, **Bernau am Chiemsee** are good bases for exploring the lake. Of the two towns, Prien is by far the larger and livelier.

The Drive » There's no car ferry to the Herreninsel. Take the hourly or half-hourly passenger ferry from Prien-Stock (€7.60 return, 15 to 20 minutes) or from Bernau-Felden (€7.90, 25 minutes, May to October). From the boat landing on Herreninsel, it's a 20-minute walk through pretty gardens to the palace.

---

⑨ Schloss Herrenchiemsee

An island just 1.5km across the Chiemsee from Prien, **Herreninsel** is home to Ludwig II's Versailles-inspired castle, **Schloss Herrenchiemsee** (📞08051-688 70; www.herren chiemsee.de; adult/child €9/free; ⏰tours 9am-6pm Apr-Oct, 9.40am-4.15pm Nov-Mar). Begun in 1878, it was never intended as a residence, but as a homage to absolutist monarchy as epitomised by Ludwig's hero, Louis XIV. Ludwig splurged more money on this palace than on Neuschwanstein and Linderhof combined, but when cash ran out in 1885, one

TOP TIP: GUEST CARD

Wherever you stay in the Alps, make sure your hotel reception supplies you with a guest card. This grants free or discounted admission to local attractions plus free use of public transport within a given area.

year before his death, 50 rooms remained unfinished. Ludwig spent only 10 days here.

The vast **Gesandten-treppe** (Ambassador Staircase), a double staircase leading to a frescoed gallery and topped by a glass roof, is the first visual knock-out on the guided tour, but that fades in comparison to the stunning **Grosse Spiegelgalerie** (Great Hall of Mirrors). This tunnel of light runs the length of the garden (98m, or 10m longer than that in Versailles).

Other highlights include the **Paradeschlaf-zimmer** (State Bedroom), featuring a canopied bed perching altar-like on a pedestal behind a golden balustrade, and the king's bedroom, the **Kleines Blaues Schlaf-zimmer** (Little Blue Bedroom), encrusted with gilded stucco and wildly extravagant carvings.

The Drive » The easy-going way to cover the 90km from Prien to Berchtesgaden is to head south to Reit im Winkl, then east almost to Bad Reichenhall on the B305 nearly all the way. Stay on the B305

to Berchtesgaden. The journey takes a little under 1¾ hours and passes through the dramatic Chiemgauer Alpen range.

---

⑩ Berchtesgaden

Wedged into Austria and framed by six formidable mountain ranges, the **Berchtesgadener Land** is a drop-dead-gorgeous corner of Bavaria. The area includes the **Watzmann** (2713m), Germany's second-highest mountain, and the pristine **Königssee**, perhaps the country's most photogenic body of water.

Away from the stunning Alpine views, Berchtesgaden has some dark tourism sights bequeathed by the Nazis who chose nearby Obersalzberg as their headquarters. **Dokumentation Obersalzberg** (📞08652-947 960; www. obersalzberg.de; Salzberg-strasse 41, Obersalzberg; adult/child €3/free, audioguide €2; ⏰9am-5pm daily Apr-Oct, 10am-3pm Tue-Sun Nov-Mar, last entry 1hr before closing) tells the story.

The **Eagle's Nest** (Kehlsteinhaus; 📞08652-29 69; www.kehlsteinhaus.de;

Classic Trip

Obersalzberg; tour €33.50; ☺ buses 8.30am-4.50pm mid-May–Oct) was built as a mountaintop retreat for Hitler, and gifted to him on his 50th birthday. It took some 3000 workers only two years to carve the precipitous 6km-long mountain road, cut a 124m-long tunnel, install a brass-panelled lift through the rock, and build the lodge itself (now a restaurant). It can only be reached by special shuttle bus from the Kehlsteinhaus bus station.

📖 p245

The Drive » It's a short 6km drive to Schönau on the northern shore of the Königssee. Electric boats depart for lake tours.

- - - - - - - - - - - - - - - -

TRIP HIGHLIGHT

⑪ Königssee

Crossing the serenely picturesque, emerald-green **Königssee** makes for some once-in-a-lifetime photo opportunities. Cradled by steep mountain walls some 5km south of Berchtesgaden, Königssee is Germany's highest

HITLER'S MOUNTAIN RETREAT

Of all the German towns tainted by the Third Reich, Berchtesgaden has a burden heavier than most. Hitler fell in love with nearby Obersalzberg in the 1920s and bought a small country home, later enlarged into the imposing Berghof.

After seizing power in 1933, Hitler established a part-time headquarters here and brought much of the party brass with him. They bought, or often confiscated, large tracts of land and tore down farmhouses to erect a 7ft-high barbed-wire fence. Obersalzberg was sealed off as the fortified southern headquarters of the NSDAP (National Socialist German Workers' Party). In 1938, British prime minister Neville Chamberlain visited for negotiations (later continued in Munich), which led to the infamous promise of 'peace in our time' at the expense of Czechoslovakia's Sudetenland.

Little is left of Hitler's Alpine fortress today. In the final days of WWII, the Royal Air Force levelled much of Obersalzberg, though the Eagle's Nest (p243), Hitler's mountaintop eyrie, was left strangely unscathed. The historical twist and turns are dissected at the impressive Dokumentation Obersalzberg (p243).

lake (603m), with pure, drinkable waters shimmering into fjordlike depths.

Escape the hubbub of the bustling lakeside tourist village of **Schönau** by taking an electric-boat tour to **St Bartholomä**, a quaint onion-domed chapel on the western shore. At some point, the boat will stop while the captain plays a horn towards the **Echo Wall** – the sound

will bounce seven times. From St Bartholomä, an easy trail leads to the wondrous **Eiskapelle** (ice chapel) in about one hour.

You can also skip the crowds by meandering along the lake shore. It's a nice and easy 3.5km return walk to the secluded **Malerwinkel** (Painter's Corner), a lookout famed for its picturesque vantage point.

Eating & Sleeping

Lindau ➊

✘ Valentin   Mediterranean €€€

(☎08382-504 3740; www.valentin-lindau.de; In der Grub 28; mains €20-25; ⏰11.30am-3pm & 5.30-11pm Tue-Sat; ⚡) With a deft hand, the chef sources local, seasonal, largely organic ingredients to go into his Med-style dishes at this chic vaulted restaurant. Dishes such as ayurvedic spinach soup, octopus with chorizo, cabbage and sweet potato, and chocolate molten cake with pumpkin ice cream are beautifully prepared and presented. Vegetarians and vegans are well catered for.

🛏 Reutemann & Seegarten   Luxury Hotel €€€

(☎08382-9150; www.reutemann-lindau. de; Ludwigstrasse 23; s €99-185, d €142-263; 🛜🏊) Wow, what a view! Facing the harbour, lighthouse and lion statue, this hotel has plush, spacious rooms done out in sunny shades, plus a pool big enough to swim laps, spa, gym and refined restaurant. It's worth paying extra for a room with a lake view.

Füssen ➋

✘ Zum Hechten   Bavarian €€

(Ritterstrasse 6; mains €8-19; ⏰10am-10pm) Füssen's best hotel restaurant keeps things regional with a menu of Allgäu staples like schnitzel and noodles, Bavarian pork-themed favourites, and local specialities such as venison goulash from the Ammertal. Post-meal, relax in the wood-panelled dining room caressing a König Ludwig Dunkel, one of Germany's best dark beers brewed by the current head of the Wittelsbach family.

🛏 Hotel Sonne   Design Hotel €€

(☎08362-9080; Prinzregentenplatz 1; s/d from €100/120; 🅿🛜) Although traditional looking from outside, this Altstadt favourite offers an unexpected design-hotel experience within. Themed rooms feature everything from swooping bed canopies to big-print wallpaper, huge pieces of wall art to sumptious fabrics. The public spaces are littered with pieces of art, period costumes and design features – the overall effect is impressive and unusual for this part of Germany.

Garmisch-Partenkirchen ➎

✘ Gasthof Fraundorfer   Bavarian €€

(☎08821-9270; www.gasthof-fraundorfer. de; Ludwigstrasse 24; mains €11-20; ⏰7am-midnight Thu-Mon, from 5pm Wed) If you've travelled to the Alps to experience yodelling, knee slapping and beetroot-faced locals squeezed into Lederhosen, you just arrived at the right address. Steins of frothing ale fuel the increasingly raucous atmosphere as the evening progresses and monster portions of plattered pig meat push belt buckles to the limit. Decor ranges from baroque cherubs to hunting trophies and the 'Sports Corner'. Unmissable.

🛏 Reindl's Partenkirchner Hof   Hotel €€

(☎08821-943 870; www.reindls.de; Bahnhofstrasse 15; s/d €100/150; 🅿🛜) Reindl's may not look worthy of its five stars from street level, but this elegant, tri-winged luxury hotel is stacked with perks, a wine bar and a top-notch gourmet restaurant. Renovated to perfection on a rolling basis, the rooms are studies in folk-themed elegance and some enjoy gobsmacking Alpine views to get you in the mood.

Berchtesgaden ➓

🛏 Hotel Edelweiss   Hotel €€

(☎08652-979 90; www.edelweiss-berchtes gaden.com; Maximilianstrasse 2; s/d €140/230; 🛜🏊) In the heart of town, the Edelweiss is a sleek affair. The style could be described as modern Bavarian, meaning a combination of traditional woodsy flair and factors such as a luxe spa, a rooftop terrace restaurant-bar with widescreen Alpine views and an outdoor infinity pool. Rooms are XL-sized and most have a balcony.

Lake Constance

20

This circular route around Lake Constance (Bodensee) takes you from lakeside cafes to baroque churches, medieval cathedrals to sandy beaches, all sharing stupendous Alpine views.

TRIP HIGHLIGHTS

104 km

Konstanz
Historical city on the Switzerland–Germany border

49 km

Meersburg
A duo of castles awaits in this pretty town

③

⑤

Friedrichshafen

① **START**

⑦ **FINISH**

Rorschach

Lindau
Easy-going town with an attractive promenade

Bregenz
Austrian lakeside city with wonderful views

0 km

180 km

7 DAYS
180KM / 112 MILES

GREAT FOR...

BEST TIME TO GO
Easter to October: winter fog doesn't obscure views and all sights are open.

 ESSENTIAL PHOTO
Aerial shots from a Zeppelin over Lake Constance.

 BEST FOR HISTORY
Meersburg's castle double act is unmissable for history fans.

20 | Lake Constance

Shared by three countries (Germany, Austria and Switzerland), Lake Constance is Central Europe's third-largest body of water. Taking in meadows and vineyards, orchards and wetlands, beaches and Alpine foothills, the lake's landscapes make a 'greatest hits' of European scenery. Add to that heaps of culture, medieval architecture and relaxed lakeside promenades and you have yourself a highly enjoyable drive with many reasons to stop along the way.

TRIP HIGHLIGHT

❶ Lindau

Lindau is also the starting point for Trip 19.

Some of the town's lesser-known attractions are also worth an hour or two of exploration. The **Peterskirche** (Oberer Schrannenplatz; ⊘ variable) is a 1000-year-old church now transformed into a war memorial, but still hiding exquisite time-faded frescos of the Passion of Christ by Hans Holbein the Elder. The cool, dimly lit

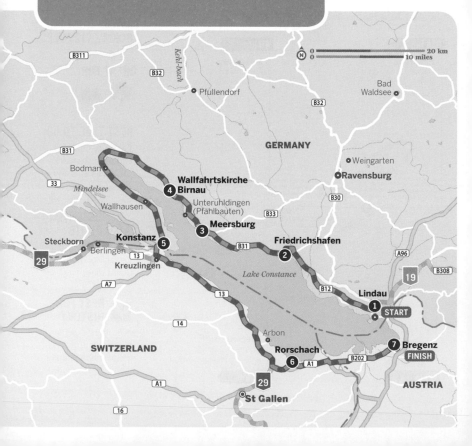

interior is a quiet spot for contemplation. Lions and voluptuous dames dance across the *trompe l'oeil* facade of the flamboyantly baroque Haus zum Cavazzen, the town's museum which is currently under renovation.

 p245, p253

The Drive » This anticlockwise route follows a simple rule: if the lake is on your right, you're going the wrong way! From Lindau take the L116 as far as Kressbronn. From there take the L334 to Eriskirch, where you join the B31 as far as Friedrichshafen. The journey is around 30km.

---

② Friedrichshafen

Zeppelins, the cigar-shaped airships that first took flight in 1900 under the stewardship of high-flying Count Ferdinand von Zeppelin, will forever be associat-

LINK YOUR TRIP

19 German Alpine Road

Both this Lake Constance route and the German Alpine Road kick off in Lindau.

29 Northern Switzerland

This route in Switzerland starts in St Gallen, only about 13km southwest of Rorschach.

COME FLY WITH ME

Real airship fans will justify the splurge on a trip in a high-tech, 12-passenger **Zeppelin NT** (📞07541-590 00; www.zeppelin-nt.de; Messestrasse 132; 30-45 min flights €255-375). Flights last between 30 and 45 minutes for trips covering lake destinations such as Schloss Salem and Lindau, while longer ones drift across to Austria or Switzerland. Take-off and landing are in Friedrichshafen. The flights aren't cheap but little beats floating over Lake Constance with the Alps on the horizon, and their slow pace means that you can make the most of the legendary photo ops.

ed with Friedrichshafen. Near the eastern end of its lakefront promenade, Seestrasse, is the **Zeppelin Museum** (www.zeppelin-museum.de; Seestrasse 22; adult/child €11/6, ☉9am-5pm daily May-Oct, 10am-5pm Tue-Sun Nov-Apr), housed in the Bauhaus-style former Hafenbahnhof, built in 1932. The centrepiece is a full-scale mock-up of a 33m section of the *Hindenburg* (LZ 129), the largest airship ever built, measuring an incredible 245m long and outfitted as luxuriously as an ocean liner. The hydrogen-filled craft tragically burst into flames, killing 36, while landing in New Jersey in 1937. Other exhibits provide technical and historical insights, including an original motor gondola from the famous *Graf Zeppelin,* which made 590 trips and travelled around the world in 21 days in 1929.

A promenade runs through the sculpture-dotted lakefront Stadtgarten park along Uferstrasse, a great spot for a picnic or stroll.

 p253

The Drive » The 19km drive from Friedrichshafen to Meersburg hugs the lakeshore most of the way as it follows the B31. En route, the town of Immenstaad is a pretty stop, its old town gathered around a small promontory and pier.

TRIP HIGHLIGHT

③ Meersburg

Tumbling down vine-streaked slopes to Lake Constance and crowned by a perkily turreted medieval castle, Meersburg lives up to all those clichéd knight-in-armour, damsel-in-distress fantasies. And if its tangle of cobbled lanes and half-timbered houses filled with jovial banter doesn't sweep you off your feet, the local Pinot noir served in its cosy *Weinstuben* (wine taverns) certainly will.

Meersburg's two castles are the town's premier attractions. Looking across Lake Constance from its high perch, the **Altes Schloss** (Schlossplatz 10; adult/concession €12.80/10; ⊘9am-6.30pm Mar-Oct, 10am-6pm Nov-Feb) is an archetypal medieval stronghold, complete with keep, drawbridge, knights' hall and dungeons. The **Neues Schloss** (www.neues-schloss-meersburg.de; Schlossplatz 13; adult/concession €5/2.50; ⊘9.30am-6pm Apr-Oct, noon-5pm Sat & Sun Nov-Mar) was built in 1710 by Prince-Bishop Johann Franz Schenk von Stauffenberg, and is a dusky-pink, lavishly baroque affair. A visit to the now state-owned palace takes in the extravagant bishops' apartments, replete with stucco work and frescos, Balthasar Neumann's elegant staircase, and gardens with inspirational lake views.

The Drive » The quickest way to go between Meersburg and the next stop, the Wallfahrtskirche Birnau, is to stick to the B31 all the way (9km). The lakefront road is not a suitable route.

---

❹ Wallfahrtskirche Birnau

The exuberant, powder-pink **Wallfahrtskirche Basilika Birnau** (Uhldingen-Mühlhofen; ⊘7.30am-7pm, to 5pm in winter) is one of Lake Constance's architectural highlights. It was built by the rococo master Peter Thumb of Vorarlberg in 1746. When you walk in, the decor is so intricate and profuse that you don't know where to look first. At some point your gaze will be drawn to the ceiling, where Gottfried Bernhard Göz worked his usual fresco magic.

The Drive » There are two ways of reaching Konstanz. The short way is to backtrack to Meersburg and take the ferry. The long way is to head to the north of the lake then southeast along the western shore, a journey of around 46km.

TRIP HIGHLIGHT

❺ Konstanz

Sidling up to the Swiss border, bisected by the Rhine and outlined by the Alps, Konstanz sits prettily on the north-western shore of Lake Constance. Roman emperors, medieval traders and the bishops of the 15th-century Council of Constance have all left their mark on this alley-woven town, which was mercifully spared the bombs of WWII.

Crowned by a filigreed spire and looking proudly back on 1000 years of history, the sandstone **Münster** (Münsterplatz 1; tower adult/child €2/1; ⊘10am-6pm, tower 10am-5pm Mon-Sat, 12.30-5.30pm Sun) was the church of the diocese of Konstanz until 1821. The cathedral's interior is an architectural potpourri of Romanesque, Gothic, Renaissance and baroque styles. It's worth ascending the tower for broad views over the city and lake. On the lake itself, the sculpture-dotted promenade lures inline skaters, cyclists, walkers and ice-cream lickers. Just 4km northeast of the centre, the **Strandbad Horn** (Eichhornstrasse 100; ⊘mid-May–Sep; 🚻) has sunbathing lawns, a kiddie pool and sports facilities.

🍴 🛏 p253, p261

TOP TIP: BODENSEE CARD

The three-day **Bodensee Erlebniskarte** (adult/child €69/41) is available at area tourist and ferry offices – it allows travel on almost all boats and mountain cableways on and around Lake Constance (including its Austrian and Swiss shores) and gets you entry to more than 160 tourist attractions and museums.

Meersburg Altes Schloss

The Drive » The border with Switzerland doesn't come straight after the bridge over the Rhine in Konstanz, but a couple of kilometres further on. Have your passport ready just in case. After that, road 13 hugs the lake's shore all the way to Rorschach, a journey of around 40km.

---

❻ Rorschach

The quiet waterfront resort of Rorschach on the Swiss side of the lake is backed by a wooded hill. Although something of a faded beauty, the town has some fine 16th- to 18th-century houses with oriel windows. Out on the lake is the 1920s Badhütte (Bathing Hut), attached to land by a small, covered bridge; it is a pleasant place for a drink.

The Drive » From Rorschach take road 7 east to the A1 highway. Stay on this until the signs for the exit to the border crossing with Austria. From there the B202 heads into Bregenz, crossing the Rhine Canal on the way. The journey is 27km long.

TRIP HIGHLIGHT

❼ Bregenz

Bregenz enjoys the most stupendous of views, with the lake spreading out like a liquid mirror; behind you the Pfänder (1064m) climbs to the Alps; to the right you see Germany, to the left the faint outline of Switzerland.

Three attractions stand out in Vorarlberg's capital. Designed by Swiss architect Peter Zumthor, the giant glass-and-steel cube of the **Kunsthaus** (www.kunsthaus-bregenz.at; Karl-Tizian-Platz; adult/child €11/free; ⊘10am-6pm Tue, Wed & Fri-Sun, to 8pm Thu; 🚼) is said to resemble a lamp, reflecting the changing light of the sky and lake. The stark, open-plan interior is perfect for rotating exhibitions of contemporary art. The striking home of the **Vorarlberg Museum** (www.vorarlbergmuseum.at; Kornmarktplatz 1; adult/child €9/free; ⊘10am-6pm Tue, Wed & Fri-Sun, to 8pm Thu) is a white cuboid that homes in on Vorarlberg's history, art and architecture. For an outdoor experience, the **Pfänder Cable Car** (www.pfaenderbahn.at; Steinbruchgasse 4; adult/child one way €7.70/3.80, return €13.20/6.60; ⊘8am-7pm) whizzes to the peak of the Pfänder, a wooded mountain rearing above Bregenz with a breathtaking panorama.

✕ 🛏 p253, p293, p303

Eating & Sleeping

Lindau ❶

✕ Grosstadt
Cafe €€

(📞08382-504 2998; www.grosstadt-lindau.de; In der Grub 27; light meals around €10; ⏰9am-11pm Tue-Sat; 🛜🍴) There's always a good buzz at this retro-flavoured cafe, full of intimate nooks and crannies and with a terrace spilling out onto the cobbles. The menu is a winning mix of speciality coffees, wraps, soups, creative salads, bagels and deli-style dishes such as marinated feta with rocket, with vegan and gluten-free options. It morphs into a chilled bar by night.

🛏 Reutemann & Seegarten
Luxury Hotel €€€

(📞08382-9150; www.reutemann-lindau. de; Ludwigstrasse 23; s €99-185, d €142-263; 🛜🏊) Wow, what a view! Facing the harbour, lighthouse and lion statue, this hotel has plush, spacious rooms done out in sunny shades, plus a pool big enough to swim laps, a spa, gym and refined restaurant. It's worth paying extra for a room with a lake view.

Friedrichshafen ❷

🛏 Aika Seaside Living
Boutique Hotel €€€

(📞07541-378 357; www.aika-cafe.de; Karlstrasse 38; d €140-220, ste €260-350; 🛜) Well, it might not be the 'seaside' exactly, but Aika comes up trumps with its large, spacious, wood-floored rooms and slick, contemporary neutral-palette suites, which come with fabulous views of the lake. The **cafe** (snacks €3-8; ⏰8.30am-8pm Mon-Fri, 9am-8pm Sat, 9.30am-8pm Sun) downstairs has one of the best terraces in town.

Konstanz ❺

✕ Tamara's Weinstube
German €

(📞07531-284 318; http://tamaras-weinstube. de; Zollernstrasse 6-8; light bites & meals €6-14; ⏰4pm-1am Mon-Sat) With stone walls, low wood beams, soft lighting and a traditional *Kachelofen* (tiled oven), this wine bar is as cosy as they come.

It's a terrific spot for an evening of Badisch wines and regional grub such as ox salad with onions and gherkins, homemade potato salad, pork knuckles and farm-fresh bratwurst.

🛏 Riva
Boutique Hotel €€€

(📞07531-363 090; www.hotel-riva.de; Seestrasse 25; s €110-230, d €200-320, ste €320-660; 🅿🛜🏊) This ultrachic contender has crisp white spaces, glass walls and a snail-like stairwell. Zen-like rooms with hardwood floors feature perks like free minibars. A rooftop pool, spa area, gym, and gourmet restaurant and terrace overlooking the lake seal the deal.

Bregenz ❼

✕ Kornmesser
Austrian €€

(📞05574-548 54; www.kornmesser.at; Kornmarktstrasse 5; 2-course lunch €9.40, mains €19-35; ⏰9am-midnight Tue-Sun) Dine on local favourites in the vaulted interior or chestnut-shaded beer garden of this 18th-century baroque *Gästehaus*. These include pork knuckle with bread dumplings and potato salad, roast local trout with parsley potatoes, boiled beef with horseradish, pasta with picked-the-same-day chanterelles, and an 'emperor's pancake' (with stewed plums).

✕ Wirtshaus am See
Austrian €€

(📞05574-422 10; www.wirtshausamsee.at; Seepromenade 2; mains €15-27; ⏰9am-midnight; 🍴) Snag a table on the lakefront terrace at this mock half-timbered villa, dishing up local specialities such as buttery Bodensee whitefish and venison ragout. Vegetarian options abound. It's also a relaxed spot for quaffing a cold one. Service can be hit-and-miss.

🛏 Schwärzler
Hotel €€

(📞05574-49 90; www.schwaerzler.s-hotels. com; Landstrasse 9; d €165-275; 🅿🛜🏊) This turreted, ivy-clad place is a far cry from your average business hotel. Contemporary rooms are done out in earthy hues and blond wood, with comforts including bathrobes, flat-screen TVs and minibars. Regional produce from organic farms features on the breakfast buffet, and there's an indoor pool and sauna area.

Fantastic Road

21

This loop lives up to its name, taking you through a fantasy land of enchanting forests, gingerbread villages, turreted castles and mirror-like Alpine lakes.

TRIP HIGHLIGHTS

598 km

Baden-Baden
Home to a palatial spa and lavish casino

Heidelberg

START/ FINISH

9

● Stuttgart

● Tübingen

Breisach

6 **5**

Konstanz
Spectacularly set on the shores of Lake Constance

322 km

Meersburg
A medieval Schloss, and a baroque one too

305 km

**4–6 DAYS
753KM / 468 MILES**

GREAT FOR...

BEST TIME TO GO
June to August offers the loveliest summer weather.

 ESSENTIAL PHOTO

Schloss Hohentübingen's terrace overlooks the river, old town and vine-streaked hills beyond.

 BEST FOR FOODIES

Black Forest gateau on its home turf.

Driving through the Black Forest

255

21 | Fantastic Road

On this ring encircling the German state of Baden-Württemberg, you'll be dazzled by its jewels: the ancient university city of Heidelberg, a string of storybook castles, sparkling Alp-framed lakes, a lush island-set garden, and a swathe of thick Black Forest. Treasures include half-timbered villages huddled around cobbled squares, and the yesteryear grandeur of Baden-Baden, with its temple-like spa and opulent casino.

❶ Heidelberg

Spirited Heidelberg is famed for its centuries-old university. The three-room **Universitätsmuseum** (www.uni-heidelberg. de; Grabengasse 1; adult/child incl Studentenkarzer €3/2.50; ⏰10am-6pm Tue-Sun Apr-Sep, to 4pm Tue-Sat Oct-Mar), inside the Alte Universität building, has paintings, portraits, photos and documents about the university's mostly illustrious history.

From 1823 to 1914, students convicted of misdeeds such as public inebriation, duelling, loud nocturnal singing or freeing the local pigs were sent to its student jail, the **Studentenkarzer**

(Student Jail; ☎06221-541 2813; www.uni-heidelberg.de; Auginergasse 2; adult/child incl Universitätsmuseum €3/2.50; ⏰10am-6pm Tue-Sun Apr-Oct, to 4pm Mon-Sat Nov-Mar), for at least 24 hours. Judging by the inventive wall graffiti, some found their stay highly amusing. Delinquents were let out to attend lectures or take exams. In certain circles, a stint in the Karzer was considered a rite of passage.

Heidelberg's student atmosphere peaks in its pubs, including its most historic, **Zum Roten Ochsen** (Red Ox Inn; www. roterochsen.de; Hauptstrasse 217; ⏰5pm-midnight Mon-Wed, from 11.30am Thu-Sat), with black-and-white

frat photos on its dark wooden walls and names carved into the tables.

The Drive » Zooming along 120km of autobahn is the easiest way to reach Stuttgart. Southwest of Heidelberg take the A5 south for 9km. Join the eastbound A6 for 52km, and turn off onto the southbound A81 for another 52km.

✕ ⇌ p199

---

❷ Stuttgart

The city where Bosch invented the spark plug and Daimler pioneered the gas engine has plenty to interest road-trippers, not least its two high-powered motoring museums. The **Mercedes-Benz Museum** (📞0711-173 0000; www.mercedes-benz. com, Mercedesstrasse 100; adult/concession €10/5; ⏱9am-6pm Tue-Sun, last admission 5pm; Ⓢ Neckarpark) takes a chronological spin through the Mercedes empire. Look out

LINK YOUR TRIP

15 **Bergstrasse**
Pick up the castle-lined, mountain-backed Bergstrasse in Heidelberg.

22 **Schwarzwald-hochstrasse**
Baden-Baden is the starting point for a glorious drive through the Black Forest along the Schwarzwaldhochstrasse.

for legends like the 1885 Daimler Riding Car, the world's first gasoline-powered vehicle, and the record-breaking Lightning Benz that hit 228km/h at Daytona Beach in 1909. At the **Porsche Museum** (☏0711-9112 0911; www.porsche.com/museum; Porscheplatz 1; adult/concession €8/4; ⊕9am-6pm Tue-Sun; ⑤Neuwirtshaus), groovy audioguides race you through the history of Porsche from its 1948 beginnings. Stop to glimpse the 911 GT1 that won Le Mans in 1998.

The Drive » From Stuttgart, it's 43km south via the B27 to Tübingen.

- - - - - - - - - - - - - - - -

❸ Tübingen

In this bewitchingly pretty city, cobbled lanes lined with half-timbered townhouses twist up to a turreted 16th-century castle, **Schloss Hohentübingen** (☏07071-297 7579; www.unimuseum.uni-tuebingen.de; Burgsteige 11; tour adult/concession €5/3; ⊕10am-6pm Wed-Sun May-Sep, to 5pm Oct-Apr). An ornate Renaissance gate leads to the courtyard and the laboratory where Friedrich Miescher discovered DNA in 1869. Inside the castle, view the world's oldest figurative artworks, the locally unearthed 35,000-year-old Vogelherd figurines, at the **Museum Alte Kulturen** (adult/concession

€5/3; ⊕10am-5pm Wed, Fri-Sun, to 7pm Thu).

✂ 🛏 p261

The Drive » Back on the B27, drive south for 25km. At the Hechingen-Süd exit, take the K7111 (which becomes the K7110) for 2.3km to reach the lower and upper car parks for Burg Hohenzollern, from where it's an 800m or a 600m walk, respectively, to the castle.

- - - - - - - - - - - - - - - -

❹ Burg Hohenzollern

Rising dramatically from an exposed crag, its medieval battlements and silver turrets often veiled in mist, neo-Gothic **Burg Hohenzollern** (www.burg-hohenzollern.com; adult/concession tour €12/8, grounds admission without tour €7/5; ⊕tours 10am-5.30pm mid-Mar–Oct, to 4.30pm Nov–mid-Mar) dates from 1867. It's the ancestral seat of the Hohenzollern family, the first and last monarchical rulers of the short-lived second German Empire (1871–1918).

The Drive » From Burg Hohenzollern, it's 110km southeast to Meersburg. When you cross the Danube at Sigmaringen, look out for the stunning Schloss Sigmaringen (rarely open to the public). The B31 bringing you into Meersburg skirts Lake Constance's eastern shore.

- - - - - - - - - - - - - - - -

TRIP HIGHLIGHT

❺ Meersburg

Tumbling down vine-laced slopes to Lake Constance, Meersburg's

ROMANBABAKIN / GETTY IMAGES ©

tangle of cobbled lanes and half-timbered houses are the stuff of medieval fantasies. Looking across the lake from its lofty perch, the **Altes Schloss** (Schlossplatz 10; adult/concession €12.80/10; ⊕9am-6.30pm Mar-Oct, 10am-6pm Nov-Feb) is an archetypal medieval stronghold, complete with keep, drawbridge, knights' hall and dungeons. Founded by Merovingian king Dagobert I in the 7th century, the fortress is among Germany's oldest. The bishops of Konstanz used it as a summer residence between 1268 and 1803.

Baden-Baden (p260) Old town

In 1710 Prince-Bishop Johann Franz Schenk von Stauffenberg, perhaps tired of the dinginess and rising damp, swapped the Altes Schloss for the dusky-pink, lavishly baroque **Neues Schloss** (www.neues-schloss-meersburg.de; Schlossplatz 13; adult/concession €5/2.50; ⊙9.30am-6pm Apr-Oct, noon-5pm Sat & Sun Nov-Mar). A visit to the now state-owned palace takes in the extravagant bishops' apartments, replete with stucco work and frescos, Balthasar Neumann's elegant staircase, and gardens with inspirational lake views.

The Drive » From Meersburg's harbour, take the car ferry across Lake Constance to the B33 and follow it into Konstanz (10km including the ferry ride).

TRIP HIGHLIGHT

❻ Konstanz

Konstanz is a highlight on a road filled with highlights, with its stunning location on the northwestern shore of Lake Constance, magnificent architecture and a fascinating history spanning Roman emperors, medieval traders and the bishops of the 15th-century Council of Constance. It also has a spirited student scene.

See p250 for details of the city's attractions.

✕ ⨳ p253, p261

The Drive » Take the B33 northwest for 50km and turn left (southwest) onto the B31. Pass beautiful Freiburg (well worth a stop if you have time); 6km later turn left onto the A5 towards Basel for 12km, before taking the B31 for 11km to reach Breisach.

---

❼ Breisach

Breisach is where the Black Forest meets the French border. Lording over the town, the Romanesque and Gothic **St Stephansmünster**

259

DETOUR: MAINAU ISLAND

Start: ⑥ Konstanz

From Konstanz, it's a quick 6km drive north via the B33 and L219 to the car park for Mainau Island, which is reached by a pedestrian-only causeway. (If you want to leave the car behind for a while, you can also take a ferry here from Konstanz.)

Jutting out over the lake, the lusciously green islet of Mainau is a 45-hectare Mediterranean **garden** (www.mainau.de; adult/concession summer €21.50/12.50, winter €10.50/6.50; ⏰10am-7pm late Mar-late Oct, to 5pm rest of year) dreamed up by the Bernadotte family, relatives of the royal house of Sweden.

Crowds especially flock on weekends to admire sparkly lake and mountain views from the baroque castle, and to wander sequoia-shaded avenues and hothouses bristling with palms and orchids. Crowd-pullers include a butterfly house, an Italian Cascade integrating patterned flowers with waterfalls, and a petting zoo. Tulips and rhododendrons bloom in spring, hibiscus and roses in summer.

(Münsterplatz; ⏰9am-5pm Mon-Sat) shelters a faded fresco cycle, Martin Schongauer's *The Last Judgment* (1491), and a magnificent altar triptych (1526) carved from linden wood.

Breisach's cobbled streets are lined with pastel-painted houses, and you'd never guess that 85% of the town was flattened in WWII, so successful has been the reconstruction. Vauban's star-shaped French fortress-town of Neuf-Brisach (New Breisach), which made the Unesco World Heritage list in 2008, sits 4km west of Breisach.

The Drive » Vineyards fan out around you on this stretch of the trip. Head north via the L104 to reach the A5. Take it north towards Offenburg for 39km and link up with the B33. Following the B33 east brings you to Gengenbach (a 77km drive in total), within the Black Forest.

---

⑧ Gengenbach

Chocolate-box Gengenbach's chief 'sight' is its scrumptious Altstadt (old town) of half-timbered houses framed by vineyards and orchards. It's especially atmospheric during its Christmas festivities.

🛏 p261

The Drive » It's a 96km journey to Baden-Baden. Take the B33 south; at Biberach, wind northeast for 35km to reach the high-altitude B500 (aka the Schwarzwaldhochstrasse or Black Forest High Road, which you can explore on Trip 22). For the next 46km, views stretch over the mist-wreathed Vosges Mountains, heather-flecked forests and glacial lakes.

TRIP HIGHLIGHT

⑨ Baden-Baden

Baden-Baden recalls the grandeur of yesteryear with its colonnaded buildings and turreted Art Nouveau villas beneath a backdrop of forest-covered mountains.

Gleaming with marble and glistening with mosaics, the palatial 19th-century Friedrichsbad (p265) thermal baths put the *baden* (bathe) in Baden.

Marlene Dietrich called Baden-Baden's sublime **casino** (☎07221-302 40; www.casino-baden-baden. de; Kaiserallee 1; admission €5, guided tour €7; ⏰2pm-2am Sun-Thu, to 3.30am Fri & Sat, guided tours 9.30-11.45am Apr-Oct, 10am-11.30am Nov-Mar) 'the most beautiful casino in the world'. Gents must wear a jacket and tie. To marvel at the opulence, take a guided tour.

🍴 🛏 p261, p269

The Drive » From Baden-Baden, it's a quick 90km back to Heidelberg. Take the B500 (Schwarzwaldhochstrasse) northwest for 6.3km and turn northeast onto the A5. Along the way, you'll pass the town of Karlsruhe, which was the model for Washington, DC.

Eating & Sleeping

Tübingen ❸

✗ Neckarmüller — Pub Food €€

(☎07071-278 48; www.neckarmueller.de; Gartenstrasse 4; mains €9-20; ⏱10am-1am Mon-Sat, to midnight Sun) Overlooking the Neckar, this cavernous microbrewery is a summertime magnet for its chestnut-shaded beer garden. Come for home brews by the metre and beer-laced dishes from (tasty) Swabian roast to (interesting) tripe stew.

🛏 Hotel am Schloss — Historic Hotel €€

(☎07071-929 40; www.hotelamschloss.de; Burgsteige 18; s/d from €125/150; P🛜) So close to the castle you can almost touch it, this flower-bedecked hotel has dapper rooms ensconced in a 16th-century building. The hotel's cosy restaurant **Mauganeschtle** (mains €12-27; ⏱noon-2.30pm & 6pm-midnight) excels in hearty Swabian grub.

Konstanz ❻

🛏 Glückseeligkeit Herberge — Guesthouse €

(☎07531-902 2075; www.herberge-konstanz.de; Neugasse 20; s €35-60, d €70-80; 🛜) What a sweet deal this little guesthouse is. Housed in a period building in the Altstadt, it shelters petite but attractively decorated rooms. The attic room has direct access to the roof terrace, which peers over a jumble of rooftops to the cathedral spire. There's also a shared lounge, kitchen and patio. E-bikes available to rent.

Gengenbach ❽

🛏 Die Reichsstadt — Boutique Hotel €€€

(☎07803-966 30; www.die-reichsstadt.de; Engelgasse 33; d from €120; P🛜) This boutique stunner on Engelgasse wings you to storybook heaven. Its 16th-century exterior conceals a pure, contemporary aesthetic, where clean lines, natural materials and subtle cream-caramel shades are enlivened with eye-catching details. A spa, sparkling wine on arrival, free fruit in your room and one of the top restaurants in town complete this pretty picture.

Baden-Baden ❾

✗ Café König — Cafe €

(Lichtentaler Strasse 12; cake €3.50-5, lunch specials €11-19; ⏱8.30am-6.30pm) Liszt and Tolstoy once sipped coffee at this venerable cafe, which has been doing a brisk trade in Baden-Baden's finest cakes, tortes, pralines and truffles for over 250 years. Black Forest gateau topped with clouds of cream; fresh berry tarts; or moist nut cakes – oh, decisions!

✗ Schneider's Weinstube & Vinothek — German €€€

(☎07221-976 6929; www.schneiders-weinstube.de; Merkurstrasse 3; mains €14-25; ⏱5-11pm Mon-Sat) A charmingly old-school choice, Schneider's brings you the best of Badisch food and Pinot wines to the table. You'll receive a heartfelt welcome in the warmly lit space, where the menu swings with the seasons – from pike-perch with potato salad to braised wild boar with cranberry sauce. Check out the daily specials on the blackboard.

🛏 Hotel Belle Epoque — Luxury Hotel €€€

(☎07221-300 660; www.hotel-belle-epoque.de; Maria-Viktoria-Strasse 2c; s €155-185, d €240-305, ste €390-685; 🛜) Nestling in manicured parkland, this neo-Renaissance villa is one of Baden-Baden's most characterful five-star pads. Antiques lend old-world opulence to the individually designed rooms. Rates include afternoon tea, with scones, cakes and fine brews served on the terrace or by the fireplace.

Schwarzwald-hochstrasse

22

What it says on the tin: the Black Forest High Road meanders scenically past glacial lakes, toytown villages and the gentle folds of valleys and forests that seem to roll on to infinity.

TRIP HIGHLIGHTS

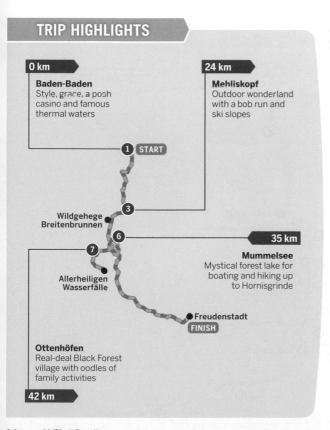

0 km

Baden-Baden
Style, grace, a posh casino and famous thermal waters

24 km

Mehliskopf
Outdoor wonderland with a bob run and ski slopes

1 START

3

Wildgehege
Breitenbrunnen

6

7

35 km

Mummelsee
Mystical forest lake for boating and hiking up to Hornisgrinde

Allerheiligen
Wasserfälle

●Freudenstadt
FINISH

Ottenhöfen
Real-deal Black Forest village with oodles of family activities

42 km

2–4 DAYS
60KM / 37 MILES

GREAT FOR...

BEST TIME TO GO
Spring to autumn for seasonal colour (flowers and foliage).

📷 ESSENTIAL PHOTO
Snap the Black Forest peaks wreathed in morning mist.

☑ BEST FOR FAMILIES
Mehliskopf for its zippy bob run and high-rope course.

22 Schwarzwald-hochstrasse

Road trips in the deep, dark Black Forest don't get any lovelier than the Schwarzwaldhoch-strasse. Why? This is a road with altitude, where the views over hill and dale are constant. Wind down the window for pine-fresh air as you wiggle south from the spa town of Baden-Baden to Freudenstadt, passing heather-flecked woodlands, luscious meadows, waterfalls, lakes and stout farmhouses. Autumn brings a dash of gold to the picture.

TRIP HIGHLIGHT

❶ Baden-Baden

Baden-Baden's air of old-world luxury and curative waters have attracted royals, the rich and celebrities over the years – Obama and Bismarck, Queen Victoria and Victoria Beckham included. This chic Black Forest town boasts grand colonnaded buildings and whimsically tur-reted Art Nouveau villas spread across the forested hillsides. Top billing goes to the grand neoclassical

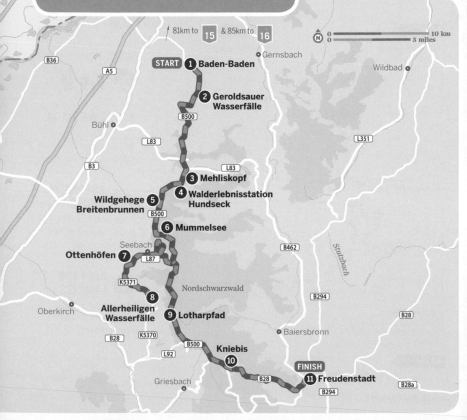

Trinkhalle (Pump Room; Kaiserallee 3; ⏰10am-6pm Mon-Sat, 2-5pm Sun), a pump room embellished with 19th-century frescos of local legends, the sublime gilded casino (p260) and the architecturally innovative **Museum Frieder Burda** (📞07221 398 980, www.museum-frieder-burda. de; Lichtentaler Allee 8b; adult/concession €14/11; ⏰10am-6pm Tue-Sun), whose stellar collection features Picasso, Gerhard Richter and Jackson Pollock. If the sun's out, join the locals for a lazy mooch along the **Lichtentaler Allee**, a 2.3km ribbon of greenery shadowing the sprightly Oosbach, studded with fountains and carpeted with flowers.

 p261, p269

LINK YOUR TRIP

15 **Bergstrasse**
From Baden-Baden, drive 86km north to Wiesloch and the Bergstrasse, a road trip taking in castles and vineyards aplenty.

16 **German Castle Road**
Like nothing better than a good castle? You'll be in your element on this history-packed road trip. Hook onto it in Heidelberg, 90km north of Baden-Baden.

SPA TIME

The bath-loving Romans were the first to discover the healing properties of Baden-Baden's springs in the city they called Aquae Aureliae. Rheumatism, arthritis, respiratory complaints, skin problems – all this and a host of other ailments can be healed, apparently, by this mineral-rich spring water. To take the waters yourself, you could abandon modesty (and clothing) to wallow in thermal waters at **Friedrichsbad** (📞07221-275 920; www.carasana.de; Römerplatz 1; 3hr ticket €25; ⏰9am-10pm, last admission 7pm), a palatial 19th-century marble-and-mosaic-festooned spa, with a strict regime of hot-and-cold bathing, dunking and scrubbing. If you'd rather keep your bathing togs on, slip over to **Caracalla Spa** (📞07221-275 940; www.carasana.de; Römerplatz 11; 2/3hr €16/19, day ticket €23; ⏰8am-10pm, last admission 8pm), a modern glass-fronted spa with a cluster of indoor and outdoor pools, grottos and surge channels.

The Drive » The B500 south of Baden-Baden soon begins its steady climb through high meadows and spruce, pine and larch forest. After 7.5km, just after Gasthaus Auerhahn, bear left onto Geroldsauerstrasse, which soon becomes Wasserfallstrasse. It's a further 2km drive to Geroldsauer Wasserfälle.

---

❷ Geroldsauer Wasserfälle

Word has it that German composer Brahms and French painter Courbet had a soft spot for the wispy **Geroldsauer Wasserfälle** (Wasserfallstrasse), which plunge over mossy boulders into a green pool. The 1.5km walk through forest and along the Grobbach stream is deliciously cool on a hot day and looks freshly minted for a kids' picture book about water sprites.

The falls are at their loveliest when the rhododendrons are in bloom (early May to June).

The Drive » Backtrack to the B500 and follow it as it meanders south, affording bucolic views over forested hills, to Mehliskopf, 14km away.

TRIP HIGHLIGHT

❸ Mehliskopf

The slopes of 1007m **Mehliskopf** (www.mehliskopf. de; bob adult/concession €4.10/3.50, cart €4, day ski pass adult/concession €24/21, tower free; ⏰bob 10am-6pm Wed-Sun year-round, carts 10am-6pm Sat & Sun Apr-Nov, high-rope course 10am-6pm Apr-Nov, ski lift 9am-8pm late Nov-Mar) are a magnet for families seeking low-key outdoor adventure. You can whiz downhill year-round on the bob run, picking up speeds of up to 40km/h on its hairpin bends and 360-degree loop, or on the downhill carts (over 14-year-olds only). There's also a high-rope course in the forest and a lookout tower, with far-reaching views across the Northern Black Forest and the Rhine Plain. In winter, the focus switches to the snow park's rails and obstacles, and downhill skiing.

The Drive » Sidling up to Mehliskopf is the peak of Hundseck – your next stop.

❹ Walderlebnisstation Hundseck

A sure-fire hit with the kids, this **forest discovery area** has child-geared trails including a circular 500m hunting path and a 2km quiz path, as well as a shorter barefoot path for feeling different textures underfoot.

The Drive » Press on south along the ever-panoramic B500, veering right onto the L86 after around 5km. After a couple of kilometres you'll reach the Wildgehege Breitenbrunnen.

❺ Wildgehege Breitenbrunnen

If wildlife encounters rank highly on your wish list, factor in a stop at this **game reserve** (Breitenbrunnen, Sasbachwalden; ☺ dawn to dusk) to come eye to eye with stags, roe deer and wild boar.

The Drive » Head back to the B500 for the dreamy drive overlooking a ripple of wooded hills to Mummelsee, around 3.5km south.

TRIP HIGHLIGHT

❻ Mummelsee

This glacial **cirque lake** (☺ lookout tower 10.30am-5pm Sat & Sun) makes a beautiful splash on a vast tract of forest. Lore has it that an underwater king and nymphs dwell in its inky depths – and indeed the lake is pure Grimm fairy-tale stuff. You can pedal across it by boat or stroll its shores. Should you want to ramble further, hike 1.5km up to 1164m Hornisgrinde, the highest peak in these parts, commanding far-reaching views over the Black Forest from its lookout tower.

🛏 p269

The Drive » From Mummelsee, bear south past slopes that fill with skiers in winter, then turn right onto the L87 (Ruhesteinstrasse) for the drive to Ottenhöfen, 14km away.

TRIP HIGHLIGHT

❼ Ottenhöfen

As story-book Black Forest villages go, **Ottenhöfen** (www.ottenhoefen -tourismus.de) fits the bill nicely with its plethora of lovingly restored watermills (best explored on the 12km Mühlenweg), slender-spired church and farmhouses snuggled among low-rise, wooded hills. Climbers and hikers can head up to the knobbly peak of Karlsruher Grat.

NATIONALPARK SCHWARZWALD

An outdoor wonderland of heather-speckled moors, glacial cirque lakes, deep valleys, mountains and near-untouched coniferous forest, the **Nationalpark Schwarzwald** (Black Forest National Park; 📞07449-929 980; www.nationalpark-schwarzwald.de; Schwarzwaldhochstrasse 2, Seebach; ☺10am-6pm Tues-Sun May-Sep, to 5pm Oct-Apr;), which finally got the seal of approval (national park status) on 1 January 2014, is the Black Forest at its wildest and untamed best. Nature is left to its own devices in this 100-sq-km pocket in the Northern Black Forest, tucked between Baden-Baden and Freudenstadt and centred on the Schwarzwaldhochstrasse (Black Forest High Road), the Murgtal valley and the Mummelsee.

Hiking and cycling trails abound, as do discovery paths geared towards children. Stop by the information centre in Seebach for the low-down and to pick up maps. Details of guided tours and online maps are also available on the website.

Mummelsee

The surrounding area is criss-crossed with family-friendly walking trails and mountain-bike routes.

The Drive » The K5371 is a minor country road leading southeast of Ottenhöfen to Allerheiligen, 7.5km away.

---

8 Allerheiligen Wasserfälle

Allerheiligen's 90m-high **waterfalls** (Allerheiligen 3, Oppenau) spill in silky threads over several cascades. From here, a short, round trail leads over bridges and up steps through the wooded gorge to a ruined Gothic abbey – an evocative sight with its nave open to the sky.

The Drive » From Allerheiligen, take the winding K5370 north back to the B500, then turn right heading south, where you'll pass Schliffkopf Wellness & Nature Hotel en route to the Lotharpfad. It's a 16km drive in total.

---

9 Lotharpfad

Hurricane Lothar swept across Europe in 1999, flattening some parts of the Northern Black Forest: trees fell like dominoes in wind speeds of up to 200km/h. The Lotharpfad is an 800m adventure trail that gives an insight into how the area is now being reforested.

The Drive » Back behind the wheel, drive gently south to reach the little village of Kniebis, 7km distant.

---

10 Kniebis

Serene and family-friendly, **Kniebis** (www. kniebis.de) backs onto a terrific landscape for all manner of outdoor activities – from hiking and biking to cross-country skiing and sledding. To cool off in summer, head over to the forest-rimmed

LOCAL KNOWLEDGE: GOURMET PIT STOP

Swinging along country lanes 6km north of Freudenstadt brings you to Baiersbronn. It looks like any other Black Forest town, snuggled among meadows and wooded hills, but on its fringes sit two of Germany's finest restaurants, both holders of the coveted three Michelin stars.

Schwarzwaldstube (☑07442-4920; www.traube-tonbach.de; Tonbachstrasse 237, Baiersbronn-Tonbach; tasting menus €165-245, cookery courses around €200; ☺noon-1.30pm Thu-Sun, 7-9pm Wed-Sun) commands big forest views from its rustically elegant dining room. Here Harald Wohlfahrt performs culinary magic, while carefully sourcing and staying true to French cooking traditions.

Claus-Peter Lumpp has consistently won plaudits for his brilliantly composed, French-inflected menus at **Restaurant Bareiss** (☑07442-470; www.bareiss.com; Hermine-Bareiss-Weg 1, Baiersbronn-Mitteltal; lunch menu €125, dinner menus €198-245; ☺noon-2pm & 7-9.30pm Wed-Sun). Dishes that appear deceptively simple on paper become things of beauty – rich in textures and aromas and presented with an artist's eye for detail.

Waldschwimmbad (www.waldschwimmbad-kniebis.de; Strassburger Strasse 95; adult/concession €3/1.80; ☺1pm-7pm Mon-Fri, from 11am Sat & Sun late May–mid-Sep; 🚻), with its outdoor pool, kids' splash area and volleyball court.

The Drive ›› It's an easy 11km drive east on the B28, past forested hills, pastures and farmhouses, to Freudenstadt, marking the southern terminus of the Schwarzwaldhochstrasse.

⑪ Freudenstadt

Duke Friedrich I of Württemberg built a new capital in Freudenstadt in 1599, which was bombed to bits in WWII. Though its centre is underwhelming, statistics lovers will delight in ticking off Germany's biggest square (216m by 219m, for the record), **Marktplatz**, whose arcades harbour rows of shops and cafes with alfresco seating, and the 17th-century red-sandstone **Stadtkirche** (☺10am-5pm), with an ornate 12th-century Cluniac-style baptismal font, Gothic windows, Renaissance portals and baroque towers. The glass-fronted **Panorama-Bad** (www.panorama-bad.de; Ludwig-Jahn-Strasse 60; adult/concession 3hr pass €7.30/6.30; ☺9am-10pm Mon-Sat, to 8pm Sun) is a relaxation magnet with pools, steam baths and saunas.

✕ 🛏 p269

Eating & Sleeping

Baden-Baden ❶

✖ Weinstube im Baldreit　German €€

(☎07221-231 36; Küferstrasse 3; mains
€12-20; ⏱5-10pm Tue-Sat) Well hidden down
cobbled lanes, this wine-cellar restaurant is
worth looking for. Baden-Alsatian fare such as
Flammkuchen (Alsatian pizza) topped with Black
Forest ham, Roquefort and pears is expertly
matched with local wines. Eat in the ivy-swathed
courtyard in summer, the vaulted interior in
winter.

🛏 Hotel am Markt　Historic Hotel €€

(☎07221-270 40; www.hotel-am-markt-baden.
de; Marktplatz 18; s €65-90, d €105-130, apt
€110-140; P 🛜) Sitting pretty in front of the
Stiftskirche, this hotel, which is almost three
centuries old, has 23 homey, well-kept rooms.
It's quiet apart from your wake-up call of church
bells, but then you wouldn't want to miss out on
the great breakfast.

🛏 Hotel
Belle Epoque　Luxury Hotel €€€

(☎07221-300 660; www.hotel-belle-epoque.
de; Maria-Viktoria-Strasse 2c; s €155-185,
d €240-305, ste €389-685; 🛜) Nestling in
manicured parkland, this neo-Renaissance
villa is one of Baden-Baden's most characterful five-star pads. Antiques lend old-world
opulence to the individually designed rooms.
Rates include afternoon tea, with scones,
cakes and fine brews served on the terrace or
by the fireplace.

Mummelsee ❻

🛏 Berghotel
Mummelsee　Guesthouse €€€

(☎0/842-992 86; www.mummelsee.de;
Schwarzwaldhochstrasse 11; s €80-130, d €130-
190; P 🛜) Sitting prettily on the shores of
Mummelsee, this chalet-style lodge has rooms
decked out in modern-country style, with warm
hues, local pine furnishings and balconies – the
pick of which overlook the lake and forest.

Warmed by a tiled oven, the wood-panelled
restaurant dishes up regional fare (including a
decent Black Forest gateau). Unwind in the little
spa area and sauna.

Allerheiligen Wasserfälle ❽

🛏 Schliffkopf
Wellness & Nature Hotel　Hotel €€€

(☎07449-9200; www.schliffkopf.de; Schliffkopf;
incl half board s s/d/ste from €170/265/360;
P 🛜 🏊) Right in the wooded heart of the
Black Forest National Park, this hilltop hotel is
an appealing pick, with spacious, warm-toned
rooms (some big enough to accommodate
families), a spa, a sauna and an outdoor pool.
Splashing out on a wellness suite gets you a
whirlpool bathtub. Rates include a five-course
dinner that plays up seasonal, farm-fresh food.

Freudenstadt ⓫

✖ Turmbräu　German €€

(www.turmbraeu.de; Marktplatz 64; mains €6-25;
⏱11am-midnight Sun-Thu, to 3am Fri & Sat) For
a lively night out in Freudenstadt, this is your
place, with a microbrewery that doubles as a
beer garden. Sit in ye-olde barn to munch hearty
grub such as goulash, stubby pork knuckles
with sauerkraut, and *Bierkrustenbraten* (pork
roast with beer sauce) while guzzling Turmbräu
brews – a 5L barrel costs €39.

🛏 Hotel Grüner Wald　Spa Hotel €€€

(☎07441-860 540; www.gruener-wald.de;
Kinzigtalstrasse 23, Lauterbad; s €95-105, d
€175-215; P 🛜 🏊) Nuzzling between forest
and meadows, this eco-conscious spa hotel
in Lauterbad, 2km south of Freudenstadt, is
a terrific pick for a relaxing break, with warm
toned, country-style rooms done out in wood
and natural fabrics, affording knock-out views
from their balconies. The spa has an indoor
pool, relaxation area with waterbeds, saunas
and steam room. There's a pretty garden with
hammocks.

STRETCH YOUR LEGS
MUNICH

Start: Marienplatz

Finish: Englischer Garten

Distance: 4km / 2.5 miles

Duration: Three hours

This walk follows a route around the main sights in Munich's historical city centre. It takes in some of the Bavarian capital's finest churches, its top palace and its busiest piazzas, passing some of Central Europe's best shopping opportunities along the way.

Take this walk on Trip

Marienplatz

Leave your car at one of the city's many park-and-ride sites (see www.parkund ride.de) and take the S-Bahn into the Altstadt (old town). This city-centre walk kicks off at the heart and soul of Munich's Altstadt, the Marienplatz. This piazza, a popular gathering spot, is anchored by the Mariensäule (Mary's Column), built in 1638 to celebrate victory over Swedish forces during the Thirty Years' War.

The Walk ≫ Head along Rindermarkt, past the Peterskirche with its climbable tower and out onto the expanse of the Viktualienmarkt.

Viktualienmarkt

The Viktualienmarkt is a feast of flavours and one of Central Europe's finest gourmet markets, with fresh fruits and vegetables, piles of artisan cheeses, hams and jams, and chanterelles and truffles on display. Its **beer garden** (Viktualienmarkt 6; ☺9am-10pm) has been a Munich institution since 1807.

The Walk ≫ Head northwest along Rosental until you reach Sendlinger Strasse. Take a left here and walk on – the Asamkirche is on your right.

Asamkirche

The pocket-sized, late-baroque **Asam-kirche** (Sendlinger Strasse 32; ☺9am-6pm), built in 1746, is as rich and epic as a giant's treasure chest. Its creators, the brothers Cosmas Damian Asam and Egid Quirin Asam, dug deep into their considerable talent box to swathe every inch of wall space with gilt garlands and docile cherubs, false marble and oversize barley-twist columns.

The Walk ≫ Retrace your steps along Sendlinger Strasse for 100m until you reach Hackenstrasse on the left. Wind your way north until you hit pedestrianised Kaufingerstrasse. The Frauenkirche is just beyond.

Frauenkirche

The landmark **Frauenkirche** (Church of Our Lady; www.muenchner-dom.de; Frauenplatz 1; ☺7.30am-8.30pm), built between 1468 and 1488, is Munich's spiritual heart. No other building in the central city

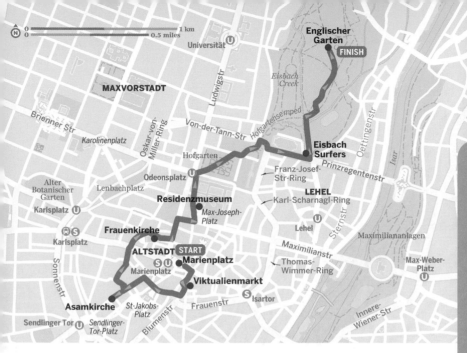

may stand taller than its onion-domed twin towers (99m).

The Walk » From the Frauenkirche's eastern end, head along Albertgasse then take a left into Weinstrasse until you reach the tramlines of Perusastrasse and Maximilianstrasse. Residenzstrasse and the Residenz entrance are on your left.

Residenz

Home to Bavaria's Wittelsbach rulers from 1508 until WWI, the Residenz is Munich's number-one attraction. The amazing treasures, as well as all the trappings of the rulers' lifestyles over the centuries, are on display at the **Residenzmuseum** (www.residenz-muenchen. de; Residenzstrasse 1; adult/concession/under 18yr €7/6/free; 9am-6pm Apr–mid-Oct, 10am-5pm mid-Oct–Mar, last entry 1hr before closing), which takes up around half of the palace. It takes at least two hours to see everything.

The Walk » Follow Residenzstrasse until you reach Odeonsplatz. Cross the exquisite Hofgarten diagonally until you reach Prinzregentenstrasse.

Eisbach Surfers

The last sport you might expect to see being practised in central Munich is surfing, but go to the southern tip of the English Garden at Prinzregenten-strasse and you'll see a crowd leaning over a bridge to cheer on wetsuit-clad daredevils hanging on an artificial wave in the Eisbach Stream.

The Walk » The Eisbach wave is at one of the entrances to the Englischer Garten, which extends north from here.

Englischer Garten

The sprawling English Garden is among Europe's biggest city parks, and a popular playground for both locals and visitors. Of its attractions, the one that may be of most interest post-walk is the **Chinesischer Turm** (www.chinaturm. de; Englischer Garten 3; 10am-11pm late Apr-Oct), Munich's oldest beer garden (1791).

The Walk » The nearest S-Bahn (train) station is at Marienplatz, while the nearest U-Bahn (metro) station is at the southern end at Odeonsplatz.

Austria

AUSTRIA IS A ROAD-TRIPPER'S FANTASY LAND. Not only are there spectacular backdrops of spellbinding landscapes and storybook architecture, opportunities to get out and experience them abound.

Along these routes, you can scale soaring peaks, ski year-round, scuba-dive crystal-clear glacial lakes, raft white-water rapids, pelt down toboggan runs and delve into glittering ice caves and salt mines.

When you've had enough thrills and spills, Austria's multitude of cultural pursuits span medieval castles to monumental palaces, art-filled museums and magnificent churches, as well as the remains of Roman settlements and sobering WWII sites. You can taste cheese at Alpine dairies, schnapps at distilleries, and beer and wine in monasteries where they're still made by monks. Or just hop aboard a horse-drawn carriage to clip-clop through cobbled, lamp-lit city streets.

Vienna View from Stephansdom (p333)
VERONICKA / SHUTTERSTOCK ©

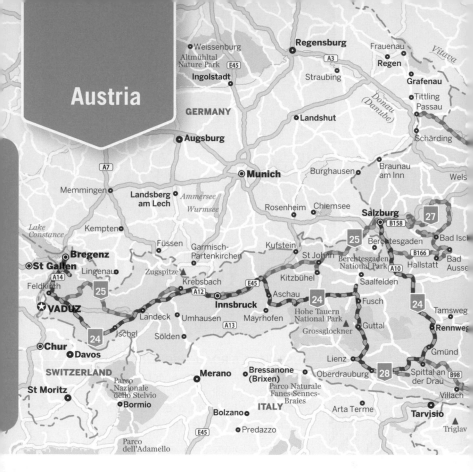

Austria

GERMANY

SWITZERLAND

ITALY

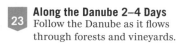

23 Along the Danube 2–4 Days
Follow the Danube as it flows through forests and vineyards.

24 Grossglockner Road 5–7 Days
Twist and turn along three of Austria's most spectacular mountain passes.

25 Tyrol & Vorarlberg 5–7 Days
Walk through wildflower-filled pastures and savour local produce on this Alpine route.

26 Castles of Burgenland 2–4 Days
Visit castles and palaces along with celebrated wineries between Vienna and Graz.

27 Salzkammergut 5–7 Days
Spin around the Salzkammergut's jewel-like lakes beneath towering snow-capped mountains.

28 Carinthian Lakes 2–4 Days
Swim, boat, waterski or just unwind along 'Austria's Riviera', the Carinthian Lakes.

DON'T MISS

Vienna

With its resplendent palaces, magnificent museums and opera house, Austria's capital is the belle of the country's ball.
Trips 23 26

Lake Swimming

Many of Austria's Alp-framed lakes reach temperatures of up to 28°C in summer.
Trips 24 25 26 27 28

Salzburg

Famed for its starring role in *The Sound of Music,* Salzburg's Unesco-listed Altstadt (old town) is a treasure.
Trips 24 25 27

Skiing

Austria is synonymous with pure-white powder pistes. You can also ski the Stubai Glacier, near Innsbruck, in summer.
Trip 24

Hiking

Through forests, up waterfall trails, down gorges, along wildflower-strewn meadows... You'll find some of the best hiking in Austria.
Trips 24 25

Along the Danube

23

Follow the beautiful Danube as it flows from the German city of Passau by the Austrian border through farmland, forest and vineyard-streaked hillsides to Austria's majestic capital, Vienna.

TRIP HIGHLIGHTS

205 km

Dürnstein
Richard the Lionheart was imprisoned here in a now-ruined castle

293 km

Vienna
View Vienna by foot, horse-drawn carriage or Ferris wheel

START
Passau

Linz

4

Melk

7

9

Krems an der Donau

10 FINISH

St Florian
Visit the abbey's exuberant basilica

92 km

Stift Göttweig
This Unesco-listed abbey serves its own monk-made wines

219 km

2–4 DAYS
293KM / 198 MILES

GREAT FOR...

BEST TIME TO GO
Aim for summer: many places close between November and March.

 ESSENTIAL PHOTO
The dazzling interior of St Florian's abbey.

 BEST FOR ART
Linz' contemporary Lentos gallery.

23 Along the Danube

Immortalised in the stirring *Blue Danube* waltz by Austrian composer Johann Strauss II, this magnificent river ripples with the reflections of dense green forests, hilltop castles and ribbons of vineyards, particularly on its prettiest stretch, the Wachau, between Melk and Krems an der Donau. Along the river's course are plenty of surprises too, including the cutting-edge city of Linz, and two superb monasteries producing, respectively, sublime beer and wine.

❶ Passau

Just inside the German border, Passau's pastel-shaded Altstadt (old town) sits atop a narrow peninsula jutting into the confluence of three rivers: the Danube, the Inn and the Ilz. Christianity generated prestige as Passau evolved into the largest bishopric in the Holy Roman Empire, as testified by the mighty cathedral **Dom St Stephan** (Domplatz; ⊘6.30am-7pm).

Stroll the old town, which remains much as

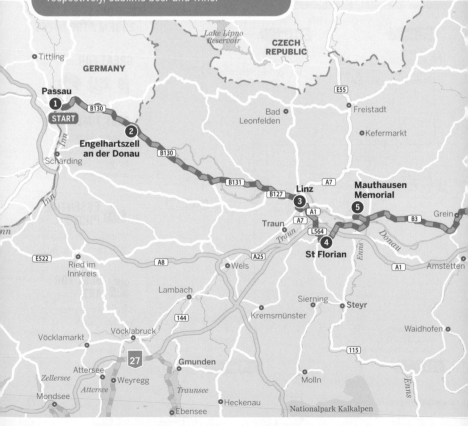

it was when the powerful prince-bishops built its tight lanes, tunnels and archways with an Italianate flourish.

 p233, p283

The Drive » Cross the Inn River where it joins the Danube and head east on the ST2125 which, 3.3km later, becomes the B130 on entering Austria, and follows the Danube's southern bank. On your right, you'll pass Burg Krempelstein, built on the site of a Roman watch-house. It's 26km all-up to Engelhartszell an der Donau.

---

❷ Engelhartszell an der Donau

The little riverside village of Engelhartszell an der Donau is home to one of only eight licensed Trappist breweries outside Belgium, and the only one in Austria. At the 1293-founded abbey **Engelszell** (www.stift-engelszell. at; Stiftstrasse 6; ☉ church 8am-7pm Apr-Oct, to 5pm Nov-Mar, shop 9am-5pm Apr-Oct, shorter hours rest of year), you can purchase monk-made

LINK YOUR TRIP

26 Castles of Burgenland
Vienna is the starting point of this castle-strewn route.

27 Salzkammergut
From Passau, it's 115km southwest to Salzburg, from where you can explore the Salzkammergut's mountain-ringed lakes.

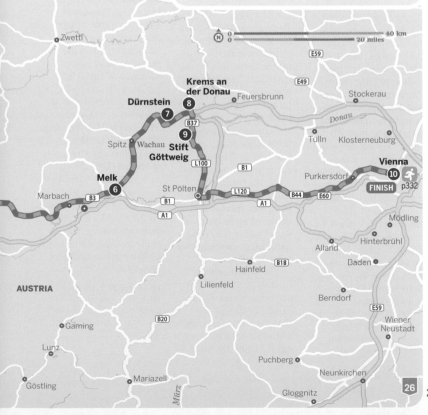

brews (dark Gregorius, amber Benno, and blond Nivard); the shop also sells liqueurs and cheeses produced here. Adjoining the shop is the abbey's gorgeous rococo church, completed in 1764.

The Drive >> Take the B130; at Aschach an der Donau, cross the river on the B131, and continue east to Ottensheim to join the B127 to Linz (52km in total).

- - - - - - - - - - - - - - - - -

❸ Linz

The Austrian saying *In Linz beginnt's* (It begins in Linz) sums up this technology trailblazer. Its leading-edge **Ars Electronica Center** (www. aec.at; Ars-Electronica-Strasse 1; adult/child €9.50/7.50; ⏱9am-5pm Tue, Wed & Fri, to 7pm Thu, 10am-6pm Sat & Sun) has labs for interacting with robots, animating digital objects, converting your name to DNA and (virtually) travelling to outer space. After dark, the LED glass skin kaleidoscopically changes colour. Directly across the Danube is Linz' world-class contemporary-art gallery, the glass-and-steel **Lentos** (www.lentos.at; Ernst-Koref-Promenade 1; adult/child €8/4.50; ⏱10am-6pm Tue, Wed & Fri-Sun, to 9pm Thu), with works by Warhol, Schiele and Klimt, among others.

But it's not all new in Austria's third-largest city: the **Mariendom** (www.dioezese-linz.at; Her-

renstrasse 26; ⏱7.30am-7pm Mon-Sat, 8am-7.15pm Sun) is a neo-Gothic giant of a cathedral with a riot of pinnacles, flying buttresses and filigree traceried windows.

🍴 🛏 p283

The Drive >> Take the A1 southeast to Ebelsberg, then continue on the L564 to St Florian (21km all-up).

- - - - - - - - - - - - - - - - -

TRIP HIGHLIGHT

❹ St Florian

Rising like a vision above St Florian is its magnificent abbey, **Augustiner Chorherrenstift** (www. stift-st-florian.at; Stiftstrasse 1; tours €10.50; ⏱tours 11am, 1pm & 3pm May–mid-Oct). Dating to at least 819, it has been occupied by the Canons Regular, living under Augustinian rule, since 1071. Today its imposing yellow-and-white facade is overwhelmingly baroque.

Compulsory guided tours of the abbey's interior take in the resplendent apartments adorned with rich stuccowork and frescos, including 16 emperors' rooms (once occupied by visiting popes and royalty) and a galleried library housing 150,000 volumes.

The **Stiftsbasilika** (www.stift-st-florian.at; Stiftstrasse 1; tours €10.50; ⏱tours 11am, 1pm & 3pm May–mid-Oct) is an exuberant affair with an altar carved from 700 tonnes

of pink Salzburg marble, and a gold 18th-century organ.

The Drive >> Head northeast on the L566 to join the B1. Follow it for 7.5km then turn east on the B123 to cross the Danube, before turning west on the B3. After 2.4km take the L1411 for 2.5 signposted kilometres to the Mauthausen Memorial (22km in total).

- - - - - - - - - - - - - - - - -

❺ Mauthausen Memorial

Nowadays Mauthausen is a peaceful small town on the north bank of the Danube, but in WWII, the Nazis turned the quarrying centre into the **KZ Mauthausen** concentration camp. Prisoners were forced into slave labour in the granite quarry and many died on the so-called *Todesstiege* (stairway of death) leading from the quarry to the camp. Some 100,000 prisoners perished or were executed in the camp between 1938 and 1945. The complex is now a **memorial** (📞07238-2269-0; www.mauthausen-memorial. org; Erinnerungsstrasse 1; ⏱9am-5.30pm Mar-Oct, to 3pm Tue-Sun Nov-Feb); English-language audioguides relate its sobering history. It's not recommended for under 14s.

The Drive >> Travelling east for 76km brings you to Melk. Along the river at Grein, look out for the dramatic castle Greinburg rising to your left.

St Florian Augustiner Chorherrenstift

⑥ Melk

Historically, Melk was of great importance to the Romans and later to the Babenbergs, who built a castle here. In 1089 the Babenberg margrave Leopold II donated the castle to Benedictine monks, who converted it into the fortified **Stift Melk** (Benedictine Abbey of Melk; www.stiftmelk.at; Abt Berthold Dietmayr Strasse 1; adult/child €12.50/6.50, with guided tour €14.50/8.50; ☺9am-5.30pm, tours 10am-4pm Apr-Oct). Fire destroyed the original edifice; today its monastery church dominates the complex

with its twin spires and high octagonal dome. The baroque-gone-barmy interior has regiments of cherubs, gilt twirls and polished faux marble. The theatrical high-altar scene depicts St Peter and St Paul (the church's two patron saints).

The Drive » The Wachau is the loveliest stretch along the mighty river's length: both banks here are dotted with ruined castles and terraced with vineyards. From Melk, follow the river northeast along the nothern bank for 28km, passing medieval villages Spitz, Wösendorf in der Wachau and Weissenkirchen, to reach Dürnstein.

TRIP HIGHLIGHT

⑦ Dürnstein

Picturesque Dürnstein is best known for the **Kuenringerburg** – the now-ruined castle above the town where Richard the Lionheart (Richard I of England) was imprisoned from 1192 to 1193, before being moved to **Burg Trifels** in Germany.

Of the 16th-century buildings lining Dürnstein's hilly, cobbled streets, the **Chorherrenstift** (www.stiftduernstein.at; Stiftshof; adult/child €6.50/4; ☺9am-6pm Mon-Sat, 10am-6pm Sun May-Oct) is

TOP TIP: DANUBE CRUISES

Floating past vine-covered banks crowned by castles gives you a different perspective of the river. From Linz and Passau, **Wurm & Noé** (☎0851-929 292; www.donauschiffahrt.eu; Höllgasse 26; city tour €8.90) operates cruises between Regensburg, Germany, and Vienna from March to early November. Ticket prices vary according to how many stops you stay on board.

the most impressive. It's all that remains of the former Augustinian monastery originally founded in 1410, and received its baroque facelift in the 18th century.

The Drive 》 Head east along the river on the B3 for 7.5km to reach Krems an der Donau.

❽ Krems an der Donau

Against a backdrop of terraced vineyards, Krems has an attractive cobbled centre and gallery-dotted **Kunstmeile** (Art Mile; www.kunstmeile-krems.at). Its flagship is **Landesgalerie NÖ** (☎02732-908 010; www.landesgalerie-noe.at; Museumsplatz 1; adult/child €10/3.50; ⏰10am-6pm Tue-Sun), a brand-new futuristic structure containing ever-changing exhib-itions of edgy modern art and contemporary installations.

✖ 🛏 p283

The Drive 》 Leave Krems an der Donau on the B37 and cross the southbound L100.

Stift Göttweig is well-signposted (9km altogether from Krems).

TRIP HIGHLIGHT

❾ Stift Göttweig

Surrounded by grape-laden vines, Unesco World Heritage–listed **Stift Göttweig** (Göttweig Abbey; ☎02732-855 81-0; www.stiftgoettweig.at; Furth bei Göttweig; adult/child €8.50/5; ⏰10am-6pm Apr-Oct) was founded in 1083, but the abbey you see today is mostly baroque. Highlights include the Imperial Staircase with a heavenly ceiling fresco painted by Paul Troger in 1739, and the over-the-top baroque interior of the Stiftskirche (which has a Kremser Schmidt work in the crypt). Best of all is the opportunity to sip wine made here by the monks – including an exquisite Messwein rosé – on the panoramic garden terrace above the valley (you can also buy it at the abbey's shop).

The Drive 》 From Stift Göttweig, it's 79km to Vienna. The most scenic route,

through farmland and forest, is south on the L100 to St Pölten, then east on the L120 to join the eastbound B44 at Ebersberg. Continue through the Wienerwald to the Austrian capital.

TRIP HIGHLIGHT

❿ Vienna

Renowned for its imperial palaces, baroque interiors, opera houses and magnificent squares, Vienna is also one of Europe's most dynamic urban spaces. The best way to experience its blend of old and new is on a walking tour (p332).

A wonderfully atmospheric (if touristy) alternative is clip-clopping aboard a **Fiaker** (20/40/60min tour €55/80/110; ⏰10am-9pm), a traditional-style open carriage drawn by a pair of horses. Drivers point out places of interest en route. Lines of horses, carriages and bowler-hatted drivers can be found at Stephansplatz, Albertinaplatz and Heldenplatz at the Hofburg.

Or survey the city from Vienna's 65m-high, 1897-built Ferris wheel, the **Riesenrad**. It's located at the **Prater** (www.wiener-prater.at; 🚼; Ⓤ Praterstern), a sprawling park encompassing meadows, woodlands, and an amusement park (the **Würstelprater**), between the Danube and Danube Canal.

✖ 🛏 p283 , p311

Eating & Sleeping

Passau ❶

✗ Heilig-Geist-Stifts-Schenke
Bavarian €€

(📞0851-2607; www.stiftskeller-passau.de; Heilig-Geist-Gasse 4; mains €12-22; ⏱11am-11pm, closed Wed & Thu; 🛜) Not only does this historical inn have a succession of walnut-panelled ceramic-stove-heated rooms, a candlelit cellar (from 6pm) and a vine-draped garden, but the food is equally inspired. Amid the river fish, steaks and seasonal dishes there are quite gourmet affairs such as beef fillet in flambéed cognac sauce. Help it all along with one of the many Austrian and German wines in stock.

🛏 Hotel Schloss Ort
Boutique Hotel €€

(📞0851-340 72; www.hotel-schloss-ort.de; Im Ort 11; s/d from €70/90; 🅿🛜) The most characterful place to sleep in Passau, this 800-year-old medieval palace by the Inn River conceals a soothingly tranquil boutique hotel, stylishly done out with polished timber floors, crisp white cotton sheets and wrought-iron bedsteads. Many of the 18 rooms enjoy river views and breakfast is served in the vaulted restaurant.

Linz ❸

✗ k.u.k. Hofbäckerei
Cafe €

(Pfarrgasse 17; dishes €3-6; ⏱6.30am-6.30pm Mon-Fri, 7am-12.30pm Sat) The Empire lives on at this gloriously frozen-in-time cafe in a timber-framed building dating from 1371. Here Fritz Rath bakes some of the best Linzer Torte in town – rich, spicy and with a wonderful crumbly lattice pastry. In summer, the best seats are in the shady courtyard.

🛏 Hotel am Domplatz
Design Hotel €€

(📞0732-773 000; www.hotelamdomplatz.at; Stifterstrasse 4; d/ste from €160/325; 🅿❄🛜) Adjacent to the neo-Gothic Mariendom (ask for a room overlooking the cathedral), this glass-and-concrete cube filled with striking metal sculptures has 69 streamlined, Nordic-style white and blond-wood rooms with semiopen

bathrooms, and two suites. Wind down with a view in the rooftop spa. In fine weather, head to the cathedral-facing terrace for breakfast (€19), which includes a glass of bubbly.

Krems an der Donau ❽

🛏 Hotel Alte Poste
Hotel €€

(📞02732-822 76; www.altepost-krems.at; Obere Landstrasse 32; s €40-65, d €70-100; 🛜) If you are on a budget and want to stay centrally, the 23 rooms at this historic 500-year-old post inn by the Steinertor (the medieval gateway into the old town) are for you. Basic but well-kept, rooms are gathered around an enchanting courtyard. Immaculate bathrooms are shared and rates include breakfast.

Vienna ❿

✗ Bierhof
Austrian €€

(📞01-533 44 28; www.bierhof.at; 01, Haarhof 3; mains €11-25; ⏱11.30am-10pm Mon-Sat, to 9pm Sun; 🛜; Ⓤ Herrengasse) A narrow passageway opens to a courtyard where umbrella-shaded tables beneath the trees make a charming spot to dine on homemade classics like Eiernockerl (flour-and-egg dumplings), Tiroler Gröstl (pork, potatoes and bacon, topped with a fried egg), Tiroler Leber (liver dumplings with apple sauce and green beans) and Wiener schnitzel with parsley potatoes. The midweek lunch menu costs just €7.90.

🛏 Grand Ferdinand Hotel
Design Hotel €€

(📞01-918 80; www.grandferdinand.com; 01, Schubertring 10-12; dm/d/ste from €30/175/470; ❄🛜🖾; 🚋2, 71 Schwarzenbergplatz) An enormous taxidermied horse stands in the reception area of this ultrahip hotel. The Grand Ferdinand is shaking up Vienna's accommodation scene by offering parquet-floored eight-bed dorms with mahogany bunks alongside richly coloured designer rooms with chaise longues and chandeliered suites with private champagne bars. Breakfast (€29) is served on the panoramic rooftop terrace, adjacent to the heated, open-air infinity pool.

Classic Trip

Grossglockner Road

24

Austria's most exhilarating trip takes you on a wild roller-coaster drive over three legendary Alpine passes and packs in outdoor activities from year-round skiing to windsurfing and white-water rafting.

TRIP HIGHLIGHTS

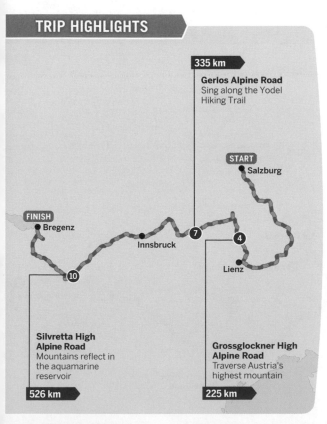

335 km

Gerlos Alpine Road
Sing along the Yodel Hiking Trail

START
Salzburg

FINISH
Bregenz

Innsbruck

Lienz

Silvretta High Alpine Road
Mountains reflect in the aquamarine reservoir

526 km

Grossglockner High Alpine Road
Traverse Austria's highest mountain

225 km

5–7 DAYS
711KM / 442 MILES

GREAT FOR...

BEST TIME TO GO
The peak time to tackle this trip is midsummer.

ESSENTIAL PHOTO
Europe's highest waterfalls, the three-tiered Krimmler Wasserfälle.

BEST FOR DRIVERS
The Grossglockner's 36 heart-in-your-mouth hairpin bends.

Classic Trip

24 Grossglockner Road

Fair warning: if you're a faint-hearted driver (or passenger), this probably isn't the trip for you. (Take the gentler Tyrol & Vorarlberg route instead.) But if you're up for a serious adventure, this Austrian classic provides an opportunity to experience epic scenery, invigorating Alpine sports and dizzying mountain passes with so many switchbacks they're used by high-performance car manufacturers and championship race drivers as test tracks.

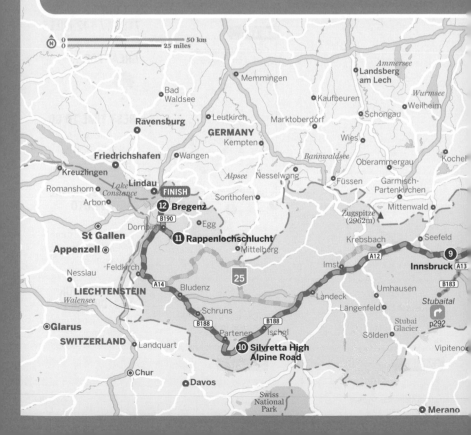

❶ Salzburg

Salzburg's **trophy sights** (p302) huddle in the pedestrianised, Unesco World Heritage–listed Altstadt (old town). The tangled lanes are made for a serendipitous wander, leading to hidden courtyards and medieval squares framed by burgher houses and baroque fountains. You'll also see plenty of icons from the evergreen musical *The Sound of Music* (p319).

Beyond **city strolling** (p330), there are plenty of opportunities to get active, from swimming at **Freibad Leopoldskron** (Leopoldskronstrasse 50; adult/child €5/2.80; 🕑9am-7pm May–mid-Sep;), Salzburg's biggest lido, with diving boards, waterslides and volleyball, to hiking up Salzburg's rival mountains, the 540m

Mönchsberg and 640m **Kapuzinerberg**. Both mountains are thickly wooded and criss-crossed by walking trails, with photogenic views of the Altstadt's right bank and left bank respectively.

🍴 🛏 p303, p321

LINK YOUR TRIP

25 Tyrol & Vorarlberg

To make a mega-circuit of the Austrian Alps, pick up the Tyrol & Vorarlberg route in Bregenz.

28 Carinthian Lakes

Wind around the Carinthian Lakes from lively Lienz.

Classic Trip

The Drive ≫ It's 47km south from Salzburg on the B159 to Werfen, mostly along the Salzach River. After passing through a wide valley, you'll enter a tight, steep gorge; follow it until Werfen.

----

❷ Werfen

More than 1000m above Werfen in the Tennengebirge mountains is **Eisriesenwelt** (www.eisriesenwelt.at; Eishohlenstrasse 30; adult/child €12/7, incl cable car €24/14; ⊗8am-4pm Jul & Aug, to 3pm May, Jun, Sep & Oct). Billed as the world's largest accessible ice caves, this spectacle spans 30,000 sq metres and 42km of narrow passages. A highlight is the cavernous **Eispalast** (ice palace), where the frost crystals twinkle when a magnesium flare is held up to them. Wrap up for subzero temperatures. Photography is not permitted inside the caves.

On a wooded clifftop beneath the majestic peaks of the Tennengebirge range formidable **Burg Hohenwerfen** (Hohenwerfen Fortress; www.salzburg-burgen.at; adult/child/family €12.50/7/30, incl lift €16.50/9.50/39.50; ⊗9am-5pm May-Sep, shorter hours Mar, Apr & Oct) dates from 1077. Time your visit to be at the castle by 3:15pm for the falconry show.

🛏 p293

The Drive ≫ Take the A10 south to the Millstätter See (which you can visit on Trip 28 through the Carinthian Lakes) and turn west onto the B100/E66 through the Drau Valley to Lienz (166km in total).

----

❸ Lienz

Ringed by Dolomite peaks, Lienz straddles the Isel and Drau Rivers, and lies just 40km north of Italy. An ancient **Roman settlement**, today it's a famed ski town (for its Zettersfeld and Hochstein peaks, and especially its 100km of cross-country trails), but it has an energetic vibe year-round.

If you want to get up into the mountains, **Bergstatt** (📞0664 516 5835; Kranewitweg 5; trips per adult/child from €80/60) has guides who can lead you on half-day, full-day and multiday rock climbing, *via ferrata* or summit trips.

The Drive ≫ Take the B107 north, passing picturesque villages including Winklern (with a wonderful alpine hotel, p293) and Heiligenblut (look for the needle-thin spire of its pilgrimage church) to the Grossglockner High Alpine Road toll gates (43km in total).

TRIP HIGHLIGHT

❹ Grossglockner High Alpine Road

A stupendous feat of 1930s engineering, the 48km **Grossglockner Road** (www.grossglockner.at; day ticket car/motorbike €36.50/26.50; ⊗6am-8pm May, 5am-9.30pm Jun-Aug, 6am-7.30pm Sep & Oct) swings giddily around 36 switchbacks, passing lakes, forested slopes and glaciers as it traverses the heart of the Hohe Tauern National Park, peaking at the bell-shaped **Grossglockner** (3798m), Austria's highest mountain.

En route, flag-dotted **Kaiser-Franz-Josefs-Höhe** (2369m) has memorable views of Grossglockner and the rapidly retreating Pasterze Glacier (best appreciated on the short and easy Gamsgrubenweg and Gletscherweg trails). Allow time to see the glacier-themed exhibition at the visitor centre and the crystalline Wilhelm-Swarovski observatory.

Get your camera handy for **Fuscher Törl** (2428m), with super views on both sides of the ridge, and Fuscher Lacke (2262m), a gemstone of a lake nearby. A small exhibition documents the construction of the road, built by 3000 men over five years during the Great Depression.

A 2km side road corkscrews up to **Edelweiss Spitze** (2571m), the road's highest viewpoint. Climb the tower for 360-degree views of more than 30 peaks topping 3000m.

Between toll gates, all attractions are free. Check the forecast before you hit the road, as the drive is not much fun in heavy fog, snow or a storm. It's often bumper-to-bumper by noon, especially in July and August; beat the crowds by setting out early.

The Drive ≫ Descend the Grossglockner on the B107 to Bruck and take the B311 northeast to Zell am See.

---

⑤ Zell am See

Resort town Zell am See's brightly painted chalets line the shore of the deep-blue Zeller See, framed by the Hohe Tauern's snow-capped peaks.

Mountain breezes create ideal conditions for windsurfing on the lake; **Windsurfcenter Zell Am See** (📞0664 644 36 95; www.windsurfcenter.info; Seespitzstrasse 13; 2hr beginner course €40; ⏰dawn-dusk May-Sep) rents equipment and runs courses.

The Drive ≫ From the lake, it's 54km to the Krimmler Wasserfälle. Head west on the B168 and B165 to Krimml; when you arrive in the town the waterfalls come into view.

---

⑥ Krimmler Wasserfälle

Europe's highest falls, at 380m, are the thunderous, three-tier **Krimmler Wasserfälle** (Krimml Falls; 📞06564-72 12; www.wasserfaelle-krimml.at; adult/child €4/1; ⏰9am-5pm mid-Apr–Oct). The **Wasserfallweg** (Waterfall Trail), which starts at the ticket office and weaves uphill through mixed forest, has up-close viewpoints. It's

TOP TIP: ALPINE ROAD TOLLS

Be aware that this trip's three top-draw drives – Grossglockner High Alpine Road, Gerlos Alpine Road and Silvretta High Alpine Road – incur hefty tolls. There's also a smaller toll on the detour to the Stubaital. Toll booths accept cash and credit cards.

4km one way (about a 2½-hour round-trip walk).

The Drive ≫ From the falls, it's 7.7km (and eight hairpin bends) to the Gerlos Alpine Road toll gates.

TRIP HIGHLIGHT

⑦ Gerlos Alpine Road

Open year-round, the **Gerlos Alpine Road** (www.gerlosstrasse.at; car/motorcycle €9.50/6.50) winds 12km through high moor and spruce forest, reaching an elevation of 1630m. The lookout above the turquoise Stausee (reservoir) is a great picnic stop, with a tremendous vista of the Alps.

If you have the urge to burst out into song as you skip through wildflower-strewn meadows, take the 4.8km-long **Jodel Wanderweg** (Yodel Hiking Trail; www.jodelweg.at; Wald-Königsleiten) in Königsleiten. You can go it alone and practise your high notes at eight stops with giant cowbells, alpine horns and listen-repeat audio clippings. Alternatively, join a free guided sing 'n' stroll hike with trail

founder Christian Eder. The three-hour ambles begin at 10.30am every Wednesday from late June to mid-September at the Dorfbahn (adult/child €9/4.50) cable-car station; reserve by 5pm the previous day by phone.

The Drive ≫ Continue west on the B165, passing the reservoir Durlassboden, before descending to Zell am Ziller along six hairpin bends (63km in total).

---

⑧ Zell am Ziller

At the foot of knife-edge Reichenspitze (3303m), Zell am Ziller is a former gold-mining centre and popular ski base.

Year-round, you can take a wild toboggan ride on the 1.45km-long **Arena Coaster** (www.zillertalarena.com; Zillertal Arena; adult/child coaster only €5.40/3.60, incl cable car €24.90/12.50; ⏰9.30am-6pm late Jun-early Sep, shorter hours rest of year; ♿), which incorporates both a 360-degree loop and a 540-degree loop. It's accessible by cable car or a steep 1.5km walk.

Aktivzentrum Zillertal (📞0664 5059594; www.aktivzentrum-zillertal.at; Freizeitpark Zell; ♿) offers

Classic Trip

WHY THIS IS A CLASSIC TRIP
MARC DI DUCA, WRITER

Awe-inspiring mountainscapes and adrenaline-pumping activities abound on this Alpine itinerary, but the ultimate draw is the drive itself, peaking with its trio of dizzying high-altitude switchback passes – the Grossglockner High Alpine Road, Gerlos Alpine Road and Silvretta High Alpine Road. This is a route that reminds you that the highlight of road-tripping isn't the destination but the journey.

Above: Skiing, Innsbruck
Right: Krimmler Wasserfälle (p289)
Left: Bergisel ski jump tower, Innsbruck

JIMMYR / GETTY IMAGES ©

summertime paragliding, white-water rafting on the Ziller, canyoning, *via ferrata* climbing and llama trekking.

🛏 p293, p303

The Drive » Zell am Ziller sits 60km from Innsbruck. Take the B169 north then the A12 west to the city.

⑨ Innsbruck

Hit Innsbruck's **cultural attractions**, then head up to its ski jump, the **Bergisel** (www.bergisel. info; adult/child €9.50/4.50; ⏰9am-6pm Jun-Oct, 10am-5pm Wed-Mon Nov-May), for a spectacular city and mountain panorama. Rising above Innsbruck like a celestial staircase, the glass-and-steel structure was designed by Iraqi architect Zaha Hadid.

Hadid also designed the space-age funicular **Nordkettenbahnen** (www. nordkette.com; single/return to Hungerburg €5.40/9, to Seegrube €18.60/31.10, to Hafelekar €20.70/34.50; ⏰Hungerburg 7.15am-7.15pm Mon-Fri, 8am-7.15pm Sat & Sun, Seegrube 8.30am-5.30pm daily, Hafelekar 9am-5pm daily), which whizzes from the Congress Centre to the slopes every 15 minutes. Walking trails head off in all directions from Hungerburg and Seegrube.

✕ 🛏 p293

The Drive » Leave Innsbruck on the westbound A12 and veer southwest on the B188, passing a string of ski towns, to the Silvretta High Alpine Road toll gates (118km all-up).

Classic Trip

TRIP HIGHLIGHT

⑩ Silvretta High Alpine Road

Silhouetted by the glaciated Silvretta range and crowned by the 3312m arrow of Piz Buin, the Montafon Valley remains one of the most unspoilt in the Austrian Alps.

The 23km-long **Silvretta High Alpine Road** (www.silvretta-bielerhoehe.at; car/motorcycle €16.50/13.50; ☺early Jun–late Oct) twists and turns beneath peaks rising to well over 2500m before climbing over the 2036m Bielerhöhe Pass via 34 knuckle-whiteningly tight switchbacks. At the top of the pass, the **Silvretta Stausee** (2030m), an aquamarine reservoir, mirrors the surrounding peaks on bright mornings.

The Drive » It's 100km to Rappenlochschlucht. Continue on the B188 and join the A14 at aromatic Bludenz (home to the Milka chocolate factory; there's an outlet shop but alas, no tours). Continue northwest to Dornbirn, from where Rappenlochschlucht is 4km southeast on Gütlestrasse.

⑪ Rappenloch-schlucht

The **Rappenlochschlucht** (Rappenloch Gorge; www.rappenlochschlucht.at) was gouged out by the Dorn-

DETOUR: STUBAITAL

Start: ⑨ **Innsbruck**

Slip out of sandals and into skis at year-round skiing magnet, Stubai Glacier. A one-day summer **ski pass** (www.stubaier-gletscher.com) costs €43/21.50 per adult/child and covers 26 lifts accessing 62km of slopes. Ski shops are plentiful; ski or snowboard and boot rental costs around €30/15 per adult/child. Summer skiing is between 2900m and 3300m and is dependent on weather conditions.

Lower down in the Stubai Valley, the **Wildewasser-weg** waterfall trail wends for 9.2km (one way) to Sulzenau Glacier. En route, it passes the spectacular Grawa falls; there's a cafe with a panoramic viewing deck at its base.

The Stubai Glacier is just 38km south of Innsbruck. Take the A13 south to the toll gates (€3 per car including passengers); keep right to take the B183 southwest along the valley.

birner Ache. From the car park, there's a 375m trail to the **Staufensee**, a turquoise lake.

At the bottom of the Rappenlochschlucht, a 19th-century cotton mill is the unlikely home of the world's largest collection of Rolls-Royces at the **Rolls-Royce Museum** (www.rolls-royce-museum.at; Gütle 11a; adult/child €6/3; ☺10am–6pm Tue-Sun).

The Drive » Return to Dornbirn and head north on the B190 for 16km to Bregenz.

⑫ Bregenz

Bregenz sits on the shores of Lake Constance, Europe's third-largest lake. The views here are extraordinary: before you the mirror-like lake; behind you,

1064m-high mountain the Pfänder; to the right, Germany; to the left, Switzerland.

A **cable car** (www.pfaenderbahn.at; Steinbruchgasse 4; adult/child one way €7.70/3.80, return €13.20/6.60; ☺8am–7pm) glides up the Pfänder. At the top, a 30-minute circular trail brings you close to wildlife at the year-round **Alpine Game Park Pfänder** (www.pfaender.at; ☺sunrise-sunset).

Some 5km south of central Bregenz, where the Rhine flows into Lake Constance, is the nature reserve **Rheindelta** (www.rheindelta.org; Hard). Its mossy marshes, reeds and woodlands attract more than 300 bird species.

✕ 🛏 p253, p293 , p303

Eating & Sleeping

Werfen ②

🛏 Weisses Rössl Pension €

(📞06468-52 68; www.weisses-roessl-werfen.
at; Markt 39; s/d/tr/q €45/80/100/120;
P 📶) In the village centre, this good-value
pension has great views of the fortress and the
Tennengebirge from its rooftop terrace. Rooms
are a blast from the 1970s, but all are large and
cosy with sofas and cable TV.

Winklern

**🛏 Hotel
Tauernstern** Chalet €€

(📞04822-248; www.tauernstern.at; Winklern
24, Winklern im Mölltal; s €55-80, d €105-125, ste
€135-145, half board €15; **P** 📶) Sweeping valley
views extend from the timber balconies of this
mountain-set gem. Four-poster pine-and-stone
beds, in-room fridges, a sauna and spa built
from local wood and slate, and an exceptional
gourmet restaurant using ingredients from
local farms all make Tauernstern a fabulous pit
stop before tackling the Grossglockner High
Alpine Road.

Zell am Ziller ⑧

🛏 Hotel Englhof Boutique Hotel €€

(📞05282-31 34; www.englhof.at; Zellbergeben
28; s/d €75/120; 📶) Beautiful blond-wood-
panelled, white-linen-dressed rooms (many
with balconies) and amenities like free DVD
rental make Englhof a superb place to stay.
But what really seals the deal is its in-house
gourmet restaurant and world-class cocktail
bar with Austria's second-largest collection of
spirits (over 1400 varieties), mixing incredible
cocktails like a Bloody Mary with frozen
cherry tomatoes and barbecued black-pepper
seasoning.

Innsbruck ⑨

✕ Die Wilderin Austrian €€

(📞0512-56 27 28; www.diewilderin.at;
Seilergasse 5; mains €12-20; ⊙5pm-midnight
Tue-Sun) Take a gastronomic walk on the wild
side at this modern-day hunter-gatherer of
a restaurant, where chefs take pride in local
sourcing and using top-notch farm-fresh and
foraged ingredients. The menu sings of the
seasons, be it asparagus, game, strawberries or
winter veg. The vibe is urbane and relaxed.

**🛏 Hotel Weisses
Kreuz** Historic Hotel €€

(📞0512-594 79; www.weisseskreuz.at; Herzog-
Friedrich-Strasse 31; s €65-105, d €100-180;
P @ 📶) Beneath the arcades, this atmospheric Altstadt hotel has played host to guests
for 500 years, including a 13-year-old Mozart.
With its wood-panelled parlours, antiques and
twisting staircase, the hotel oozes history with
every creaking beam. Rooms are supremely
comfortable, staff are charming and breakfast
is a lavish spread.

Bregenz ⑫

🛏 Schwärzler Hotel €€

(📞05574-49 90; www.schwaerzler.s-hotels.
com; Landstrasse 9; d €165-275; **P** 📶 ⊠) This
turreted, ivy-clad place is a far cry from your
average business hotel. Contemporary rooms
are done out in earthy hues and blond wood,
with comforts including bathrobes, flat-screen
TVs and minibars. Regional produce from
organic farms features on the breakfast buffet,
and there's a 400-sq-metre pool and a sauna
area. Parking costs €7.

Tyrol & Vorarlberg

Opportunities for outdoor pursuits abound here in the Alps, but there are also plenty of gentler pleasures, from rambles through wildflower-filled meadows to foodie tastings and artistic treasures.

25

TRIP HIGHLIGHTS

37 km

Feldkirch
Home to a medieval old town and fairy-tale castle

383 km

Salzburg
Resplendent Salzburg is the storybook vision of Austria

FINISH
11

START
Bregenz
Schoppernau
7 8
2
Landeck
St Anton am Arlberg

Stift Stams
Monumental abbey topped by twin silver cupolas

179 km

Innsbruck
Mountain-ringed city filled with art and architectural treasures

203 km

5–7 DAYS
383KM / 295 MILES

GREAT FOR...

BEST TIME TO GO
Year-round is possible; you'll need snow tyres and chains in winter.

  ESSENTIAL PHOTO
Innsbruck's Gothic Hofkirche.

BEST FOR FOODIES
The Bregenzerwald Käsestrasse (Bregenz Forest Cheese Road).

Tyrol & Vorarlberg

As you drive east from opera-festival-famed Bregenz on the shores of Lake Constance, you'll discover a different side of the Alps to the dizzying drives on and around the Grossglockner Road. On this food- and culture-filled trip through mountain valleys you'll visit Alpine dairies, schnapps distilleries and a medieval-castle-housed brewery, as well as dazzling, art-adorned palaces and churches.

❶ Bregenz

In a postcard-perfect setting on the shores of Lake Constance, framed by towering Alps, Bregenz offers plenty of swimming, boating and walking opportunities.

The white cuboid **Vorarlberg Museum** (www.vorarlbergmuseum.at; Kornmarktplatz 1; adult/child €9/free; ☺10am-6pm Tue, Wed & Fri-Sun, to 8pm Thu) is emblazoned with what appears to be 16,656 flowers (actually PET bottle bases imprinted in concrete). Permanent

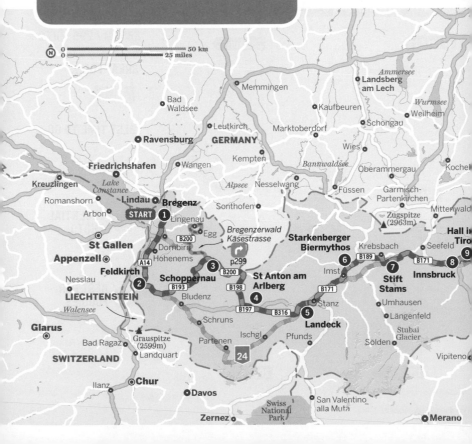

exhibitions home in on Vorarlberg state's history, art and architecture, with archaeological finds from Roman Brigantium, and paintings by Angelika Kauffmann.

Bregenz is most famous for the **Bregenzer Festspiele** (Bregenz Festival; ☎05574-40 76; www.bregen zerfestspiele.com; ☺mid-Jul– mid-Aug), when opera is performed on a floating stage on the lake.

Palm-shaded **Beach Bar Bregenz** (www.wirts hausamsee.at; Seepromenade 2; ☺4pm-midnight Mon-Fri, from 2pm Sat, from 11am Sun late Apr-early Sep) is perfect for enjoying cool cocktails and chilled DJ beats in a *Strandkorb* (wicker basket chair). Open-air cinema nights regularly take place.

✕ ⊨ p253, p293, p303

The Drive ≫ It's a quick 33km zip from Bregenz via the southbound A14 to Feldkirch.

TRIP HIGHLIGHT

❷ Feldkirch

On the banks of the turquoise Ill River, Feldkirch sits at the foot of wooded

LINK YOUR TRIP

24 **Grossglockner Road**

Salzburg is the starting point for an action-packed trip through the Alps.

27 **Salzkammergut**

Set off from Salzburg to the Salzkammergut's sparkling mountain-ringed lakes.

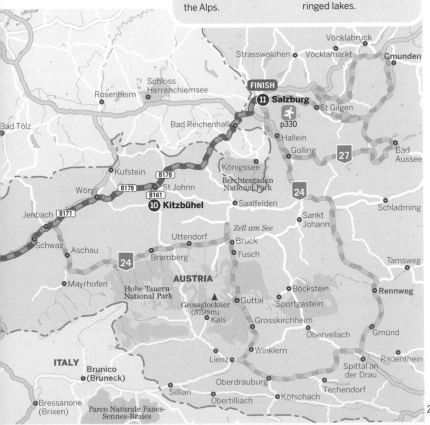

mountains, vineyards and a castle-crowned hill. Its cobbled, arcaded lanes and pastel-coloured townhouses wing you back to late-medieval times. Towers surviving from the old fortifications include the 40m-high **Katzenturm** (Hirschgraben), where a bell weighing 7500kg still tolls.

Red-turreted **Schloss Schattenburg** (www.schattenburg.at; Burggasse 1; adult/child €7/3.50; ⌚9am-5pm Mon-Fri, from 10am Sat & Sun) is straight out of a fairy tale. Once the seat of the counts of Montfort, the castle now houses a small museum displaying religious art, costumes and weaponry.

Distinguished by its slender spire, Feldkirch's cathedral, **Domkirche St Nikolaus** (Domplatz; ⌚8am-6pm), has a large, forbidding interior complemented by late-Gothic features and dazzling stained glass.

✕ p303

The Drive » You'll know you're in the Alps on this 50km drive. From Feldkirch, take the B190 southeast, then the precipitous B193 northwest up to Schoppernau. Wind down your car windows to hear the melodic clinging of cow bells.

3 Schoppernau

Discover cheese-making secrets (including why Emmentaler is holey) at show dairy **Bergkäserei Schoppernau** (www.bergkaeserei.at; Unterdorf 248; ⌚8.30-11.30am & 3-6pm Mon-Fri, to 5pm Sat). It's famed for its award-winning tangy *Bergkäse,* matured for up to 12 months. (And if it's not open, don't worry, a vending machine dispenses *Bergkäse* along with handmade butter, *Spätzle* noodles and fried onion round the clock.)

If the dairy whets your appetite for more melt-in-your-mouth cheese produced from the mountains' pristine pastures, set off from Schoppernau on a detour of the Bregenzerwald Käsestrasse (Bregenz Forest Cheese Road).

The Drive » From Schoppernau, it's an ultra-scenic 47km through deep valleys, steep ascents and switchback descents along the B200 and B198 to St Anton am Arlberg.

4 St Anton am Arlberg

In 1901 St Anton am Arlberg founded the first ski club in the Alps and downhill skiing was born. Strung out along the northern bank of the Rosanna River at the foot of 2811m-high Valluga, in winter St Anton is a cross between a ski bum's utopia and Ibiza in fast-forward mode – the terrain fierce, the nightlife hedonistic.

Walking in the mountains through meadows full of wildflowers and grazing cattle is the most popular summertime activity. A handful of cable cars and lifts (€5 to €23 one way, €6 to €25 return) rise to the major peaks. If you're planning to hike, pick up a detailed booklet and map from the **tourist office** (☎05446-226 90; www.stantonamarlberg.com; Dorfstrasse 8; ⌚8am-noon & 1-5pm Mon-Fri, 9am-noon Sat & Sun). Also consider purchasing a Wanderpass (3-/7-day pass €34/39), providing unlimited access to all lifts, or a St Anton Card (3-/7-day pass €55/77), which offers the same benefits plus entrance to the town's indoor and outdoor swimming pools.

The Drive » A 25km deep valley drive via the B197 and B316 brings you to Landeck.

5 Landeck

Landeck is an ordinary town with an extraordinary backdrop: framed by an amphitheatre of forested peaks, it's bordered by the fast-flowing Inn and Sanna Rivers, and presided over by a hilltop medieval castle that's visible from afar, 13th-century **Schloss Landeck** (www.schlosslandeck.at; Schlossweg 2; adult/child €7.70/2; ⌚10am-5pm mid-Apr–late Oct, 1-5pm mid-Dec–early Jan; 👪). Its museum showcases everything from Celtic figurines to hand-carved *Krampus* (devil) masks; there's also an art gallery here. Sweeping views over Landeck and the Lechtaler

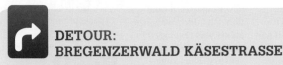

DETOUR:
BREGENZERWALD KÄSESTRASSE

Start: ❸ **Schoppernau**

Explore the Bregenzerwald's rolling dairy country and local *Sennereien* (dairy farms) on the **Bregenzerwald Käsestrasse** (Bregenz Forest Cheese Road; www. kaesestrasse.at), which refers to the cheese-producing region rather than a specific route.

From Schoppernau, it's a 49km round trip. Country lanes lead to the pretty village of Egg en route to Lingenau. Peek inside the huge cellars of the ultramodern **Käsekeller Lingenau** (www.kaesekeller.at; Zeihenbühel 423, Lingenau; ⊗10am-6pm Mon-Fri, 9am-5pm Sat, shorter hours in winter) to see robots brushing wagon-wheel-sized cheeses with salt water, watch a free 12-minute film (in English) and savour a tasting (three cheeses €5, with local wine €8).

Book ahead to take a factory tour of **Käse-Molke Metzler** (☑05512-30 44; www. molkeprodukte.com; Bruggan 1025, Egg; ⊗8am-noon & 1.30-6pm Mon-Fri, 8am-noon Sat). Tours costing €13.50/6.75 per adult/child include a lavish buffet of cheeses like creamy *Wälderkäsle*, made from cow's and goat's milk. If you'd like to try milking the goats and cows as well, the price is €25/12.50.

Old farmhouses tiled with wood shingles and studded with scarlet geraniums crowd the narrow streets of Schwarzenberg. Contemplate neoclassical art in the **Angelika Kauffmann Museum** (www.angelika-kauffmann.com; Brand 34, Schwarzenberg; adult/child €7.50/5.50; ⊗10am-5pm Tue-Sun). Admission covers entry to the neighbouring **Heimat Museum** (Heritage Museum), a pristine Alpine chalet. Displays focus on rural 19th-century life with traditional painted furniture, extraordinary headwear, hunting paraphernalia and filigree iron crosses. Dine on cheesy *Kässpätzle* (hand-rolled noodles with cheese, topped with crispy fried onion) in the wood-panelled parlour or garden at **Gasthof Hirschen** (☑05512-29 44; www.hotel-hirschen-bregenzerwald.at; Hof 14, Schwarzenberg; d €190-260, ste €261-310; P 🛜) – or consider staying the night.

From Schwarzenberg, head southeast via peaceful Au back to Schoppernau.

Alps extend from the tower.

In summer, the **Venet** (www.venet.at; adult/child one way €14.40/8.20, return €16.50/9.80; ⊗8am-5pm) cable car zooms up to Krahberg (2208m), where there's a web of marked walking trails.

A roller coaster of water thrashes the limestone cliffs at **Zammer Lochputz** (www. zammer-lochputz.at; adult/

child €4.50/3.50; ⊗9.30am-5.30pm May-Sep, 10am-5pm Sat-Mon Oct), a gorge 4km northeast of Landeck, across the Inn River from Zams. Leading up through pine forest, a 2.9km round-trip trail passes viewpoints and interesting rock formations – look out for the head of a bull and a nymph.

The Drive » Travel via the B171 for 20km to Imst. Starkenberger

Biermythos is 2.3km north of Imst just off the B189.

- - - - - - - - - - - - - - - - - -

❻ Starkenberger Biermythos

At 200-year-old brewery **Starkenberger Biermythos** (☑05412-662 01; www. starkenberger.at; Griesegg 1, Tarrenz; tour adult/child €7/free; ⊗10am-5pm Tue-Sun May-Oct, 10am-noon & 1-4pm Tue-Fri Nov-Apr), housed in a medieval castle, tours take you through the brewing process and include a beer tasting. If you can't get enough of the stuff, you can even bathe in it by prior reservation – it does wonders for the complexion, apparently. A two-person beer bath costs €250 per couple.

The Drive » Take the northeast-bound B189 for 22km to the village of Krebsbach, then head south, crossing the Inn River, to reach Stams (29km all-up).

TRIP HIGHLIGHT

❼ Stift Stams

Monumental ochre-and-white abbey **Stift Stams** (www.stiftstams.at; Stiftshof 3; tours adult/child €12.50/6; 🕙 guided tours hourly 9-11am & 1-5pm Mon-Sat, 1-5pm Sun Jun-Sep, 4pm Thu Oct-May) was founded in 1273 by Elisabeth of Bavaria, the mother of Konradin, the last of the Hohenstaufens. It's set in pristine grounds, with a facade topped by twin silver cupolas, a final flourish added when the abbey was revamped in baroque style in the 17th century. The exuberant church interior is dominated by the high altar: the intertwining branches of this version of the 'tree of life' support 84 saintly figures surrounding an image of the Virgin. Near the entrance is the Rose Grille, an exquisite iron screen made in 1716. Crane your neck to admire the ceiling's elaborate stucco-work, gilding and frescos.

Marmalade, juice, honey, liqueurs and schnapps made on the premises can be bought from the **Kloster shop** (🕙9am-noon & 1-5pm Mon-Sat, 1-5pm Sun Jun-Sep, 9am-noon & 2-5pm Mon-Sat Oct-May), plus bread that's freshly baked here on Monday, Wednesday and Friday.

The Drive » Travel along the eastbound B171 for 37km to Innsbruck. Approaching the city you'll pass its airport – the views of planes descending into the valley are amazing.

TRIP HIGHLIGHT

❽ Innsbruck

The mountains surrounding Innsbruck beg to be explored but the city itself is also filled with treasures.

Innsbruck's pride and joy is the Gothic **Hofkirche** (www.tiroler-landesmuseum.at; Universitätsstrasse 2; adult/child €7/free; 🕙9am-5pm Mon-Sat, 12.30-5pm Sun), one of Europe's finest royal court churches. It was commissioned in 1553 by Ferdinand I, who enlisted top artists of the age such as Albrecht Dürer, Alexander Colin and Peter Vischer the Elder. Top billing goes to the empty black-marble sarcophagus of Emperor Maximilian I (1459–1519), a masterpiece of German Renaissance sculpture.

Built for Emperor Maximilian I, golden oriel ('awning') **Goldenes Dachl & Museum** (Golden Roof; Herzog-Friedrich-Strasse 15; museum adult/child €4.80/2.40; 🕙10am-5pm May-Sep, Tue-Sun Oct & Dec-Apr) glitters with 2657 fire-gilt copper tiles. Inside, look for the grotesque tournament helmets designed to resemble the Turks of the rival Ottoman Empire.

The cupola-crowned **Hofburg** (Imperial Palace; www.hofburg-innsbruck.at;

TIROLER SCHNAPSROUTE

For another flavour-packed detour, set out on the **Tiroler Schnapsroute** (www.schnapsroute.at). Like the Bregenzerwald Käsestrasse, this isn't a single road but instead refers to a region.

On a sunny plateau dotted with apple and plum orchards, the village of **Stanz** has just 204 residents but over 50 schnapps distilleries where you can taste and buy the local firewater.

From Landeck, it's a 2.5km drive northwest to Stanz. If you're still thirsty, other Schnapsroute villages include Grins, Elbigenalp, Prutz, Pfunds, Imsterberg and Arzl.

Innsbruck Hofkirche

Rennweg 1; adult/child €9.50/ free; ⊘9am-5pm) was built as a castle for Archduke Sigmund the Rich in the 15th century, expanded by Emperor Maximilian I in the 16th century and given a baroque makeover by Empress Maria Theresia in the 18th century.

Amid beautiful gardens, Renaissance **Schloss Ambras** (www. schlossambras-innsbruck.at; Schlosstrasse 20; palace adult/ child €12/free, gardens free; ⊘ palace 10am-5pm, gardens 6am-dusk, closed Nov; 🚻) was acquired in 1564 by Archduke Ferdinand II, then ruler of Tyrol, who trans-

formed it from a fortress into a palace. Don't miss the Spanische Saal (Spanish Hall), the dazzling armour collection and the gallery's Velázquez and van Dyck originals.

✕ 🛏 p293, p303

The Drive » From Innsbruck it's just a 10km trip east to Hall in Tirol along the B171 on the Inn River's northern bank.

----

⑨ Hall in Tirol

Tucked beneath the Alps, medieval Hall prospered from salt in the 13th century. You can visit a reconstructed salt mine, complete with galleries, tools and shafts,

on a 45-minute guided tour at the **Bergbau Museum** (www.hall-wattens. at; Fürstengasse; adult/child €5/3; ⊘ tours 11.30am Mon, Thu & Sat).

Hall's winding lanes, lined with pastel-coloured townhouses that are lantern-lit after dark, are made for ambling. Bordering the main square is Hall's 15th-century **Rathaus** (Town Hall, Oberer Stadtplatz). Its distinctive courtyard is complete with crenellated edges and mosaic crests.

At **Burg Hasegg** (www. muenz-hall.at; Burg Hasegg 6; adult/child tower €5.50/4.50, mint €8/5.50, combined ticket

€11.50/8; ⏱10am-5pm Tue-Sun; ♿), a staircase spirals up 186 steps to the 5th floor for panoramic views. The castle had a 300-year career as a mint for silver *Thalers* (coins; the root of the modern word 'dollar'). Its history is unravelled in the Münze Hall, displaying water-driven and hammer-striking techniques; kids can mint their own coins here.

The Drive » It's a 92km drive from Hall in Tirol to Kitzbühel. East along the B171 along the widening valley, you'll pass Wattens, home to Austria's Swarovski crystal. From the village of Wörgl the incline ramps up. Turn east on the B178, passing beneath the awe-inspiring Kaisergebirge mountains, before heading south at St Johann on the B161 to Kitzbühel.

- - - - - - - - - - - - - - - - -

⑩ Kitzbühel

Kitzbühel began life in the 16th century as a silver and copper mining town, and preserves a charming medieval centre despite its winter persona. Ever since Franz Reisch slipped on skis and whizzed down the slopes of Kitzbüheler Horn in 1893, so christening Austria's first Alpine ski run, Kitzbühel has carved out its reputation as one of Europe's foremost ski resorts.

In summer, it's a four-hour (14km) hike one way, or a speedy cable-car ride to the **Alpine Flower Garden** (⏱8.30am-5pm May-Sep). Arnica, edelweiss and

purple bellflowers are among the 400 alpine blooms flourishing here atop Kitzbüheler Horn. A road also twists up to the mountain (toll per car €6, plus €3 per person).

The **Museum Kitzbüh-el** (www.museum-kitzbuehel. at; Hinterstadt 32; adult/child €7/free; ⏱10am-5pm Fri-Wed, to 8pm Thu Apr-late Sep, reduced hours late Sep-Mar) traces Kitzbühel's heritage from its Bronze Age mining beginnings onwards. The big emphasis is on winter sports, and pays tribute to home-grown legends like ski racing champ Toni Sailer and winter landscape painter Alfons Walde.

✖ 🛏 p303

The Drive » Kitzbühel sits 85 fabulously scenic kilometres from Salzburg. Head northeast on the B161 then B178, passing the white-water rafting village of Lofer, and cross the German border (the road becomes the B21). On your left you'll see an opaque turquoise lake, the Saalachsee, before reaching Bad Reichenhall. The road crosses back into Austria and brings you into Salzburg.

- - - - - - - - - - - - - - - - -

TRIP HIGHLIGHT

⑪ Salzburg

Salzburg is storybook Austria, and easily explored on a walking tour (p330). Beside the fast-flowing Salzach River are the Altstadt's mosaic of domes and spires, and the formidable 900-year-old clifftop fortress, the **Festung Hohensalzburg**

(www.salzburg-burgen.at; Mönchsberg 34; adult/child/ family €10/5.70/22.20, incl funicular €12.90/7.40/28.60; ⏱9.30am-5pm Oct-Apr, 9am-7pm May-Sep), reached by the glass **Festungsbahn funicular** (Festungsgasse 4; one way/return adult €6.90/8.60, child €3.70/4.70; ⏱9am-8.30pm May-Sep, to 5pm Oct-Apr), with the mountains beyond. This dazzling backdrop inspired the lordly prince-archbishops and home-grown genius Mozart.

You can visit the great composer's 1756 birthplace, the **Mozarts Geburtshaus** (Mozart's Birthplace; www.mozarteum. at; Getreidegasse 9; adult/child €11/3.50; ⏱9am-5.30pm Sep-Jun, 8.30am-7pm Jul & Aug), as well as his one-time residence, the **Mozart-Wohnhaus** (Mozart's Residence; www.mozarteum. at; Makartplatz 8; adult/child €11/3.50; ⏱9am-5.30pm Sep-Jun, 8.30am-7pm Jul & Aug); both house museums.

Other unmissable stops include Salzburg's baroque cathedral, the **Dom** (www.salzburger-dom. at; Domplatz; guided tours €5; ⏱8am-7pm Mon-Sat, from 1pm Sun May-Sep, shorter hours Oct-Apr), and the **Salzburg Museum** (www.salzburg museum.at; Mozartplatz 1; adult/child €9/3; ⏱9am-5pm Tue-Sun; ♿), inside the baroque Neue Residenz palace, along with famed *The Sound of Music* sights (p319).

✖ 🛏 p303, p321

Eating & Sleeping

Bregenz ❶

Goldener Hirschen Austrian €€

(☎05574-428 15; www.hotelweisseskreuz.at; Kirchstrasse 8; lunch €8.20, mains €9-22; ⏱11am-10pm Wed-Mon) Austrian through and through, this restaurant in the **Weisses Kreuz** (☎05574-498 80; Römerstrasse 5; s €98-125, d €125-275, ste €175-335; P 📶) has bags of rustic charm, with its high beamed ceilings and jovial crowd of locals. The kitchen rolls out well-prepared classics such as Carinthian cheese noodles, boiled beef with horseradish, homemade dumplings with sauerkraut and pork roast with cumin-beer sauce. There's a garden courtyard for fine-weather dining.

Feldkirch ❷

Gutwinski Austrian €€€

(☎05522-721 75; www.gutwinski.cc; Rosengasse 4-6; mains €26-34, 4-course menu €59; ⏱noon-2pm & 6-10pm Tue-Sat) In fine weather, head to Gutwinski's tree-shaded terrace to dine on classics such as *Wiener schnitzel* with parsley potatoes and cranberry compote, or brighter, more inventive dishes such as Arctic char with ginger mousse and gin-laced cucumber, and crème brûlée with lavender ice cream. When it's chilly, the candlelit, champagne-kissed interior, with high-back velvet chairs and banquettes, makes an ideal refuge.

Innsbruck ❽

Markthalle Market €

(www.markthalle-innsbruck.at; Herzog-Siegmund-Ufer 1-3; ⏱7am-6.30pm Mon-Fri, to 1pm Sat) Fresh-baked bread, Tyrolean cheese, organic fruit, smoked ham and salami – it's all under one roof at this riverside covered market.

Grand Hotel Europa Luxury Hotel €€

(☎0512-59 31; www.grandhoteleuropa.at; Südtiroler Platz 2; s €115-155, d €140-220; P ❄ @ 📶) This luxurious pile opposite the station has been given a facelift. Pared-down chic now defines the rooms, though old-world grandeur lingers in the opulent Baroque Hall and wood-panelled restaurant. Mick Jagger and Queen Elizabeth II are famous past guests.

Kitzbühel ❿

Huberbräu Stüberl Austrian €€

(☎05356-656 77; Vorderstadt 18; mains €9-19; ⏱8am-11.30pm Mon-Sat, from 9am Sun; 👪) An old-world Tyrolean haunt with vaults and pine benches, this tavern favours substantial portions of Austrian classics, such as schnitzel, goulash and dumplings, cooked to perfection. Cash only.

Hotel Edelweiss Hotel €€

(☎05356-752 52; www.edelweiss-kitzbuehel.at; Marchfeldgasse 2; d incl half board €120-150; P 📶) Near the Hahnenkammbahn, Edelweiss oozes Tyrolean charm with its green surrounds, Alpine views, sauna and cosy interiors. Your kindly hosts Klaus and Veronika let you pack up a lunch from the breakfast buffet and also serve delicious five-course dinners.

Salzburg ⓫

Imlauer Sky Austrian €€

(☎0662-88 978 666; www.imlauer.com; Rainerstrasse 6, Imlauer Hotel Pitter; mains €20-34; ⏱11.30am-1.30am) From the lofty vantage point of this slickly modern, glass-fronted rooftop restaurant, Salzburg spreads out before you in all its glory – it's particularly spectacular after dark when the fortress lights up. Service is attentive and the menu swings from steaks and surf 'n' turf to well-executed classics such as *Wiener schnitzel* and *Tafelspitz* (braised beef with horseradish).

Hotel & Villa Auersperg Boutique Hotel €€€

(☎0662-88 94 40; www.auersperg.at; Auerspergstrasse 61; s €145-195, d €175-305, ste €240-355; P @ 📶) This charismatic villa and hotel duo fuses late 19th-century flair with contemporary design in rooms featuring wood floors, muted colours and Nespresso machines. Guests can relax by the lily pond in the vine-strewn garden or in the rooftop wellness area with its sauna, tea bar and mountain views. Local organic, vegan and gluten-free produce features at breakfast.

Castles of Burgenland

26

Studded with fortified castles and lavish palaces, the countryside you'll traverse on this route is also threaded by vineyards that produce some of Austria's finest wines.

TRIP HIGHLIGHTS

2–4 DAYS
228KM / 220 MILES

GREAT FOR...

BEST TIME TO GO
May to September offers the most idyllic weather.

ESSENTIAL PHOTO
Buttercup-yellow Schloss Esterházy.

BEST FOR FOODIES
Vienna's Naschmarkt.

46 km

Petronell-Carnuntum
Explore the remains of the Roman town of Carnuntum

START
Vienna
2

95 km

Rust
Home to reed-filled lakeshores and outstanding wines

3
Burg Forchtenstein
Burg Lockenhaus
Burg Güssing

FINISH 9

228 km

Graz
This vibrant city has a spectacular riverside setting

26 | Castles of Burgenland

Austria's showpiece capital, Vienna, sets the stage for a dramatic voyage through this region's turbulent history. You'll visit the remains of the major political and military centre in the Roman Empire's northeastern territory, and a string of hilltop-perched castles (some reached by funicular or cable car), built as strongholds against marauding invaders, before finishing in the country's second-largest city, spirited Graz.

---

❶ Vienna

Take in the Austrian capital's majestic sights on a walking tour (p332), or aboard a traditional Fiaker (horse-drawn carriage).

Vienna's splendour peaks at the Habsburgs' opulent summer palace, Unesco World Heritage–listed **Schloss Schönbrunn** (☑01-811 13-0; www.schoenbrunn.at; 13, Schönbrunner Schlossstrasse 47; adult/child Imperial Tour €16/11.50, Grand Tour €20/13, Grand Tour with guide €24/15; ☺8am-6.30pm Jul & Aug, to 5.30pm Apr-Jun, Sep & Oct, to 5pm Nov-Mar; Ⓤ Schönbrunn, Hietzing). Of its 1441 rooms, 40 are open to the public. The fountain-filled, French-style formal gardens shelter the world's oldest zoo, the 1752-founded **Tiergarten**, as well as a 630m-long hedge maze, and the **Gloriette**, whose roof offers panoramas over the palace grounds and beyond.

Grand *Kaffeehäuser* (coffee houses) aside, the best place to *nasch* (snack) is the historic **Naschmarkt** (www.wien.gv.at; 06, Linke & Rechte Wienzeile; ☺6am-7.30pm Mon-Fri, to 5pm Sat; ☑; Ⓤ Karlsplatz, Kettenbrückengasse), with food-laden stalls, delis, sit-down cafes and take-away stands.

✕ 🛏 p283, p311

The Drive ≫ The 37km drive from Vienna is unavoidably industrial until you clear the city's outskirts. Take the A4 southeast for 19km. After passing the airport, take the exit to the B9 and follow it eastwards for a further 18km.

- - - - - - - - - - - - - - - -

TRIP HIGHLIGHT

❷ Petronell-Carnuntum

The Roman town of Carnuntum was the most important political and military centre in the empire's northeast; with a population of 50,000 people at its peak, it made Vienna look like a village in comparison. The town developed around AD 40 and was abandoned some 400 years later.

The three main Roman attractions are covered by one ticket (adult/child €12/6). Modern-day Petronell-Carnuntum is home to the fascinating

LINK YOUR TRIP

23 **Along the Danube**
From Vienna, you can follow the Danube to Passau, just over the German border, to do this route in reverse.

28 **Carinthian Lakes**
Graz is the starting point for a drive around the crystal-clear Carinthian Lakes.

open-air museum **Freilichtmuseum Petronell** (www.carnuntum.at; Hauptstrasse 1a; ⊙9am-5pm mid-Mar–mid-Nov), with buildings painstakingly reconstructed using ancient techniques, including a cloth merchant's house, an upper-class city mansion and Roman public baths. Situated 2.7km east, the grass-covered **Amphitheater Bad Deutsch-Altenburg** (www.carnuntum.at; Wienerstrasse 52; ⊙9am-5pm mid-Mar–mid-Nov) seated 15,000. The spa town of Bad Deutsch-Altenburg, a further 1km northeast, harbours archaeological finds at the **Museum Carnuntinum** (www.carnuntum. at; Badgasse 40-46; ⊙9am-5pm mid-Mar–Nov).

The Drive » The 49km drive southwest to Rust becomes increasingly picturesque. Travel through farmland via the B211 and E60 to the vast lake Neusiedler See. Here, you enter wine country, with vineyards covering the hillsides. Wine villages along this stretch of the B50 that offer tastings and cellar-door sales include Purbach am See, Donnerskirchen and Oggau am Neusiedler See.

- - - - - - - - - - - - - - - - -

TRIP HIGHLIGHT

❸ Rust

The reed-filled lake and hidden boatsheds of the charming village of Rust give it a sleepy, swampy feel on a steamy day. From the end of March, dozens of storks make their homes on chimneys

in town to rear their young. The clacking of expectant parents can be heard until late August.

The tower of the central **Katholische Kirche** (Haydengasse; ⊙10.30am-noon & 2.30-5pm Mon-Sat, 3-5pm Sun) is a good vantage point for observing storks. For a close-up view, check out the **webcam** (or 'nestcam') outside the tourist office, located at the Rathaus (town hall) on Conradplatz.

In 1524 the emperor granted local vintners the right to display the letter 'R' on their wine barrels and today the corks still bear this distinctive insignia. Wineries where you can sample the local drop are scattered through the village's streets.

🛏 p311

The Drive » Driving northwest along the B52 for 15km through rolling countryside ribboned with vineyards brings you to Eisenstadt's Schloss Esterházy.

- - - - - - - - - - - - - - - - -

❹ Schloss Esterházy

Dating from the 14th century, giant, sunny yellow **Schloss Esterházy** (www.esterhazy.at; Esterházyplatz 1; adult/child €12/6; ⊙10am-5pm mid-Mar–Apr & Oct, 10am-6pm May-Sep, 10am-5pm Fri-Sun Nov–mid-Mar; P), in Burgenland's small capital, Eisenstadt, received one makeover in baroque and a later one in the neoclassical style. Many

of the 256 rooms are occupied by the provincial government, but several can be seen on tours. The highlight is the frescoed **Haydn Hall**, where during Joseph Haydn's employment by the Esterházys from 1761 to 1790 the great composer conducted an orchestra on a near-nightly basis. Haydn's music accompanies you as you walk past exhibitions on his life and work. Austria's largest **wine museum** is also here, along with a *Vinothek* serving local vintages.

The Drive » It's 26km through mostly open countryside to Burg Forchtenstein via the B50.

- - - - - - - - - - - - - - - - -

❺ Burg Forchtenstein

Straddling a dolomite spur, **Burg Forchtenstein** (www.esterhazy.at; Melinda Esterházy-Platz 1; adult/ child each attraction €12/10, highlight tour €18/16; ⊙10am-6pm late Mar-Oct) was built in the 14th century and enlarged in 1635 by the Esterházys (who still own it today). Apart from a grand view from its ramparts, the castle's highlights include an impressive collection of armour and weapons, portraits of regal Esterházys in the **Ahnengalerie**, and spoils from the Turkish wars (it was the only castle in the area not to fall to the Turks). Its **Schatzkammer** contains a rich

Rust Storks' nest

collection of jewellery and porcelain.

The Drive » From Burg Forchtenstein, head up into heavily forested hills on the L223. Join the southbound L149 to Kirchschlag in der Buckligen Welt, then head southeast on the B55 (54km in total).

---

❻ Burg Lockenhaus

Burg Lockenhaus
(📞02616-239 40; www.ritterburg.at; Günserstrasse 5; adult/child €9/4; ☉9am-6pm May-Oct, reduced hours winter) is infamous for its former resident Elizabeth Báthory, aka the 'Blood Countess'. During her reign of terror early in the 17th century, she

reputedly tortured and murdered over 600 mainly peasant women for her own sadistic pleasure. The castle has long been cleansed of gruesome horrors but still contains an impressive torture chamber, complete with an iron maiden.

📖 p311

The Drive » Head south on the B56 for 66km, skirting the Hungarian border, before following the road west to Güssing.

---

❼ Burg Güssing

Arresting **Burg Güssing** (📞03322-434 00; www.burgguessing.info;

Batthyanystrasse 10; adult/child €7.50/4; ☉9am-5pm Tue-Sun Easter–mid-Nov; 🅿) rises dramatically over the Strembach River and peaceful town, reached by a modern 100m **funicular railway** (Schrägaufzug; one-way/return €2/4; ☉10am-5pm Tue-Sun Easter-Oct). A mix of ruins and renovations, the castle contains plenty of weapons from the Turks and Hungarians, striking portraits from the 16th century and a tower with 360-degree views of the surrounding countryside.

The Drive » You'll traverse hilly forest and farmland on this scenic stretch. Take the

WINES OF BURGENLAND

Burgenland's wine is some of Austria's finest, due to the 300 days of sunshine per year, rich soil and excellent drainage. Although classic white varieties have a higher profile, the pick of the local wines is arguably the red *Blaufränkisch,* whose 18th-century pedigree here predates its arrival in the Danube region and Germany.

Eiswein (wine made from grapes picked late and shrivelled by frost) and selected late-picking sweet or dessert wines are being complemented by *Schilfwein,* made by placing the grapes on reed *(Schilf)* matting so they shrivel in the heat.

Southern Burgenland is best known for *Uhudler,* a typically rosé-coloured wine with a distinctly fruity taste.

B57 southwest to Heiligenkreuz im Lafnitztal. Continue south on the L116, grazing the Hungarian border (literally across the road), and rejoin the B57. The L207 then L224 travel northwest, passing the delightful swimming and pedal-boating lake Seebad Riegersburg, before heading uphill to Schloss Riegersburg (50km altogether).

- - - - - - - - - - - - - - - - - -

❽ Schloss Riegersburg

Perched on a 200m-high rocky outcrop, **Schloss Riegersburg** (☏03153-82 131; www.dieriegersburg.at; Riegersburg 1; adult/child/family €19/11/45; ☺9am-6pm May-Sep, 10am-6pm Apr & Oct) is a hugely impressive 13th-century castle built due to invading Hungarians and Turks; today it houses a Hexenmuseum

on witchcraft, a Burgmuseum featuring the history of the Liechtenstein family, who acquired it in 1822, and an impressive collection of weapons. A war memorial is a reminder of fierce fighting in 1945, when Germans occupying the castle were attacked by Russian troops.

A cable car on the north side whisks you up in 90 seconds (uphill/downhill €4/2); it costs €2 to walk up the footpath.

The Drive ≫ From Riegersburg, it's just 57km north via the B66 and west via the B65 to the lively city of Graz.

- - - - - - - - - - - - - - - - - -

TRIP HIGHLIGHT

❾ Graz

Austria's second-largest city bursts with energy

thanks to its spirited student population. Surrounding the fast-flowing river gushing through its centre is a vision of green parkland, red rooftops, Renaissance courtyards and baroque palaces, plus innovative modern designs.

Rising 473m, **Schlossberg** (one way €2.40; ☒4, 5 Schlossbergplatz) is the site of the original fortress where Graz was founded. It's topped by the city's most visible icon – the **Uhrturm** (clock tower). Its wooded slopes can be reached by bucolic (and strenuous) paths, but also by lift or Schlossbergbahn funicular.

Graz' elegant palace, **Schloss Eggenberg** (☏0316-8017 95 32; www.museum-joanneum.at; Eggenberger Allee 90; adult/child €15/6; ☺tours hourly 10am-4pm, except 1pm Tue-Sun Apr-Oct, exhibitions 10am-5pm Tue-Sun Apr-Oct; ☒1 Schloss Eggenberg), was created for the Eggenberg dynasty in 1625. Admission is via a highly worthwhile guided tour during which you'll learn about each room's idiosyncrasies, the stories portrayed by the frescos and the Eggenberg family itself.

 p311 , p329

Eating & Sleeping

Vienna ❶

✖ Figlmüller
Austrian €€

(☎01-512 61 77; www.figlmueller.at; 01, Wollzeile 5; mains €13-21; ⏱11am-9.30pm; 🛜; Ⓤ Stephansplatz) Vienna would simply be at a loss without Figlmüller. This famous *Beisl* (bistro pub) has a rural decor and some of the biggest and best schnitzels in the business. Wine is from the owner's vineyard, but no beer is served. Its popularity has spawned a second location nearby on **Bäckerstrasse** (☎01-512 17 60; 01, Bäckerstrasse 6; ⏱11am-9.30pm) with a wider menu (and drinks list).

✖ Meierei im Stadtpark
Austrian €€

(☎01-713 31 68; www.steirereck.at; 03, Am Heumarkt 2a; mains €19-22, set breakfasts €21-25; ⏱8am-11pm Mon-Fri, 9am-7pm Sat & Sun; 🅿; Ⓤ Stadtpark) In the green surrounds of Stadtpark, the Meierei is most famous for its goulash served with lemon, capers and creamy dumplings, and its selection of 120 types of cheese. Served until noon, the bountiful breakfast features gastronomic showstoppers such as poached duck egg with forest mushrooms and pumpkin, and corn waffles with warm tomato salad and sheep's cheese.

🛏 Hotel Rathaus Wein & Design
Boutique Hotel €€

(☎01-400 11 22; www.hotel-rathaus-wien.at; 08, Lange Gasse 13; d/tr/f from €115/135/280; ❄🛜; 🚇2 Rathaus, Ⓤ Rathaus) Each of the 39 open-plan, minimalist-chic rooms at this boutique hotel is dedicated to an Austrian winemaker and the minibars are stocked with premium wines from the growers themselves. With clever backlighting, rooms reveal a razor-sharp eye for design, especially the opalescent ones with hybrid beds and bathtubs. Some rooms overlook the inner courtyard space.

Rust ❸

🛏 TiMiMoo Boutique Hotel Bürgerhaus
Boutique Hotel €€€

(☎02685-6162; www.timimoo.at; Hauptstrasse 1; ste €275-310; 🅿🛜) With spiral staircases

inside a 1537 former bakery and Biedermeier-style rooms with vaulted ceilings and drapes around the beds, this sweetly nostalgic hotel is pretty and cluttered with antiques faux and real, creating an impressive place to stay. The theme continues out in the extensive gardens, service is top-notch and children are superbly catered for.

Burg Lockenhaus ❻

🛏 Burghotel Lockenhaus
Historic Hotel €€

(☎02616-23 94; www.ritterburg.at; s/d €100/140; 🅿🛜) Burghotel Lockenhaus has antique furnished rooms, and a sauna. Breakfast costs €8; there's an extra €15 supplement for heating from October to March. Apartments with kitchenettes attached to the castle wall are also available (€161, including breakfast).

Graz ❾

✖ Der Steirer
Austrian €€

(☎0316-70 36 54; www.der-steirer.at; Belgiergasse 1; weekday lunch menu €8.90, mains €11-24; ⏱11am-midnight; 🅿; 🚋1, 3, 6, 7 Südtiroler Platz) This neo-*Beisl* and wine bar has a beautiful selection of Styrian dishes, including great goulash, crispy *Backhendl* (fried breaded chicken) and seasonal game dishes, all done in a simple, contemporary style. Its Styrian tapas concept is a nice way to sample local flavours.

🛏 Schlossberg Hotel
Hotel €€

(☎0316-807 00; www.schlossberg-hotel.at; Kaiser-Franz-Josef-Kai 30; s/d from €120/160; 🅿@🛜🐾; 🚋4, 5 Schlossbergbahn) Central but just removed from the action, four-star Schlossberg is blessed with a prime location tucked below its namesake. Rooms are well sized, and, individually decorated and with eccentric elegance. The hotel brings together three historic buildings so even the architecture is gently idiosyncratic. A small rooftop pool and vertiginous terraced garden make a stay here completely memorable. Breakfast isn't included in the rates.

Salzkammergut

27

The Salzkammergut's gemstone-coloured lakes glittering beneath the soaring, snow-capped Alps set the scene for a magical drive between enchanting villages along the waters' edge.

TRIP HIGHLIGHTS

137 km

St Wolfgang
Take a steam train high above town

Kammer

Traunkirchen

START/ FINISH

Salzburg

9

Bad Ischl

11 **10**

Hallstatt
Salzkammergut's prettiest village, home to an intriguing salt mine

195 km

Obertraun
Explore the dazzling Dachstein ice caves

190 km

**5–7 DAYS
282KM / 175 MILES**

GREAT FOR...

BEST TIME TO GO

The lakes are at their sparkling best from June to September.

 ESSENTIAL PHOTO

D-o-w-n through the glass floor of the 5 Fingers viewing platform.

 BEST FOR HISTORY

Salt mine Salzwelten, detailing the area's 'white gold'.

27 Salzkammergut

Captivating scenery is reason enough to set out on this trip, but the Salzkammergut's beauty goes well below the surface. You'll explore iridescent ice caves and fascinating salt mines, and visit magnificent churches, including the wedding-scene church from *The Sound of Music*. Fans of the iconic musical can visit a multitude of other filming locations on this trip, particularly in romance-steeped Salzburg.

----

❶ Salzburg

A walking tour (p330) is an ideal way to discover this exquisite city.

Along with architectural standouts (p302) and outdoor activities (p287), some of Salzburg's most magnificent buildings featured in *The Sound of Music*, and can be visited on a DIY tour (p319). They include the stately baroque square, the **Residenzplatz**, with its horse-drawn carriages and palatial **Residenz** (www.domquartier.at;

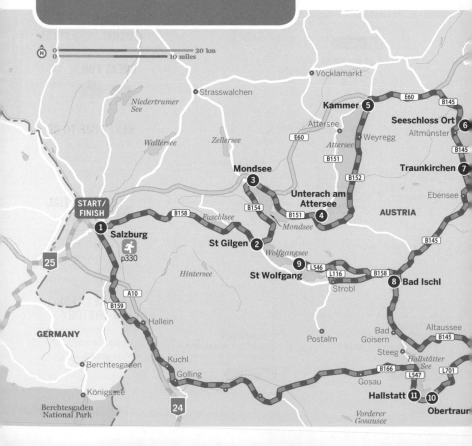

Residenzplatz 1; DomQuartier ticket adult/child €13/5; ⏰10am-5pm Wed-Mon Sep-Jun, to 6pm daily Jul & Aug). Another splendid palace, the **Schloss Mirabell** (Mirabellplatz 4; ⏰Schloss Mirabell 8am-6pm, Marble Hall 8am-4pm Mon, Wed & Thu, 1-4pm Tue & Fri, gardens 6am-dusk), was built by Prince-Archbishop Wolf Dietrich for his mistress Salome Alt in 1606 and given an early 18th-century baroque makeover that included its lavish, stucco Marmorsaal (Marble Hall). Benedictine convent,

1300-year-old **Stift Nonnberg** (Nonnberg Convent; Nonnberggasse 2; ⏰6.45am-dusk), has beautiful Romanesque frescos.

A highlight is Hellbrunn Park at early 17th-century Italianate villa **Schloss Hellbrunn** (www.hellbrunn.at; Fürsten-weg 37; adult/child/family €12.50/5.50/26.50, gardens free; ⏰9am-9pm Jul & Aug, to 5.30pm May, Jun & Sep, to 4.30pm Apr & Oct; 🅿), the summer palace built by Markus Sittikus as an escape from his Residenz duties.

🍴 🛏 p303, p321

The Drive » It's 28km from Salzburg along the eastbound B158, past resort lake the Fuschlsee, to St Gilgen.

- - - - - - - - - - - - - - - -

❷ St Gilgen

St Gilgen's historic centre, 400m west of the Wolfgangsee's shore, huddles around Mozart-platz and the photogenic Rathaus (old town).

Mozart's mother was born in St Gilgen and the family is the focus at St Gilgen's **Mozarthaus**

(📞06227-202 42; www.mozart haus.info; Ischlerstrasse 15; adult/child €4/2; ⏰10am-4pm Tue-Sun Jun-Sep), especially Mozart's sister 'Nannerl', also an accomplished composer and musician.

Cosy little museum **Muzikinstumente-Museum der Völker** (Folk Music Instrument Museum; www.hoerart.at; Aberseestrasse 11; adult/child €4/2.50; ⏰9-11am & 3-6pm Mon-Thu, 9-11am Fri, 3-6pm Sun early Jan-May, 9-11am & 3-7pm Tue-Sun Jun–mid-Oct, 9-11am & 2-5pm Dec-early Jan, closed mid-Oct–Nov) is home to 1500 musical instruments from all over the world, collected by a family of music teachers; there are opportunities to hear and play the instruments.

The eclectic collection at the **Heimatkundliches Museum** (📞06227-79 59; www.heimatkundliches -museum-sankt-gilgen.at; Pichlerplatz 6; adult/child €4/2.50; ⏰10am-noon & 3-6pm Tue-Sun Jun-Sep) spans embroidery (origi-nally manufactured in the building) to animal specimens (about 4700) and religious objects.

Grünau
Heckenau
Habernau
Almsee
Seehaus

raunsee

ltausseer See
Bad Aussee
Kammer See
Grundlsee
Salzkammergut
Bad Mitterndorf

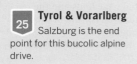

LINK YOUR TRIP

24 Grossglockner Road
This adventure-filled trip also starts in Salzburg.

25 Tyrol & Vorarlberg
Salzburg is the end point for this bucolic alpine drive.

The Drive » Leaving St Gilgen, take the B154 northeast past the small Krottensee. At its northern end, you'll enter a tight, forested mountain pass, then descend to the Mondsee. Continue northwest along the lakeshore to the town of Mondsee at the lake's northwestern end (14km in total).

----

❸ Mondsee

The lively – if touristy – town of Mondsee extends along the northern tip of the crescent-shaped, warm-water lake of the same name.

A must-see for *The Sound of Music* lovers is the 15th-century Gothic former monastery **Basilica Minor St Michael** (www.pfarre-mondsee.com; Kirchengasse 1; by donation; ☺9am-7pm). Its lemon-yellow baroque facade (added in 1740) and interior, centred on a soaring high altar, featured in the Captain and Maria's wedding scene in the film. Pope John Paul II upgraded it from a parish church to a *basilica minor* in 2005.

Next door to the basilica, the **Museum Mondseeland und Pfahlbaumuseum** (www.museum-mondsee.at; Marschal-Wrede-Platz; adult/child €4/2; ☺10am-6pm Tue-Sun Jul & Aug, to 5pm Tue-Sun May, Jun & Sep, 10am-5pm Sat & Sun Oct) has displays on Stone Age finds and the monastic culture of the region.

Segelschule Mondsee (☏06232-354 82 00; www.segelschule-mondsee.at;

Robert Baum Promenade 3; rental per half-day windsurfing €50, kayaking €35, SUP €50, sailboat per hour/half-day from €10/35; ☺9am-6pm May-Sep) offers windsurfing, kayaking and sailing-boat rental as well as courses.

The Drive » From Mondsee it's a 13km drive, taking the B151 along the Mondsee's northern shoreline, flanked by farmland with picturesque swimming spots en route, to Unterach am Attersee.

----

❹ Unterach am Attersee

The Attersee is the largest of the Salzkammergut's lakes. The village of Unterach am Attersee has little in the way of sights but is a relaxing spot to swim or rent a SUP (stand-up paddle-board) from **SUP Attersee** (☏699 8113 83 17; www.sup-attersee.at; Strandbad Litzlberg, Litzlberg; equipment rental per hour/day €12/50; ☺11am-7pm Jul-Aug).

From Unterach am Attersee, you can cruise on the lake with **Attersee-Schifffahrt** (☏07666-78 06; www.atterseeschifffahrt.at; ☺early Apr-Oct), which runs a five-stop southern lake tour (adult/child €11/5.50, one hour 10 minutes), an 11-stop southern lake tour (€17/8.50, 2½ hours), and an 18-stop full lake tour (€20/10, 3½ hours).

The Drive » Take the B152 along the Attersee's southern then eastern shores for 24km to

Kammer (signposted Kammer-Schörfling am Attersee, with its neighbouring town of Schörfling).

----

❺ Kammer

A treat for art lovers, Kammer, on the shores of the Attersee, is home to the **Gustav Klimt-Themenweg**, a 2km-long lakeside trail including information boards with prints of works by symbolist painter Gustav Klimt (1862–1918), a seminal Vienna Secession movement member. Klimt spent regular spells on the Attersee, painting many of his renowned landscapes here; the trail passes

Seeschloss Ort

his summer residences. There are also some boards in other lake settlements.

The **Gustav Klimt Zentrum** (📞0664 8283 990; www.klimt-am-attersee.at; Hauptstrasse 30; adult/child €7/4; 🕙10am-4pm Wed-Sun May–mid-Jun & early Sep-late Oct, daily mid-Jun–early Sep) rents audioguides for the trail (€3). High-tech multimedia exhibits here provide an overview of Klimt's life and works on the Attersee; the museum also has a cinema screening informative films (mainly in German with English subtitles). There's often an original on-loan work displayed here.

The centre neighbours privately owned **Schloss Kammer**, dating from the mid-13th century.

From Kammer, Attersee-Schifffahrt runs a seven-stop northern lake tour (adult/child €11/5.50, 1 hour 10 minutes).

The Drive » A 24km drive brings you to Seeschloss Ort. From Kammer, follow the A1 east and exit onto the B145. Just south of Gmunden, as the road descends to the Traunsee, you'll spot Seeschloss Ort out in the lake.

- - - - - - - - - - - - - - - -

❻ Seeschloss Ort

On the Traunsee's eastern side, pretty nature reserve Toscana Park forms

a backdrop to **Seeschloss Ort** (📞07612-7944 00; www.schloss-ort.at; Orth 1; adult/child €5/free; 🕙9.30am-4.30pm Easter-Oct). Reached by a pedestrian bridge, this lake-set castle on a small island is believed to have been built on the ruins of a Roman fortress. Dating from 909 or earlier, it was rebuilt in the 17th century after a fire. There's a picturesque courtyard, a late-Gothic external staircase and sgraffito from 1578. You can walk around the outside for free.

The Drive » Traunkirchen lies 10km south of Seeschloss Ort on the Traunsee just off the B145.

7 Traunkirchen 8 Bad Ischl 9 St Wolfgang

7 Traunkirchen

Traunkirchen sits on a picturesque spit of land on the western shore of the Traunsee, guarded by immense mountain peaks. A beautiful 450m path wends around the headland. There's a great **paddling pool** in the lake for kids.

In the Pfarrkirche (Parish Church) is the wooden **Fischerkanzel** (Fisherman's Pulpit; ✆07617-2214; Klosterplatz 1; ⏰8am-5pm), carved in 1753 and depicting the miracle of the fishes, with the Apostles standing in a tub-shaped boat and hauling in fish-laden nets.

There are plenty of lake cruises; to explore under your own steam you can rent pedal boats and electric boats from **Schiff-fahrt Loidl** (✆0664 371 56 46; www.schifffahrt-traunsee. at; Ortsplatz; pedal/electric boat rental per hour €10/15; ⏰10am-6pm May-Sep).

✗ 🏠 p321

TOP TIP: SALZKAMMERGUT SAVINGS

Save money by picking up a **Salzkammergut Erlebnis-Card** (Salzkammergut Adventure Card; €4.90), available from tourist offices and hotels. The nontransferable card offers discounts of up to 30% at popular attractions, sights and activities for 21 days. Details of seasonal savings and conditions are available on the comprehensive website www.salzkammergut.at.

The Drive » It's 22km from Traunkirchen southwest on the B145 to Bad Ischl. As you come into Ebensee, you'll cross the Traun River; 3km south of Ebensee, you'll cross the river again and follow its northern bank.

---

8 Bad Ischl

This spa town's reputation was enhanced after the Habsburg Princess Sophie took an infertility cure here in 1828. Within two years she had given birth to Emperor Franz Josef I, who made Bad Ischl his summer home for the next 60 years. The fateful letter he signed declaring war on Serbia, sparking WWI, bore a Bad Ischl postmark.

The **Stadtmuseum** (✆06132-254 76; www.stadtmuseum.at; Esplanade 10; adult/child €5.50/2.70; ⏰2-7pm Wed, 10am-5pm Thu-Sun Apr-Oct & Dec, 10am-5pm Fri-Sun Jan-Mar, closed Nov) showcases Bad Ischl's history inside the building where Franz Josef and Princess Elisabeth

of Bavaria were engaged (the day after they met at a ball).

Franz Josef's Italianate **Kaiservilla** (✆06132-232 41; www.kaiservilla.at; Jainzen 38; adult/child €15/7.50, grounds only €5.10/4.10; ⏰9.30am-5pm May-Sep, 10am-4pm Apr & Oct, 10am-4pm Sat & Sun Dec, 10am-4pm Wed Jan-Mar, closed Nov) was bought by Sophie as an engagement present for her son and Elisabeth. Tours give illuminating insights into the family's life.

The Drive » St Wolfgang sits 16km west from Bad Ischl via the B158 and the L116 and L546.

TRIP HIGHLIGHT

9 St Wolfgang

Charming St Wolfgang slinks down the steep banks of the Wolfgang-see. Its narrow streets can get clogged with day trippers but early evenings offer tranquil strolling along the forested lakeshore past creaking wooden boathouses.

St Wolfgang became famous as a place of pilgrimage, and the faithful still come to the **Wallfahrtskirche** (Pilgrimage Church; ✆06138-23 21; www.pfarre-sankt-wolfgang. at; Markt; €1; ⏰8am-7pm May-Sep, to 5pm Oct-Apr), a 14th-century pilgrim church. It's a spectacular gallery of religious art, with glittering altars (from Gothic to baroque), an extravagant pulpit, a

AUSTRIA 27 SALZKAMMERGUT

DIY SALZBURG SOUND OF MUSIC TOUR

Did you know that there were 10, not seven, Trapp children, the eldest of whom was Rupert (so long Liesl)? Or that in 1938 the Trapp family left quietly for the United States instead of climbing every mountain to Switzerland?

No matter. Sing as you stroll on a self-guided tour of *The Sound of Music* filming locations. Let's start at the very beginning:

The Hills Are Alive The opening scenes were actually filmed around the Salzkammergut lakes. Maria makes her twirling entrance on Alpine pastures just across the German border in Bavaria.

A Problem Like Maria Nuns waltzing on their way to mass at Benedictine Stift Nonnberg (p315) is fiction, but it's a fact that the real Maria von Trapp intended to become a nun here.

Have Confidence Residenzplatz (p314) is where Maria playfully splashes the spouting horses of the Residenzbrunnen fountain.

So Long, Farewell The grand rococo palace Schloss Leopoldskron, a 15-minute walk from Festung Hohensalzburg, is where the lake scene was filmed. Its Venetian Room was the blueprint for the Trapp's lavish ballroom, where the children bid their farewells.

Do-Re-Mi The Pegasus fountain, the steps with fortress views, the gnomes...the Mirabellgarten at Schloss Mirabell (p315) might inspire a rendition of 'Do-Re-Mi', especially if there's a drop of golden sun.

Sixteen Going on Seventeen Liesl and Rolf's glass-paned pavilion hides out in Hellbrunn Park at Schloss Hellbrunn.

Edelweiss and Adieu The Felsenreitschule (Summer Riding School) is the backdrop for the Salzburg Festival in the movie, where the Trapp Family Singers win the audience over with 'Edelweiss' and give the Nazis the slip with 'So Long, Farewell'.

Climb Every Mountain To, erm, Switzerland. Or content yourself with Alpine views from Untersberg, which appears briefly at the end of the movie when the family flees the country.

fine organ and countless statues and paintings.

The lovable crimson-coloured steam train that appeared with Maria and the children in *The Sound of Music,* the **Schafbergbahn** (www.wolfgangseeschifffahrt.at; Schaf-bergbahnstrasse; adult/child one way €28.10/14.10, return €39.60/19.80; ◈May-Oct), chugs from St Wolfgang to the summit of the 783m-high Schafberg.

During the season there are seven departures daily, starting from 9.15am, then hourly from 10am to 3pm. Journey time is 40 minutes one way.

The Drive » The prettiest drive from St Wolfgang back to Bad Ischl is along the narrow L546 through undulating open countryside. From Bad Ischl, head south on the B145 to Bad Aussee, and take the L701 west on a tight, heavily forested descent before crossing the

Traun River into Obertraun (53.5km all-up).

- - - - - - - - - - - - - - - - - - -

TRIP HIGHLIGHT

⑩ Obertraun

Obertraun offers easy access via cable car to the extraordinary **Dachstein Eishöhle** (www.dachstein-salzkammergut.com; adult/child all cable car sections plus caves €48.20/26.60, one section plus caves €42.60/23.40; ◈9.20am-3.30pm late

Apr–mid-Jun & mid-Sep–Oct, to 4pm mid-late Jun, to 5pm late Jun–mid-Sep). Millions of years old, these glittering ice caves extend into the mountain for almost 80km in places. Dress warmly! Also here is the non-ice **Mammuthöhle** (www.dachstein-salzkam mergut.com; adult/child all cable car sections plus caves €48.20/26.60, one section plus caves €42.60/23.40; ⊙9.20am-3.30pm late Apr–mid-Jun & mid-Sep–Oct, to 4pm mid-late Jun, to 5pm late Jun–mid-Sep), among the deepest and longest caves in the world.

Another cable car runs up to the 2109m-high **Krippenstein** (www. dachstein-salzkammergut.com; cable car return adult/child €32/17.60; ⊙mid-Jun–Oct) and its vertigo-inducing **5 Fingers viewing plat-form**, protruding from a sheer cliff face. Each 'finger' has a different form, with one reminis-cent of a diving board. A glass floor allows you to peer below your feet into a gaping void.

Allow a whole day to see one or both caves and the viewpoint. A **combination ticket** for all three, including cable cars, is €41.90/23.10 per adult/child.

The Drive » From Obertraun it's just 4.5km to Hallstatt via the L547 along the southern edge of the beautiful Hallstätter See.

- - - - - - - - - - - - - - - - -

TRIP HIGHLIGHT

⑪ Hallstatt

Hallstatt's pastel-coloured houses cast shimmering reflections onto the glassy waters of the Hallstätter See.

The village is strung along a narrow stretch of land between the towering mountains and lakeshore. The **Beinhaus** (Bone House; Kirchenweg 40; adult/child €1.50/0.50; ⊙10am-5pm May-Oct, 11.30am-3.30pm Wed-Sun Nov-Apr), a small charnel house, contains rows of neatly stacked skulls, painted with decorative designs and the names of their former owners. It stands in the grounds of the 15th-century Catholic **Pfarrkirche** (Parish Church), which has some attractive Gothic frescos and three winged altars inside.

Salt in the surround-ing hills have made it a centre of salt mining. The Hallstatt Period (800 to 400 BC) refers to the early Iron Age in Europe, named after the village and the Iron Age settlers and Celts who worked the salt mines here.

The fascinating **Salzwelten** (☎06132-200

24 00; www.salzwelten.at; Salzbergstrasse 21; funicular return & tour adult/child/family €34/17/71; ⊙9.30am-2.30pm early Mar-late Mar & late Sep–mid-Dec, to 4.30pm late Mar-late Sep) is situated high above Hallstatt on Salzberg (Salt Mountain). Tours (in English and German) detail how salt is formed and the his-tory of mining, and take visitors into the depths on miners' slides – the longest is 60m. The Hall-stätter Hochtal (Hallstatt High Valley) near the mine was also an Iron Age burial ground. Audioguides from the base station of the **funicular** (www.salzwelten. at; single/return adult €10/18, child €5/9; ⊙9am-6pm Apr-Sep, to 4.30pm Oct-early Jan & early Feb-late Mar, closed early Jan-early Feb) to the mine take you through the numbered stations and explain the site and rituals of burial.

✗ ⧉ p321

The Drive » Take the L547 north along the cliff-framed Hallstätter See until you reach the Gosaubach River. Then head west on the B166 through the Gschütt mountain pass and the hot-air ballooning town of Gosau to Lindenthal. Take the B162 northwest to Golling an der Salzach, then the B159 north to return to Salzburg (77km in total).

Eating & Sleeping

Salzburg ❶

✖ Bärenwirt
Austrian €€

(📞0662-42 24 04; www.baerenwirt-salzburg.
at; Müllner Hauptstrasse 8; mains €12-20;
🕐11am-11pm) Sizzling and stirring since 1663,
Bärenwirt is Austrian through and through.
Go for hearty *Bierbraten* (beer roast) with
dumplings, locally caught trout or organic wild-
boar bratwurst. A tiled oven warms the woody,
hunting-lodge-style interior in winter, while the
river-facing terrace is a summer crowd-puller.
The restaurant is 500m north of Museumplatz.

✖ Alter Fuchs
Austrian €€

(📞0662-88 20 22; www.alterfuchs.at; Linzer
Gasse 47-49; lunch €6.90, mains €10-17;
🕐noon-midnight Mon-Sat; 🍴) This sly old fox
prides itself on no-nonsense Austrian fare –
schnitzel, roast pork with dumplings, cordon
bleu and the like. Bandana-clad foxes guard
the bar in the vaulted interior, and there's a
courtyard for good-weather dining. In the cosy
Stube (parlour) out back, scribbling on the walls
(chalk only, please) is positively encouraged.
Service can be hit or miss.

🛏 Villa Trapp
Hotel €€

(📞0662-63 08 60; www.villa-trapp.com;
Traunstrasse 34; s €75-135, d €90-280, ste €165-
565; P🎧) Marianne and Christopher have
transformed the original von Trapp family home
into a beautiful guesthouse (for guests only, we
might add). The 19th-century villa is elegant,
if not *quite* as palatial as in the movie, with
tasteful wood-floored rooms and a balustrade
for sweeping down à la Baroness Schräder.

Traunkirchen ❼

✖ Restaurant Bootshaus
Austrian €€€

(📞07617-22 16; www.dastraunsee.at;
Klosterplatz 4; mains €48, 4-/6-/7-course
menu €89/109/119; 🕐6-9pm Thu, Fri & Mon,
noon-2pm & 6-9pm Sat & Sun) A stunningly

converted *Bootshaus* (boat house) at the lake's
edge with panoramic views is the setting for
locally sourced ingredients given the gourmet
treatment by chefs Lukas Nagl and Michael
Kaufmann: Traunsee freshwater crayfish along
with lake fish or, moving away from the lake,
organic lamb prepared in various styles are the
order of the day in this very highly acclaimed
restaurant. Sublime wine pairings are available.
It is inside the Seehotel Das Traunsee.

🛏 Seehotel Das Traunsee
Hotel €€€

(📞07617-221 60; www.dastraunsee.at;
Klosterplatz 4; s €147, d €245-280, rooftop
ste €316; P🍴🎧) Seehotel Das Traunsee
is the prime address in Traunkirchen. It's
contemporary, bright and with a stunning
location on the lake, where you can relax on
deck chairs in warm weather and listen to the
lapping waves.

Hallstatt ⓫

✖ Restaurant zum Salzbaron
European €€

(📞06134-826 30; www.gruenerbaum.cc;
Marktplatz 104; mains €22-33; 🕐noon-10pm;
🎧🍴) One of the best gourmet acts in town,
the Salzbaron is perched alongside the lake
inside the **Seehotel Grüner Baum** (s €150,
d €250-380, ste €450; 🍴🎧) and serves a
seasonal pan-European menu – the wonderful
local trout features strongly in summer.

🛏 Hallstatt Hideaway
Boutique Hotel €€€

(📞0677 617 105 18; www.hallstatt-hideaway.
com; Dr Friedrich-Morton-Weg 24; ste €270-480;
🍴🎧) Six splendidly modern, beautifully
textured private suites make up what is the
region's most stylish accommodation choice.
While prices reflect the varying sizes and
facilities of each of the suites, they all have their
own particular appeal – be that Alpine charm,
a stuccoed ceiling or contemporary design
pieces and killer terraces with hot tub in the
penthouse.

Carinthian Lakes

28

This spin through the Carinthian Lakes region not only offers stunning Alpine scenery but the opportunity to get out on – and into – the sparkling clear waters.

TRIP HIGHLIGHTS

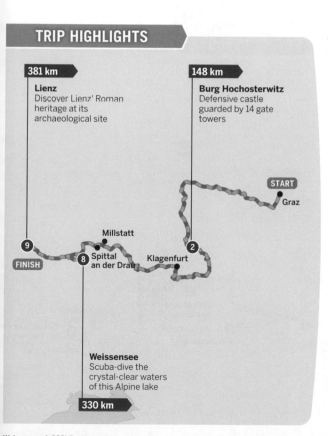

381 km

Lienz
Discover Lienz' Roman heritage at its archaeological site

148 km

Burg Hochosterwitz
Defensive castle guarded by 14 gate towers

START
Graz

Millstatt

9
FINISH

8
Spittal an der Drau

Klagenfurt

2

Weissensee
Scuba-dive the crystal-clear waters of this Alpine lake

330 km

2–4 DAYS
381KM / 270 MILES

GREAT FOR...

BEST TIME TO GO
May to September offers the best weather for boating and swimming.

ESSENTIAL PHOTO

Lake views from the top of the Aussichtsturm Pyramidenkogel.

BEST FOR FAMILIES
'Miniature world' Minimundus.

---

28 Carinthian Lakes

On this multilake trip in the country's summer playground, dubbed 'Austria's Riviera', water babies of all ages can swim, boat, waterski and wakeboard, as well as scuba-dive high up in the Alps at Weissensee, the country's highest swimmable glacial lake. Along the way, you'll discover a wealth of cultural attractions too, from Roman archaeological finds to medieval castles, a splendid Benedictine abbey and cutting-edge contemporary art galleries.

1 Graz

Austria's second-largest city might be famed for its historic treasures, including palatial **Schloss Eggenberg** (p310), but you'll find edgy new art and architecture here too.

Inside the Joanneumsviertel museum complex, the **Neue Galerie** (☏0316-8017 91 00; www.museum-joanneum.at; adult/child €9.50/3.50; ☺10am-5pm Tue-Sun; ᚘ1, 3, 4, 5, 6, 7 Hauptplatz) has a stunning collection showcasing richly textured and colourful

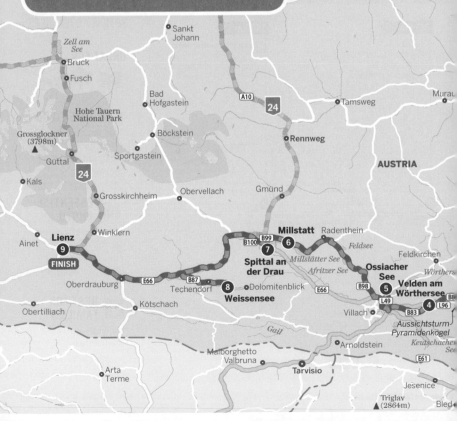

works by painters such as Ernst Christian Moser.

World-class contemporary-art space **Kunsthaus Graz** (☎0316-8017 92 00; www.museum-joanneum.at; Lendkai 1; adult/child €9.50/3.50; ⏱10am-5pm Tue-Sun; 🚊1, 3, 6, 7 Südtiroler Platz) looks something like a space-age sea slug. Exhibitions here change every three to four months.

In the middle of the Mur River, floating landmark **Murinsel** (🚻; 🚊4, 5 Schlossplatz/Murinsel, 🚊1, 3, 6, 7 Südtiroler Platz) is a curvilinear metal and plastic island/bridge containing a cafe, kids' playground and a small stage.

🍴 🛏 p311, p329

The Drive » Avoid the faster but tunnel-dominated highways and drive the scenic 170km to Burg Hochosterwitz through farmland and mountains. Take the B70 then B77 northwest to Judenburg and join the B317. Take the L84 past the Längsee and head east on the B82; the castle's car park is a 3km drive uphill.

TRIP HIGHLIGHT

❷ Burg Hochosterwitz

Storybook fortress **Burg Hochosterwitz** (☎04213-2010; www.burg-hochosterwitz.com;

LINK YOUR TRIP

24 **Grossglockner Road**

Pick up this dizzying Alpine drive in Lienz.

26 **Castles of Burgenland**

This castle- and winery-lined route ends in Graz.

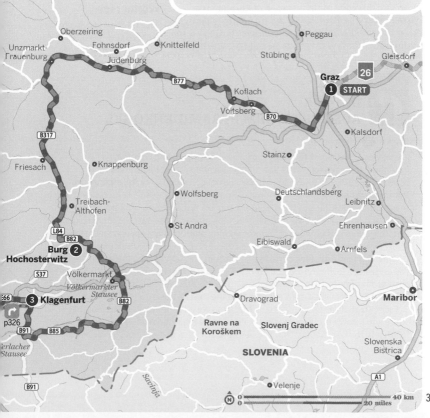

Hochosterwitz 1; adult/child incl tour €15/8; ⊙9am-6pm May–mid-Sep, 10am-5pm mid-Sep–Oct) rises from the slopes of a Dolomite mountain, with 14 gate towers on the path up to the final bastion. The towers were built between 1570 and 1586 by its former owner, Georg Khevenhüller, to ward off invading Turks. Each gate presented different challenges to attackers – some have embedded spikes, which could be dropped straight through unwary invaders passing underneath.

From the car park a lift (€6), sometimes out of service, ascends to the castle; otherwise it's a steep but smooth-going 620m walk.

The Drive » From the base of the hill, head east to Brückl then southeast on the B82, past the Völkermarkter Stausee, to join the westbound B85 to the Ferlacher Stausee. The B91 leads north to Klagenfurt (84km in total).

- - - - - - - - - - - - - - - - -

❸ Klagenfurt

Busy Klagenfurt isn't comparable with Graz or Vienna but it's still an enjoyable, sunny city that offers easy access to the beautiful Wörthersee, which, due to its thermal springs, is one of the region's warmer lakes, averaging 21°C in summer.

At the town's western limit is the wide green space of **Europapark** (🏛). Its family-friendly *Strandbad* (beach) on the shores of the Wörthersee

offers splashy fun. The park's biggest draw is **Minimundus** (www.mini mundus.at; Villacher Strasse 241; adult/child €19/10; ⊙9am-6pm Apr, Oct & Nov, to 7pm May, Jun & Sep, to 10pm Jul & Aug; **P**), a 'miniature world' with 140 replicas of the world's architectural icons, downsized to a scale of 1:25.

 p329

The Drive » Take the B83 west along the Wörthersee's northern shore for 16.5km, through the resort town of Pörtschach am Wörthersee to Velden am Wörthersee.

- - - - - - - - - - - - - - - - -

❹ Velden am Wörthersee

The Wörthersee stretches from east to west between Klagenfurt and Velden.

⟳ DETOUR: AUSSICHTSTURM PYRAMIDENKOGEL

Start: ❸ Klagenfurt

Phenomenal views over the sparkling lakes and surrounding countryside extend from the Pyramidenkogel. The 851m-high mountain is topped by a stunning contemporary 70.6m tower (the world's highest of its kind), the **Aussichtsturm Pyramidenkogel** (☑04273-24 43; www.pyramidenkogel.info; Linden 62, Keutschach am See; adult/child €14/6.50, slide ride €4; ⊙9am-9pm Jul & Aug, 9am-8pm Jun, 10am-7pm May & Sep, 10am-6pm Oct, Mar & Apr, 10am-5pm Nov-Feb), made of steel with wooden beams spiralling up its exterior. Two of its three viewing platforms are open; one, the lower-level Sky Box, is glass encased.

After climbing 441 steps or riding the glass lift and taking in the panoramas, you can return to ground level on Europe's highest covered **slide**, down 120 tube-enclosed metres (on a mat), dropping 52m in about 20 seconds at speeds of up to 25km/h. Recover with a drink in the cafe at the tower's base.

From Klagenfurt, it's an 18km side trip: head west to the Wörthersee's southern shore and follow the L96 along the lakefront to Reifnitz. Turn left on the L97B and follow it to the lake, Keutschach See. Take the L97C northwest until you reach the tower.

Millstatt Bell towers, Stift Millstatt

The Wörthersee's top nightlife resort, Velden is also the venue of various high-adrenaline sports events on summer weekends (this is the country that invented Red Bull, after all). It's a vibrant place packed with people of all ages enjoying everything from ice creams to cocktails.

Paragliding, waterskiing, wakeboarding and electric boat rental are all offered by lakeside beach club **Strand Club** (☏04274-511 01; www.strand club.com; Seepromenade 15; ☺activities dawn-dusk Apr-Oct, bar 7am-midnight Apr-Oct). Afterwards, relax at the bar and adjoining cafe.

The Drive ⟫ Continue west on the B83 and take the L49 north, passing Burg Landskron, which has summer falconry shows, to Annenheim, on the western shores of the Ossiacher See (18km all-up).

⑤ Ossiacher See

The pretty Ossiacher See has plenty of lake swimming and boating opportunities.

Boats run by **Ossiachersee Schifffahrt** (☏0699-15 077 077; www. ossiachersee-schifffahrt. at; day ticket adult/child €14.90/7.50; ☺up to 8 services daily Apr-Oct) complete a criss-cross 2½-hour circuit between St Andrä and Steindorf as part of a regular service. The company also runs half-day lake tours.

The Drive ⟫ It's a 39km drive from Annenheim to Millstatt. Head northwest on the B98. En route you'll pass the Afritzer See and the Feldsee, as well as the northern shore of the Millstätter See, to reach Millstatt.

⑥ Millstatt

Stretching 12km long but just 1.5km wide, the Mill-

stätter See, Carinthia's second-largest lake, was gouged out during the Ice Age around 30,000 years ago and has temperatures of 22°C to 26°C in summer. Millstatt is the most appealing of its small towns.

Swimming, boating and water sports aside, Millstatt's main attraction is its Romanesque Benedictine abbey, **Stift Millstatt** (www.stiftsmu seum.at; Stiftsgasse 1; adult/ child €3.90/2.50; ☺10am-4pm mid-Jun–Sep). Founded in 1070, it contains the Stiftsmuseum, an attractive 11th-century abbey church and a graveyard. The abbey grounds and magnificent arcades and cloisters are free to enter.

The Drive ⟫ The 9km drive from Millstatt follows the Millstätter See shore on the B98 before veering south through a steep forested valley on the B99 to Spittal an der Drau.

❼ Spittal an der Drau

Spittal is a key economic and administrative centre in upper Carinthia. Its name comes from a 12th-century hospital and refuge that once succoured travellers here.

Adjoining a small but attractive park with splashing fountains and bright flowerbeds is the impressive Italianate palace **Schloss Porcia & Museum für Volkskultur** (Local Heritage Museum; 📞04762-28 90; www.museum-spittal.com; Burgplatz 1; adult/child €8/4; ⊙9am-6pm mid-Apr–Oct, 1-4pm Mon-Thu Nov–mid-Apr). Inside, arcades line a central courtyard used for summer theatre performances. The top floors contain the Local Heritage Museum, which has extensive displays about the region.

The Drive » Traversing 44km along a farmed valley framed by towering snow-capped Alps via the B100 and B87 brings you to the least developed of Carinthia's lakes, the Weissensee.

TRIP HIGHLIGHT

❽ Weissensee

Wedged within a glacial cleft in the Gailtal Alps,

the pristine nature reserve Weissensee holds Austria's highest swimmable glacial lake, with an altitude of 930m and summer temperatures of above 20°C. Just 1km-or-so wide in most parts, it stretches for almost 12km.

Boat services on Weissensee operated by **Weissensee Schifffahrt** (www. schifffahrt-mueller.at; 1-8 stops €2.50-8.50, day ticket €13.50; ⊙up to 10 services daily mid-May–mid-Oct) are as much an excursion through the picturesque landscape as a way of getting around the lake.

The crystal-clear waters offer incredible visibility for dazzling views of the lake's 22 fish species. **Yachtdiver** (📞0664 460 40 80; www. yachtdiver.at; Techendorf 55; dives from €15; ⊙9am-6pm) runs scuba-diving trips for experienced divers and courses for beginners, as well as ice-diving expeditions in winter.

The Drive » Take the B87 back to the B100 and head west to lively Lienz (a 48km journey).

TRIP HIGHLIGHT

❾ Lienz

Towering **Dolomite peaks** rise like an amphitheatre around Lienz.

The Romans settled here some 2000 years ago. Their legacy is explored at the regional history museum inside the medieval castle **Schloss Bruck** (www. museum-schlossbruck.at; Schlossberg 1; adult/child €8.50/2.50; ⊙10am-6pm Jul & Aug, to 4pm Tue-Sun Sep & Oct, to 5pm Tue-Sun Jun), and at the archaeological site **Aguntum** (www.aguntum. info; Stribach 97; adult/child €7/4, combined entry with Schloss Bruck €11.50/9.50; ⊙9.30am-4pm Jun-Sep, closed Sun May & Oct; ♿), where excavations are unearthing details of this two-millenia-old *municipium,* which was a centre of trade and commerce under Emperor Claudius. Visit the glass-walled museum to learn more before exploring the ruins. An exhibition features fun elements such as traditional Roman recipes.

The town's medieval cobbled centre is an atmospheric place to stroll.

✕ 🛏 p329

Eating & Sleeping

Graz ❶

✘ Caylend   Fusion €€

(☎0316-71 15 15; www.caylend.at; Stigergasse 1; mains €13-29; ⊙4pm-midnight Wed-Fri, noon-midnight Sat & Sun; 🚊1, 3, 6, 7 Südtiroler Platz) Backlighting, a streamlined design and primary colours lend a contemporary feel to this vaulted, wood-floor bistro and wine bar, with ever-exciting fusion cuisine. Dishes range from the Austro-exotic such as 24-hour-smoked pork belly with wild garlic and cream cheese, to the Australo-exotic, kangaroo steaks (albeit with *Spätzle*) and beef flaps 'Caylend style'. There's a huge selection of Austrian wines to match.

✘ Landhauskeller   Austrian €€

(☎0316-83 02 76; www.landhaus-keller.at; Schmiedgasse 9; mains €17-36; ⊙noon-1am Mon-Wed, to 2am Thu-Sat; ✍; 🚊1, 3 ,4, 5, 6, 7 Hauptplatz) What started as a spit-and-sawdust pub in the 16th century has evolved into a darkly atmospheric, super-stylish restaurant serving modern takes on Styrian or national specialities. As well as favourites like *Tafelspitz* (prime boiled beef), you'll find some vegetarian options and ragout, and the full range of meats, plus seafood, all prepared creatively.

🛏 Hotel zum Dom   Hotel €€

(☎0316-82 48 00; www.domhotel.co.at; Bürgergasse 14; s €100-160, d €145-175; 🅿😊❄🛜; 🚊30 Palais Trauttmansdorff/Urania, 🚊1, 3, 4, 5, 6, 7 Hauptplatz) Ceramics and other objects feature throughout the Hotel zum Dom, whose individually furnished rooms are traditional but far from bland. Bonus: they come either with steam/power showers or whirlpool tubs; one even has a terrace whirlpool. Prices vary considerably; check online.

Klagenfurt ❸

✘ Restaurant Maria Loretto   Austrian €€

(☎0463-244 65; www.restaurant-maria-loretto.at; Lorettoweg 54; mains €18-28; ⊙10am-midnight Wed-Mon; 🛜) Situated on a headland above the Wörthersee, this restaurant near the *Strandbad* (beach) has bags of lakeside character and is generally regarded by locals as one of the town's best. It does good trout and fish grills, though don't expect Mediterranean lightness of touch, as dishes come with a solid Austrian richness. Reserve for an outside table.

🛏 Lemon 7   Hotel €

(☎0463-577 93; 10 Oktober Strasse 11; dm/s/d €27/55/80; 🛜) Arranged around a plant-filled vaulted atrium in a 400-year-old building, the freshly renovated rooms are simple and modern and their wooden, almost ecclesiastical furnishings add warmth and character. A good budget find.

Lienz ❾

✘ Kirchenwirt   Austrian €€

(☎04852-625 00; Pfarrgasse 7; mains €9-30; ⊙9am-11.30pm Wed-Mon; 🛜) On a hill opposite the Stadtpfarrkirche St Andrä, this atmospheric restaurant does a selection of local dishes, served under vaulting or on the streamside terrace. The menu specialises in filling, heavy Austrian fare.

🛏 Goldener Fisch   Hotel €€

(☎04852-621 32; www.goldener-fisch.at; Kärntner Strasse 9; d from €115; 🅿🛜) The chestnut-tree-shaded beer garden is a big draw at this family-friendly hotel. The rooms are light and modern, though nothing fancy and sometimes on the small side. After a day on the slopes you can wind down in the sauna and herbal steam baths. Breakfast is a filling set-up for a day of physical activity.

STRETCH YOUR LEGS SALZBURG

Start/Finish: Stift Nonnberg

Distance: 6.4km

Duration: Three to four hours

This walk is Salzburg in a nutshell, taking you high above its rooftops and spires, up to its whopper of a fortress, down to the Salzach River and over to Mozart's birthplace and the palaces and churches of its resplendent, Unesco-listed Altstadt (old town).

Take this walk on Trips

Stift Nonnberg

With views to make you yodel out loud, the Benedictine convent **Stift Nonnberg** (Nonnberggasse 2; ☺6.45am-dusk) found fame as the nunnery in *The Sound of Music*. There are no problems like Maria nowadays, just peace and a beautiful rib-vaulted church.

The Walk ≫ There is an underground car park at Unipark Nonntal, a five-minute walk southeast of Stift Nonnberg. Walking on from Stift Nonnberg, take the high, panoramic Festungsgasse, peer out over the spires and domes of Salzburg, then make the stiff final climb to the fortress.

Festung Hohensalzburg

Every inch the storybook fortress, clifftop Festung Hohensalzburg (p302) proudly guards 900 years of history. Roam the ramparts for far-reaching views over the city's spires, the Salzach River and the mountains.

The Walk ≫ Skirt the top of Mönchsberg along shady wooded trails, following the signs for Museum der Moderne.

Museum der Moderne

Straddling Mönchsberg's cliffs, the contemporary glass-and-marble **Museum der Moderne** (www.museumdermoderne. at; Mönchsberg 32; adult/child €8/6, combined ticket with Rupertinum €12/8; ☺10am-6pm Tue & Thu-Sun, to 8pm Wed; 👬) shows first-rate temporary exhibitions. While you're up here, linger over lunch at **M32** (www.m32. at; mains €24-32; ☺9am-11pm Tue-Sun; 🍴).

The Walk ≫ Your scenic walk continues along Mönchsberg, with cracking views of the city that occasionally open up to the distant mountains. As you descend, you reach Augustiner Bräustübl.

Augustiner Bräustübl

Who says monks can't enjoy themselves? Since 1621, monastery-run brewery **Augustiner Bräustübl** (www. augustinerbier.at; Augustinergasse 4-6; ☺3-11pm Mon-Fri, 2.30-11pm Sat & Sun) has been serving potent homebrews in Stein tankards in the vaulted hall and beneath the chestnut trees in the 1000-seat beer garden.

The Walk ≫ Cross Müllner Hauptstrasse and amble down to the Kaipromenade shadowing

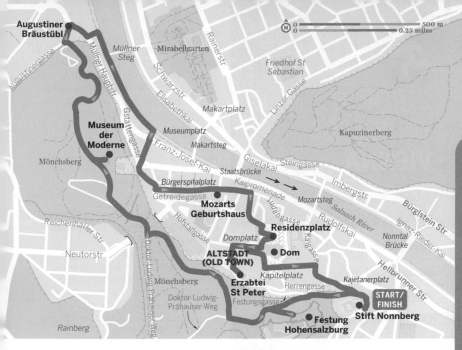

the Salzach River, then turn right to cross Museumsplatz and Gstättengasse. You'll emerge on shop-lined, sign-crammed Getreidegasse.

Mozarts Geburtshaus

Wolfgang Amadeus Mozart, Salzburg's most famous son, was born in Mozarts Geburtshaus (p302) in 1756 and spent the first 17 years of his life here.

The Walk >> Continue straight then veer right onto the regal, cafe-dotted Alter Markt to reach Residenzplatz.

Residenzplatz

With its horse-drawn carriages and palace, this stately baroque square is the Salzburg of a thousand postcards. Its centrepiece is the Residenzbrunnen, a fountain ringed by horses and topped by Triton. Allow ample time for a romp of the **Residenz** (www.domquartier.at; DomQuartier ticket adult/child €13/5; ⊙10am-5pm Wed-Mon Sep-Jun, to 6pm daily Jul & Aug), the crowning glory of Salzburg's new DomQuartier.

The Walk >> No need to walk far – Residenzplatz sidles up to Domplatz.

Dom

Gracefully crowned by a copper dome and twin spires, the **Dom** (www.salzburger -dom.at; guided tours €5; ⊙8am-7pm Mon-Sat, from 1pm Sun May-Sep, shorter hours Oct-Apr) stands out as a masterpiece of baroque art. Bronze portals symbolising faith, hope and charity lead into the cathedral.

The Walk >> Stroll west along Franziskanergasse, then turn left and left again to Erzabtei St Peter.

Erzabtei St Peter

A Frankish missionary named Rupert founded abbey church and monastery **Erzabtei St Peter** (www.stift-stpeter.at; Sankt-Peter-Bezirk 1-2; catacombs adult/child €2/1.50; ⊙church 8am-noon & 2.30-6.30pm, cemetery 6.30am-7pm, catacombs 10am-12.30pm & 1-6pm) in around 700, making it the oldest in the German-speaking world. The cemetery is home to the catacombs, cave-like crypts hewn out of the Mönchsberg cliff face.

The Walk >> It's a 12-minute walk east back to the starting point, Stift Nonnberg.

STRETCH YOUR LEGS
VIENNA

Start/Finish: Café Central

Distance: 3.4km

Duration: Four hours

Vienna's grandeur unfolds in all its glory on this city stroll, from the timeless elegance of its *Kaffeehäuser* (coffee houses) to its monumental Hofburg palace, museums, parks and opulent opera house, as well as magnificent churches.

Take this walk on Trips

Café Central

Park just around the corner on Freyung and fortify yourself with coffee and a slice of chocolate-truffle *Altenbergtorte* cake at grand **Café Central** (www.cafecentral.wien; 01, Herrengasse 14; ⊙7.30am-10pm Mon-Sat, from 10am Sun; 🚇; ⓤHerrengasse), adorned with marble pillars, arched ceilings and glittering chandeliers.

The Walk ⟫ Walk southeast on Herrengasse for 350m, then through the Michaelertor entrance gate to the imposing Hofburg.

Hofburg

Nothing symbolises Austria's culture and heritage more than the **Hofburg** (www.hofburg-wien.at; 01, Michaelerkuppel; 🚋D, 1, 2, 71 Burgring, ⓤHerrengasse), seat of the Habsburgs from 1273 to 1918. Its oldest section is the 13th-century Schweizerhof (Swiss Courtyard). The palace owes its size and architectural diversity to sections added by different rulers over the years.

The Walk ⟫ It's a 750m stroll southwest through Heldenplatz, passing the twin museums Naturhistorisches and Kunsthistorisches on Maria-Theresien-Platz, to the MuseumsQuartier.

MuseumsQuartier

The **MuseumsQuartier** (www.mqw.at; 07, Museumsplatz; ⊙information & ticket centre 10am-7pm; 🚋49 Volkstheater, ⓤMuseumsquartier, Volkstheater) is a remarkable ensemble of museums, cafes, restaurants and bars inside former imperial stables. With over 60,000 sq metres of exhibition space, the complex is one of the world's most ambitious cultural spaces.

The Walk ⟫ Head southeast through the MuseumsQuartier's arched laneways, passing the Leopold Museum and Kinder Museum, to Mariahilfer Strasse. Turn left and continue 350m northeast to the Burggarten.

Burggarten

The **Burggarten** (Castle Garden; www.bundesgaerten.at; 01, Burgring; ⊙6am-10pm Apr-Oct, 7.30am-5.30pm Nov-Mar; 🚋D, 1, 2, 71 Burgring, ⓤMuseumsquartier) is a leafy oasis amid the city's hustle and bustle.

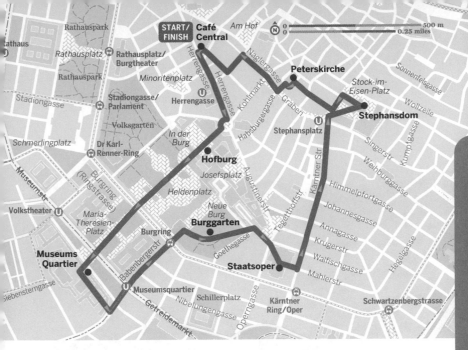

The marble statue of Mozart is the park's most famous tenant, but there's also a statue of Emperor Franz Josef. Don't miss the **Schmetterlinghaus** (butterfly house), and the **Palmenhaus** bar, housed in a beautifully restored *Jugendstil* (Art Nouveau) palm house.

The Walk » From the gardens' northeastern edge, walk southeast on Hanuschgasse for 200m to the city's resplendent opera house, the Staatsoper.

Staatsoper

The neo-Renaissance **Staatsoper** (www. wiener-staatsoper.at; 01, Opernring 2; tour adult/child €9/4; D, 1, 2, 62, 71 Kärntner Ring/ Oper, Karlsplatz) is Vienna's foremost opera and ballet venue. Built between 1861 and 1869, it initially appalled the Viennese public, earning the nickname 'stone turtle'. Performances here are unforgettable; you also can visit its museum and/or take a guided tour.

The Walk » Head north on Kärntner Strasse for 600m to the Stephansdom, and pause to check out the glorious tiled roof, with its dazzling row of chevrons and Austrian eagle.

Stephansdom

Vienna's soaring, filagreed Gothic masterpiece, **Stephansdom** (www.stephans kirche.at; 01, Stephansplatz; adult/child incl audioguide or guided tour €6/2.50, all-inclusive ticket €14.90/3.90; 9-11.30am & 1-4.30pm Mon-Sat, 1-4.30pm Sun, English tours 10.30am Mon-Sat; Stephansplatz), has stood here since the 12th century.

The Walk » Take Goldschmiedgasse northwest for 230m to Petersplatz and the domed Peterskirche.

Peterskirche

The **Peterskirche** (www.peterskirche.at; 01, Petersplatz; 7am-8pm Mon-Fri, 9am-9pm Sat & Sun; Stephansplatz) was built in 1733. Interior highlights include a fresco on the dome painted by JM Rottmayr and a golden altar depicting the martyrdom of St John of Nepomuk.

The Walk » Head northwest on Graben and Naglergasse for 200m. Turn left onto Haarhof for 90m, then right onto Wallnerstrasse for 80m; Café Central is in front of you.

Switzerland

A PLACE OF HEART-STOPPING NATURAL BEAUTY AND HEAD-SPINNING EFFICIENCY, Switzerland lies in the centre of Europe yet exhibits a unique blend of cultures. Dazzling outdoor scenery – such as the ever-admired Alps, pristine lakes, lush meadows and chocolate-box chalets – combines with local traditions, cosmopolitan cities and smooth infrastructure. In short, Switzerland makes it easy for you to dive deep into its heart: distances are manageable and variety is within easy reach. You can be perusing a farmers market for picnic provisions in the morning, then feasting on them on a mountaintop come lunchtime. At nightfall, try gazing at stars in the night sky from cosy digs or revelling in the cultural offerings of one of Switzerland's urbane cities.

Switzerland

29 **Northern Switzerland 3 Days**
Architectural marvels and epic water features colour this oft-overlooked northern delight.

30 **Lake Geneva & Western Switzerland 4 Days**
A glorious lake, stunning vineyards, enchanting villages and fairy-tale castles.

31 **Geneva to Zürich 7 Days**
Mountains, pastures, lakes and small-town charm, bookended by Switzerland's biggest cities.

Classic Trip
32 **The Swiss Alps 7 Days**
The greatest of the great outdoors: perfect peaks, gorgeous glaciers, verdant valleys.

DON'T MISS

The Matterhorn

Symbol of Switzerland, this magical mountain demands to be photographed. See it for yourself in Trip **32**

Lavaux

Swiss wine is a well-kept secret, but this dreamy Unesco-listed spot will have you wanting to share its charms with the world. Trip **30** **31**

Rheinfall

Its thunderous roar is the perfect soundtrack to the panoramic lift to the Kanzelli viewing platform, part of Trip **29**

Züri-West

Switzerland dispenses with its staid reputation in this hip neighbourhood full of great bars, clubs, cafes and restaurants. Trip **31**

Tremola Road

All hairpin bends and cobblestones, this section of the historic St Gotthard Pass is a true joyride. Trip **33**

 Graubünden & Ticino 5 Days
Big-sky wilderness, off-the-beaten-track beauty, pretty towns and unique local flavours.

Northern Switzerland

29

Combine Switzerland's natural and artificial wonders with this art- and architecture-rich trip through the powerhouse north, all with a distinct Swiss-German accent.

TRIP HIGHLIGHTS

244 km

Basel
Design-driven museum capital with an arty edge

102 km

Stein am Rhein
Sublime old town with charm in spades

Schaffhausen

6

4

St Gallen
START

7

Ligerz
FINISH

Rheinfall
Europe's biggest waterfall knows how to grab your attention

124 km

3 DAYS
355KM / 220 MILES

GREAT FOR...

BEST TIME TO GO
Any time of year, although the warmer months are best.

ESSENTIAL PHOTO
The half-timbered heart of Stein am Rhein.

BEST FOR CULTURE
From St Gallen's rococo ebullience to Basel's myriad museums and architectural gems.

Basel Rathaus (town hall; p344)

29 Northern Switzerland

The best of Switzerland is blended to perfection with a little northern exposure. This route allows travellers to tiptoe off the tourist trail and experience lesser-known places such as Appenzell before returning for the heavy-hitting urban pleasures of museum-rich Basel. Impressive natural wonders like the Rheinfall compete with architectural jaw-droppers such as St Gallen's Stiftsbibliothek, while tucked-away vineyards delight the senses.

❶ St Gallen

St Gallen's riotously beautiful rococo library, **Stiftsbibliothek** (www. stibi.ch; Klosterhof 6d; adult/child Sfr12/9, audioguide Sfr5; ⏱10am-5pm), in its Catholic abbey, is a must-see. The 16th-century library (one of the world's oldest), along with the monastery complex, forms a Unesco World Heritage site. Filled with 170,000 priceless books and manuscripts painstakingly handwritten by monks in the Middle Ages, it's a dimly

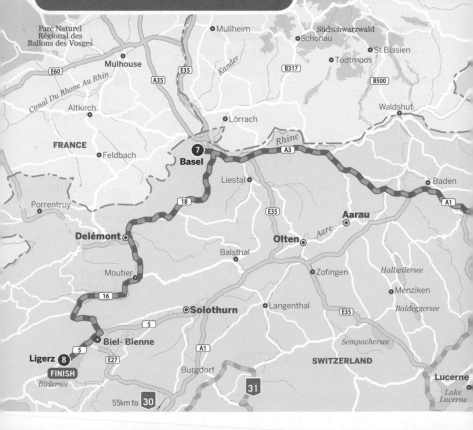

lit confection of ceiling frescos, stucco, cherubs and parquetry.

The Drive » Driving through the verdant countryside from St Gallen, take gently winding Rte 443 for 19km to Appenzell's centre.

- - - - - - - - - - - - - - - - - -

❷ Appenzell

Appenzell is a feast for the eyes and the stomach. Behind the gaily decorative pastel-coloured facades of its traditional buildings lie cafes, *confiseries* (sweets and cake shops), cheese shops, delicatessens,

butchers and restaurants offering local specialities. It's also perfect for a lazy wander along the **Sitter River** or through the photogenic **Altstadt** (old town) with its **Landsge-meindeplatz** featuring elaborately painted

hotels and restaurants. **Brauerei Locher** (www. brauquoell.ch; Brauereiplatz 1; visitor centre free, beer tasting Sfr8.50; ☺1-5pm Mon, 10am-12.15pm & 1-5pm Tue-Fri, 10am-5pm Sat & Sun Apr-Oct, shorter hours winter) is great for brew lovers, or come to

LINK YOUR TRIP

30 **Lake Geneva & Western Switzerland**

Head south from Ligerz for 77km to Gruyères, the end of Trip 30, which you can easily reverse.

31 **Geneva to Zürich**

Geneva lies 145km southwest of Ligerz, allowing a loop through the country, back to the north.

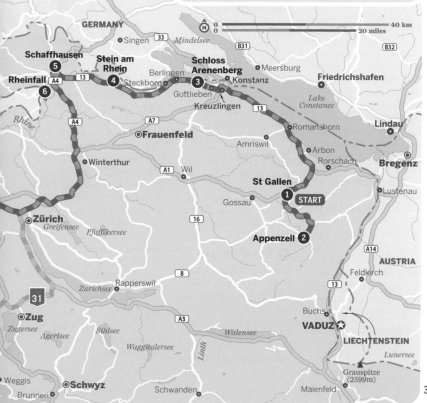

grips with local history at the **Appenzell Museum** (Hauptgasse 4; adult/child Sfr7/3; ⊙10am-noon & 1.30-5pm Mon-Fri, 11am-5pm Sat & Sun Apr-Oct, shorter hours rest of year) nearby.

 p345

The Drive » Retrace your drive to St Gallen (Rte 447), then head to Arbon (the A1 and A1.1) on Lake Constance's shore. From Arbon drive to Romanshorn, then take Rte 13 to Schloss Arenenberg, on the Untersee – 70km in all.

❸ Schloss Arenenberg

Lake Constance (Bodensee) is the German Mediterranean, with a mild climate, gardens and palm trees. Nicknamed the 'Swabian Sea', Central Europe's third-largest lake straddles Switzerland, Germany and Austria. It's a cool place to wind down. The lakeside road (Rte 13) between Kreuzlingen and Stein am Rhein is dotted with quaint half-timbered villages such as **Gottlieben**, **Steckborn** and **Berlingen**. Near the latter is **Schloss Arenenberg** (www.napoleonmuseum.tg.ch; Salenstein; adult/child Sfr15/5; ⊙10am-5pm Apr-Oct, closed Mon rest of year), a handsome lakefront mansion in beautiful grounds where France's Napoleon III grew up.

The Drive » Departing the castle, continue on lakeside Rte 13 for 18km to Stein am Rhein.

TRIP HIGHLIGHT

❹ Stein am Rhein

Stein am Rhein appears to have leaped from the pages of a fable, with its leafy river promenade and gingerbread houses. The effect is overwhelming in cobblestone **Rathausplatz**, hailed as Switzerland's most beautiful town square: houses, some half-timbered, others covered in frescos, line up for a permanent photo op with the fresco-festooned **Rathaus** (town hall) soaring above. Situated between the Rathaus and the Rhine is the **Klostermuseum St Georgen** (www.klostersanktgeorgen.ch; Fischmarkt 3; adult/child Sfr5/free; ⊙10am-5pm Tue-Sun Apr-Oct), on the site of a Benedictine monastery built in 1007. Today's cloister and magnificent *Festsaal* (grand dining room) are largely a late-Gothic creation.

 p345

The Drive » It's a straightforward 20km, 20-minute drive along Rte 13 to Schaffhausen, passing small towns and agricultural holdings.

❺ Schaffhausen

Quaint medieval Schaffhausen is known for ornate frescos and oriel bay windows (called *Erker*), which grace its old town houses. The colourful frescos of 17th-century **Zum Goldenen Ochsen**

(Vorstadt 17) and 16th-century **Zum Grossen Käfig** (Vorstadt 45) depict the parading of Turkish sultan Bajazet in a cage by the triumphant Mongol conqueror Tamerlane. A block east, eye-catching 1492 **Haus zum Ritter** (Vordergasse 65) boasts a detailed Renaissance-style fresco of a knight. Good city **walking tours** (adult/child Sfr14/10; ⊙2pm Sat May–mid-Oct) leave the tourist office in summer. The 16th-century circular **Munot** (⊙8am-8pm May-Sep, 9am-5pm Oct-Apr) fortress lords it over a vineyard-streaked hill.

Rhine Falls

Completed in 1103, **Allerheiligen Münster** (All Saints' Cathedral; Münsterplatz; ☉10am-noon & 2-5pm Tue-Sun, cloister 7.30am-8pm Mon-Fri, 9am-8pm Sat & Sun), with its beautifully simple cloister, is a rare Romanesque specimen in Switzerland. The art collection of **Museum zu Allerheiligen** (www.aller heiligen.ch; Klosterstrasse 16; adult/child Sfr12/free; ☉11am-5pm Tue-Sun) has works by Otto Dix and Lucas Cranach the Elder.

The Drive » Taking Rte 4, it's a very quick trip (5.5km) to Rheinfall, with parking at Schloss Laufen.

TRIP HIGHLIGHT

6 Rheinfall

Ensnared in wispy spray, thunderous **Rheinfall** (Rhine Falls; www.rheinfall.ch) might not compete with Niagara in height (23m), width (150m) or flow (700 cu metres per second in summer), but Europe's largest plain waterfall is stunning nonetheless. Trails thread up and along its shore, and viewpoints provide photo ops.

The 1000-year-old medieval castle **Schloss Laufen** (www.schlosslaufen. ch; adult/child Sfr5/3; ☉8am-7pm Jun-Aug, shorter hours rest of year) overlooks the falls at closer quarters. Buy a ticket at its souvenir shop to walk or take the lift down to the **Känzeli viewing platform** to fully appreciate the crash-bang spectacle.

During summer, **ferries** (www.rhyfall-maendli. ch; adult/child Sfr20/10) flit in and out of the water at the falls' bottom. The best is the round trip that stops at the tall rock in the middle of the falls, from where you can climb to the top.

The Drive » Get on the A4, then change to the A1 and eventually the A3 to get to Basel as quick as possible (128km).

❼ Basel

Business-minded Basel's delightful medieval old town is centred on **Marktplatz**, dominated by the astonishingly vivid red facade of the 16th-century **Rathaus** (Town Hall; ☎061 267 81 81; Marktplatz 9; ☺8am-5pm Mon-Fri). Blending Gothic exteriors with Roman-esque interiors, the 13th-century **Münster** (Cathedral; ☎061 272 91 57; www.baslermuenster.ch; Münsterplatz 9; ☺10am-5pm Mon-Fri, to 4pm Sat, 11.30am-5pm Sun Apr-Oct, shorter hours rest of the year except Advent; ℗) was largely rebuilt after a 1356 earthquake. Renaissance humanist Erasmus of Rotterdam (1466–1536) lies buried in the northern aisle. For views, climb the soaring Gothic **towers**, or visit leafy **Münster Pfalz** for sublime Rhine watching.

The astounding private turned public collection, **Fondation Beyeler** (☎061 645 97 00; www.fondation-beyeler.ch; Baselstrasse 101, Riehen; adult/concession Sfr25/12; ☺10am-6pm Thu-Tue, to 8pm Wed; ℗), assembled by former art dealers Hildy and Ernst Beyeler, is housed in a light-filled, open-plan building designed by Renzo Piano. It has works by Picasso, Rothko, Miró and Max Ernst.

Built by Ticino architect Mario Botta, **Museum Jean Tinguely** (☎061 681 93 20; www.tinguely.ch; Paul Sacher-Anlage 2; adult/student/child Sfr18/12/free; ☺11am-6pm Tue-Sun; ℗) showcases the playful, mischievous and wacky concoctions of sculptor turned mad scientist Tinguely. Pop across the German border to the dazzling **Vitra Design Museum** (☎+49 7621 702 3500; www.vitra.com/en-hu/campus; Charles-Eames-Strasse 2, Weil am Rhein; adult/child Vitra Campus €17/15, Design Museum only €11/9, architecture tour €14/10; ☺10am-6pm). The main building, designed by Frank Gehry, is surrounded by ever-expanding installations by other cutting-edge architects.

✕ 🛏 p345

The Drive » For this last drive, enjoy the longer and slower (95km, 1¾ hours) route through the lush Jura countryside: Rte 18 to Delémont, Rte 16 to Biel/Bienne and finally scenic Rte 5 along the beautiful vineyard- and village-lined Bielersee to Ligerz.

❽ Ligerz

This hidden delight sees lush green vines stagger down the steep hillside towards Lake Biel's northern shore. The quaint lakeside hamlet of Ligerz is, simply put, a heavenly place to savour local wines in relaxed surrounds. There's a small **wine museum** (Rebbaumuseum am Bielersee 'Hof'; ☎032 315 21 32; www.rebbaumuseum.ch; Bielstrasse 66, La Neuveville; adult/child Sfr6/free; ☺1.30-5pm Sat & Sun May-Oct; ℗) and the old-fashioned **Vinifuni funicular** (☎032 315 12 24; www.vinifuni.ch; adult one way Sfr4.60) climbs through the vines to hilltop Prêles. On clear days, views across the vines to the snow-capped Bernese Alps are a revelation. A 30-minute lakeside walk to Twann reaches **Vinothek Viniterra Bielersee** (☎032 315 77 47; www.viniterra-bielersee.ch; Im Moos 4, Twann-Tüscherz; ☺5-9pm Tue-Fri, 2-8pm Sat, 2-7pm Sun).

✕ 🛏 p345

ACID BASE

In 1943 a chemist for Sandoz, Albert Hofmann (1906–2008), accidentally absorbed an experimental compound through his fingertips while searching for a migraine cure and took the world's first 'acid trip'. Hofmann's discovery was soon taken up by artists and writers such as Aldous Huxley, and by the 1960s flower-power generation.

Basel remains the epicentre of the Swiss multibillion-franc pharmaceutical industry; industry giants like Roche and Novartis are based here.

Eating & Sleeping

Appenzell ②

✗ Gasthaus Linde — Swiss €€

(☎071 787 13 76; Hauptgasse 40; mains Sfr20-30; ☺noon-2pm & 7-10pm Fri-Wed) This warm, wood-panelled tavern oozes local character and does excellent Appenzell beer fondue. More adventurous diners can tuck into offal specialities.

Stein am Rhein ④

✗ Burg Hohenklingen — Swiss €€

(☎052 741 21 37; www.burghohenklingen.com; Hohenklingenstrasse 1; mains Sfr30-58; ☺10am-midnight Tue-Sat, to 6pm Sun, closed late Dec) For medieval atmosphere, you can't beat this 12th-century hilltop fortress, with superb views over Stein am Rhein. Tuck into Swiss classics in the *Rittersaal* (Hall of Knights). It's a 30-minute uphill walk from the old town.

🛏 B&B Stein am Rhein — B&B €

(☎052 741 45 44; Bollstieg 22; s/d/f from Sfr80/115/160; ℗ 🛜) Huddled away in a green, quiet corner of town is this charming B&B. The kindly Keller family make you feel instantly at home in their chalet with bright, well-kept rooms kitted out with pine furnishings. Families are *wilkommen*, and biking and kayaking tours can be arranged.

Basel ⑦

✗ Volkshaus Basel — Brasserie €€

(☎061 690 93 00; www.volkshaus-basel.ch; Rebgasse 12-14; mains Sfr33-46; ☺restaurant 11.30am-2pm & 6-10pm Mon-Fri, 6-10pm Sat, bar 10am-midnight Mon-Wed, to 1am Thu-Sat)

This stylish Herzog & de Meuron–designed venue is part resto-bar, part gallery and part performance space. For relaxed dining, head for the atmospheric beer garden, in a shady, cobblestoned courtyard. The menu ranges from brasserie classics to more innovative offerings. The hip bar is open 10am to 1am Monday to Saturday.

🛏 Hotel Krafft — Hotel €€

(☎061 690 91 30; www.krafftbasel.ch; Rheingasse 12; s Sfr145-230, d Sfr250-450, ste Sfr300-500; 🛜) Design-savvy urbanites will love this renovated historic hotel. Sculptural modern chandeliers dangle in the creaky-floored dining room overlooking the Rhine, and minimalist Japanese-style tea bars adorn each landing of the spiral stairs.

Ligerz ⑧

✗ Restaurant Aux Trois Amis — Swiss €€

(☎032 315 11 44; www.aux3amis.ch; Untergasse 17; 4-7 course menu Sfr85-115; ☺11.30am-11pm Wed-Sat, to 5pm Sun) A quintessential village bistro with a centuries-old vined facade. In summer, its tree-shaded terrace heaves with punters eating, drinking and gazing at the tumbling vines and the slate-blue water rippling towards St Peter's Island.

🛏 Hotel Kreuz — Hotel €€

(☎032 315 11 15; www.kreuz-ligerz.ch; Hauptstrasse 17; s/d from Sfr120/185; ℗ 🛜) This lakefront hotel in an old patrician's house with painted shutters has been run by the same welcoming family for generations. It has a Renaissance soul and a garden by the water (swimming allowed). Its bistro serves wine produced from its own vines and great local dishes.

Lake Geneva & Western Switzerland

30

By turns hugging the shore of Lake Geneva and venturing into the lush dairy lands of French-speaking Switzerland, this trip offers dazzling views, rare wines and bucolic bliss.

TRIP HIGHLIGHTS

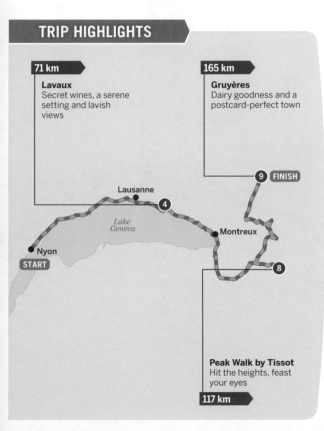

71 km

Lavaux
Secret wines, a serene setting and lavish views

165 km

Gruyères
Dairy goodness and a postcard-perfect town

9 **FINISH**

Lausanne

4

Lake Geneva

Montreux

Nyon

START

8

Peak Walk by Tissot
Hit the heights, feast your eyes

117 km

4 DAYS
165KM / 108 MILES

GREAT FOR...

BEST TIME TO GO
From May to September, when the vineyards put on a show.

ESSENTIAL PHOTO
Lavaux' terraced vineyards overlooking Lake Geneva.

BEST FOR FOODIES
Lausanne's dining scene has come into its own and fondue is a regional staple.

Lake Geneva & Western Switzerland

Touring Lake Geneva (Western Europe's biggest lake, known as Lac Léman to locals) is a treat; the 570-sq-km lake is the region's summer playground, embellished by the Alps, historic vineyards, chic urban centres, petite *plages* (beaches), beautiful villages, classic castles and the constant play of light and wind upon its surface. Plus, this is the perfect spot to enjoy rare wines, fondue and heavenly meringues under double cream.

---

1 Nyon

The wine-producing region between Lausanne and Geneva is known as La Côte (The Coast). From Geneva to Nyon is a 40-minute trip (24km) via Rte 1, which skirts the lake. Of Roman origin, Nyon is a pretty fishing village pierced at its hilltop heart by the white turrets of a textbook castle. **Château de Nyon** (☎022 316 42 73; www.chateaudenyon.ch; Pl du Château; adult/child Sfr8/free; ☺2-5pm Tue-Sun Nov-Mar, from 10am Apr-Oct;

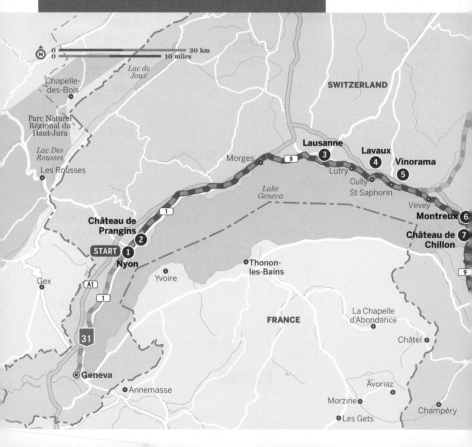

P **⋔**) was begun in the 12th century, modified 400 years later and now houses the **Le Caveau de Nyon** (⏎022 361 95 25; www.caveaudenyon.ch; Pl du Château 5; ⏰2-9pm Fri & Sat, 11am-8pm Sun), where you can taste five Nyon wines (and charcuterie) for Sfr25. Don't miss the view of Lake Geneva from the terrace. Nyon's ancient history is on display at the **Musée Romain** (Roman Museum; ⏎022 361 75 91; www.mrn.ch; Rue Maupertuis 9; adult/child Sfr 8/6; ⏰10am-5pm Tue-Sun Apr-Oct, 2-5pm Tue-Sun Nov-Mar; **P**), in the foundations of a 1st-century basilica.

🛏 p353

The Drive » From Rte 1 in Nyon, it's a short hop (3km) through the leafy landscape to Château de Prangins. Drive along Rte 1, continuing until the château's car park (make a right turn just after the bus stop named 'Prangins, Les Abériaux'. You'll need to walk from there (signed).

---

❷ Château de Prangins

A stone's throw from Nyon, charming 18th-century **Chateâu de Prangins** (⏎058 469 38 90; www.chateaudeprangins.ch; Av du Général Guiguer 3, Prangins; adult/child Sfr10/free; ⏰10am-5pm Tue-Sun; **P**) houses one of the branches of the **Musée National Suisse**. Swiss history from 1730 to 1920 is covered in satisfying detail, and the lovely *potager* (vegetable garden) and nature trail warrant exploration.

The Drive » Avoid the motorway and stick with Rte 1

for just under an hour (36km). You'll be rewarded with views of the lake, verdant countryside, small towns, orchards and some impressive hedges that stand between you and the discreetly super-rich.

---

❸ Lausanne

One of Switzerland's lovelier cities, Lausanne has overcome a reputation for culinary stagnation and now has a buzzing food scene, with solid drinking choices. Dominated by the grand Gothic **Cathédrale de Notre Dame** (⏎021 316 71 60; www.patrimoine.vd.ch; Pl de la Cathédrale; ⏰9am-7pm Apr-Sep, to 5.30pm Oct-Mar), the city has a full cultural calendar, pretty lakefront, delightful **old town** and fab food **market** (Lausanne Market; Place de la Riponne; ⏰Wed & Sat 8am-2pm). Must-see sights also include the wonderful **Musée Olympique** (⏎021 621 65 11; www.olympic.org/museum; Quai d'Ouchy 1; adult/child Sfr18/10; ⏰9am-6pm daily May–mid-Oct, 10am-6pm Tue-Sun mid-Oct–Apr;

LINK YOUR TRIP

31 **Geneva to Zürich** Head north for 32km via the A12 from Gruyères to beautiful bilingual Fribourg, in the same canton.

32 **The Swiss Alps** The fastest route to Arosa, starting point of the A to Z of Swiss Alps, is 330km, heading west along the A1 then the A3.

(P) (🚹) and **Fondation de l'Hermitage** (📞021 320 50 01; www.fondation-hermitage. ch; Rte du Signal 2; adult/child Sfr19/5; 🕙10am-6pm Tue, Wed & Fri-Sun, to 9pm Thu).

✕ 🛏 p353

The Drive ≫ Take Rte 9 for a few kilometres until just after Lutry. Turn left on Rte Petite Corniche, passing through petite medieval towns such as Aran and Epesses. The road becomes Rte de la Corniche, taking you up to Chexbres. From there, drive east back down to the lakeside, then head west along Rte 9 to St-Saphorin.

TRIP HIGHLIGHT

4 **Lavaux**

East of Lausanne, the 830-hectare serried ranks of 800-plus-year-old **vineyards** stagger up the steep terraced slopes of Lake Geneva to form the Lavaux wine region. They're sufficiently magnificent to be a Unesco World Heritage site. Walking between vines and tasting wines are key reasons to explore the string of villages beaded along this 40km stretch of fertile and wealthy shore. This drive starts as a loop of sorts once you reach **Lutry**, heading up into the vines and villages, before heading down and back along the shore. The prettiest town here and the focus of untold 'I could live here' fantasies is **St-Saphorin**, a little gem with closely packed centuries-old

houses, narrow streets, wine cellars, a church dating from 1530 and a great lunch-spot auberge (inn).

✕ 🛏 p353

The Drive ≫ It's a 1.4km, two-minute drive from St-Saphorin to Vinorama. You may even want to walk it, so that you can take advantage of the wine tasting then walk off its effects.

----

5 **Vinorama**

Lavaux Vinorama (📞021 946 31 31; www.lavaux-vino rama.ch; Rte du Lac 2, Rivaz; 🕙10.30am-8.30pm Mon-Sat, to 7pm Sun, closed Mon & Tue Nov-Jun) marries edgy modern architecture with the region's best tipples (some 260 of them). It sits in a designer bunker fronted by a 15m-long bay window, decorated with 6000 metallic pixels inspired by the veins of a vine leaf. Find it at the foot of a terraced vineyard by the lake. Wine-tasting packages cost from Sfr13 to Sfr22, and platters of local cheese or dry sausage cost Sfr13 or Sfr14 respectively.

The Drive ≫ It's an easy 14km drive along Rte Cantonal (Rte 9) to Montreux. For the hotel, turn left onto Av de Alpes (100m after Hôtel Villa Toscane). Continue until the roundabout and take the fourth exit for Rue de la Gare (heading up), then continue until you take a slight left onto Rue du Pont, eventually turning left onto Rue du Temple.

----

6 **Montreux**

No place does palm trees and yellow awnings better than Montreux on a sunny day. The town's golden microclimate and prized position belie the fact that the place is fairly quiet outside of the **Montreux Jazz Festival** (www.montreuxjazzfestival. com; 🕙late Jun–mid-Jul). The main draw is the **Queen studio experience** (www.mercuryphoenixtrust. com; Rue du Théâtre 9, Casino Barrière de Montreux; 🕙10.30am-10pm), where fans of Queen and the beloved Freddie Mercury get a kick out of seeing the studio where Queen

Tissot Peak Walk (p352)

recorded numerous albums (they owned the joint from 1979 to 1993). Evocative memorabilia includes Freddie's handwritten lyrics and flamboyant Zandra Rhodes stage wear, plus the original mixing desk. At lakefront Place du Marché, in front of the town's covered market, there's a 3m-tall **statue** of Freddie, 'lover of life, singer of songs'.

✗ ⌂ p353

The Drive ⟩⟩ Drive along Rte 9 for 3km until you reach the castle, located in Veytaux (parking available).

❼ Château de Chillon

The magnificent 13th-century fortress **Château de Chillon** (☏021 966 89 10; www.chillon.ch; Av de Chillon 21; adult/child Sfr13.50/7; ☺9am-7pm Apr-Sep, 9.30am-6pm Jan-Mar & Oct, 10am-5pm Nov & Dec, last entry 1hr before close) is a maze of courtyards, towers and halls filled with arms, period furniture and artwork. The landward side is heavily fortified, but lakeside presents a gentler face. Don't miss the medieval frescos in the Chappelle St Georges and the spooky Gothic dungeons. The fortress gained fame in 1816 when Byron wrote 'The Prisoner of Chillon', a poem about François Bonivard, thrown into the dungeon for his seditious ideas and freed by Bernese forces in 1536. Byron carved his name into the pillar to which Bonivard was supposedly chained.

The Drive ⟩⟩ From Château de Chillon, Rte 9 heads east to exit 17. From here take Rte 11 through Aigle (making sure to catch sight of its castle surrounded by vineyards), before ascending via the same winding road through forested countryside topped with rocky peaks to Col du Pillon (parking), just past Les Diablerets. All told, it's 38km (about 45 minutes).

TEN O'CLOCK & ALL IS WELL!

From the height of Lausanne's cathedral bell tower, a *guet* (night watchman) still calls out the hours into the night, from 10pm to 2am. Four times after the striking of the hour he calls out: *'C'est le guet! Il a sonné dix, il a sonné dix!'* (Here's the night watchman! It's 10 o'clock, it's 10 o'clock!). In earlier times the *guet* kept a lookout for fires around town and other dangers. He was also charged with making sure that townsfolk were well behaved during solemn moments of church services.

`TRIP HIGHLIGHT`

8 Peak Walk by Tissot

Opened in 2014, the feat of engineering known as **Peak Walk** (Les Diablerets; ⊘9am-4.30pm, closed 2 weeks mid-Oct) allows you to stroll between sky-scraping peaks and feast on views of iconic mountains such as Eiger, Mönch, Jungfrau, the Matterhorn and Mont Blanc. The 107m-long span has viewfinders (with names of the peaks) that overlook the famous Glacier3000 ski station. From the car park at Col du Pillon, take the **cable car** (return adult/ child Sfr80/40) to Cabane and then to the Mario Botta–designed station at Scex Rouge (15 minutes; 2971m).

The Drive » Rte 11 and Rte 190 connect Col du Pillon with Gruyères (55km, 70 minutes) through countryside and quaint chalet-filled villages (Les Mosses has a sweet wood-shingled church). From Col du Pillon, retrace your drive on Rte 11 and follow signs to Bulle. From Montbovon, the road skirts the train tracks, but just past Estavannens, take a left (Rte de Gruyères).

- - - - - - - - - - - - - - -

`TRIP HIGHLIGHT`

9 Gruyères

This dreamy village of 15th to 17th-century houses tumbling down a hillock has a cobblestone heart and the postcard-perfect **Château de Gruyères** (☏026 921 21 02; www.chateau-gruyeres. ch; Rue du Château 8; adult/ child Sfr12/4; ⊘9am-6pm Apr-Oct, 10am-5pm Nov-Mar) as its crowning glory. The hard AOC Gruyère cheese (the 's' is dropped for the cheese) has been made for centuries in the surrounding Alpine pastures; learn all about it at **La Maison du Gruyère** (☏026 921 84 00; www. lamaisondugruyere.ch; Pl de la Gare 3, Pringy-Gruyères; adult/ child Sfr7/6; ⊘9am-6.30pm Jun-Sep, to 6pm Oct-May), with daily cheesemaking demonstrations, a shop and information about area walks. It's 1.5km from Gruyères, in Pringy.

✗ p353

Eating & Sleeping

Nyon ❶

🛏 La Barcarolle   Hotel €€

(📞022 365 78 78; www.labarcarolle.ch; Rte de Promenthoux, Prangins; s/d from Sfr155/175; 🅿🌼@🛜🏊) Rooms at this lakeside property (3km from Nyon) are spacious, comfortable and stylish, but it's the magnificent views of Lake Geneva, the Alps and Mont Blanc that make this place extra special. Enjoy them from many balconied rooms, the bar, the restaurant or when wandering the manicured grounds.

Lausanne ❸

🍴 Le Pointu   Cafe €

(📞021 351 14 14; www.le-pointu.ch; Rue Neuve 2; mains Sfr13-23; ⏰7am-midnight Mon-Wed, to 1am Thu, to 2am Fri, 9am-2am Sat, 10am-3pm Sun) In a turreted belle époque building on a street corner, this cafe-restaurant is a talking point, with its boho vibe, green ceiling lit by bare bulbs, beautiful tilework and vintage-style furniture. Drop by for a coffee, cocktail, gourmet salad or open sandwich. Weekend brunches are worth raving about, with blueberry pancakes and açaí smoothie bowls.

🛏 BnB Lausanne   B&B €

(📞021 616 77 22; www.bnblausanne. ch; Av Édouard Dapples 23; d/tr/q from Sfr100/120/130; 🛜) A warm *bienvenue* awaits at this early 20th-century apartment turned B&B, centrally located for exploring downtown Lausanne. Besides three well-looked-after rooms, with wood floors, warm colours, original paintings and antique furnishings, there is a guest lounge where you can grab a tea or coffee. Swiss produce features at breakfast. It's a couple of minutes' walk from the train station.

Lavaux ❹

🍴 Auberge de l'Onde   Swiss €€€

(📞021 925 49 00; www.aubergedelonde.ch; Centre du Village, St Saphorin; bar mains Sfr28-42, rotisserie mains Sfr38-62; ⏰noon-2pm & 7-9.30pm Wed-Sun) In the delightful village of St Saphorin, you'll find wonderful rotisserie meats and imaginative Med-influenced dishes.

🛏 Hotel Lavaux   Hotel €€

(📞021 799 93 93; www.hotellavaux.ch; Rte Cantonal; s/d from Sfr105/135; 🅿🛜) Perfectly placed for views across the lake or the famous Lavaux vineyards, this hotel has sleekly simple and contemporary rooms and a summer terrace designed for sundowners. If arriving by train, alight at Cully and walk east for 1.5km, or catch a (less frequent) train to Epesses.

Montreux ❻

🍴 MontreuxJazz Cafe   International €€

(📞021 962 13 00; www.montreuxjazzcafe.com; Av Claude Nobs 2; mains Sfr25-50; ⏰11.30am-10.30pm) If you can't stay in the **Fairmont Le Montreux Palace** (www.fairmont.com/Montreux; d/ste from Sfr360/750), why not pop into this jazzy cafe-bar to soak up the surrounds? Sip a Bellini and enjoy global dishes from seabass ceviche to soy-marinated rack of lamb. Smart casual dress is required.

🛏 Tralala Hôtel   Boutique Hotel €€

(📞021 963 49 73; www.tralalahotel.ch; Rue du Temple 2; s/d/ste from Sfr130/190/250; 🌼🛜) This old town boutique hotel references Montreux' extraordinary musical heritage. The 35 stylish rooms have three sizes – S ('Small and Sexy'), L or XL – and each pays homage to a different artist, such as David Bowie.

Gruyères ❾

🍴 Chez Boudji   Swiss €€

(📞026 921 90 50; www.boudji.ch; Gite d'Avau 1, Broc; mains Sfr13-27; ⏰11.30am-2.30pm & 5.30-9pm May-Oct, 24hr Jul & Aug) Visitors love the authenticity of this Swiss mountain chalet with a panoramic terrace overlooking the Alps. Linger there in anticipation of the cheesy goodness you're about to consume. This is stodgy, hearty food, such as chalet soup. The rich local cheese enlivening each simple dish is indescribably enjoyable.

Geneva to Zürich

31

Connect the dots between Switzerland's two biggest cities as you drive through its enigmatic heartland, historic cities, spine-tingling ascents and a world-famous mountain trio.

TRIP HIGHLIGHTS

0 km

Geneva
Cosmopolitan city and old town grace galore

481 km

Zürich
Culturally vibrant city with a post industrial edge

FINISH
9

Bern

Lucerne

Fribourg

1
START

Stanserhorn
An open-air cable car; the perfect Lake Lucerne panorama

402 km

7 DAYS
481KM / 292 MILES

GREAT FOR...

BEST TIME TO GO
Late spring, summer and autumn, when the light and weather are best.

ESSENTIAL PHOTO
The verdant Emmental region exemplifies pastoral perfection.

BEST FOR CULTURE
Zürich's mighty museums and relentless nightlife are intoxicating.

31 Geneva to Zürich

Rather than take a straight line from Geneva to Zürich, this trip gives you room to roam some of Switzerland's finest sights: small cities with charming old towns, heaven-sent lakes with dreamy views, winding roads through countryside bucolic and wild, an adventure capital with the perfect setting, a train ride to the top of Europe, and scenic ascents that will have you gasping – all bookended by Switzerland's cultural capitals.

TRIP HIGHLIGHT

1 Geneva

Cosmopolitan Geneva is a rare blend: a multicultural population chattering in every language under the sun, a distinctly French feel, one of the world's most expensive cities, a stronghold of the Protestant Reformation, a synonymity with numbered bank accounts and a humanitarian haven.

With a whole day and night, schedule time for Geneva's magnificent **old town** (see our Walking Tour on p388). For waterside attractions, make a beeline for the emblematic **Jet d'Eau** (Quai Gustave-Ador) and the egalitarian

Bains des Pâquis (☑022 732 29 74; www.bains-des-paquis.ch; Quai du Mont-Blanc 30; pools adult/child Sfr2/1, sauna, hammam & Turkish baths Sfr20; ⊙9am-9.30pm).

Plenty of museums will tempt you: among the best are the **Musée d'Art Moderne et Contemporain** (Museum of Modern & Contemporary Art MAMCO); ☑022 320 61 22; www.mamco.ch; Rue des Vieux-Grenadiers 10; adult/child Sfr8/free; ⊙noon-6pm Tue-Fri, 11am-6pm Sat & Sun; ☐Musée d'Art Moderne), the **Musée International de la Croix-Rouge et du Croissant-Rouge** (International Red Cross & Red Crescent Museum; ☑022 748 95 11; www.redcrossmuseum.ch; Av de la Paix 17; adult/child

Sfr15/7; ⊙10am-6pm Tue-Sun Apr-Oct, to 5pm Nov-Mar) and the lavish timepieces of **Patek Philippe Museum** (☑022 707 30 10; www.patekmuseum.com; Rue des Vieux-Grenadiers 7; adult/child Sfr10/free; ⊙2-6pm Tue-Fri, 10am-6pm Sat). For a behind-the-scenes glimpse of the UN or the Large Hadron Collider, prebook a tour

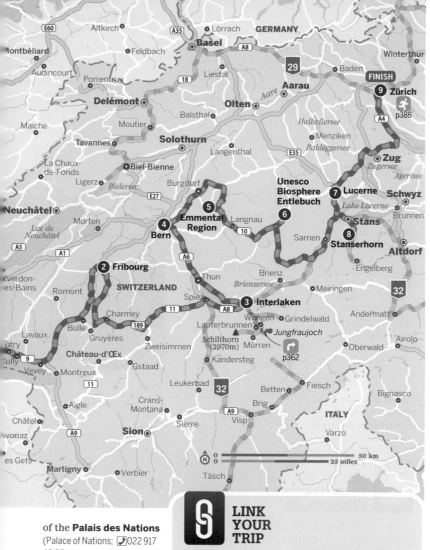

of the **Palais des Nations**
(Palace of Nations; ☎022 917
48 96; www.unog.ch; Av de la
Paix 14; adult/child Sfr12/7;
🕐10am-noon & 2-4pm Mon-
Sat Apr-Aug, Mon-Fri Sep-Mar;
guided tours 10.30am, noon,
2.30pm & 4pm) or **CERN**
(☎022 767 84 84; www.cern.
ch; Meyrin; 🕐 guided tours in
English 11am & 1pm Mon-Sat),
respectively.

🖊 LINK YOUR TRIP

29 Northern Switzerland

From end-point Zürich
it's an easy one-hour,
85km drive east to start-
point St Gallen.

32 The Swiss Alps

It's a two-hour
(147km) drive eastward
from Zürich to Arosa,
the starting point of the
Alpine whirl.

🍴 p360, p363

The Drive » Head west via
the A1 until the A9 (follow signs

to Vevey/Montreux). Take exit 11 and follow signs for Lutry. From Lutry, take Rte 9 (direction Vevey) until Cully, then head up Rte de la Corniche to Chexbres. Next follow Rte du Genevrex and get on the A9, followed by the A12 to Fribourg (143km total).

----

❷ Fribourg

Nowhere is Switzerland's language divide felt more keenly than in Fribourg (Freiburg or 'Free Town'), a medieval city where inhabitants on the west bank of the Sarine speak French, and those on the east bank of the Sanne speak German. Sights that merit a look-see include the bohemian **Espace Jean Tinguely – Niki de Saint Phalle** (☑026 305 51 40; www.mahf. ch; Rue de Morat 2; adult/child Sfr7/free; ◷11am-6pm Wed & Fri-Sun, to 8pm Thu), the evocative **old town** filled with Gothic facades, the **Musée d'Art et d'Histoire** (Museum of Art & History;

☑026 305 51 40; www.mahf. ch; Rue de Morat 12; adult/child Sfr10/8; ◷11am-6pm Tue, Wed & Fri-Sun, to 8pm Thu) and the outsize **Cathédrale de St Nicolas de Myre** (St Nicolas Cathedral; ☑026 347 10 40; www. cathedrale-fribourg.ch; Rue des Chanoines 3; tower adult/child Sfr3.50/1; ◷7.30am-7pm Mon-Sat, 9am-9pm Sun, tower 10am-5pm Mon-Sat, 1-5pm Sun Apr-Oct) with its 74m-tall **tower**. Make time for a couple of the city's bohemian cafe-bars, such as Le Port (p363) or **Café Culturel de l'Ancienne Gare** (CCAG; ☑026 322 57 72; www.cafeanciennegare.ch; Esplanade de l'Ancienne-Gare 3; ◷9am-11.30pm Mon-Thu, to 3am Fri, 1.30pm-3am Sat, 1.30-8pm Sun).

 p363

The Drive » We've chosen a longish (103km, one hour and 50 minutes) scenic route along winding roads through lovely small towns and unspoiled countryside in Fribourg and

Bern cantons. Head to the village of Charmey via Rte 189, then to Boltingen. Take Rte 11 to Speiz on Lake Thun, then follow Rte 8 to Interlaken.

----

❸ Interlaken

Once Interlaken made the Victorians swoon with mountain vistas from the chandelier-lit confines of grand hotels; today it makes daredevils scream with adrenaline-loaded adventures. Straddling the glittering Lakes Thun and Brienz and dazzled by the pearly whites of Eiger, Mönch and Jungfrau, the scenery is mind-blowing.

LOCAL KNOWLEDGE: FRIBOURG'S FILTHY FUNICULAR

Nowhere else in Europe does a funicular lurch up the mountainside with the aid of sewage water (on certain days it smells as you'd expect). Constructed in 1899 and managed by the Cardinal Brewery until 1965 (when the municipality took over), the **Funiculaire de Fribourg** (Sfr3; ◷7am-8pm Mon-Sat, 9.30am-8pm Sun Jul & Aug, 9.30am-7pm Sep-Jun) links the lower town with the upper. It runs every six minutes, and the ride in one of two counterbalancing water-powered carriages from the lower Pertuis station (121m; Place du Pertuis) to the upper station (618m; Rte des Alpes) takes two minutes.

View from Stanserhorn (p361)

Check out views from **Harder Kulm** (www.jungfrau.ch/harderkulm; adult/child Sfr32/16), or try daredevil activities with **Outdoor Interlaken** (📞033 826 77 19; www.outdoor-interlaken.ch; Hauptstrasse 15; 🕐8am-7pm), organised in advance. Leave the car in Interlaken after overnighting and head to the Top of Europe (Jungfraujoch) very early next morning.

✗ 🛏 p363

The Drive » From Interlaken it's a one-hour (54km) drive via Lake Thun's Seestrasse, past turreted Schloss Oberhoffen and Art Nouveau meets neo-Renaissance Schloss Hünegg.

After Thun, you'll get to Bern quickly via the A6.

- - - - - - - - - - - - - - - - - - -

❹ Bern

Wandering through the picture-postcard **old town**, with its laid-back, riverside air, it's hard to believe that Bern (Berne in French) is the Swiss capital, but it is, and a Unesco World Heritage site to boot. The flag-festooned, cobbled centre, rebuilt in grey-green sandstone after a devastating 1405 fire, is a delight, with 6km of covered arcades, cellar shops and bars, and fantastical folk figures frolicking on

16th-century fountains, such as the **Kindlifresser-brunnen** (Kornhausplatz). Be sure to visit Bern's **Münster** (www.bernermuenster.ch; Münsterplatz 1; tower adult/child Sfr5/2; 🕐10am-5pm Mon-Sat, 11.30am-5pm Sun Apr–mid-Oct, noon-4pm Mon-Fri, 10am-5pm Sat, 11.30am-4pm Sun mid-Oct–Mar); the famous **Bären Park** (Bear Park; 📞031 357 15 15; www.tierpark-bern.ch; Grosser Muristalden 6; 🕐8am-5pm), the architecturally daring **Zentrum Paul Klee** (📞031 359 01 01; www.zpk.org; Monument im Fruchtland 3; adult/child Sfr20/7; 🕐10am-5pm Tue-Sun); and the well-endowed

ISLAND DINING IN GENEVA

Genevan living is easy in summer: a constant crowd throngs the lakefront quays to hang out in pop-up terrace bars such as **La Terrasse** (☑079 685 96 21; www.laterrasse. ch; Quai Wilson 31a; ☺8am-midnight Apr-Sep), the fashionista spot by the water to see and be seen. Meander away from Quai du Mont-Blanc to uncover a beloved trio of summertime shacks on the water's edge – alfresco and effortlessly cool.

The right-bank address is refreshingly casual: Rhône-side **Terrasse Le Paradis** (☑076 715 83 70; www.terrasse-paradis.ch; Quai Turrettini; ☺9am-9pm Jun-Sep) is the type of cafe that practically begs you to pull out a book and stay all day in deckchairs arranged down steps to the water, while sipping beakers of homemade *citronnade* (lemonade). 'Paradise' does not serve alcohol, but green mint tea flows and the wholly affordable sandwiches, salads and legendary tabbouleh hit the spot.

Le Bateau Lavoir (☑022 321 38 78; www.bateaulavoir.ch; Passerelle des Lavandières; ☺11am-midnight Mon-Thu, 11am-1am Fri, 5pm-1am Sat May-Sep) is an eye-catching boat with rooftop terrace moored between the old market hall and Pont de la Coulouvrenière. Its cabin-size dining area cooks fondue and basic local dishes, the crowd is hip and there is a 360-degree lake view. Its design and name evoke the wash-house boats – yes, where undies etc were washed – that floated here in the 17th century.

Then there is **La Barje** (☑022 344 83 56; www.labarje.ch; Promenade des Lavandières; ☺11am-midnight Mon-Fri, from 3pm Sat, from noon Sun Apr-Sep), not a barge at all but a vintage caravan with tin roof and candy-striped facade, parked on the grassy banks of the Rhône near the Bâtiment des Forces Motrices. The beer and music are plentiful, outside concerts and art performances pull huge crowds, and proceeds go towards helping young people in difficulty.

Kunstmuseum (Museum of Fine Arts; ☑031 328 09 44; www.kunstmuseumbern.ch; Hodlerstrasse 8-12; adult/child Sfr10/5; ☺10am-9pm Tue, to 5pm Wed-Sun).

✖ ⊨ p363

The Drive » Leave via the A6 and take Krauchthalstrasse (35 minutes, about 24km) through verdant countryside to Burgdorf. From Burgdorf to Affoltern im Emmental, 6km to the east, is a scenic drive past old farmsteads bedecked with flower boxes, neat woodpiles and kitchen gardens. Rte 23 between Affoltern and Langnau im Emmental is 21km (25 minutes).

❺ Emmental Region

After so much city time, the postcard-perfect landscapes of rural Switzerland beckon: time for the bucolic idyll of the Emmental region, where holey Emmental (Swiss) cheese is produced. To see the iconic cheese being made, head to **Emmentaler Schaukäserei** (Emmental Open Cheese Dairy; ☑034 435 16 11; www. emmentaler-schaukaeserei. ch; Schaukäsereistrasse 6; ☺9am-6.30pm Apr-Oct, to 5pm Nov-Mar) in Affoltern.

The region's gateway towns of Burgdorf and Langnau im Emmental preside over a mellow patchwork of quiet villages, grazing cows and fabulous farm chalets with vast barns and overhanging roofs, strung out along the Emme's banks. Burgdorf (literally 'castle village') is split into an Upper and Lower Town. The natural highlight of the Oberstadt (Upper Town) is the 12th-century **Schloss** (castle), with its drawbridge, thick stone walls and trio of museums.

The Drive » From Langnau im Emmental, take Rte 10 for 30 minutes (23km), crossing from Bern canton to Lucerne canton, to reach Schüpfheim, the heart of the Entlebuch biosphere.

⑥ Unesco Biosphere Entlebuch

The 39,000-plus-sq-km **Entlebuch area** (www.biosphaere.ch; a mixed mountain-and-highland ecosystem) was declared a Unesco Biosphere Reserve in 2001. Far from being a lonely wilderness outpost, the reserve is home to some 17,000 people keen to preserve their traditional dairy-farming lifestyle. The landscape of karst formations, sprawling moors (some 25% of the area), alpine pastures and mountain streams, which rise from 600m to some 2350m above sea level, makes for stirring scenery. The park office is in Schüpfheim.

The Drive » Driving through Entlebuch from Schüpfheim, take the Panoramastrasse (which deserves to be more famous) to the town of Giswil (Obwalden canton; 50 minutes, 37km). Next, follow the signs to Lucerne (Luzern in German) along the A8 (30 minutes, 30km).

⑦ Lucerne

Recipe for a gorgeous Swiss city: take a cobalt lake ringed by mountains of myth (Pilatus, Rigi), add a well-preserved medieval **old town** (Altstadt), then sprinkle with covered bridges **Kapellbrücke** (Chapel Bridge) and **Spreuerbrücke** (Spreuer Bridge; btwn Kasernenplatz & Mühlenplatz), sunny plazas, candy-coloured houses and waterfront promenades. Legend has it that an angel with a light showed the first settlers where to build a chapel in Lucerne, and today it still has amazing grace.

One minute it's nostalgic – its emotive **lion monument** (Löwendenkmal; Denkmalstrasse), the next highbrow, with concerts at acoustic marvel **Kultur und Kongresszentrum** (KKL; ☏041 226 79 50; www.kkl-luzern.ch; Europaplatz; guided tour adult/child Sfr15/9; ☺ticket counter 9am-6.30pm Mon-Fri, 10am-4pm Sat) and the peerless Picasso collection of **Museum Sammlung Rosengart** (☏041 220 16 60; www.rosengart.ch; Pilatusstrasse 10; adult/child Sfr18/10; ☺10am-6pm Apr-Oct, 11am-5pm Nov-Mar). Crowd-pleasers such as **Verkehrshaus** (Swiss Museum of Transport; ☏041-375 75 75; www.verkehrshaus.ch; Lidostrasse 5; adult/child Sfr32/12; ☺10am-6pm Apr-Oct, to 5pm Nov-Mar; 🚻) and the surrounding natural wonders never fail to impress, while balmy summers and golden autumns ensure this 'city of lights' shines constantly.

✕ p363

The Drive » A fast 15-minute, 15km journey along the A2 will get you from Lucerne to Stans' Stansstaderstrasse 19, for the journey up to Stanserhorn.

TRIP HIGHLIGHT

⑧ Stanserhorn

Looming above the lake, 1898m Stanserhorn (www.stanserhorn.ch) boasts 360-degree vistas of **Lake Lucerne**, **Mt Titlis**, **Mt Pilatus** and the **Bernese Alps**, among others. Getting to the summit is half the fun. The journey starts with a ride on a vintage 19th-century funicular from Stans to Kälti; from here, the nearly transparent **CabriO** (☏041 618 80 40; www.cabrio.ch; Stansstaderstrasse 19; adult/child return Sfr74/37; ☺mid-Apr–early Nov), launched in 2012 as the world's first cable car with an open upper deck, takes you the rest of the way, offering amazing on-the-go views.

On sunny days or when many travellers are expected, book an online 'boarding pass' to confirm your time of departure and subsequent return.

At the summit there's the star-shaped **Rondorama**, the region's only revolving restaurant, which rotates 360 degrees every 43 minutes. Kids love the nearby **marmot park**, where the critters can be observed in a near-natural habitat.

The Drive » Retrace your route along the A2 and head toward Lucerne before changing to the A4 and following the signs to Zürich (50 minutes, 65km).

DETOUR: JUNGFRAUJOCH: THE TOP OF EUROPE

Start: ❸ Interlaken

Presided over by monolithic Eiger, Mönch and Jungfrau (Ogre, Monk and Virgin), the crown jewels of Bernese Oberland's Alpine scenery will make your heart skip a beat.

The 'big three' peaks have an enduring place in mountaineering legend, particularly the 3970m Eiger, whose fearsome north wall remained unconquered until 1938. Today, it takes only 2½ hours from Interlaken Ost by train to **Jungfraujoch** (3454m), Europe's highest station.

From Kleine Scheidegg (the last stage of the journey), the train burrows through the Eiger before arriving at the **Sphinx meteorological station**. Opened in 1912, the tunnel took 3000 men 16 years to drill. Along the way, the Eigerwand and Eismeer stops have panoramic windows offering glimpses across rivers of crevassed ice.

Good weather is *essential* for this journey; check beforehand on www.jungfrau. ch and always take warm clothing, sunglasses and sunscreen. Within the Sphinx weather station there's a nice sculpture gallery, restaurants, indoor viewpoints and a souvenir shop. Outside there are views of the 23km-long **Aletsch Glacier**. On cloudless days, the views stretch as far as the Black Forest in Germany.

When you tire (as if!) of the view, you can zip across the frozen plateau on a flying fox, dash downhill on a sled or snow disc, or enjoy a bit of tame skiing or boarding at the **Snow Fun Park** (⊘11am-5pm early May–mid-Oct; 👆).

If you cross the glacier along the prepared path, in around an hour you reach the **Mönchsjochhütte** (☑033 971 34 72; www.moenchsjoch.ch; dm Sfr31, incl half-board Sfr69; ⊘late Mar–mid-Oct) at 3650m, where hardcore rock climbers psych themselves up to tackle Eiger or Mönch.

TRIP HIGHLIGHT

❾ Zürich

Culturally vibrant, efficiently run and set at the meeting of river and lake, Zürich is constantly recognised as one of the world's most liveable cities. It's a savvy, hard-working financial centre, yet Switzerland's largest and wealthiest metropolis has an artsy, post-industrial edge. Much of the old town, with its winding lanes and quaint squares, is lovingly intact. Must-see sights include the glorious **Fraumünster** (www. fraumuenster.ch; Stadthausquai 19; incl audioguide Sfr5; ⊘10am-6pm Mar-Oct, to 5pm Nov-Feb; 🚊6, 7, 10, 11, 14 to Paradeplatz), with its Marc Chagall stained-glass windows; the **Grossmünster** (www.grossmuenster.ch; Grossmünsterplatz; ⊘10am-6pm Mar-Oct, to 5pm Nov-Feb; 🚊4, 15 to Helmhaus) with its salt-and-pepper-shaker steeples; and the excellent **Kunsthaus** (☑044 253 84 84; www.kunsthaus.ch; Heimplatz 1; adult/child Sfr16/ free; ⊘10am-6pm Tue & Fri-Sun, to 8pm Wed & Thu; 🚊5, 8, 9, 10 to Kunsthaus), which holds an impressive permanent collection. For contemporary cool, walk around Züri-West (p386). In summer, the fun revolves around lake and river pools like **Seebad Utoquai** (☑044 251 61 51; www.bad-utoquai.ch; Utoquai 49; adult/child Sfr8/4; ⊘7am-8pm mid-May–late Sep; 🚊2, 4, 10, 11, 14, 15 to Kreuzstrasse), **Frauenbad** (☑044 211 95 92; Stadthausquai; adult/ child Sfr8/4; ⊘9am-7.30pm May-Sep; 🚊2, 5, 8, 9, 10, 11, 14, 15 to Bürkliplatz) and **Männerbad** (☑044 211 95 94; Badweg 10; ⊘11am-7pm Mon-Thu & Sun, to 6.30pm Fri, to 5.30pm Sat Jun-Sep; 🚊2, 8, 9, 13, 14, 17 to Sihlstrasse).

✖ p363

Eating & Sleeping

Geneva ❶

✕ Living Room — International €€

(☎022 909 60 65; www.ritzcarlton.com; 11 Quai du Mont-Blanc, Ritz Carlton; mains Sfr29-45, 3-course lunch Sfr35; ⏱7-10pm Mon-Fri, noon-2pm & 7-10pm Sat & Sun) Tasteful decor in a gold-kissed, dining room, refined service, glorious views of Lake Geneva, and a menu that puts creative riffs on seasonal ingredients all make the Living Room a winner. The chef gets experimental with market-fresh Swiss and Mediterranean produce in dishes pulled off with flair.

Fribourg ❷

✕ Le Port — Cafe €

(☎026 321 22 26; www.leport.ch; Planche-Inférieure 5; ⏱10am-11pm Tue-Sun May-Oct) No address better reflects Fribourg's creative spirit. Squirrelled away in a former gas warehouse on the banks of the Sarine, the Port bursts with energy. On summer days Fribourgeois hang out on its tree-shaded, riverbank terrace and dine on seasonal lunchtime platters (Sfr20).

🛌 Hotel Alpha — Boutique Hotel €

(☎026 322 72 72; www.alpha-hotel.ch; Rue du Simplon 13; s/d from Sfr100/120; 🅿🛜) There's something wonderful about this simple hotel that's hard to put your finger on. The compact, modern rooms may lack air-conditioning but design smarts and incredible staff have made excellent use of the building's good bones to make it a quiet, cosy haven – with enormous pillows, muted tones and sensible pricing. Love.

Interlaken ❸

🛌 Hotel Alphorn — Hotel €€

(☎033 822 30 51; www.hotel-alphorn.ch; Rothornstrasse 29a; s Sfr120-160, d Sfr160-225; 🅿🛜) Supercentral yet peaceful, the Alphorn is a five-minute toddle from Interlaken West station. Decorated in cool blues and whites, the rooms are spotlessly clean, but you'll need to fork out an extra Sfr10 for a balcony.

Bern ❹

✕ Altes Tramdepot — Swiss €€

(☎031 368 14 15; www.altestramdepot.ch; Grosser Muristalden 6, Am Bärengraben; mains Sfr17-35; ⏱11am-12.30am Mon-Fri, from 10am Sat & Sun) At this cavernous microbrewery, classic beer grub like schnitzel, *Bauernrösti* (fried potatoes topped with an egg) and sausages with sauerkraut compete against wok-cooked curries and *tarte flambée* for your affection, and the microbrews go down a treat.

🛌 Hotel Landhaus — Hotel €

(☎031 348 03 05; www.landhausbern.ch; Altenbergstrasse 4; dm/s/d from Sfr38/90/130; 🅿🛜) Fronted by the river and old town spires, this well-run boho hotel offers a mix of stylish six-bed dorms, family rooms and doubles. Its buzzing ground-floor cafe and terrace attracts a cheery crowd. Breakfast (included with private rooms) costs Sfr12 extra for dorm-dwellers.

Lucerne ❼

✕ Grottino 1313 — Italian €€€

(☎041 610 13 13; www.grottino1313.ch; Industriestrasse 7; lunch menus from Sfr22, dinner menus Sfr66-78; ⏱11.30am-2pm Mon-Fri, 6-11.30pm daily) Offering a welcome escape from Lucerne's tourist throngs, this relaxed yet stylish restaurant south of the train station serves 'surprise' menus. The herb-fringed front patio is lovely in summer; the candlelit interior exudes sheer cosiness on a chilly evening.

Zürich ❾

✕ Alpenrose — Swiss €€

(☎044 431 11 66; www.restaurantalpenrose.ch; Fabrikstrasse 12; mains Sfr25-32; ⏱9am-11.30pm Tue-Fri, from 5pm Sat & Sun; 🚋3, 4, 6, 10, 11, 13, 15, 17 to Quellenstrasse) The Alpenrose exudes cosy Old World charm, and its cuisine lives up to the promise. Hearty Swiss classics, like herb-stuffed trout with homemade *Spätzli* (egg noodles) and buttered carrots, are exquisitely prepared and presented, and accompanied by a good wine list and a nice selection of desserts.

The Swiss Alps

32

From Arosa to Zermatt, this zig-zagging trip is the A to Z of Switzerland's astounding Alpine scenery, with majestic peaks, formidable panoramas, cable-car rides and local charm.

TRIP HIGHLIGHTS

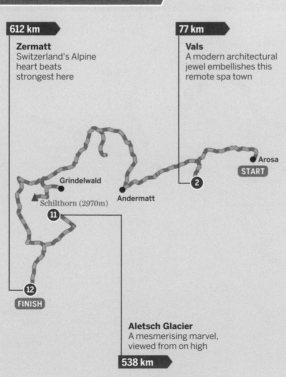

612 km

Zermatt
Switzerland's Alpine heart beats strongest here

77 km

Vals
A modern architectural jewel embellishes this remote spa town

Grindelwald

Schilthorn (2970m)

Andermatt

Arosa
START

FINISH

Aletsch Glacier
A mesmerising marvel, viewed from on high

538 km

---

7 DAYS
612KM / 333 MILES

GREAT FOR...

BEST TIME TO GO

This trip can be done year-round, although certain mountain passes may be closed to vehicular traffic.

 ESSENTIAL PHOTO

The Matterhorn.

 BEST FOR OUTDOORS

Whatever the season, the Alps offer activities galore.

Classic Trip

32 The Swiss Alps

A natural barrier, the Alps are both a blessing and a burden when it comes to tripping around Switzerland. The soul-stirring views are stupendous, but you have to either go over, around or through them to get to the next one. Starting in Graubünden's Arosa and finishing in Valais' Zermatt, this trip visits five cantons via hairpin bends, valley highways, tunnels, passes and cable cars to bring you the best.

❶ Arosa

Framed by the peaks of **Weisshorn**, **Hörnli** and moraine-streaked **Schiesshorn**, Arosa is a great Alpine all-rounder: perfect for downhill and cross-country skiing in winter, hiking and downhill biking in summer, and heaps of family activities year-round. Although only 30km southeast of Chur (Switzerland's oldest city), getting here involves 180-degree hairpin bends so challenging that Arosa cannot be reached

by postal buses. Once here, you may want to revel in the beauty of the Mario Botta–designed **Tschuggen Bergoase Spa** (Sonnenbergstrasse; www.tschuggen.ch; Tschuggen Grand Hotel; nonguest morning/evening pass Sfr65; ⏲7am-9pm), an architectural statement built at the foot of the mountains. The structure's recurring leaf-shaped motifs look particularly striking when illuminated at night.

✕ p376

The Drive » The trip from Arosa to Vals takes 79km and 1¾ hours. Head back towards Chur, then take Rte 19 to Ilanz for the delightful road that passes through Uors and St Martin before arriving at Vals (1252m). About 2km short of the village, you emerge into Alpine pastures, liberally scattered with chalets and shepherds' huts.

- - - - - - - - - - - - - - - - - - -

TRIP HIGHLIGHT

❷ Therme Vals

Shadowing the course of the babbling Glogn (Glenner) stream south, the luxuriantly green Valsertal (Vals Valley) is full of sleepy hamlets and thundering waterfalls. **Vals** stretches 2km along its glittering stream. The secret of this chocolate-box village and its soothing waters is out since Basel-born architect Peter Zumthor transformed **Therme Vals** (☎058 7132 011; www.7132therme.com; adult/child Sfr80/52; ⏲11am-8pm) into a temple of cutting-edge cool. Using 60,000 slabs of local quartzite, Zumthor created one of the country's most enchanting thermal spas. Aside from heated indoor and outdoor pools, this grey-stone labyrinth hides watery nooks and crannies, cleverly lit and full of cavernous atmosphere. Drift away in the bath-warm Feuerbad (42°C) and perfumed Blütenbad, sweat it out in the steam room, and cool down in the teeth-chattering Eisbad.

🛏 p376

The Drive » Return to Ilanz, then continue on Rte 19 to Disentis/Mustér (50km, 55 minutes).

LINK YOUR TRIP

30 **Lake Geneva & Western Switzerland**

Zermatt is three hours (245km) east of Geneva, the starting point of Trip 30.

31 **Geneva to Zürich**

Arosa is a two-hour drive east (147km) on the A3 from Zürich, the end point of Trip 31.

Classic Trip

③ Disentis Abbey

Disentis/Mustér's Benedictine monastery, **Kloster Disentis** (www. kloster-disentis.ch; Via Claustra 1; museum adult/child Sfr10/5; ⊙ museum 8.30-5pm), rising like a vision above town, has a lavishly stuccoed baroque church attached. A monastery has stood here since the 8th century, but the present immense complex dates from the 18th century. Enter the **Klostermuseum**, crammed with memorabilia, left of the church entrance. Head left upstairs to the **Marienkirche**, a chapel with Romanesque origins now filled with ex-votos from people seeking (or giving thanks for) a miraculous intervention from the Virgin Mary. If you're peckish, a handy (and very good-value) on-site cafe/takeaway has soups, salads and specialities.

The Drive >> Disentis is an exhilarating (40 minutes, 32km) drive along Rte 19 and the twisting Oberalp Pass (2044m), which connects Graubünden and Uri cantons. In winter, the pass is closed to cars, but a car train connects Sedrun on Rte 19 and Andermatt (three services daily in winter, two in spring). Reservations are essntial (www. matterhorngotthardbahn.ch).

LOCAL KNOWLEDGE: ZUMDORF

If the grand scale of this trip seems overwhelming, the antidote surely lies in a quick detour to Switzerland's smallest village, **Zumdorf**: little more than a cluster of small buildings on the Furkastrasse and a population counted on one hand. Despite its diminutive size, it has **Restaurant Zum Dörfli** (☏041 887 01 32; www.zumdoerfli.ch; Furkastrasse, Zumdorf; mains Sfr26-40), specialising in Swiss dishes (especially rösti) and venison (in season). Find it 6km southwest of Andermatt.

④ Andermatt

Blessed with austere mountain appeal, Andermatt (Uri canton) contrasts low-key village charm (despite a recent five-star development) with big wilderness. Once an important staging-post on the north–south St Gotthard route, it's now bypassed by the tunnel. It remains a major crossroads near four major passes (Susten, Oberalp, St Gotthard and Furka), making it a terrific base for **hiking** and **cycling**. The tourist office supplies free booklets.

One popular hike leads from the Oberalp Pass to sparkly **Lai da Tuma**, the source of the Rhine; the 11km round trip takes three to four hours, with 500m elevation gain. A walk around and along **Gotthardstrasse** reveals textbook dark-wood central-Swiss architecture, often weighed down with either geraniums or snow.

Skiers in the know flock to 2963m **Gemsstock** (www.skiarena.ch), reached by the Gemsstockbahn cable car (set to reopen in 2020), for the snow-sure winter slopes.

🛏 p376

The Drive >> Take Rte 2 to Göschenen, then get on the A2/E35 and follow the signs for Lucerne. The road skirts the bottom of Lake Uri for lovely water views. Continue to exit 33 (Stans-Süd), then follow Rte 374 to Engelberg (one hour, 77km in total).

⑤ Engelberg

Wonderful **Engelberg** (literally 'Angel Mountain'), backed by the glacial bulk of **Mt Titlis** (www.titlis.ch; central Switzerland's tallest mountain) and frosted peaks, which feature in many a Bollywood production, is divine. After visiting the 12th-century Benedictine **Engelberg**

Monastery (Kloster Engelberg; ☑041 639 61 19; www.kloster-engelberg.ch; church admission free, tours adult/child Sfr8/free; ⏱1hr tour 4pm Mon-Sat), get closer to the heavens via the world's first revolving **cable car** (www.titlis.ch/en/tickets/cable-car-ride; adult/child return Sfr92/46; ⏱8.30am-5pm). It pirouettes over the dazzling **Titlis Glacier**, peaks rising like shark fins ahead, before you step out onto Titlis station's **terrace** (3020m), with a panorama that stretches to Eiger, Mönch and Jungfrau in the Bernese Oberland. For even more thrilling views, take the adjacent **Cliff Walk** (www.titlis.ch/en/glacier/cliff-walk) – opened in 2012, this 100m-long, 1m-wide, cable-supported swinging walkway is Europe's highest suspension bridge.

There are some 360km of marked hiking trails in and around Engelberg. For gentle ambles and gorgeous scenery, head for **Brunni** across the valley. Its **cable car** (www.brunni.ch; one way/return Sfr20/32, incl chairlift Sfr29/44) goes up to Ristis at 1600m, where a chairlift takes you to the Swiss Alpine Club's refurbished **Brunni Hütte**. From here, you can choose to watch a magnificent sunset before spending the night.

🛏 p375

The Drive » Retrace your route to the A2, heading west, before turning onto the A8 (direction Interlaken), and continuing alongside bright-blue Brienzersee to Giessbachfälle. One hour and 10 minutes, 71km.

- - - - - - - - - - - - - - - - -

❻ Giessbachfälle

Illuminating the firs Slike a spotlight in the dark, the misty **Giessbachfälle** (Giessbach Falls) plummet 500m over 14 rocky ridges. **Europe's oldest funicular**, dating to 1879, creaks up from the boat station (one way/return Sfr6/9), but it's only a 15-minute walk up to the

---

AROUND GRINDELWALD: FIRST

From Grindelwald, a cable car zooms up to **First**, the trailhead for 100km of paths, half of which stay open in winter. You can trudge up to **Faulhorn** (2681m; 2½ hours), even in winter, via the cobalt **Bachalpsee** (Lake Bachalp). As you march along the ridge, the unfolding views of the Jungfrau massif are entrancing. Stop for lunch and 360-degree views at Faulhorn. You might like to continue to Schynige Platte (another three hours) and return by train.

Other great walks head to **Schwarzhorn** (three hours), **Grosse Scheidegg** (1½ hours), **Unterer Gletscher** (1½ hours) and **Grindelwald** itself (2½ hours).

First has 60km of well-groomed pistes, which are mostly wide, meandering reds suited to intermediates. The south-facing slopes make for interesting skiing through meadows and forests. Freestylers should check out the kickers and rails at **Bärgelegg** or have a go on the superpipe at **Schreckfeld station**.

Faulhorn happens to be the starting point for **Europe's longest toboggan run**, accessible only on foot. Bring a sled to bump and glide 15km over icy pastures and through glittering woodlands all the way to Grindelwald via Bussalp. Nicknamed 'Big Pintenfritz', the track lasts around 1½ hours, depending how fast you slide.

Year-round, you can get your pulse racing on the **First Flyer**, a staggeringly fast zip-line from First to Schreckfeld. The mountains are but a blur as, secure in your harness, you pick up speeds of around 84km/h.

The **First Cliff Walk** is a summit trail with a 40m-long suspension bridge, climbing stairs and an observation deck, with suitably impressive views of the local landscape and the jaw-dropping mountains.

Classic Trip

WHY THIS IS A CLASSIC TRIP
WRITER SALLY O'BRIEN

Even though I now call Switzerland home, the Alpine scenery still has an other-worldly effect on me. The abundance of snow-capped peaks, mountains with fairy-tale names that 'pop up' at numerous vantage points, time-defying glaciers, gravity-defying railways. And then there's the moment you catch sight of the Matterhorn...

Above: Gornergratbahn (p372)
Right: First Cliff Walk (p369)
Left: Giessbachfälle (p369)

most striking section of
the falls.

The Drive » Get back onto
the A8 and follow it along
the Brienzersee until exit 25
(Wilderswil/Grindelwald), then
continue as the road winds its
way through rural countryside
up to Grindelwald (39km, 45
minutes).

- - - - - - - - - - - - - - - - -

❼ Grindelwald

Grindelwald's sublime
natural assets are film-
set stuff – the chiselled
north-face features
of **Eiger**, the glinting
tongues of **Oberer** and
Unterer Glaciers, and
the crown-like peak of
Wetterhorn. Skiers and
hikers cottoned onto
its charms in the late
19th century, making
it one of Switzerland's
oldest resorts. It has lost
none of its appeal, with
geranium-studded cha-
lets and verdant pastures
aplenty.

Turbulent waters carve
a path through craggy
Gletscherschlucht
(Glacier Gorge; www.
grindelwaldsports.ch; adult/
child Sfr19/10; ⏲9.30am-
6pm Sat-Thu, to 10pm Fri), a
30-minute walk south
of the centre. A footpath
weaves through tunnels
hacked into cliffs veined
with pink and green
marble. It's justifiably a
popular spot for canyon
and bungee-jumping
expeditions.

Grindelwald is out-
standing **hiking** territory,
veined with trails that
command arresting

Classic Trip

views to massive north faces, crevasse-filled glaciers and snow-capped peaks. Reach high-altitude walks by taking cable cars from the village.

✕ p375

The Drive ›› Follow the signs to Lauterbrunnen, which is 20km (15 minutes) away by car.

- - - - - - - - - - - - - - - - - -

❽ Lauterbrunnen

Laid-back Lauterbrunnen's wispy **Staubbachfall** (Staubbach Falls; ⏰8am-8pm Jun-Oct) inspired both Goethe and Byron to pen poems to their ethereal beauty. Today the postcard-perfect village, nestled in the valley of 72 waterfalls – including the **Trümmel-**

bachfälle (Trümmelbach Falls; www.truemmelbach-faelle.ch; adult/child Sfr11/4; ⏰9am-5pm Apr-Jun & Sep-Oct, 8.30am-6pm Jul & Aug) – attracts a less highfalutin crowd. Hikes heading into the mountains from the waterfall-laced valley include a 2½-hour uphill trudge to car-free **Mürren** and a more gentle 1¾-hour walk to **Stechelberg**. In winter, glide past frozen waterfalls on a well-prepared 12km cross-country trail.

The Drive ›› Head to Stechelberg (10 minutes, 6km), where you'll leave the car (paid parking available) and take the cable car to Schiltorn (adult/child Stechelberg–Schilthorn return Sfr102/51).

- - - - - - - - - - - - - - - - - -

❾ Schilthorn

There's a tremendous 360-degree, 200-peak panorama from the 2970m Schilthorn, best

appreciated from the **Skyline viewing platform** or **Piz Gloria revolving restaurant** (☎033 856 21 50; www.schilthorn.ch; Höheweg 2; mains Sfr21-45; ⏰8am-5pm). On a clear day, you can see from **Titlis** around to **Mont Blanc**, and across to the German Black Forest.

Some visitors seem more preoccupied with practising their delivery of the line, 'The name's Bond, James Bond', because scenes from *On Her Majesty's Secret Service* were shot here in 1968–69. The **Bond World 007** interactive exhibition gives you the chance to pose for photos secret-agent style, and relive movie moments in a helicopter and bob sled.

The Drive ›› When you descend to Stechelberg, head to Kandersteg via the road down to Interlaken. Get on the A8/Rte 11, then take exit 19 (direction

---

THE HIGH LIFE

Charming as Zermatt is, heading out of town and up to the mountains is a rush like no other. Europe's highest cogwheel railway, the **Gornergratbahn** (www.gornergrat. ch; Bahnhofplatz 7; return adult/child Sfr98/49; ⏰7am-6.18pm), has climbed picture-postcard scenery to Gornergrat (3089m) – a 30-minute journey – since 1898. Sit on the right-hand side to gawp at the Matterhorn. Tickets allow you to get on and off en route; there are restaurants at **Riffelalp** (2211m) and **Riffelberg** (2582m). In summer an extra train runs once a week at sunrise and sunset – the most spectacular trips of all.

Views from Zermatt's cable cars are all remarkable, but the **Matterhorn Glacier Paradise** (Schluhmattstrasse; www.matterhornparadise.ch; ⏰8.30am-4.50pm; return adult/child Sfr100/50) is the icing on the cake. Ride Europe's highest-altitude cable car to 3883m and marvel at 14 glaciers and 38 mountain peaks over 4000m from the Panoramic Platform (only open in good weather). Don't miss the **Glacier Palace**, an ice palace complete with glittering ice sculptures and an ice slide to swoosh down bum first. End with exhilarating snow tubing outside in the snowy surrounds.

LOCAL KNOWLEDGE: WINE TIME

The canton of Valais, which features so much of Switzerland's stunning Alpine scenery, is also the country's largest and best wine producer. Sampling it in situ at the end of a day's driving is a great idea.

Drenched in extra sunshine and light from above the southern Alps, much of the land north of the Rhône river in western Valais is planted with vines. Unique to the Valais are the *bisses* (narrow irrigation channels) that traverse the vineyards.

Dryish white Fendant, the perfect accompaniment to fondue and raclette, and best served crisp cold, is the region's best-known wine, accounting for two-thirds of Valais wine production. Dôle, made from Pinot noir and Gamay grapes, is the principal red blend and is full bodied, with a firm fruit flavour.

When ordering wine in a wine bar or restaurant, use the uniquely Swiss approach of *deci* (decilitre – ie a 10th of a litre) multiples. Or just order a bottle...

Spiez/Kandersteg/Adelboden). The 60km trip takes one hour.

- - - - - - - - - - - - - - - - -

⑩ Kandersteg

Turn up in Kandersteg in anything but muddy boots and you'll attract a few odd looks. Hiking is the town's raison d'être, with 550km of surrounding trails. An amphitheatre of spiky peaks studded with glaciers and jewel-coloured lakes, such as **Blausee** (www.blausee.ch) and **Oeschinensee** (www.oeschinensee.ch; cable-car one way/return Sfr22/30; ☺9am-5pm; 🅿), creates a sublime natural backdrop to the rustic village of dark-timber chalets.

In winter there are more than 50km of cross-country ski trails, including the iced-over Oeschinensee. The limited 15km of downhill skiing suits beginners

and Kandersteg's frozen waterfalls attract ice climbers.

🛏 p375

The Drive » Take the BLS Lötschberg Tunnel, which connects with Goppenstein (in Valais) at regular intervals daily; it takes 15 minutes and costs from Sfr25 per car if booked online. From Goppenstein, head east from Rte 9. Once past Brig, the deep valley narrows and the landscape switches to rugged wilderness, with a string of bucolic villages of timber chalets and onion-domed churches. It's 47km all-up.

- - - - - - - - - - - - - - - - -

TRIP HIGHLIGHT

⑪ Aletsch Glacier

The Aletsch Glacier is a seemingly never-ending, 23km-long swirl of ice with deep crevasses that slices past thundering falls, jagged spires of rock and pine forest. It stretches from Jungfrau in the Bernese Oberland to a plateau above the Rhône

and is, justly so, a Unesco World Heritage site.

Picture-postcard riverside **Fiesch** on the valley floor is the best place to access it. From the village, ride the **cable car** (www.eggishorn.ch; Furkastrasse; adult/child return from Fiesch Sfr45/22.50) up to **Fiescheralp** and continue up to **Eggishorn** (2927m). Streaming down in a broad curve around the **Aletschhorn** (4195m), the glacier is just like a frozen six-lane superhighway. In the distance to the north rise the glistening summits of Jungfrau (4158m), Mönch (4107m), Eiger (3970m) and Finsteraarhorn (4274m). To the southwest of the cable-car exit, you can spy Mont Blanc and the Matterhorn.

🛏 p375

The Drive » It takes one hour (56km) to get from Fiesch to Täsch via Rte 19 to Visp, then

Classic Trip

the winding rural road to Täsch itself. Park the car here before boarding the train to car-free Zermatt.

- - - - - - - - - - - - - - - - - -

TRIP HIGHLIGHT

⑫ Zermatt

You can almost sense the anticipation on the train from Täsch. As you arrive in car-free Zermatt, the pop-up-book effect of the one-of-a-kind Matterhorn (4478m) works its magic. Like a shark's fin it rises above the town, with moods that swing from pretty and pink to dark and mysterious. Since the mid-19th century, Zermatt has starred among Switzerland's glitziest resorts. Today skiers cruise along well-kept pistes, spellbound by the scenery, while style-conscious darlings flash designer threads in the town's swish lounge bars.

Meander main-strip **Bahnhofstrasse** with its boutiques and stream of horse-drawn sleds or carriages and electric taxis, then head towards the noisy Vispa River along **Hinterdorfstrasse**. This old-world street is crammed with archetypal Valaisian timber granaries propped up on stone discs and stilts to keep out pesky rats; look for the fountain commemorating Ulrich Inderbinen (1900–2004), a Zermatt-born mountaineer who climbed the Matterhorn 370 times, the last time at age 90.

A walk in Zermatt's **Mountaineers' Cemetery** (Kirchstrasse) in the garden of St Mauritius Church is sobering. Numerous gravestones tell of untimely deaths on Monte Rosa, the Matterhorn and Breithorn. In July 2015 a **memorial** to 'the unknown climber' was unveiled to mark the 150th anniversary of the Matterhorn's first ascent.

The **Matterhorn Museum** (☏027 967 41 00; www.zermatt.ch/museum; Kirchplatz; adult/child Sfr10/5; ⏰11am-6pm Jul-Sep, 3-6pm Oct–mid-Dec, 3-7pm mid-Dec–Mar, 2-6pm Apr-Jun) provides a fascinating insight into Valaisian village life, the dawn of tourism in Zermatt and the lives the Matterhorn has claimed. Short films portray the first successful ascent of the Matterhorn on 14 July 1865, led by Edward Whymper, a feat marred by tragedy on the descent when four team members crashed to their deaths in a 1200m fall down the North Wall. The infamous rope that broke is on display.

✖ p375

Eating & Sleeping

Arosa ❶

✖ Burestübli   Swiss €€

(☎081 377 18 38; www.arlenwaldhotel.ch; Hotel Arlenwald, Prätschli; mains from Sfr25; ⏱8am–midnight) This woodsy chalet on the forest edge affords magical above-the-treetop views. Come winter, it's beloved by ruddy-faced sledders who huddle around pots of gooey fondue, butter-soft steaks and mugs of *Glühwein* (mulled wine). The marvellously eccentric chef prides himself on using first-rate local produce.

Vals ❷

🛏 7132 Hotel   Design Hotel €€€

(☎058 7132 000; www.7132.com; d from Sfr600; 🅿🛜) In this 1960s colossus, rooms have been revamped under the design skills of world-famous architects. Check out the website and pick your package. 7132 also features three restaurants and a bar.

Andermatt ❹

🛏 River House Boutique Hotel   Design Hotel €€

(☎041 887 00 25; www.theriverhouse.ch; Gotthardstrasse 58; s/d from Sfr135/180; 🅿🛜) At this stylish eco-hotel in a 250-year-old building, the Swiss-American owners have used local materials to create unique and beautiful rooms with inlaid parquet floors and beams, some with river views. The on-site restaurant (mains from Sfr25) features local produce, plus Swiss wines.

Engelberg ❺

🛏 Ski Lodge Engelberg   Hotel €€

(☎041 637 35 00; www.skilodgeengelberg.com; Erlenweg 36; s/d/tr/q Sfr150/270/360/450; 🅿🛜) This delightful, centrally located lodge fuses Art Nouveau flair with 21st-century comforts in smart rooms (including family rooms). Après-ski activities include a sauna, gazing at snowy peaks from an outdoor hot tub and sharing ski tips over the excellent New Nordic cuisine.

Grindelwald ❼

✖ Memory   Swiss €€

(☎033 854 31 31; Dorfstrasse 133; mains Sfr18-35; ⏱9am-11.30pm) Always packed, the Eiger Hotel's unpretentious restaurant rolls out tasty Swiss grub such as rösti, raclette and fondue, as well as – titter ye not – 'horny' chicken with a spicy 'Christian' sauce. Try to bag a table on the street-facing terrace.

Kandersteg ❿

🛏 The Hayloft   B&B €

(☎033 675 03 50; www.thehayloft.ch; Altes Bütschels Hus; s/d/tr Sfr60/120/180) Picture a dark-wood, 500-year-old chalet snuggled against the hillside, flower-strewn meadows where cows graze placidly, views of waterfalls and glaciers – ahhh...this place sure is idyllic! The farm turned B&B serves delicious breakfasts and dinners (Sfr30).

Aletsch Glacier ⓫

🛏 Fiesch Youth Hostel   Hostel €

(www.youthhostel.ch/en/hostels/fiesch; Sport Ferien Resort; dm with shared bathroom from Sfr35 per person, d with private bathroom Sfr100; 🅿🛜) This complex plays host to 1001 activities. It is very well run, has spotless rooms and is an ideal spot to drop your bags for the night after a trip to Eggishorn and Aletsch Glacier. Perfect for families and a bargain to boot, including breakfast in the rates.

Zermatt ⓬

✖ Schäferstube   Swiss €€

(☎027 966 76 00; www.julen.ch/en/restaurant-schaeferstube; Riedstrasse 2; mains Sfr11-63; ⏱6-11pm) Just the kind of warm, rustic, snugly lit hut where you'll pray for the flakes to fall in winter. The Schäferstube is as traditional as they come, with low timber ceilings, huge cowbells and hunting trophies galore. Expect succulent cuts of lamb, cooked on a charcoal grill, alongside Valais raclette and cheese fondue.

Graubünden & Ticino

33

Graubünden is raw natural beauty; broad-shouldered Alpine grandeur married with unique local culture. Meanwhile, Ticino's dolce vita tempers Alpine scenery with Italian flair.

TRIP HIGHLIGHTS

490 km

St Gotthard Pass
Thrilling touring, twinned with sweeping views

101 km

Swiss National Park
Wilderness wonderland at the edge of Switzerland

START
Chur

Davos

4

13
FINISH

St Moritz

Bellinzona
11

410 km

Locarno
Lake Maggiore's sweet sanctuary

**5 DAYS
490KM / 345 MILES**

GREAT FOR...

BEST TIME TO GO
Spring or summer.

 ESSENTIAL PHOTO

Sublimely pretty Val Fex.

 BEST FOR CULTURE

Graubünden is home to Romansch, an official Swiss language spoken regularly by only 60,000 people.

155 km to 29

33 Graubünden & Ticino

The wild beauty of Switzerland dominates, tracing valley floors sheltered by hulking mountains, pristine forests and brilliantly blue lakes. Cities on this route are reassuringly relaxed and even a bit retro, the villages embrace their quiet appeal, and at the end of it all climbs one of Europe's most exciting drives. Start in Graubünden, with its unique language and identity, then finish with a hearty ciao bella in riviera-rich Ticino.

❶ Chur

The Alps rise like an amphitheatre around Chur, Switzerland's oldest city, inhabited since 3000 BC.

The **Bündner Kunstmuseum** (Museum of Fine Arts; ☎081 257 28 68; www. buendner-kunstmuseum.ch; Bahnhofstrasse 35; adult/child Sfr15/free; ⏰10am-5pm Tue-Sun, to 8pm Thu) in the neoclassical Villa Planta gives an insight into the artistic legacy of Graubünden-born Alberto Giacometti (1877–1947) and his talented contemporaries, including Giovanni Segantini and Ernst Ludwig Kirchner.

The city's most iconic landmark is **Martinskirche** (St Martin's Church;

Kirchgasse 12), with its distinctive spire and clock face. The 8th-century church was rebuilt in the late-Gothic style in 1491 and is dramatically lit by a trio of Augusto Giacometti **stained-glass windows**.

Chur is a 1¼-hour drive from Zürich along the A3, passing the fantastically fjord-like **Walensee**. The limestone Churfirsten mountains rise like an iron backdrop along the lake's north flank, occasionally interrupted by a coastal hamlet or upland pasture and, about halfway along the lakefront, seemingly cracked open by **Seerenbachfälle**, Switzerland's highest waterfall.

The Drive ⟩⟩ Chur to Tamina Therme is a simple 18-minute, 20km drive along the A13.

❷ Bad Ragaz

The graceful little spa town of Bad Ragaz opened in 1840 and attracted the bath-loving likes of Douglas Fairbanks and Mary

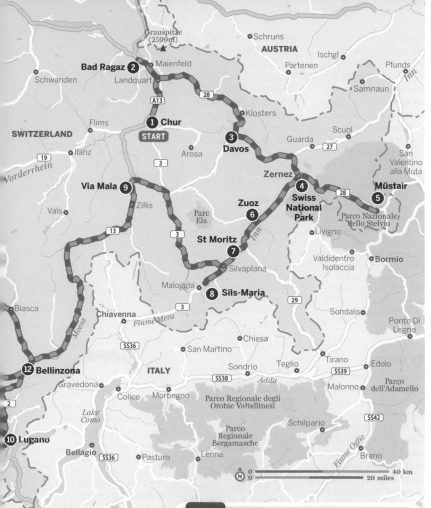

Pickford. The fabled waters are said to boost the immune system and improve circulation. The sleek and stylish **Tamina Therme** (☏081 303 27 40; www.taminatherme. ch; Hans-Albrecht-Strasse; weekday ticket adult/child Sfr40/22; ☺8am-10pm Sun-Thu, to 11pm Fri), **a couple of kilometres south of Bad**

LINK YOUR TRIP

29 **Northern Switzerland**

End point St Gotthard Pass is a 2½-hour drive northeast from St Gallen, starting point of Trip 29.

31 **Geneva to Zürich**

Starting point Chur is only a 75-minute (120km) drive southeast from Zürich, end point of Trip 31.

Ragaz, has several pools for wallowing in the 36.5°C thermal waters, as well as massage jets, whirlpools, saunas and an assortment of treatments and massages, not to mention Alp views and a good cafe. Dine and sleep in nearby Maienfeld (p385).

The Drive » From Maienfeld, take Landstrasse for 5km to turn left onto the N28 road east from Landquart. Here you enter the broad Prättigau Valley, which stretches east to Davos for 39km. This high Alpine country is punctuated by villages and burned-wood Walser houses built by these rural folk since migrating here from eastern Valais from the 13th century onward.

- - - - - - - - - - - - - - - -

❸ Davos

Davos is more cool than quaint, but what the resort lacks in Alpine prettiness, it makes up for with seductive skiing and a great après-ski scene. It is also the annual meeting point for the crème de la crème of global capitalism, the World Economic Forum. Davos also inspired Thomas Mann to pen *The Magic Mountain*.

Davos' giant cube of a museum, **Kirchner Museum** (☏081 410 63 00; www.kirchnermuseum. ch; Promenade 82; adult/child Sfr12/5; ☺11am-6pm Tue-Sun), showcases the world's largest Ernst Ludwig Kirchner (1880–1938) collection, with some 50

paintings. The German Expressionist painted extraordinary scenes of the area around Davos, which he called home from 1918. When the Nazis classified Kirchner a 'degenerate artist' and emptied galleries of his works, he was overcome with despair and took his own life in 1938.

🛏 p385

The Drive » Turn onto Rte 28 (Flüelastrasse), continuing for 34km (40 minutes) until you reach Zernez, where the headquarters of the Swiss National Park are located. This route includes, weather permitting, the Flüela Pass (2383m). If the pass is closed, you'll need to travel through the Vereina Tunnel (car train) from Selfranga to Sagliains (www.rhb. ch/en/car-transporter).

- - - - - - - - - - - - - - - -

❹ Swiss National Park

Spanning 172 sq km, Switzerland's first and only national park (established 1 August 1914) is a nature-gone-wild swathe of dolomitic peaks, shimmering glaciers, larch woodlands, pastures, waterfalls and high moors strung with topaz-blue lakes. It's a real glimpse of the Alps before the dawn of tourism.

Some 80km of well-marked hiking trails lead through the park, where, with a little luck and decent binoculars, ibex, chamois, marmot and

VIDALIDALI / GETTY IMAGES ©

golden eagle can be sighted. The **Swiss National Park Centre** (☏081 851 41 41; www.nationalpark.ch; exhibition adult/child Sfr7/3; ☺8.30am-6pm Jun-Oct, 9am-noon & 2-5pm Nov-May) in **Zernez** should be your first port of call for information on activities and accommodation. An audioguide gives you the low-down on conservation, wildlife and environmental change. The tourist office here can also provide details on park hikes.

Zernez itself is an attractive cluster of stone chalets, outlined by the profile of its baroque

church and the stout medieval tower of its castle, **Schloss Wildenberg**.

The Drive » The views between Zernez and Müstair along Rte 28 are stupendous, with wild Alpine scenery and the Ofen/Fuorn Pass (2149m). The drive takes 40 minutes (39km).

5 Müstair

Nestled in a remote corner of Switzerland, just before the Italian border, **Müstair** is one of Europe's early Christian treasures and a Unesco World Heritage site. When Charlemagne supposedly founded a monastery and a church here in the 8th century, this was a strategically placed spot below the Ofen Pass, separating northern Europe from Italy and the heart of Christendom.

Vibrant Carolingian (9th century) and Romanesque (12th century) frescos smother the interior of the church of Benedictine **Kloster St Johann** (St John's Convent; www.muestair.ch). Beneath Carolingian representations of Christ in Glory in the apses arc Romanesque stories depicting the grisly ends of St Peter (crucified), St Paul (decapitated) and St Stephen (stoned). The **museum** (adult/child Sfr12/6; ⊙9am-noon & 1.30-5pm Mon-Sat, 1.30-5pm Sun) next door takes you through part of the monastery complex, with Carolingian art and other relics.

The Drive » From Müstair to Zuoz is 56km (one hour). This is mostly retracing your drive back to Zernez along Rte 28, before heading southwest along Rte 27, which sticks close to the Inn River as it snakes through the valley floor.

6 Zuoz

Little Zuoz is a quintessential Engadine town, with colourful **sgraffito**

LOCAL KNOWLEDGE:
MUST-TRY BÜNDNER SPECIALITIES

Pizokel Stubby wheat-and-egg noodles, seasoned with parsley and often served with speck, cheese and onions.

Bündnerfleisch Seasoned and air-dried beef or game.

Capuns A hearty dish consisting of egg pasta and sausage or *Bündnerfleisch,* which is wrapped in chard, flavoured with herbs and cooked in milky water.

Maluns Potatoes soaked for 24 hours, then grated and slowly roasted in butter and flour. Apple mousse and Alpine cheese add flavour.

Nusstorte Caramelised nut tart usually made with walnuts.

Bündner Gerstensuppe Creamy barley soup with smoked pork, beef, speck, leeks, celery, cabbage, carrots and potatoes.

houses, flower boxes bursting with geraniums and Augusto Giacometti **stained-glass windows** illuminating the church chancel. Though skiing is fairly limited (albeit good), Zuoz is unquestionably one of the Oberengadin's prettiest towns, and a great place to unwind for a night.

🛏 p385

The Drive » Follow Rte 27 for 18km along the valley path, admiring the landscape of broad-shouldered mountains and small towns.

----

❼ St Moritz

Switzerland's original winter wonderland and the cradle of Alpine tourism, St Moritz has been luring royals, celebrities and serious money since 1864. With its shimmering aquamarine lake, emerald forests and aloof mountains, the town looks a million dollars, which you could probably drop during a quick shopping spree on **Via Serlas**.

The real riches lie outdoors with superb carving on **Corviglia** (2486m), hairy black runs on **Diavolezza** (2978m) and miles of **hiking** and **biking** trails when the snow melts.

 p385

The Drive » Part of the 10km-long drive (take Rte 27, then Rte 3) from St Moritz to Sils-Maria skirts the startlingly turquoise, wind-buffeted Silvaplanersee, a kitesurfing and windsurfing mecca. Sils-Maria is situated between Silvaplanersee and another equally beautiful lake, the Silsersee.

----

❽ Sils-Maria

Sils-Maria (Segl in Romansch) is a cluster of pastel-painted, slate-roofed chalets set against a backdrop of rugged, glacier-capped mountains. German philosopher Friedrich Nietzsche spent his summers here from 1881 to 1888 writing, including *Thus Spake Zarathustra.* Housed in a geranium-bedecked chalet, the little memorabilia-filled **Nietzsche Haus** (✆081 826 53 69; www.nietzschehaus.ch; Via da Marias 67; adult/child Sfr8/free; ◷3-6pm Tue-Sun Jun-Oct & Dec-Apr) was his summer retreat.

Nearby car-free **Val Fex** features high pastures freckled with wildflowers in summer and streaked gold with larch forests in autumn, and a glacier crowning a host of rocky peaks. Nietzsche, Thomas Mann and Marc Chagall were among those who found the space here to think and dream.

Reaching the valley is an experience in itself, whether you hike (around 2½ hours from Sils-Maria) or arrive by horse-drawn carriage. For the latter, head to Dorfplatz in Sils-Maria from where carriages depart. The scenic journey for up to four people costs from Sfr60/100 one-way/return to Fex-Platta, Sfr70/120 to Fex-Cresta and Sfr90/160 to Hotel Fex; exact times and prices depend on group numbers.

🛏 p385

The Drive » Head back past the Silvaplanersee, then turn left onto Rte 3. This takes you to the Julier Pass (open year-round; 2284m) and then up towards Thusis. Next head south on Rte 13, which you drive along for just under 5km to get to Via Mala (64km total, one hour and 10 minutes).

- - - - - - - - - - - - - - - -

❾ Via Mala

The narrow, breathtakingly sheer and narrow gorge Via Mala ('Bad Path') was once part of a pack-mule trail to Italy. Today you can descend to its depths (some cliffs reach 300m) via 321 steps and try to imagine what an arduous and inhospitable schlep this must have been back in the day.

The Drive » Head to Lake Lugano via Rte 13 and watch as the landscape changes from stoic Graubünden mountains to the velvety hills of Ticino, via the San Bernardino Pass (2066m). It takes around two hours and 130km.

- - - - - - - - - - - - - - - -

❿ Lugano

Ticino's lush, mountain-rimmed Lago di Lugano (Lake Lugano) isn't its only liquid asset. The largest city in the canton is also the country's third-most-important banking centre. Suits aside, Lugano is a vivacious city, with chic boutiques, bars and pavement cafes, all huddling in the spaghetti maze of steep cobblestone streets that untangle at the edge of the lake and along the flowery promenade.

For a bird's-eye view of Lugano and the lake, head for the hills. A funicular from Cassarate hauls you to the summit of the 925m **Monte Brè** (www.montebre.ch; funicular one way/return Sfr16/25; ☺9am-7pm) from March to December. The peak is the trailhead for hiking and mountain-biking trails that grant expansive views of the lake and reach deep into the Alps.

🛏 p385

The Drive » Hop on the A2 heading north. Take exit 48 (Monte Ceneri) and then Rte 2 and A13, following the signs to Locarno (45 minutes, 43km).

- - - - - - - - - - - - - - - -

TRIP HIGHLIGHT

⓫ Locarno

With its palm trees and much-vaunted 2300 hours of sunshine a year,

SCHLOSS SCHAUENSTEIN

Lauded as one of Switzerland's greatest chefs, Michelin-starred Andreas Caminada is king of fairy-tale **Schloss Schauenstein** (www.schauenstein.ch), which has featured in San Pellegrino's list of the world's 50 best restaurants. The rarefied experience belies the simplicity of many of the ingredients, often local, all handled with imagination and exquisite technique. The excellent wine list features many of Switzerland's best vintages, along with international offerings.

The castle's **guesthouse** (rooms/suites from Sfr370/580, breakfast Sfr42) features three rooms decorated with sleek contemporary furnishings and three suites that combine period fixtures and modern features. The manicured grounds come with an outdoor pool and terrace.

Reserve well in advance for both (up to eight months), or try your luck with listings of last-minute table cancellations via the website. Find it in Fürstenau, just off Rte 13 from Chur, before Thusis and Via Mala.

Locarno, the lowest town in Switzerland, attracts sun lovers to its warm, Mediterranean-style setting, and has done so since the late 19th century.

The impossibly photogenic **Santuario della Madonna del Sasso** (www. madonnadelsasso.org; Via Santuario 2; ☺7.30am-6.30pm) overlooks the town and is a must-see. It was built after the Virgin Mary supposedly appeared in a vision to a monk, Bartolomeo d'Ivrea, in 1480. There's a highly adorned church and several rather rough, near-life-size statue groups (including one of the Last Supper) in niches on the stairway. The best-known painting in the church is *La Fuga in Egitto* (Flight to Egypt), painted in 1522 by Bramantino. A **funicular** (one way/return adult Sfr4.80/7.20, child Sfr2.20/3.60; ☺8am-10pm May, Jun & Sep, to midnight Jul & Aug, to 9pm Apr & Oct, to 7.30pm Nov-Mar) runs every 15 minutes from the town centre past the sanctuary to Orselina, but a more scenic, pilgrim-style approach is the 20-minute walk up the chapel-lined Via Crucis (take Via al Sasso off Via Cappuccini).

The Drive » Take the A13 then Rte 13; follow the signs to Bellinzona (30 minutes, 24km).

⓬ Bellinzona

At the convergence of several Alpine valleys, Bellinzona is visually striking. Its three grey-stone medieval castles have attracted everyone from Swiss invaders to British painter William Turner.

The main one, **Castelgrande** (www.bellinzonese -altoticino.ch; Via Salita Castelgrande; ☺grounds 10am-6pm Mon, 9am-10pm Tue-Sun; Murata 10am-7pm), rising from a rocky central hill, was a Roman frontier post and Lombard defensive tower. It's now one of Bellinzona's best places to eat, and wandering the vineyard-surrounded grounds is unforgettable.

The three castles didn't stop Swiss-German confederate troops from overwhelming the city in 1503, thus deciding Ticino's fate for the following three centuries. Castelgrande is the easiest castle to access, but both **Castello di Montebello** (www. bellinzonese-altoticino.ch; Salita al Castello di Montebello; castle free, museum adult/child Sfr5/2; ☺10am-6pm Apr-Oct, 10.30am-4pm Nov-Mar) and **Castello di Sasso Corbaro** (www.bellinzonese -altoticino.ch; Via Sasso Corbaro; castle free, museum & tower adult/child Sfr5/2; ☺10am-6pm Apr-Oct, 10.30am-4pm Nov-Mar) reward the effort.

✗ p385

The Drive » On the A2, take exit 41 (direction Nufenen/Bedretto/Passo San Gottardo) before continuing on Rte 2 towards San Gottardo (one hour, 72km).

 TRIP HIGHLIGHT

⓭ St Gotthard Pass

An exhilarating drive if ever there was one, this famous mountain pass (2108m) at the heart of Europe connects cantons Ticino and Uri (namely, Andermatt). It can be bypassed by the tunnel (road and train), but if you want spectacular scenery and a sense of really getting over the Alps, then take the famous cobblestone **Tremola Road**. On the southern side of the pass, it connects the highest point with the Italian-speaking town of Airolo via 37 tortuous twists, and is a must. Once at the top, visit the **Museo Nazionale San Gottardo** (☎091 869 15 25; www.passosangottardo. ch; ☺9am-6pm Jun-Oct). This museum covers the commercial, political and cultural significance of the pass and is housed in a former customs house and hotel. Note that the museum is currently closed for renovations, and is scheduled to reopen in August 2021. From here, you can connect with Andermatt easily.

Eating & Sleeping

Maienfeld

✗ Schloss Brandis — Swiss €€

(📞081 302 24 23; www.schlossbrandis.ch; mains Sfr28-56; ⊙11am-10pm) **Schloss Brandis** is a lofty 15th-century tower, a five-minute walk northeast of Maienfeld train station, housing one of the canton's best restaurants. Sit in the beamed, lantern-lit dining room, in the garden or in the vaulted cellar, and enjoy Maienfeld Riesling soup and meatier specialities (including game in autumn).

⏨ Schlaf Fass — Guesthouse €€

(www.schlaf-fass.ch; Weingut zur Bündte; per person from Sfr90; P 🛜) Should you have overindulged on the local plonk, you can bed down in one of two giant wine barrels at Schlaf Fass, among the vineyards northeast of Maienfeld. Check the website for how this works!

Davos ③

⏨ Waldhotel Davos — Historic Hotel €€€

(📞081 415 15 15; www.waldhotel-davos.ch; Buolstrasse 3; s/d from Sfr135/215; P 🛜 ⚏) *The Magic Mountain* in Thomas Mann's eponymous 1924 novel, this built-in-1911 sanatorium turned hotel has had a stylish facelift, and even standard rooms come with sunny balconies. When you tire of mountain views, head down to the spa's saltwater pools and saunas. The restaurant matches Grisons cuisine with wines drawn from the award-winning cellar. This hotel is only open in winter.

Zuoz ⑥

⏨ Hotel Castell — Design Hotel €€

(📞081 851 52 53; www.hotelcastell.ch; Via Castell 300; d/ste from Sfr230/400; P 🛜) Design trailblazer Castell gets rave reviews for its rural-meets-minimalist interiors. Some of Europe's leading architects pooled their creativity to transform this turn-of-the-century hotel, which now boasts art-slung spaces, chic and colourful rooms and a restaurant serving seasonally inspired cuisine. Unwind with a steam or soapy massage in the hammam.

St Moritz ⑦

✗ Ecco St Moritz — Italian €€€

(📞081 836 63 00; www.giardino-mountain.ch; Giardino Mountain, Champfèr; menus Sfr215-270; ⊙7pm-midnight Wed-Sun) **The pinnacle of St Moritz' dining scene, Ecco St offers exquisitely presented dishes with strong, assured flavours.**

Sils-Maria ⑧

⏨ Hotel Fex — Hotel €€

(📞081 832 60 00; www.hotelfex.ch; Via da Fex 73; s/d from Sfr160/260; 🛜) If you fancy staying in the remote Val Fex, south of Sils-Maria, book into the grand 19th-century Hotel Fex, a mountain retreat with sensational views and a restaurant serving top-quality regional dishes (mains from Sfr19). Reaching the valley is an experience, whether you hike (2½ hours from Sils-Maria) or arrive by horse-drawn carriage.

Lugano ⑩

⏨ Guesthouse Castagnola — Guesthouse €€

(📞078 632 67 47; www.gh-castagnola.com; Salita degli Olivi 2; apt from Sfr105; P 🛜) Lodged in a beautifully restored 16th-century town house, this guesthouse features four rooms kitted out with Nespresso coffee machines and flat-screen TVs. There's also a family-friendly apartment with washing machine and full kitchen. Take bus 2 to Posta Castagnola, 2km east of the centre. A generous breakfast (Sfr10 extra) is served just down the hill at **Bar La Strada**.

Bellinzona ⑫

✗ Trattoria Cantinin dal Gatt — Italian €€

(📞091 825 27 71; www.cantinindalgatt.ch; Vicolo al Sasso 4; lunch menus Sfr18-28, mains Sfr23-47; ⊙11.30am-3pm & 6.30pm-midnight Tue-Fri, 10am-3pm & 6.30pm-midnight Sat; 👶) Slip up a cobblestone side street to find this cracking little trattoria. The brick-vaulted interior is inviting for digging into big Italian flavours courtesy of the Tuscan chef.

STRETCH YOUR LEGS
ZÜRICH

Start: Im Viadukt

Finish: Frau Gerolds Garten

Distance: 2.6km

Duration: Three hours

This tour of Zürich West (a quarter made up of former working-class districts Kreis 4 and Kreis 5, and now a hedonistic night-time playground nicknamed Züri-West) takes you through a postindustrial landscape dedicated to culture, commerce and carousing.

Take this walk on Trip

Im Viadukt

This once down-at-heel storage facility under a stone railway viaduct (hand-built by 6000 workers in the late 19th century) was reborn a decade ago as **Im Viadukt** (www.restaurant-markthalle.ch; Limmatstrasse 231; mains Sfr18-48; ⊙9am-11pm Mon, to midnight Tue-Sat; 🚋3, 4, 6, 10, 11, 13, 15, 17 to Dammweg), with local shops, hip eateries and a food market with great coffee.

The Walk » After perusing Im Viadukt, it's a quick 300m stroll from the market's Limmatstrasse entrance up to the Migros Museum.

Migros Museum

In the former **Löwenbräu-Areal brewery**, the well-funded **Migros Museum** (www.migrosmuseum.ch; Limmatstrasse 270; adult/child Sfr12/free, combined ticket with Kunsthalle Sfr20; ⊙11am-6pm Tue, Wed & Fri, to 8pm Thu, 10am-5pm Sat & Sun; 🚋3, 4, 6, 10, 11, 13, 15, 17 to Dammweg) focuses on innovative artwork, with exhibitions on interesting themes. The collection was started in the 1950s by Gottlieb Duttweiler, founder of the Migros chain of supermarkets, Switzerland's largest retailer. Upstairs, **Kunsthalle Zürich** (www.kunsthallezurich.ch; adult/child Sfr12/free, combined ticket with Migros Museum Sfr20; ⊙11am-6pm Tue, Wed & Fri, to 8pm Thu, 10am-5pm Sat & Sun) has contemporary art exhibitions.

The Walk » From the Migros Museum, continue up Limmatstrasse, then cross Hardstrasse into Hardturmstrasse. Veer left along Förrlibuckstrasse and follow it before turning left at Duttweilerstrasse. The 1.2km-long walk passes the city's industrial heritage (the MAN plant) and its industro-glam present (cafes and eateries).

Museum Für Gestaltung

Exhibitions at this impressive **design museum** (www.museum-gestaltung.ch; Toni-Areal, Pfingstweidstrasse 96; adult/child Sfr12/free; ⊙10am-5pm Tue & Thu-Sun, to 8pm Wed; 🚋3, 4, 6 to Toni-Areal) feature anything from classic photographers to plastic

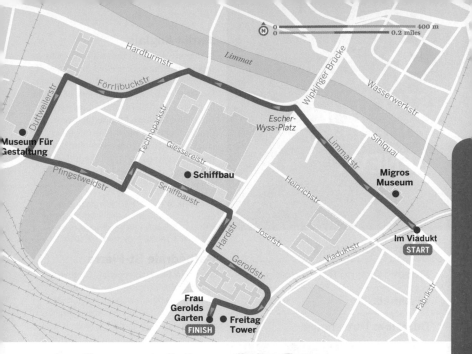

garbage. The permanent collection of 500,000-odd objects covers four categories: graphics, design, applied art and posters. Find it in its new home, the Schaudepot.

The Walk ⟩⟩ From the design museum, walk to the end of Duttweilerstrasse, turn left and follow Pfingstweidstrasse. Turn left at Technoparkstrasse and right at Schiffbaustrasse.

Schiffbau

Once a mighty shipyard fabricating lake steamers and turbine-engine parts, the enormous **Schiffbau** (Schiffbaustrasse; 🚋 3, 8 to Schiffbau) now plays host to the impressive three-staged **Schauspielhaus** (📞ticket office 044 258 77 77; www.schauspielhaus.ch) theatre, a slick restaurant and a jazz club.

The Walk ⟩⟩ From Schiffbaustrasse turn right onto Hardstrasse. Cross it, then turn left into Geroldstrasse, whose illegal clubs started the quarter's night-time rebirth. Follow U-shaped Geroldstrasse (the bottom of which almost connects with the tail end of Im Viadukt) to the Freitag skyscraper.

Freitag Tower

Zürich's Freitag brothers recycle truck tarps into chic bags. Every item is original. This flagship **Freitag store** (www.freitag.ch; Geroldstrasse 17; ⏲10.30am-7pm Mon-Fri, 10am-6pm Sat; 🚋3, 4, 6 to Schiffbau) is pure industrial whimsy – 19 shipping containers stacked 26m high. Its rooftop has spectacular city views.

The Walk ⟩⟩ From the top of the Freitag tower, descend to street level and walk a few metres.

Frau Gerolds Garten

The wildly popular addition to Zürich's scene that is **Frau Gerolds Garten** (www.fraugerold.ch; Geroldstrasse 23/23a; ⏲bar-restaurant 11am-midnight Mon-Sat, noon-10pm Sun Apr-Sep, 6pm-midnight Mon-Sat Oct-Mar, market & shops 11am-7pm Mon-Fri, to 6pm Sat year-round; ⑤Hardbrücke) is pure fun. Strewn with shipping containers, multicoloured lights and sandwiched between flower beds and a rail yard, it has numerous eating and drinking options, and even some hip shops. In winter, its restaurant moves indoors to a pavilion.

387

STRETCH YOUR LEGS
GENEVA

Start: Jardin Anglais

Finish: Place du Bourg-de-Four

Distance: 2km

Duration: Three hours

Geneva's beautiful Vieille Ville (old town) is the perfect spot for a charmingly edifying stroll, thanks to its mix of sights and a history lesson worthy of its status as one of the Protestant Reformation's key cities.

Take this walk on Trip

Jardin Anglais

Before strolling up the hill to the old town, visit the flower clock in Geneva's waterfront **garden** (Quai du Général-Guisan), landscaped in 1854 on the site of an old lumber-handling port and merchant yard. The **Horloge Fleurie** (Flower Clock), Geneva's most photographed clock, is crafted from 6500 plants and has ticked since 1955. Its second hand, 2.5m long, is claimed to be the world's longest.

The Walk » From the clock, cross Quai du Général-Guisan. Head south through the shopping district to Cour de St-Pierre, which faces the cathedral. It's about a seven-minute stroll.

Cathédrale St-Pierre

Begun in the 11th century, Geneva's **cathedral** (www.cathedrale-geneve.ch; Cour de St-Pierre; towers adult/child Sfr5/2; 9.30am-6.30pm Mon-Sat, noon-6.30pm Sun Jun-Sep, 10am-5.30pm Mon-Sat, noon-5.30pm Sun Oct-May) is predominantly Gothic with an 18th-century neoclassical facade. In 1536–64, Protestant John Calvin preached here; see his uncomfortable-looking seat in the north aisle. Inside the cathedral, 77 steps spiral up to the attic – a fascinating glimpse at its architectural construction – from where another 40 lead to the top of the panoramic **northern and southern towers**. Views of the old town and the Jet d'Eau are marvellous. In summer, free carillon (5pm) and organ (6pm) concerts fill the cathedral and its surrounding square with music.

The Walk » Exit the cathedral and head for the Site Archéologique de la Cathédrale St-Pierre; a few dozen footsteps should cover it.

Site Archéologique de la Cathédrale St-Pierre

This small **archaeological site** (www.site-archeologique.ch; Cour de St-Pierre 6; adult/child Sfr8/4; 10am-5pm) in the basement of Cathédrale St-Pierre has 4th-century mosaics in the Roman crypt, and the tomb of an Allobrogian chieftain. Its

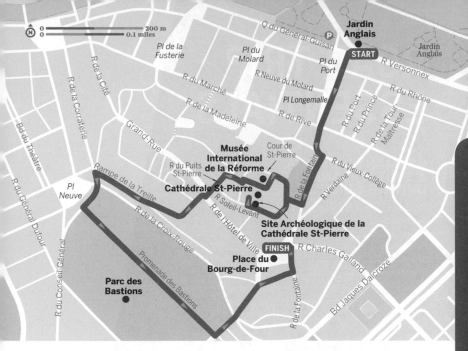

entrance is at the right of the cathedral's main portico.

The Walk » Head to the other side of the cathedral (a one-minute walk) to spend an hour at the Reformation Museum.

Musée International de la Réforme

This modern **museum** (www.musee -reforme.ch; Rue du Cloître 4; adult/child Sfr13/6; ⊙10am-5pm Tue-Sun) in an 18th-century mansion has state-of-the-art exhibits on the Reformation: printed bibles, the emergence of 16th-century Geneva as 'Protestant Rome', John Calvin and present-day Protestantism. A combined ticket covering the museum, Cathédrale St-Pierre and Site Archéologique de la Cathédrale St-Pierre is Sfr18/10 per adult/child.

The Walk » From Cour de St-Pierre, walk down Rue Otto Barblan. Turn left onto Rue du Puits-St-Pierre and continue past Maison Tavel (the city's longest-standing private residence, now a museum) to the bottom of Rue Henri Fazy. It overlooks Parc des Bastions and has the world's

longest bench. Turn down Rampe de la Treille and follow it to the park's gates.

Parc des Bastions

It's all statues – plus free life-size chess boards hosting lively games – in green Parc des Bastions. A laid-back stroll with locals along its tree-lined promenade reveals the 4.5m-tall po-faced figures of Bèze, Calvin, Farel and Knox on **Reformation Wall**, which stretches for 100m. There are play facilities for kids and a skating rink in winter.

The Walk » From Promenade des Bastion's eastern end, walk along Rue St-Léger. Continue under the bridge and ahead until Place du Bourg-de-Four ends at the fountained terrace area.

Place du Bourg-de-Four

Eateries, bars and locals crowd Place du Bourg-de-Four, Geneva's oldest square. In summer it's filled to bursting with gossiping local denizens. Stalwart **La Clémence** (www.laclemence.ch; Place du Bourg-de-Four 20; ⊙7am-1am Mon-Thu, 7am-2am Fri, 8am-2am Sat, 8am-1am Sun) is a popular place to linger over a coffee.

ROAD TRIP ESSENTIALS

Germany, Austria & Switzerland Driving Guide

With stunning landscapes, superb highways and spectacular, vertigo-inducing mountain passes and hairpin bends, this region is made for road-tripping.

DRIVING LICENCE & DOCUMENTS

Drivers must carry the following at all times:

➡ passport or EU national identity card

➡ valid EU driving licence or International Driving Permit

➡ car-ownership papers

➡ Green Card issued by your insurers as proof of third-party insurance

INSURANCE

Third-party liability insurance is compulsory for all vehicles, including cars brought from abroad. Normally, private cars registered and insured in another European country do not require additional insurance, but check with your insurer before leaving home. You could face huge costs by driving when uninsured or underinsured. People can be fussy about their cars and even nudging someone's bumper may result in you having to pay for a new one.

Keep a record of who to contact at your insurance company in case of a breakdown or accident.

HIRING A CAR

To hire a car in Austria, you'll need to be at least 19. In Germany and Switzerland it's usually 25. Region-wide, you need a credit card and a driving licence issued at least one year before.

If you plan to take your car across a country border, tell the rental company beforehand and double-check for add-on fees and age requirements.

All car-hire companies provide mandatory third-party liability insurance, but prices and conditions for collision-damage waiver insurance (CDW) vary greatly – CDW is optional, but driving without it is not recommended. Purchasing CDW reduces the deductible/excess you'll be liable for if your car is damaged or stolen. Your credit card may cover CDW if you use it to pay for the rental; verify conditions and details with your card issuer.

International car-hire companies have branches at airports, major train stations and larger towns. Rates vary considerably. Child or infant safety seats may be hired for about €5 per day; reserve when booking.

Reserve cars in advance online: prebooked and prepaid packages are cheaper than on-the-spot rentals. If you're

Driving Fast Facts

Right or left? Drive on the right

Manual or automatic? Manual

Legal driving age 18

Top speed limit On some motorways no limit in Germany, 130km/h in Austria, 120km/h in Switzerland

Signature cars BMW Coupé, Volkswagen Beetle

Road Trip Websites

AUTOMOBILE ASSOCIATIONS

ADAC (www.adac.de) Germany's main motoring organisation; roadside-assistance available to members of its affiliates, including Britain's AA, the AAA in the US and Canada's CAA.

ÖAMTC (www.oeamtc.at) Free 24-hour breakdown service to members in Austria; reciprocal agreements with motoring clubs abroad.

Swiss Touring Club (www.tcs.ch) Driving in Switzerland.

ROAD RULES

AA (www.theaa.com)

RAC (www.rac.co.uk)

MAPS & TRAFFIC INFO

ADAC (www.maps.adac.de) Online route planner for entire region.

Swiss Motorways (www.autobahnen.ch) Real-time traffic information for Switzerland.

---

flying into Geneva Airport in Switzerland, it's cheaper to rent on the French side.

Rental cars with automatic transmission are rare; book well in advance.

International car-hire companies:

Alamo (www.alamo.com)

Avis (www.avis.com)

Budget (www.budget.com)

Europcar (www.europcar.com)

Hertz (www.hertz.com)

National (www.nationalcar.com)

Sixt (www.sixt.com)

Internet-based discount brokers:

Auto Europe (www.autoeurope.com)

DriveAway Holidays (www.driveaway.com.au)

Easycar (www.easycar.com)

Holiday Autos (www.holidayautos.co.uk)

BRINGING YOUR OWN VEHICLE

➡ Any foreign vehicle entering Germany, Austria or Switzerland must display a sticker or licence plate identifying its country of registration.

➡ Right-hand-drive vehicles brought from the UK or Ireland must have deflectors affixed to headlights to avoid dazzling oncoming traffic.

MAPS

➡ Even if your car has a navigation system, a good map or road atlas is essential, especially when negotiating the labyrinth of country roads.

➡ Maps costing a few euros are sold at bookstores, train stations, airports and petrol stations. Publishers include **Freytag & Berndt** (www.freytagberndt.com), **ADAC** (www.adac.de) and **Falk** (www.falk.de).

ROAD CONDITIONS

The region has an excellent network of well-built, well-signposted and well-maintained roads comprising autobahn (*autoroutes* in French-speaking Switzerland), national roads, narrow country lanes and corkscrew mountain passes.

Autobahn (highways or motorways beginning with A, signalled by white-on-blue signs in Germany and Austria, white-on-green signs in Switzerland) Multilane divided highways, kitted out every 40km to 60km with elaborate service areas with petrol stations, toilets and restaurants.

Autobahns are free to use in Germany. In Austria and Switzerland, motorists must buy a motorway-tax sticker (vignette in German and French, *contrassegno* in Italian) to display on the windscreen. Buy vignettes in advance from motoring organisations or in situ (in cash) at border crossings, petrol stations, Austrian post offices and Tabak shops.

In Austria a vignette costs €9.20/26.80/ 89.20 for 10 days/two months/one calendar year. In Switzerland, motorists pay Sfr40, valid for one year, from 1 December to 31 January of the following year. A separate vignette is required for trailers and caravans.

For more information, see www.asfinag.at (Austria) and www.vignette.ch (Switzerland).

Bundesstrassen (*routes nationales* in French-speaking Switzerland) Secondary 'B' roads.

Landstrassen (L) Local roads designed for scenic rides rather than speed.

Alpine mountain passes Many passes in Austria and Switzerland are blocked by snow from October or November to May. Conditions are posted at the foot of each pass and signs (a criss-crossed white tyre on a blue circular background) indicate if snow chains are compulsory; always carry snow chains when motoring in mountainous areas.

Major Swiss Alpine passes are negotiable year-round, albeit by tunnel for part of the year – this is the case at the Great St Bernard, St Gotthard and San Bernardino passes.

In Austria and Switzerland some roads and tunnels demand an additional toll (not covered by the motorway vignette).

In Switzerland, putting your car on a train to traverse the Furka Pass (www.matterhorn gotthardbahn.ch), Lötschberg Tunnel (www. bls.ch) or Vereina Tunnel (www.rhb.ch) costs Sfr20 to Sfr40.

ROAD RULES

Enforcement of traffic laws is strict. Region-wide, speed- and red-light cameras and radar traps are common and notices are sent to the car's registration address. For many infractions fines are doled out on the spot.

Road Distances (km)

	Bregenz	Berlin	Bremen	Hanover	Dresden	Düsseldorf	Frankfurt	Hamburg	Munich	Stuttgart	Geneva	Zürich	Chur	Bern	Basel	St Gallen	Salzburg	Vienna	Linz
Berlin	681																		
Bremen	687	376																	
Hanover	571	273	115																
Dresden	553	187	460	357															
Düsseldorf	550	568	290	278	550														
Frankfurt	370	507	376	327	451	205													
Hamburg	777	282	115	150	453	425	482												
Munich	170	576	696	629	457	564	392	777											
Stuttgart	205	613	591	495	492	387	183	650	228										
Geneva	356	1020	1049	1106	938	743	646	1151	529	454									
Zürich	101	758	787	844	674	560	384	889	267	192	292								
Chur	87	851	770	695	758	678	492	884	261	290	409	118							
Bern	210	892	807	864	809	597	407	1004	443	331	171	125	242						
Basel	180	795	710	767	712	503	310	907	346	234	267	113	228	97					
St Gallen	32	702	770	628	521	564	410	597	205	248	371	81	102	204	191				
Salzburg	374	679	845	929	508	729	535	933	133	359	678	401	360	506	463	339			
Vienna	670	808	964	844	673	855	655	984	374	592	923	670	650	784	746	600	301		
Linz	507	648	804	684	513	695	495	824	214	432	763	510	490	624	586	439	138	189	
Innsbruck	193	751	857	741	575	733	548	947	164	378	480	277	187	341	343	199	181	477	314

393

Speed Limits

➜ Unless signposted otherwise, a limit of 50km/h applies in towns and built-up areas; this often drops to 30km/h in residential areas.

➜ Maximum speed is 100km/h on single-lane freeways and national roads; this drops to 80km/h on main roads outside towns in Switzerland and to 70km/h on some country roads in Austria.

➜ The speed limit on autobahn is 120km/h in Switzerland and 130km/h in Austria (110km/h at night between 10pm and 5am, except on the A1 between Vienna and Salzburg and the A2 between Vienna and Villach).

➜ In theory there is no speed limit on some sections of German autobahn. However, there are numerous stretches where slower speeds of 130km/h or even 100km/h apply.

Headlights

Switzerland Headlights must be turned on at all times, day and night.

Germany & Austria Use headlights after dusk, in the dark or when visibility is poor.

Region-wide Use dipped headlights in tunnels.

Winter Tyres

Austria Compulsory from 1 November to 15 April.

Switzerland & Germany Not obligatory but pretty much essential in winter.

Alcohol

Region-wide The blood-alcohol limit is 0.05% (0.5g per litre of blood) – the equivalent of two standard glasses of wine for a 75kg adult.

Austria The limit drops to 0.01% for drivers who have held their licence for less than two years.

Germany No alcohol is tolerated for drivers aged under 21 or those who have held their licence for less than two years.

Child Seats

➜ Up to age 12 (age 14 in Austria), children shorter than 1.5m must use a size-appropriate car seat or booster.

➜ Children cannot ride in the front until age 13 in Germany and 14 in Austria.

➜ Providing they are strapped in the appropriate seat or booster for their weight, children of any age can ride in the front seat in Switzerland.

Other Rules

➜ All passengers, front and back, must wear seat belts.

➜ Mobile phones may only be used with a hands-free kit or speakerphone.

➜ Give priority to traffic, including bicycles, approaching from the right (unless a priority road sign indicates otherwise).

➜ Stationary trams have priority; wait behind while tram passengers board and alight.

➜ On mountain roads the ascending vehicle has priority; Swiss postal buses always have right of way.

➜ All vehicles in Germany must carry a breakdown warning triangle and first-aid kit; in Austria you also need a reflective jacket. In Switzerland only the warning triangle is required by law, but the other items are recommended.

Green in the City

To decrease air pollution, some Austrian and German cities have low-emissions environmental zones that may only be entered by cars displaying an Umweltplakette or environmental badge. This includes foreign vehicles. Buy the sticker (€32) online from www.feinstaub vignette.de. Badgeless drivers caught in green zones are fined €80.

PARKING

➜ Street parking in city centres, often limited to up to two hours, is controlled by parking meters from 8am to 7pm Monday to Saturday. Buy a ticket at the coin-fed ticket machine and display it on your dashboard.

➜ For all-day city parking, pay to park in a car park or garage; some close at night.

➜ Region-wide, public car parks allocate special parking spaces for women, extra well lit and close to exits.

Driving Problem-Buster

I can't speak German/French/Italian; will that be a problem? German is the dominant language – learn at least the basics before arriving. Road signs are mostly international and English is widely spoken in Germany and Austria (less so in Switzerland).

What should I do if my car breaks down? Safety first: turn on your warning lights, put on your reflective vest (required by law in Austria) and place a reflective triangle 30m to 100m behind your car to warn approaching motorists. Call the local automobile association (or phone number listed on your insurance) for breakdown assistance, or walk to the nearest orange roadside call box, placed every 2km on most autobahn.

What if I have an accident? For minor accidents with no injuries, fill out a European Accident Statement, included in rental-car glove compartments. Report the accident afterwards to your insurance and/or rental-car company. If necessary, call the police (112).

What should I do if I am stopped by the police? Show your passport (or EU national identity card), driving licence and proof of insurance.

Do I need to buy a vignette, even if I am only using the Swiss/Austrian autobahn for a few kilometres? Unfortunately, yes. And don't even think about not sticking it on your windshield (for a friend to reuse) or only partially affixing it. An unstuck vignette is considered invalid by road police and will incur an on-the-spot fine of up to €240/Sfr100 in Austria/Switzerland.

Is it dangerous driving on German autobahn with no speed limit? It can be if you don't keep your wits about you. If you're unaccustomed to high speeds, be extra careful when passing another vehicle. It takes only seconds for a car appearing far away in the rear-view mirror to close in at 200km/h or more. Pass as quickly as possible, then quickly return to the right lane

FUEL

➡ Petrol stations, mainly self-service, are ubiquitous except in sparsely populated rural areas. Petrol is sold in litres.

➡ Unleaded (bleifrei, sans plomb, senza piombo) petrol is standard and diesel is widely available.

➡ Filling up is most expensive at autobahn/autoroute rest stops, cheapest at hypermarkets and large supermarkets.

SAFETY

Never leave anything valuable in your car, even in the boot (trunk). Thieves often identify and target rental cars.

RADIO

➡ In Germany, private Berlin radio station **Flux FM** (www.fluxfm.de) has a catchy mix of indie rock, alternative rock and interesting newcomers. For mainstream rock and pop, try **Radio 1** (www.radioeins.de).

➡ News in English in Germany is aired by **BBC World Service** (90.2 FM); find US news bulletins on **Rock Star** (87.9 FM; www.rocksender.de).

➡ In Austria, cruise to traffic news and drivable tunes with **Hitradio Ö3** (http://oe3.radio.net).

➡ Pick up Switzerland's English-language radio station, **WRS** (www.worldradio.ch), around Lake Geneva.

Germany, Austria & Switzerland Travel Guide

GETTING THERE & AWAY

AIR

International Airports
Rental cars are available at all international airports listed following.

Germany
Frankfurt, Düsseldorf and Munich airports are the main gateways for overseas air traffic. Berlin is accessible through **Tegel** (TXL; ☑030-6091 1150; www.berlin-airport.de; 🚇Flughafen Tegel) and **Schönefeld** (SXF; ☑030-6091 1150; www.berlin-airport.de; 🚈Airport-Express, RE7 & RB14, 🚊S9, S45) airports; Berlin Brandenburg, still under construction, will come online in the next few years.

Düsseldorf International Airport (DUS; ☑0211-4210; www.dus.com; 🚈Düsseldorf Flughafen)

Frankfurt Airport (FRA; ☑180-6 372 4636; www.frankfurt-airport.com; Hugo-Eckener-Ring; 🚆; 🚈Flughafen Regionalbahnhof)

Hamburg Airport (Flughafen Hamburg Helmut Schmidt; HAM; ☑040-507 50; www.hamburg-airport.de; Flughafenstrasse; 🚈Hamburg Airport)

Köln Bonn Airport (CGN; Cologne Bonn Airport; ☑2203 40-4001; www.koeln-bonn-airport.de; Kennedystrasse; 🚈Köln/Bonn Flughafen)

Munich Airport (MUC; ☑089-975 00; www.munich-airport.de)

Stuttgart Airport (SGT; ☑0711-9480; www.stuttgart-airport.com)

Austria
Vienna is the main hub, but international flights to smaller airports or **Airport Bra-**

tislava (BTS; ☑02-3303 3353; www.bts.aero; Ivanská cesta), 60km east of Vienna, can be cheaper.

Blue Danube Airport Linz (LNZ; ☑07221-6000; www.linz-airport.com; Flughafenstrasse 1, Hörsching)

Graz Airport (GRZ; ☑0316-290 21 72; www.flughafen-graz.at)

Innsbruck Airport (INN; ☑0512-22 52 50; www.innsbruck-airport.com; Fürstenweg 180)

Salzburg Airport (☑0662-858 00; www.salzburg-airport.com; Innsbrucker Bundesstrasse 95; 🚆)

Vienna International Airport (VIE; ☑01-700 722 233; www.viennaairport.com; 🚆)

Switzerland

Geneva (Cointrin) Airport (Aéroport International de Genève; ☑848 19 20 20; www.gva.ch)

Zürich Airport (☑043 816 22 11; www.zurich-airport.com)

CAR & MOTORCYCLE
Entering the region should be swift and painless thanks to the Schengen Agreement, which abolished passport and customs formalities between Germany, Austria, Switzerland and bordering EU countries.

TRAIN
➡ Rail services link the region with virtually every country in Europe. Main rail hubs include Munich, Vienna, Zürich and Basel. Rental cars are readily available at these and other major train stations.

➡ Book tickets and get information from **Rail Europe** (www.raileurope-world.com). **Railteam** (www.railteam.eu) is an alliance of European high-speed train operators including

German railways **Deutsche Bahn** (www.bahn.com), Austria's **ÖBB** (ww.oebb.at) and **Swiss Federal Railways** (www.sbb.ch).

➡ From the UK, hourly **Eurostar** (www.eurostar.com) trains scoot from London (St Pancras International) to Paris (Gare du Nord) in 2¼ hours or Brussels (two hours), from where you can continue by regular or high-speed train to Germany. For Vienna, go to Frankfurt then pick up a connection to Vienna. For Geneva and other Swiss cities, take a French TGV from Paris (Gare de Lyon).

➡ **The Man in Seat 61** (www.seat61.com) is a useful train-travel resource.

DIRECTORY A–Z

ACCESSIBLE TRAVEL

➡ The region is fairly progressive when it comes to barrier-free travel. Access ramps and/or lifts are available in many public buildings, including train stations, museums, concert halls and cinemas.

➡ Trains, trams, underground trains and buses are increasingly accessible; train stations have a mobile lift for boarding trains and city buses are ramp-equipped.

➡ Some car-rental agencies offer hand-controlled vehicles and vans with wheelchair lifts; reserve well in advance.

For information, contact the national tourist boards or these organisations:

Deutsche Bahn Mobility Service Centre (www.bahn.com) Train access information and route-planning assistance.

Mobility International Switzerland (www.mis-ch.ch)

ACCOMMODATION

From simple mountain huts to five-star hotels fit for royalty – you will find a wide choice of accommodation. Standards are high, and even basic accommodation is likely to be clean and comfortable. Tourist offices keep lists and details.

Seasons

➡ Seasonal variations are common in holiday regions, less in the cities where rates are generally constant year-round. Exceptions are Christmas and New Year.

Practicalities

Time The region uses the 24-hour clock and is on Central European Time, one hour ahead of GMT/UTC. During daylight-saving time (last Sunday in March to last Sunday in October) it's two hours ahead.

TV & DVD TV is DVB-T (digital) and PAL (analogue); DVDs are zone 2.

Floors 'Ground floor' is street level. The 1st floor (2nd floor in the US) is the floor above that.

Weights & Measures Metric system.

➡ In 'business' cities such as Munich, Geneva and Zürich, pricier weekday rates drop slightly at weekends.

➡ In mountain resorts prices are seasonal: low season (mid-September to mid-December and mid-April to mid-June) is the cheapest time to visit, mid-season (January to mid-February and mid-June to early July and September) begins to get pricey, and high season (July, August, Christmas, and mid-February to Easter) is the busy period.

Reservations

➡ Book in advance during high season in July, August, Christmas and Easter, and between December and April in ski areas.

➡ At other times, a day or two in advance can be sufficient; a week or more in advance is recommended for Friday and Saturday nights.

➡ You'll need to confirm online after making a phone booking; many places can be booked online, often with a best-price guarantee.

➡ Many tourist offices make hotel reservations, some for a small fee, others for free.

Camping

➡ Campsites are often in a scenic out-of-the-way place by a river or lake. Facilities usually include washing machines, electricity, on-site shops and, occasionally, cooking facilities. Camping gas canisters are often available.

➡ Most campsites open April to September; a handful open year-round. Prices start at €3/Sfr10 per person, plus €6/Sfr10 for a small tent and €3/Sfr5 for a car. Pay extra for hot showers, resort tax, electricity and sewage disposal. A **Camping Card International** (www.campingcardinternational.com) may yield savings.

➡ Wild camping (*wildes camping* in German, *camping sauvage* in French) is not allowed. In Austria, free camping in camper vans is allowed in autobahn rest areas and alongside other roads, as long as you're not causing an obstruction; it's illegal to pitch a tent in these areas.

Useful organisations:

www.campingclub.at Austrian Camping Club.

www.germany.travel/camping Searchable database with detailed information on 750 German campgrounds.

www.sccv.ch Swiss Camping and Caravanning Federation.

B&Bs & Pensionen

➡ B&Bs make for some of Switzerland's most charming accommodation – a room in a private home (anything from castle to farm), which includes breakfast, often made from homemade produce.

➡ In Germany and Austria, *Pensionen* are the B&B equivalent. *Gasthöfe/Gasthäuser* (inns) are similar but usually have restaurants serving regional food to a local clientele. Amenities, room size and decor vary, often within a single establishment. What rooms lack in amenities, though, they often make up for in charm, authenticity and friendly hosts.

➡ Tourist offices have lists of B&Bs and *Pensionen* in their area – urban rarities but plentiful in the countryside.

➡ Online listing sites include www.bnb. ch, www.bed-and-breakfast.de and www. bedandbreakfast.de.

Sleeping Price Ranges

The following price ranges refer to a double room with private bathroom in high season. Hotel prices include breakfast.

€ less than €80/Sfr170

€€ €80–160 (Germany), €80–200 (Austria), Sfr170–350 (Switzerland)

€€€ more than €160/200 (Germany/Austria), more than Sfr350

Farmstays

For motorists there is no greater way to end a day on the road than by pulling into a gorgeous old farmstead, strung with geraniums in bloom and with the milk urn sitting on the doostep waiting to be filled.

Farmstays offer a great opportunity to get close to nature in relative comfort. Kids can interact with animals and help with chores. Accommodation ranges from barebones rooms with shared facilities to fully furnished holiday apartments. Minimum stays are common. Farms may be organic, dairy, equestrian or wine estates.

Germany

The German Agricultural Association inspects and quality-controls hundreds of farms and publishes details on www.land reise.de. Another source is www.land sichten.de.

Austria

➡ In rural Austria stay in a *Bauernhof* (farmhouse) with rooms or apartments to rent, often for a minimum of three nights but sometimes for one – check when booking. Nightly rates vary between €40 and €100 per person.

➡ In mountainous regions, isolated *Almhütten* (Alpine meadow huts) – usually part of a farmstead – provide a welcome break from the road and an opportunity to stretch your legs; some can only be accessed by cable car, on foot or by mountain bike on forest tracks. Most close October to April or May.

➡ *Bio-* or *Öko-* ('eco') hotels are less rural, but in picturesque settings, often with wellness facilities such as saunas and steam baths. See www.biohotels.info.

➡ Urlaub in der Almhütte (www.urlaub aufderalm.com; www.farmholidays.com) lists farmstays; contact tourist offices for local mountaintop *Almhütten*.

Switzerland

Switzerland's **Aventure sur la paille/ Schlaf im Stroh** is the ultimate roll in the hay. When the cows are out to pasture in summer, Swiss farmers charge travellers Sfr20 to Sfr30 per adult and Sfr10 to Sfr20 per child under 15 to sleep on straw in their hay barns or lofts.

➡ Farmers provide cotton under-sheets and woolly blankets, but guests need their own sleeping bags (bring a pocket torch, too).

→ Rates include a hearty farmhouse breakfast.

→ A morning shower (Sfr2) and evening meal (Sfr20 to Sfr30) are usually available for an extra charge.

Agritourism Switzerland (www.bauern hof-ferien.ch) Lists 170-odd Swiss farms offering accommodation, including farmhouses that welcome B&B guests or self-caterers keen to rent a renovated barn or cottage.

Hostels

→ Hostels (*Jugendherberge* in German, *auberge de jeunesse* in French, *alloggio per giovanni* in Italian) range from older, institutional affairs to modern establishments bordering on designer accommodation.

→ Facilities are often excellent: four- to six-bed dorms with shower/toilet, plus double and family rooms are the norm; internet facilities, free wi-fi and a restaurant or cafe are commonplace.

→ Many hostels are affiliated with **Hostelling International** (HI; www.hihostels. com), bookable by email or online. If you don't have an HI membership card from your home country, buy one for €18/Sfr22 (valid for one year) or collect six individual Welcome Stamps (€3.50/Sfr6 per night). Average nightly rates in mixed or gender-segregated dorms are about €22/Sfr35 per night, including sheets.

→ Private, independent hostels – prevalent in big German cities like Berlin, Cologne and Hamburg – attract a convivial, international crowd.

→ Indies range from classic backpacker pads with large dorms and a communal spirit to modern 'flashpacker' properties similar to budget hotels. Indie hostels have no curfew and staff tend to be savvy, multilingual and keen to help with tips and advice.

National hostelling organisations:

Deutsches Jugendherbergswerk (DJH; www.jugendherberge.de) Manages Germany's 530 HI-affiliated hostels.

Independent Hostels of Germany (www.german-hostels.de) Alliance of over 60 independent hostels in 34 German cities.

ÖJHV (www.oejhv.at) and **ÖJHW** (www.jugendherberge.at) Austria's two hostelling organisations provide info on the country's 100-plus HI-affiliated hostels.

Swiss Youth Hostels (www.youthhostel. ch) Swiss HI-affiliated hostels.

Swiss Hostels (www.swisshostels.com) These hostels tend to be more flexible in their regulations, reception times and opening hours; membership not required.

Hotels

→ You'll find everything from small family-run properties to international chains and luxurious designer abodes.

→ Increasingly popular are budget designer chains geared towards lifestyle-savvy travellers.

→ In older, family-run hotels, rooms vary dramatically in size, decor and amenities. The cheapest may have shared facilities, while others have a shower but no private toilet; only pricier ones have their own bathrooms.

→ Midrange hotels have comfortable clean rooms and a decent buffet breakfast with cold cuts of meat, cheeses, eggs and bread rolls (except in French-speaking Switzerland where croissants, bread and jam prevail). Rooms have private bathroom with shower, flat-screen TV, often a minibar, and a place to sit or a desk. Internet and wi-fi is available, usually free.

→ Luxurious, top-end places include Germany's fairy-tale castles, palaces and country manors. Mod-cons blend with baronial ambience and old-world trappings such as four-poster beds, antique armoires and heavy drapes – the stuff of road-trip dreams. See www.germany -castles-hotels.com.

→ Most hotels are entirely nonsmoking; others set aside rooms for smokers.

ELECTRICITY

→ European two-pin plugs are standard in Austria and Germany.

Type C
220V/50Hz

➡ Swiss three-pin plugs slot into recessed, three-holed, hexagonally shaped sockets. These plugs usually take the standard European two-pronged plug, but to be safe, bring an adapter for Switzerland.

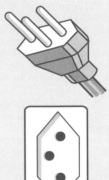

Type J
230V/50Hz

FOOD

Whether you're digging into a creamy wedge of real McCoy Black Forest gateau in southeast Germany, savouring fish on the shores of Austria's Salzkammergut's looking-glass lakes or devouring an oven-crisp rösti or cheesy fondue in the Swiss Alps, food is integral to your road-trip experience.

The region has endless eateries; categories listed here are perfect for breaking a road trip or feasting in style. You'll find cafes ranging from bakery-cafes for a quick coffee and sandwich to all-organic delis, and restaurants covering the whole spectrum from pizzeria bites to Michelin-starred finery.

Advance reservations are recommended for high-end eateries and popular, family-run rural inns.

Germany

Gaststätten & Gasthöfe Rural inns with a laid-back feel, local crowd and solid menu of *gutbürgerliche Küche* (home cooking).

Stehcafé Stand-up cafe for coffee and snacks at speed.

Cafe-Konditorei Traditional cake shop and cafe.

Ratskeller Atmospheric town-hall basement restaurant, frequented more by tourists than locals.

Imbiss Handy speed-feed stops for savoury fodder, such as wurst-in-a-bun, kebabs or pizza.

Apfelweinwirtschaft Frankfurt's historic *Ebbelwei* (apple-wine) taverns. Warm, woody and serving good honest regional fare.

Biergarten Beer garden, often with tree shade and a meaty menu.

Austria

Beisln/Gasthäuser Rural inns with homely interiors and menus packed with hearty dishes such as *Tafelspitz* (boiled beef in broth), schnitzel and goulash.

Neo-Beisln New-wave *Beisln* often with retro-cool decor and a creative, market-fresh take on classics.

Konditoreien Traditional cake-shop cafes.

Kaffeehäuser Vienna's 'living rooms' cook up delectable tortes, cakes and arm-long coffee menus; inexpensive breakfast, lunch and snacks, too.

Imbiss Snack or takeaway joint, the most famous being the Würstelstand (sausage stand).

Brauereien Many microbreweries and brewpubs serve grub, too.

Switzerland

Auberge Countryside inn serving traditional Swiss fare.

Kaffeebar Cafe in German-speaking Switzerland serving coffee and other typical drinks.

Stube Cosy bistro in rural or Alpine areas, serving traditional fare such as cheesy fondues and raclette.

Grotto Rustic, summer-cool restaurants in the Italian-speaking canton of Ticino.

Osteria Casual eatery in Ticino serving good-value, traditional fare.

LGBTQI+ TRAVELLERS

➜ Attitudes to homosexuality across the region are progressive; more so in German cities such as Berlin, Cologne, Hamburg, Frankfurt and Munich.

➜ Many cities have gay and lesbian bars, and pride marches in spring.

➜ The age of consent for gay sex is 14 in Germany and Austria, 16 in Switzerland.

Publications

Blu (www.blu.fm) Magazine with searchable, up-to-the-minute location and event listings.

L-Mag (www.l-mag.de) Bimonthly mag for lesbians.

Websites & Apps

German National Tourist Office (www.germany.travel) Dedicated LGBT pages.

My Switzerland (www.myswitzerland.com) Gay-friendly accommodation and events.

BGLAD (www.bglad.com) International online resource and directory.

Spartacus World (www.spartacusworld.com) Hip hotel, style and event guide.

Patroc Gay Travel Guide (www.patroc.com) Travel information.

INTERNET ACCESS

➜ Public wireless access points can be found at airports, train stations, some city parks, town squares and other public spaces.

➜ Some tourist offices, and many cafes and bars, sport free wi-fi and allow customers to linger with laptops.

➜ Most hotels offer free wi-fi; some have a computer guests can use to surf the internet for free or a small fee.

MONEY

ATMs

ATMs are widespread and accessible 24 hours. They accept most international bank or credit cards and have multilingual instructions. Your bank or credit-card company will usually charge a 1% to 2.5% fee, and there may also be a small charge at the ATM end.

Cash

You'll always find a better exchange rate in-country, but if arriving in the region by air late at night, bring enough euros or Swiss francs to take a taxi to your hotel.

Businesses throughout Switzerland, including most hotels and some restaurants and souvenir shops, accept euros. Change will be given in Swiss francs at that day's exchange rate.

Credit & Debit Cards

The use of credit cards is less widespread than in the UK or USA and not all shops, hotels or restaurants accept them. Euro-Card/MasterCard and Visa are the most popular.

Moneychangers

Change money at banks, airports and nearly every train station until late into the evening. Banks tend to charge 5% commission; some money-exchange bureaus don't charge commission.

OPENING HOURS

These are standard hours; hours can fluctuate by an hour or so either way:

Tipping Guide

By law restaurant and bar prices include a service charge, so there is no need to tip. In reality locals leave a bit extra if satisfied with the service, and, in Switzerland, will often round up to the nearest franc.

Bars round to nearest euro

Hotel cleaning staff €1 to €2 per day

Hotel porters €1 to €1.50 per bag

Restaurants 10%

Taxis 10% or round up to the nearest €5

Toilet attendants €0.50

Tour guides €1 to €2 per person

Banks 8am or 9am to 3pm Monday to Friday (to 4.30pm in Switzerland)

Bars 6pm or 7pm to anywhere between midnight and 4am

Cafes 7am or 8am to 11pm or midnight

Nightclubs 11pm to early morning

Post offices 8am to noon and 2pm to 6pm Monday to Friday, 8am to noon Saturday (in Germany 9am to 6pm Monday to Friday, to 1pm Saturday)

Restaurants 11am to 2.30pm and 6pm to 10pm or 11pm, five or six days a week (not before noon in Switzerland)

Shops 9am to 6.30pm or 7pm Monday to Friday, 9am to 5pm or 6pm Saturday, often late-night opening to 9pm Thursday

Supermarkets 9.30am to 8pm Monday to Saturday (shorter hours outside cities)

PUBLIC HOLIDAYS

The following public holidays (*Gesetzliche Feiertage* in German, *jours fériés* in French) are observed in the entire region:

New Year's Day 1 January

Good Friday March/April

Easter Sunday & Monday March/April

Ascension Day 40th day after Easter

Whit Sunday & Monday Seventh week after Easter

May Day 1 May

Christmas Day 25 December

St Stephen's Day 26 December

➡ In Austria and German states with predominantly Catholic populations (such as Bavaria and Baden-Württemberg), the following are also public holidays: Epiphany (6 January), Corpus Christi (10 days after Whit Sunday), Assumption Day (15 August), All Saints' Day (1 November) and Immaculate Conception (8 December).

➡ Some Swiss cantons observe their own special holidays and religious days, eg Berchtold Day (2 January), Labour Day (1 May), Corpus Christi (May or June), Assumption (15 August) and All Saints' Day (1 November).

➡ Each country celebrates its own national day with a public holiday: Swiss National Day (1 August), Day of German Unity (3 October), Austrian National Day (26 October).

SAFE TRAVEL

Germany, Austria and Switzerland are very safe countries. Visitors will generally have no trouble walking around at night in cities. Though theft and other crimes against travellers occur rarely, you should still take all the usual precautions:

Theft Keep valuables out of sight (on your person and in parked cars). Pickpockets occasionally operate on public transport and at major tourist sights.

Natural Dangers Every year people die from landslides and avalanches in the Alps. Always check weather conditions before heading out; consider hiring a guide when skiing off-piste. Before going on challenging hikes, ensure you have the proper equipment and fitness. Inform someone at your accommodation where you're going and when you intend to return.

TELEPHONE

Mobile Phones

➡ Mobile phone numbers begin with the following digits:

Germany 0151, 0157, 0170 or 0178

Austria 0650 or any higher digit up to 0699

Switzerland 076, 078 or 079

➡ All three countries use GSM 900/1800, compatible with the rest of Europe and Australia but not with the North American GSM 1900; check with your provider about roaming charges.

➜ If you're spending the bulk of your time motoring in one country, it may be cheaper to buy a local SIM card (€15 to €30) and rev it up with prepaid credit. Buy recharge cards at newsagents and supermarkets.

➜ Mobile-phone operators:

Germany O2 (www.o2online.de), T-Mobile (www.telekom.de), Vodafone (www.vodafone.de)

Austria Magenta (www.magenta.at), A1 (www.a1.net), 3 (www.drei.at)

Switzerland Salt (www.salt.ch), Sunrise (www.sunrise.ch), Swisscom Mobile (www.swisscom-mobile.ch)

Phone Codes

Calling the region from abroad Dial your country's international dialling access code, then the respective country code and the phone number *without* the initial 0.

Calling internationally from Germany, Austria or Switzerland Dial 00, the relevant country code, area code if necessary (dropping the initial 0) and telephone number.

Area codes German and Austrian telephone numbers have an area code (starting with 0 and up to six digits long). If dialling from a landline within the same town or city, you don't need to dial the area code. You must use it when calling from a *Handy* (mobile). Area codes do not exist in Switzerland, although phone numbers in the same city or region share a common three-digit prefix (which must always be dialled).

Directory enquiries From a German landline call 11828 for numbers within Germany or 11834 for numbers outside Germany; for an English-speaking operator call 11837. In Austria call 0900 11 88 77 for international directory assistance. Search for Swiss phone numbers online: http://tel.local.ch.

TOILETS

➜ Toilets in the region are sit-down affairs.

➜ Public toilets are generally clean and in reasonable supply. Free-standing 24-hour self-cleaning toilet pods are common; pay €0.50 and take no more than 15 minutes. In Switzerland, public toilets are often free, but some might charge Sfr0.50 for the use of a cubicle.

➜ Toilets in main train stations are often maintained by private companies meaning you can pay up to €1.50/Sfr2 to spend a penny.

TOURIST INFORMATION

Towns and cities have clearly signposted tourist offices (*Verkehrsbüro* in German, *office du tourisme* in French, *ufficio turistico* in Italian) where you can pick up free information and city maps, and sometimes book hotel rooms and tours. Somebody always speaks English.

National tourist boards:

German National Tourist Office (www.germany.travel)

Austria Info (www.austria.info)

Switzerland Tourism (www.myswitzerland.com)

VISAS

➜ Visas for stays of up to three months are not required for citizens of the EU, much of Eastern Europe, the USA, Canada, Australia and New Zealand. For stays exceeding 90 days in a 180-day period, contact your nearest German/Austrian/Swiss embassy or consulate and begin your visa application well in advance.

➜ Nationals from other countries need a Schengen visa. It allows unlimited travel within the entire zone for a 90-day period. Apply to the consulate of the country you are entering first, or your main destination.

➜ For up-to-date details on visa requirements, go to the **German Federal Foreign Office** (www.auswaertiges-amt.de), **Austria's Ministry of Foreign Affairs** (www.bmaa.gv.at) or the **Swiss Federal Office for Migration** (www.bfm.admin.ch).

Important Numbers

Country code Germany ☎49, Austria ☎43, Switzerland ☎41

International access code ☎00

Emergency number ☎112

Roadside assistance Germany ☎01802 22 22 22, Austria ☎120, Switzerland ☎140

Language

German is easy for English speakers to pronounce because almost all of its sounds are also found in English. If you read our coloured pronunciation guides as if they were English, you'll have no problems being understood. Note that kh is like the 'ch' in 'Bach' or the Scottish 'loch' (pronounced at the back of the throat), r is also pronounced at the back of the throat (almost like a g, but with some friction), zh is pronounced as the 's' in 'measure', and ü as the 'ee' in 'see' but with rounded lips. The stressed syllables are indicated with italics.

The sounds used in spoken French can almost all be found in English, too. There are a couple of exceptions: nasal vowels (represented in our pronunciation guides by o or u followed by an almost inaudible nasal consonant sound m, n or ng), the 'funny' *u* (ew in our guides) and the deep-in-the-throat *r*. Bearing these few points in mind and reading our pronunciation guides as if they were English, you'll be understood just fine.

GERMAN BASICS

Hello.	*Guten Tag.*	goo·ten tahk
Goodbye.	*Auf Wiedersehen.*	owf vee·der·zay·en
Yes./No.	*Ja./Nein.*	yah/nain
Please.	*Bitte.*	bi·te
Thank you.	*Danke.*	dang·ke
You're welcome.	*Bitte.*	bi·te
Excuse me.	*Entschuldigung.*	ent·shul·di·gung
Sorry.	*Entschuldigung.*	ent·shul·di·gung

Do you speak English?
Sprechen Sie Englisch? (pol)   shpre·khen zee eng·lish
Sprichst du Englisch? (inf)   shprikhst doo eng·lish

I don't understand.
Ich verstehe nicht.   ikh fer·shtay·e nikht

DIRECTIONS

Where's ...?
Wo ist ...?   vaw ist ...

How far is it?
Wie weit ist es?   vee vait ist es

Can you show me (on the map)?
Können Sie es mir (auf der Karte) zeigen?   ker·nen zee es meer (owf dair kar·te) tsai·gen

How can I get there?
Wie kann ich da hinkommen?   vee kan ikh dah hin·ko·men

Turn ...	*Biegen Sie ... ab.*	bee·gen zee ... ab
at the corner	*an der Ecke*	an dair e·ke
at the traffic lights	*bei der Ampel*	bai dair am·pel
left	*links*	lingks
right	*rechts*	rekhts

ON THE ROAD

I'd like to hire a ...	*Ich möchte ein ... mieten.*	ikh merkh·te ain ... mee·ten
4WD	*Allradfahrzeug*	al·raht·fahr·tsoyk
car	*Auto*	ow·to
motorbike	*Motorrad*	maw·tor·raht

How much is it per ...?	*Wie viel kostet es pro ...?*	vee feel kos·tet es praw ...
day	*Tag*	tahk
week	*Woche*	vo·khe

Does this road go to ...?
Führt diese Straße nach ...?   fürt dee·ze shtrah·se nahkh ...

Want More?

For in-depth language information and handy phrases, check out Lonely Planet's *German* and *French Phrasebooks*. You'll find them at **shop.lonelyplanet.com**.

(How long) Can I park here?
(Wie lange) Kann ich (vee *lang*·e) kan ikh
hier parken? heer *par*·ken

Where's a petrol station?
Wo ist eine Tankstelle? vaw ist *ai*·ne *tangk*·shte·le

I need a mechanic.
Ich brauche einen ikh *brow*·khe *ai*·nen
Mechaniker. me·*khah*·ni·ker

My car/motorbike has broken down (at ...).
Ich habe (in ...) eine ikh *hah*·be (in ...) *ai*·ne
Panne mit meinem *pa*·ne mit *mai*·nem
Auto/Motorrad. ow·to/*maw*·tor·raht

I've run out of petrol.
Ich habe kein ikh *hah*·be kain
Benzin mehr. ben·*tseen* mair

I have a flat tyre.
Ich habe eine ikh *hah*·be *ai*·ne
Reifenpanne. *rai*·fen·pa·ne

- - - - - - - - - - - - - - - - - - -
EMERGENCIES

Help!
Hilfe! *hil*·fe

I'm lost.
Ich habe mich verirrt. ikh *hah*·be mikh fer·*irt*

- - - - - - - - - - - - - - - - - - -
FRENCH BASICS

Hello.	*Bonjour.*	bon·zhoor
Goodbye.	*Au revoir.*	o·rer·vwa
Yes./No.	*Oui./Non.*	wee/non
Excuse me.	*Excusez-moi.*	ek·skew·zay·mwa
Sorry.	*Pardon.*	par·don
Please.	*S'il vous plaît.*	seel voo play
Thank you.	*Merci.*	mair·see

You're welcome.
De rien. der ree·en

Do you speak English?
Parlez-vous anglais? par·lay·voo ong·glay

I don't understand.
Je ne comprends pas. zher ner kom·pron pa

- - - - - - - - - - - - - - - - - - -
DIRECTIONS

Can you show me (on the map)?
Pouvez-vous m'indiquer poo·vay·voo mun·dee·kay
(sur la carte)? (sewr la kart)

Where's ...?
Où est ...? oo ay ...

- - - - - - - - - - - - - - - - - - -
EMERGENCIES

Help!
Au secours! o skoor

I'm lost.
Je suis perdu/perdue. zhe swee·pair·dew (m/f)

- - - - - - - - - - - - - - - - - - -
ON THE ROAD

I'd like to hire a/an ...	*Je voudrais louer ...*	zher voo·dray loo·way ...
4WD	*un quatre-quatre*	un kat·kat
automatic/ manual	*une auto- matique/ manuel*	ewn o·to· ma·teek/ ma·nwel
motorbike	*une moto*	ewn mo·to

How much is it daily/weekly?
Quel est le tarif par kel ay ler ta·reef par
jour/semaine? zhoor/ser·men

Does that include insurance?
Est-ce que l'assurance es·ker la·sew·rons
est comprise? ay kom·preez

Does that include mileage?
Est-ce que le kilométrage es·ker ler kee·lo·may·trazh
est compris? ay kom·pree

What's the speed limit?
Quelle est la vitesse kel ay la vee·tes
maximale permise? mak·see·mal per·meez

Is this the road to ...?
C'est la route pour ...? say la root poor ...

Where's a service station?
Où est-ce qu'il y a une oo es·keel ya ewn
station-service? sta·syon·ser·vees

Please check the oil/water.
Contrôlez l'huile/l'eau, kon·tro·lay lweel/lo
s'il vous plaît. seel voo play

I need a mechanic.
J'ai besoin d'un zhay ber·zwun dun
mécanicien. may·ka·nee·syun

The car/motorbike has broken down.
La voiture/moto est la vwa·tewr/mo·to ay
tombée en panne. tom·bay on pan

I had an accident.
J'ai eu un accident. zhay ew un ak·see·don

BEHIND THE SCENES

SEND US YOUR FEEDBACK

We love to hear from travellers – your comments help make our books better. We read every word, and we guarantee that your feedback goes straight to the authors. Visit **lonelyplanet. com/contact** to submit your updates and suggestions.

Note: We may edit, reproduce and incorporate your comments in Lonely Planet products such as guidebooks, websites and digital products, so let us know if you don't want your comments reproduced or your name acknowledged. For a copy of our privacy policy visit lonelyplanet.com/privacy.

ACKNOWLEDGEMENTS

Climate map data adapted from Peel MC, Finlayson BL & McMahon TA (2007) 'Updated World Map of the Köppen-Geiger Climate Classification', *Hydrology and Earth System Sciences*, 11, 1633–44.

Front cover photographs (clockwise from top):

Wallfahrtskirche St Vinzenz, Heiligenblut (near the start of the Grossglockner Road), Austria, Mathew Roberts Photography/Getty©

Johann Strauss Denkmal, Vienna, Austria, Jon Arnold/AWL©

BMW Isetta Moto Coupe, Moselle Valley, Germany, Helmut Corneli/Alamy©

Back cover photograph:

Seeschloss Ort, Traunsee, Austria, Anna Serrano/4Corners©

THIS BOOK

This 2nd edition of Lonely Planet's *Germany, Austria & Switzerland's Best Trips* guidebook was researched and written by Marc Di Duca, Anthony Ham, Anthony Haywood, Catherine Le Nevez, Ali Lemer, Craig McLachlan, Hugh McNaughton, Leonid Ragozin, Andrea Schulte-Peevers, Benedict Walker and Kerry Walker. This guidebook was produced by the following:

Destination Editors Niamh O'Brien, Brana Vladisavljevic

Senior Product Editor Sandie Kestell

Product Editor Rachel Rawling

Regional Senior Cartographer Mark Griffiths

Cartographer Alison Lyall

Book Designer & Cover Researcher Meri Blazevski

Assisting Editors Nigel Chin, Andrea Dobbin, Trent Holden, Jodie Martire, Rosie Nicholson, Lauren O'Connell, Kristin Odijk, Charlotte Orr, Susan Paterson, Mani Ramaswamy, Gabrielle Stefanos, Fionnuala Twomey

Thanks to Merle Bonefaas, Melanie Dankel, Grace Dobell, Katherine Marsh, Wibowo Rusli

INDEX

LEONID RAGOZIN

Leonid Ragozin studied beach dynamics at the Moscow State University, but for want of decent beaches in Russia, he switched to journalism and spent 12 years voyaging through different parts of the BBC, with a break for a four-year stint as a foreign correspondent for the Russian Newsweek. Leonid is currently a freelance journalist focusing largely on the conflict between Russia and Ukraine (both his Lonely Planet destinations), which prompted him to leave Moscow and find a new home in Rīga.

ANDREA SCHULTE-PEEVERS

Born and raised in Germany and educated in London and at UCLA, Andrea has travelled the distance to the moon and back in her visits to some 75 countries. She has earned her living as a professional travel writer for more than two decades and authored or contributed to nearly 100 Lonely Planet titles as well as to newspapers, magazines and websites around the world. She also works as a travel consultant, translator and editor. Andrea's destination expertise is especially strong when it comes to Germany, Dubai and the UAE, Crete and the Caribbean Islands. She makes her home in Berlin and tweets @ASchultePeevers.

BENEDICT WALKER

Benedict was born in Newcastle, New South Wales, Australia, and grew up in the 'burbs spending weekends and long summers by the beach whenever possible. Although he is drawn magnetically to the kinds of mountains he encountered in the Canadian Rockies and the Japan and Swiss Alps, beach life is in his blood. Japan was Benedict's first gig for Lonely Planet, in 2008/9, and he has been blessed to have been asked back three more times. He has since worked on numerous Lonely Planet titles, including guides to Australia, Canada, Germany and the USA. Join him on his journeys on Instagram: @wordsandjourneys.

KERRY WALKER

Kerry is an award-winning travel writer, photographer and Lonely Planet author, specialising in Central and Southern Europe. Based in Wales, she has authored/co-authored more than a dozen Lonely Planet titles. An adventure addict, she loves mountains, cold places and true wilderness. She features her latest work at https://its-a-smallworld.com and tweets @kerryawalker. Kerry's insatiable wanderlust has taken her to all seven continents and shows no sign of waning. Her writing appears regularly in publications like *Adventure Travel* magazine and she is a *Telegraph* travel expert for Austria and Wales.